ISLAM AND NEW DIRECTIONS IN WORLD LITERATURE

ISLAM AND NEW DIRECTIONS IN WORLD LITERATURE

Edited by
Sarah R. Bin Tyeer and Claire Gallien

EDINBURGH
University Press

Edinburgh University Press is one of the leading university presses in the UK. We publish academic books and journals in our selected subject areas across the humanities and social sciences, combining cutting-edge scholarship with high editorial and production values to produce academic works of lasting importance. For more information visit our website: edinburghuniversitypress.com

Edinburgh University Press Ltd
The Tun – Holyrood Road
12 (2f) Jackson's Entry
Edinburgh EH8 8PJ

First published in hardback by Edinburgh University Press 2023

Typeset in 11/15 Adobe Garamond by
IDSUK (DataConnection) Ltd

A CIP record for this book is available from the British Library

ISBN 978 1 4744 8405 3 (hardback)
ISBN 978 1 4744 8406 0 (paperback)
ISBN 978 1 4744 8408 4 (webready PDF)
ISBN 978 1 4744 8407 7 (epub)

CONTENTS

Notes on Contributors vii
Acknowledgements xii
Foreword by Jeffrey Einboden xiv

1 The World Imaginaries of Islam: Islam and New Directions in World Literature 1
Sarah R. Bin Tyeer and Claire Gallien

Tropes of Orientalism

2 *Los moros de la hueste*: Recovering the Islamicate in the Goths' Lament 57
Gregory S. Hutcheson

3 Just One Word 87
Gil Anidjar

Sensory Fluctuations: Aural, Oral, Visual and Written

4 Poems in Praise of the Prophet (*madīḥ*) as a Citizen of the Literary World 113
Walid Ghali

5 The Place and Function of Imagination in Fulani Mystical Poetry (Massina, Mali) 139
Christiane Seydou

6 Vanishing Art, Genre-making: The Uyghur Storytelling Tradition and its Heritagisation 164
Musapir

Circulation, Translation, Rereading

7 Friedrich Rückert (1788–1866) and his Poetic Translation of the Qur᾽ān 193
Georges Tamer and Cüneyd Yıldırım

8 The 'Islamic' *Arabian Nights* in World Imaginaries 217
Muhsin J. al-Musawi

9 Where is World Literature? 253
Hamid Dabashi

Secular–Non-secular

10 Praising the Prophet Muḥammad in Chinese: A New Translation and Analysis of Emperor Zhu Yuanzhang's *Ode to the Prophet* 271
Haiyun Ma and Brendan Newlon

11 A Fine Romance: Translating the *Qissah* as World Romance 295
Pasha M. Khan

12 Indonesia's *sastera profetik* as Decolonial Literary Theory 328
Nazry Bahrawi

Index 357

NOTES ON CONTRIBUTORS

Muhsin J. Al-Musawi is Professor of Arabic and Comparative Literature at Columbia University. Since 2002 he has been editor of the *Journal of Arabic Literature*. He is the recipient of the Owais Award in literary criticism (2002), and the Kuwait Prize in Arabic Language and Literature (2018). His publications cover theory, post-colonial discourse, the Arabic novel, Arabic poetry, the *Thousand and One Nights*, Orientalism, medieval Islamic knowledge and modern Arabic poetics. He has published ten major works in English, including *The Arabian Nights in Contemporary World Cultures* (2021). He has also published many books in Arabic, including six novels.

Gil Anidjar teaches in the Department of Religion and the Department of Middle Eastern, South Asian and African Studies at Columbia University. Among his books are *The Jew, the Arab: A History of the Enemy* (2003) and *Qu'appelle-t-on destruction? Heidegger, Derrida* (2017).

Nazry Bahrawi is Assistant Professor of Southeast Asian Literature and Culture at the University of Washington-Seattle. His current scholarship examines the intersections between animal fables and racial discourses in Malay–Indonesian literary texts. His articles on literary Islam, translation as cultural rewriting and Malay modernity have been published in *Critical Muslim, Green Letters, CounterText, Journal of World Literature, Journal of*

Intercultural Studies and *Literature and Theology*. He is an editor-at-large at *Wasafiri* magazine and the essay and research editor for the *Practice, Research and Tangential Activities (PR&TA)* journal.

Sarah R. Bin Tyeer is Assistant Professor at the Department of Middle Eastern, South Asian and African Studies at Columbia University. Trained in English and Comparative Literature, Classical Arabic literature (*adab*), modern Arabic literature, and Qur'ānic Studies; she was previously a Research Associate in the School of Oriental and African Studies at the University of London, UK, where she received her doctorate. Her recent publications include her monograph *The Qur'an and the Aesthetics of Premodern Prose* (2016); and chapters in the volumes: *Qur'an and Adab*: *The Shaping of Classical Literary Tradition* (2017); *The Beloved in Middle East Literature: The Culture of Love and Languishing* (2017); and *The City in Premodern and Modern Arabic Literature* (2019).

Hamid Dabashi is the Hagop Kevorkian Professor of Iranian Studies and Comparative Literature at Columbia University. Among his most recent books are *Islamic Liberation Theology: Resisting the Empire* (2008); *The World of Persian Literary Humanism* (2012); *The Shahnameh: The Persian Epic as World Literature* (2019); and *The Last Muslim Intellectual* (Edinburgh University Press, 2021).

Jeffrey Einboden is Presidential Research, Scholarship and Artistry Professor at Northern Illinois University, and prior Fellow of the National Endowment for the Humanities and the American Council of Learned Societies. A specialist in the literatures and languages of early America and the Middle East, Einboden is author of several monographs, including most recently *The Islamic Lineage of American Literary Culture* (2016); *The Qur'an and Kerygma* (2019); and *Jefferson's Muslim Fugitives: The Lost Story of Enslaved Africans, their Arabic Letters, and an American President* (2020).

Claire Gallien lectures at the University of Montpellier 3 and is member of the Institut de Recherche sur l'Age Classique et les Lumières at the CNRS. Her research focuses on early modern orientalism, Islam, but also contemporary literatures and theories pertaining to post-colonial, decolonial and translation studies. She has published extensively in these domains. Her monographs include *L'Orient anglais* (2011) and *From Corpus to Canon: Appropriating and Reconfiguring Eastern Literary Traditions in Seventeenth- and Eighteenth-Century Britain* presented for her Habilitation (Professorship) and forthcoming in print.

Walid Ghali is Associate Professor of Islamic and Arabic Studies at the Institute for the Study of Muslim Civilizations, Aga Khan University. He also leads the Aga Khan Library in the United Kingdom. His main research areas focus on Sufism and Arabic manuscript traditions. He is currently working on a research project about the Egyptian reformer Muhammad ʿAbduh (d. 1905) through newly discovered manuscripts. He published 'Sufi Shrines in Egypt's Western Desert'. His forthcoming publications are 'Humor in Islamic Literature: Vice or Virtue?' and 'The Culture of Writing Qurʾān in Lamu Archipelago' (September 2022).

Gregory S. Hutcheson is Associate Professor of Spanish in the Department of Classical and Modern Languages at the University of Louisville. He has published widely on gender and sexuality in pre-modern Spanish literature, making his most significant mark in the field with the co-edited volume *Queer Iberia: Sexualities, Cultures and Crossings from the Middle Ages to the Renaissance* (1999). In his more recent research he has turned to those rich and complex points of encounter among the diverse creeds, communities and cultures that coexisted on the pre-modern Iberia Peninsula.

Pasha M. Khan is Associate Professor and Chair in Urdu Language and Culture at McGill University. He is interested in the narrative *qissah* genre and storytelling in languages such as Urdu–Hindi, Punjabi and Persian, as well as South Asian literature more broadly. He is the author of *The Broken Spell: Indian Storytelling and the Romance Genre in Persian and Urdu* (2019) among other writings.

Haiyun Ma is Associate Professor in the Department of History at Frostburg State University, Maryland. He specialises in Islam and Muslims of China, as well as China's historical and cultural relations with the Islamic world in the Eurasian continent and the Indo-Pacific region. His recent publications include *Zhenghe Forum: Connecting China with the Muslim World* (2016).

Musapir is the pen name of an Uyghur Diaspora Scholar. Their research focuses on Uyghur literature, oral histories and traditions, folklore, and language. Their work is community-based and aims to preserve and revitalise the Uyghur language and cultural heritage, and explore the spaces of political and cultural identity within the broader Global Indigenous Movement. They grew up in southern Xinjiang and are fluent in the Uyghur language. As a diasporic scholar, they have carried this traditional knowledge abroad and displayed it in their research practice.

Brendan Newlon completed his doctorate in Religious Studies at the University of California Santa Barbara with research on religious communities and social networks, Islam and Chinese religions. His postdoctoral qualitative research at the Center for Creative Leadership focused on Jewish social sector networks and leadership development. He is a data scientist, R programmer, and expert in graph databases and semantic technologies. He has published numerous translations of Arabic and Chinese Islamic texts and didactic poems.

Christiane Seydou received her doctorate in Fula literature from INALCO. She is now Senior Research Fellow Emeritus of the CNRS (LLACAN, Langage, Langues et Cultures d'Afrique, UMR 8135). Seydou devoted her career to the study of the Fula language and literature of the Niger River in Massina (Mali). Amongst her publications are: *Dictionnaire pluridialectal des racines verbales du peul*; *Dictionnaire du fulfulde du Massina*; and bilingual editions of the most representative texts in the various literary genres present in Massina, for instance, the genre of epic with *Silâmaka et Poullôri* (1972), of profane poetry with *Bergers des mots* (1991), and sacred poetry with *La poésie mystique peule du Mali* (2008), as well as more than sixty articles presenting and analysing the literature.

Georges Tamer holds the Chair of Oriental Philology and Islamic Studies and is the director of the Bavarian Research Center for Interreligious Discourses at the University of Erlangen-Nuremberg, Germany. He focuses in his research on the hermeneutics of the Qurʾān, medieval Arab-Islamic philosophy and theology and Jewish–Christian–Islamic discourses in past and present. He published extensively in these areas.

Cüneyd Yıldırım was research assistant and lecturer at the universities of Erlangen-Nuremberg and Münster for several years before becoming an elementary and middle school teacher in the autumn of 2021. His PhD dissertation deals with the social and intellectual history of the Sufi community of the Melamiyye and was published in 2019 as *Die Melâmiyye von Rumelien. Sozial- und Ideengeschichte einer Sufi-Gemeinschaft.*

ACKNOWLEDGEMENTS

We are indebted to the Heyman Center's Edward W. Said Fellowship in 2017 for bringing Claire Gallien to the Heyman Center, Columbia University, and allowing the establishment of fruitful intellectual conversations and networks to take place. This book has been in the making since 2018, and we are grateful to our colleague Mohammad R. Salama (George Mason University) for being part of the initial stage of framing and conceptualising the project. Some of our colleagues have been with us since day one and we are truly appreciative of their intellectual and collegial presences throughout and during the difficult times of COVID-19. Michael Cooperson (UCLA) and Laetitia Nanquette (USNW) provided great insights and generous comments on the introduction. Our thanks are due to colleagues in this very volume, whom we learned from, and colleagues and mentors whom we cite and reference and perhaps have met only through books and conferences and who, without knowing it, not only contributed to the intellectual discussions in this book but also challenged us in our arguments, thereby encouraging us to strive for more clarity in thoughts and words – we are deeply grateful. Jeffrey Einboden (NIU) was supportive from the beginning and enthusiastically responded to our invitation to write a foreword to this volume.

We also extend our thanks to our wonderful editors at Edinburgh University Press, commissioning editor Emma House and assistant editor Louise Hutton for their insights, and liaising with our contributors and peer reviewers. Our due thanks also go to Nicola Ramsey, now Chief Executive, who was one of our first interlocutors at Edinburgh University Press, and was strongly supportive of the project from the early stage. To all three and to Edinburgh University Press, we are grateful.

FOREWORD

'*AGLAIT KORANE KISSÊTA*': INDIGENOUS LETTERS, ISLAMICATE WORLDS AND THE GLOBAL NORTH

Jeffrey Einboden

It is a privilege to contribute a brief foreword to this timely collection, brilliantly conceived, edited and introduced by Sarah R. Bin Tyeer and Claire Gallien, and brought to fruition despite the acute challenges presented by 2020 and 2021. Bridging polarities – aesthetic and political, historical and theoretic – this volume interrogates *Weltliteratur* via Islamicate imaginaries, confronting abstract complexities while revealing rich compositional specifics. Central to the collection is a vision of Islamicate letters as 'always and already' global in scope; as Bin Tyeer and Gallien explore in their elegant introduction, the primary sources illumined anew in this edition represent World Literatures before and beyond standard scholarly frames that have been belatedly applied from the 'Global North'.

This final phrase, implying a specifically hemispheric consciousness and critique, is aptly foregrounded in *Islam and New Directions in World Literature.* Invoking influential voices such as Aamir Mufti, the volume opens by articulating its aim to 'move beyond monocentric tendencies of World Literature' in recognition especially of the 'field' as it is 'now defined in the Global North'. It is this regional classification, charting broad zones of contact and inquiry, that I find especially intriguing. A Canadian, with rural Ontario roots, I have dedicated my own career to considering together Islamicate and North American letters, spanning lost Arabic manuscripts authored by enslaved West African Muslims, to the deep debts owed by classic New England authors to Persian Sufi poetry. The 'Global North' lineages of World Literature, as rightly recognised by Bin Tyeer and Gallien, implicate J. W. Goethe especially, whose receptions of Ḥāfiẓ were foundational to the field's formalising – receptions which later catalysed much Comparative Literature scholarship, including, admittedly, my own.[1] As a literary critic concerned with Qur'ānic legacies, but who is biographically 'northern', I find compelling the hemispheric shifts theorised by Bin Tyeer and Gallien, and performed practically within the chapters of *Islam and New Directions in World Literature*. However, the present collection's 'monocentric' critique invites us not only to broaden out beyond the 'Global North', I think, but to reimagine what this region might yet signify, attending to traditions of the North too often neglected within both Comparative Literature and Islamic Studies. In my mind, it is not only inter-hemispheric, but intra-hemispheric vistas, that are potentially opened by *Islam and New Directions in World Literature*. As the collection articulates in its introduction, Goethean legacies have long contoured the field's conceptualisation, linking *Weltliteratur* to the 'Global North' as well as 'western Europe'. But, thousands of miles northwest of Weimar, during the very decades that Goethe was reading Ḥāfiẓ, Muslim sources were inspiring other rich afterlives. As anticipated by the title to my foreword, it was at the utmost inhabited boundaries of the northern hemisphere that Islamicate imaginaries would also receive fresh expression, rendered for readers of Inuit languages.

Such Islamicate engagements in the far North, published in Indigenous languages, might seem surprising; this surprise is due not to the profound significance, and generous substance, of such engagements, however, but to a persistent lack of scholarly attention. Rich references to Islam emerge not only in Inuit languages, but in a variety of early Indigenous print sources, spanning North America, yielding receptions which have largely escaped notice, overshadowed by other legacies more often associated with the

1 Jeffrey Einboden, 'The Genesis of *Weltliteratur*: Goethe's *West-Östlicher Divan* and Kerygmatic Pluralism', *Literature and Theology* 19(3) (2005), pp. 238–50.

'Global North'. The very year after the term '*Weltliteratur*' was first invoked by Goethe – recorded as part of his 1827 conversation with Eckermann, as detailed by Bin Tyeer and Gallien below – the first sustained bilingual Indigenous newspaper in America began publication.[2] Launched in 1828, the *Cherokee Phoenix* would feature fascinating appeals to the Muslim world in its English-language columns, spanning its print run of 'six years' in Georgia.[3] Following the horrors of the 'Trail of Tears', the earliest Cherokee periodicals in Oklahoma continued to reflect interest in Islam, even forging transliterations for Arabic names and nomenclature within this Iroquoian language, introducing, for instance, the very term 'Qurʾān' into Cherokee syllabics by September 1845.[4] As the nineteenth century neared an end and the twentieth century began, Islamicate engagements surfaced increasingly in languages from the Siouan and Algonquian families, with especial attention to the Muslim world exhibited in Dakota periodicals during the 1880s and 1890s.[5]

Of all early Indigenous print heritages, it is perhaps Inuit-language publications that feature the most conspicuously *literary* appeals to Islamicate imaginaries. Readers of Kalaallisut, for instance, were offered substantive renditions from *The Thousand and One Nights* across a decade, beginning in

[2] For recognition of the *Cherokee Phoenix* as 'the first Indigenous newspaper in North America', see Gregory D. Smithers, *Native Southerners: Indigenous History from Origins to Removal* (Norman: University of Oklahoma Press, 2019), p. 137. Just in advance of the *Cherokee Phoenix*'s first issue, which was published on 21 February 1828, a short-lived hand-written Michigan periodical, engaged especially with Anishinaabe traditions – *The Muzzeniegun* – began to appear in December 1826, edited by Henry Rowe Schoolcraft, whose pages include writings authored by his wife, Bamewawagezhikaquay, known also as Jane Johnston Schoolcraft; see *The Literary Voyager or Muzzeniegun*, ed. Philip P. Mason (East Lansing: Michigan State University Press, 1962).

[3] Perhaps most powerful in this regard are columns printed in the *Cherokee Phoenix* that report on the life and death of Ibrāhīm 'Abd ar-Raḥmān, a West African Muslim, literate in Arabic, who was enslaved in America until 1828; see, for instance, *Cherokee Phoenix*, 3 December 1828, p. 2.

[4] *The Cherokee Messenger*, ed. Evan Jones (September 1845), p. 108.

[5] See, for example, the Dakota-language newspaper *Iapi Oaye*, especially the January 1881 and February 1883 issues; the former features the *shahādah*, translated into Dakota, on p. 3.

September 1865 with the publication of the first 'night' ('*únuaĸ*').[6] Beyond this famed source – which Bin Tyeer and Gallien fittingly label the 'usual suspect of the Islamicate World Literature' – lesser-known texts also helped to introduce Islamic terms into Inuit languages. My chosen title, for instance, derives from a brief biography of a Syrian man born in 1845, aptly named Ḥāfiẓ, which appeared in the Labradorian dialect, Inuttitut, at the end of the nineteenth century. Although primarily concerned with his reported conversion to Christianity, this short overview of Ḥāfiẓ's life begins by describing his original Muslim faith, including his learning that the only remaining scripture to guide humanity is Islam's sacred 'book' ('*aglait*'), namely, the 'Qur'ān alone' ('*Korane kissêta*').[7] Exceptionally, engagements with Islam would enter Inuit languages not only through prose narratives, but via the rendition of poetic sources as well. Perhaps most relevant, in light of the Goethean legacies at stake in the current collection, is the early Kalaallisut rendition of *Oberon* – a German verse epic with Islamicate interests, authored by Christoph Martin Wieland. A fixture of eighteenth-century Weimar, Wieland influenced younger *literati*, including Goethe, who admired *Oberon* intensely, even opining that this 1780 romance, whose episodic plot ranges across the Middle East, comprised 'a masterpiece of poetic art'.[8] Beginning in 1863, Wieland's poem would become Kalaallisut prose, with selections

[6] For '*únuaĸ* 1' of the *Nights*, as published in the Greenlandic newspaper *Atuagagdliutit*, please see the September 1865 issue (52), p. 812.

[7] For this Inuttitut-language biography, see *Unipkautsit Attornartut Ajokertûtsemut Kaujijaksaujune Sunatuinarne: Illiniarvingnullo Kittorngarênullo Illingajut*, ed. and trans. A. Martin (Herrnhut: G. Winterib Nenilauktangit, 1899), pp. 38–41 at p. 39. It would appear that this biography was translated into Inuttitut from a German original that appeared previously in the Basel periodical *Magazin für die neueste Geschichte der protestantischen Missions* 10(3) (1866): 33–7.

[8] For this quote, evidencing Goethe's admiration of *Oberon*, see Joseph E. Morgan, *Carl Maria Von Weber: Oberon and Cosmopolitanism in the Early German Romantic* (Lanham, MD: Rowman & Littlefield, 2014), p. 122. *Oberon*'s engagements with the Middle East are most frequently treated in studies of this poem's impact on operatic traditions; see, for example, chapter 6 of Nasser Al-Taee, *Representations of the Orient in Western Music: Violence and Sensuality* (London: Routledge, 2016), titled 'Two Hundred Years of Orientalism: Construction of the Orient in Wieland's, Wranitzky's, Weber's, and Burgess' *Oberon*'.

Scherasmin tauna imertarfik iluati-
givedlâra nelerĸartinago. „Naleganĝâ!"
Hestinut ĸaĸiniardlutiklo Scherasmin
oĸarpoĸ „imeradlarmigisa inoruseĸ ĸyt-
sauvigalogo, Vinia pikunaĸaoĸ, inutseng-
naĸaoĸ". Taima nekursektisinardlutik
audlalerikpuk udlorsuit pingasut, unuam
ilengua ĸarsuersedleitsiartardlutik, Uto-
ĸaĸ syolersortaudlune avĸosinermik uner-
soiniardlune.

OBERON

3.

Udlut sissamane ĸaĸat akorngene
ingerdleniardlutik, ĸôrĸome syonermine
tuperpeit tekorienguedlarpæk, silatainilo
anguterpeit nuname nelarsut orpît tar-
rane singuktut sekutik orpît aualeĸotei-
ne nivingarsimageit, mardluinæk pigâr-
tuk. Ujukuk tekoriaramikik ilatik iter-
sarpak; makinasuardlutik sekotik pyeit,
Hestimingnut ĸaĸigiardlutik Ujokuk
pâiJerpeit. Ujut aipe pya: „Sumut pi-

Details from the Kalaallisut translation of Christoph Martin Wieland's *Oberon* as published on successive pages within the 23 January 1863 issue of the landmark Greenlandic periodical, *Atuagagdliutit.*

published in the 'oldest Inuit periodical', the Nuuk newspaper *Atuagagdliutit*, accompanied by visual materials seemingly suggestive of *Oberon*'s settings in the Muslim world (see illustration).[9]

Fusing Inuit expression and Islamicate illustration, these pages from *Atuagagdliutit* trace aesthetic lines westward and northward, with imagined sites and scenes from the Middle East arriving to the Arctic, contributing to an Indigenous language print culture that has rarely received mention in standard accounts of *Weltliteratur*. *Oberon*'s translation seems especially illuminating,

[9] The Greenlandic *Atuagagdliutit* started to appear in January 1861, with selections from *Oberon* beginning very soon after, with portions first published in the newspaper in the 6 January 1863 issue (p. 1). The details reproduced in the illustration appear on pp. 233–5 of the 23 January 1863 issue. For *Atuagagdliutit* as the 'oldest Inuit periodical', see Louis-Jacques Dorais, *The Language of the Inuit: Syntax, Semantics, and Society in the Arctic* (Montreal: McGill-Queen's University Press, 2014), p. 208.

however, in its refusal of reductive dichotomies, with its complex trajectories evading simple oppositions of compass and culture. Multiple in media – merging Islamicate portraits, European poetry, and Arctic publication – this *Atuagagdliutit* rendition suggests how *Weltliteratur*'s expanding horizons need not obscure storied literary locales, but illumines authentically their significance. Recognising Kalaallisut receptions of the Islamicate via *Oberon* does not compress, but refract, the classic resonance of this text's hometown, with Weimar itself mapped anew within a more worldly 'Global North'. It is precisely such acts of enrichment, rather than erasure, that reflect the literary labour undertaken by the present volume. As expressed by Bin Tyeer and Gallien in their introduction, this collection avoids 'antagoniz[ing] one literature against the other', preferring instead to forge hospitable sites of fresh interpretation across hemispheres. The editors and contributors to *Islam and New Directions in World Literature* should be congratulated for such an expansive vision, as well as the practical perseverance required to realise a collection that engages a plurality of scholarly fields, and which promises to enlighten countless readers to come.

Bibliography

Dorais, Louis-Jacques, *The Language of the Inuit: Syntax, Semantics, and Society in the Arctic* (Montreal: McGill-Queen's University Press, 2014).

Al-Taee, Nasser, *Representations of the Orient in Western Music: Violence and Sensuality* (London: Routledge, 2016). ch. 6.

Einboden, Jeffrey, 'The Genesis of *Weltliteratur*: Goethe's *West-Östlicher Divan* and Kerygmatic Pluralism', *Literature and Theology* 19(3) (2005): 238–50.

Morgan, Joseph E., *Carl Maria Von Weber: Oberon and Cosmopolitanism in the Early German Romantic* (Lanham, MD: Rowman & Littlefield, 2014).

Schoolcraft. Henry Rowe (ed.), *The Literary Voyager or Muzzeniegun*, ed. Philip P. Mason (East Lansing: Michigan State University Press, 1962).

Smithers. Gregory D., *Native Southerners: Indigenous History from Origins to Removal* (Norman: University of Oklahoma Press, 2019).

1

THE WORLD IMAGINARIES OF ISLAM: ISLAM AND NEW DIRECTIONS IN WORLD LITERATURE

Sarah R. Bin Tyeer and Claire Gallien

The Imaginaries of Islam in World Literature

One of the biggest programmes and summer schools of World Literature, the Harvard Institute of World literature, is housed at Harvard University and locates to a different country every year to be then housed at its home in the third year in Boston, Harvard. The Institute of World Literature began its first chapter in 2011 in Beijing and subsequently all chapters located abroad were placed either in the Far East (Beijing, Hong Kong, Tokyo) or Europe (Copenhagen, Lisbon), the only exception to this mapping is Istanbul in 2012 – located between Europe and the Middle East. Interestingly enough, the Istanbul chapter was the only one dealing with the Islamicate (a term borrowed from Marshall Hodgson, which we will unpack and engage with, taking stock of Shahab Ahmed's critique, in due course) world literature in parts,[1] featuring the usual suspect of Islamicate World Literature: *The Thousand and One Nights*. Other seminars included Westernisation in Turkish and Russian Fiction and another on Orientalism and World Literature, befittingly in Istanbul.

[1] To explain, World Literature in capital letters refers to the discipline of World Literature, while in small letters 'world literature' refers to the corpus itself.

While these programmes are indeed a commendable effort, their trajectories are still aligned with the origins and interests of World Literature as a Goethean enterprise. Some of the multi-volume anthologies and companions published in the field of World Literature do acknowledge the presence of the Islamicate as World Literature, especially *The Longman Anthology of World Literature* (2008, 2nd edition), which seems like a pioneering effort in this regard.[2] It is a two-volume anthology; volume 1 covers a period spanning from the ancient world until the early modern period. In this volume, there is an entire section devoted to literatures from the Islamicate titled 'Classical Arabic and Islamic Literatures' with a subsection on 'Pre-Islamic Poetry' featuring a wide selection from Imrū᾽ al-Qays, al-Khansā᾽ to the Brigand Poets. Then there is a section from the Qur᾽ān composed of a wide selection of *suras* as well as a selection from Ibn Sa῾ad on 'The Prophet and his Disciples' – notwithstanding, of course, that the Prophet Muḥammad did not have 'disciples' but had companions. 'Poetry, Wine and Love' features more poetry by Abū Nuwās, Ibn al-Rūmī and al-Mutanabbī; 'Crosscurrents" includes a selection of tales from the *Thousand and One Nights*; then selections from Persian poets like Rūmī under 'Translations' and also Ḥāfiẓ as well as Firdawsī's *Shāh-nāmah.* 'Asceticism, Sufism, and Wisdom' features poets al-Ḥallāj, Ibn ῾Arabī and Farīd al-Dīn al-῾Aṭṭār. A selection from Ibn Baṭṭūṭa's travels and the founding epic of the empire of Mali *The Epic of Son-Jara* concludes this section. Other selections are spread geographically and chronologically, for instance, one finds selections from Ibn Ḥazm and Ibn Rushd and even Ibn ῾Arabī (again) under the section on medieval Europe. A couple of observations are worth mentioning regarding this selection: one woman poet features in this entire selection only in the section on pre-Islamic poetry with no other mention of women poets, or literati or scholars in later periods; there is no scarcity of them. Beside women poets with known poetry, there were entire pre-modern compendia authored by pre-modern male authors devoted solely to women's *adab* in acknowledgement such as *balāghāt al-nisā᾽* (The Eloquence of Women) by Ibn Ṭayfūr (d. 893 AD). And *ash῾ār al-nisā᾽* (The Poetry of Women), by al-Marzubānī (d. 993 AD), the latter featuring a selection of various women's poetry.

[2] Edited by David Damrosch et al.

The Norton Anthology of World Literature (2018, 4th edition) also recognises the presence of some of the literatures from the Islamicate in its table of contents. The anthology comprises three volumes, with two sections in particular mentioning Islam as a player in the field, namely, 'Circling the Mediterranean: Europe and the Islamic World' (vol. 2) and 'Encounters with Islam' (vol. 3). 'Circling the Mediterranean' contains, for instance, a selection of suras from the Qur'ān, tucked between Augustine and Beowulf, and also extracts from the *Shāh-nāmah* by Firdawsī; Ibn Zaydūn and Ibn al-ʿArabī, featuring in 'Medieval Lyrics' side-by-side with *Song of Summer*, Asad Gorgani, Walther von der Vogelweide and Alfonso X. The section also makes space for the major Persian classics Ḥāfiẓ, Rūmī, Farīd al-Dīn al-ʿAṭṭar, and for *The Thousand and One Nights*, or Ibn Baṭṭūṭa between Marco Polo and John Mandeville. If placing Ibn Baṭṭūṭa between Marco Polo and John Mandeville is a predictable choice, the organisation of other subsections, for instance, on 'Medieval Lyrics' is not. The latter brings together poets from various parts of the world that one would not have placed together if thinking only in terms of geographical and culturally bound blocks. In that sense, this anthology provides a creative reading experience. Finally, the section 'Encounters with Islam' (vol. 3) has a short extract of Evliya Çelebi's *Book of Travels* and a subsection titled 'Indian Poetry After Islam'.

Anthologies and compendia are generically bound to rely on selection, but some selections are more blatant or problematic than others in that they tend to repeat clichés or stereotypes, such as with the case of the omission of the women poets mentioned above. In addition, as genres devoted to selection, there is a risk of using under-represented literatures in the field of World Literature as mere tokens serving representation purposes. For instance, in a section devoted to 'Classical Arabic and Islamic' literature, the focus is understandably Arabic literary works but it comes with a dearth of other languages which are part and parcel of the Islamicate and with a geographical focus on Arab-speaking lands, disregarding the major production of classical Arabic literature in other parts of the world, including Africa, Southeast Asia or even China, to mention just three. It thus seems that there is a disregard for the geographical diversity that comes with Arabic and Islamic literatures and a geographical presumption that circumscribes them on the map only to Arab-speaking lands.

In the cases above, Islamicate literatures come as a quantitative addition to established lists, but are not taken as an element from which to rethink some of the field's predicaments. Therefore, it seems that the focus is expansive in its efforts rather than paradigmatic or analytical in its intentions. Another issue with anthologies comes with the binary divide between the secular and the religious. This binary was inherited from the post-Enlightenment European establishment of literature as a separate field of study in relation to the construction of the colonial empire.[3] Colonial modernity imposed a secularised reading of literature but also reconfigured indigenous literary canons.[4] Scholars are only now beginning to engage with and discuss this issue, the ramifications of which we see when reading, for instance, the *Wiley Companion to World Literature* (vol. 5a: *1920 to Early Twenty-First Century*). This understanding is mirrored in the ways in which the *Wiley Companion* selected its material. It features only one contribution about Islam as such, namely, Debjani Ganguly's chapter titled 'Salman Rushdie and the World Picture of Islam'. There are two problems with this framework: the first is to have Salman Rushdie take the only spot in the six-volume anthology to speak in the name of Islam and the framing of Islamicate literatures, acting as the 'native informant' providing 'forensic interest' as Sinan Antoon describes, rather than a literary interest.[5] The second issue has to do with the discourse. The selection and the discussion follow the well-rehearsed situating of Islam as a problem or as a question that requires an 'enlightened' and 'modernist secularist' answers to be literarily palatable:

[3] See Gauri Viswanathan's chapter, 'The Beginnings of English Literary Study', in Gauri Viswanathan, *Masks of Conquest: Literary Study and British Rule in India* (New York: Columbia University Press, 1994), pp. 23–44.

[4] Aamir Mufti, *Forget English! Orientalisms and World Literatures* (Cambridge, MA: Harvard University Press, 2016), pp. 99–145.

[5] See Sinan Antoon, 'Sinaan Antoon on the West's "Forensic Interest" in Arabic Lit', 4 March 2010, available at: https://arablit.org/2010/03/04/sinaan-antoon-on-the-wests-forensic-interest-in-the-arab-world.

> An admixture of a medieval-style morality tale and the *Arabian Nights*, the novel is a phantasmagoria of the cataclysms of global Islam. Combining motifs from two disparate narratives of Islamic worlds – the jinns from the *Arabian Nights* and Ibn Rushd, the Andalusian medieval philosopher and scholar of Aristotle – and imagining a philosophically enchanted world born of their union, Rushdie lays bare his desire to recuperate a vision of Islam that is all but lost to our age of unreason. It is a vision replete with fantasy, irreverence, reflection, spirituality, and serious scholarly exposition.[6]

The recurring placement of Islam in the world of unreason since the Enlightenment and colonial modernity has become a tired trope but one that is ultimately predictable in its rhetorical manoeuvres. It invokes an imagined, lost Golden Age, with al-Kindī (d. 873), al-Farabī (d. 950), Ibn Rushd or Averroes (d. 1198) as main representatives systematically pitted against other scholars of Islam who are misrepresented to be allegedly accused of 'closing the door of ijtihād', chief amongst them al-Ghazālī (d. 1111).[7] With these representations of Muslim thinkers and scholars, Salman Rushdie becomes a child of this lost Golden Age, a child of Averroes, a Muslim Prometheus, and the rest of the Islamicate traditions represented as lost in a backward age of unreason.

This narrative of decline found a convenient literary representative of the Islamic world of letters in the *Thousand and One Nights*, also known as *Arabian Nights* after Galland's translation, because it is full of 'fantasy' and 'irreverence' thus matching preconceptions of the 'irrational' that has been

[6] Debjany Ganguly, 'Salman Rushdie and the World Picture of Islam', in Ken Seigneurie (ed.), *A Companion to World Literature* (Hoboken, NJ: Wiley, 2019), pp. 1–11 at p. 1.

[7] For a discussion on *ijtihād* (independent reasoning) and arguments against the alleged accusations of the closure of the door after the Abbasid 'Golden Age' and with al-Ghazālī, see, Wael Hallaq, 'On the Origins of the Controversy about the Existence of Mujtahids and the Gate of Ijtihad', *Studia Islamica* 63 (1986): 129–41; Asad Q. Ahmed, 'Postclassical Philosophical Commentaries: Innovation in the Margins', *Oriens* 41 (2013): 317–48; Asad Q. Ahmed, 'Systematic Growth in Sustained Error: Dynamism of Post-Classical Rationalism', in Asad Q. Ahmed, Behnam Sadeghi and Michael Bonner (eds), *The Islamic Scholarly Tradition* (Leiden and Boston: Brill, 2011), pp. 343–78. See also Asad Q. Ahmed's opinion piece 'Islam's Invented Golden Age', *OpenDemocracy*, 28 October 2013, available at: https://www.opendemocracy.net/en/openindia/islams-invented-golden-age.

pitted against the ideas of progress and reason. This is a widespread position in Euro-American theory and reading of the *Nights*, as found in Marina Warner's *Stranger Magic*, where the tales speak to the irrational buried in the Western unconscious:

> The cross-fertilisation between our own culture and cultures which have been deemed irrational and unenlightened has been more pervasive and influential than has been acknowledged or understood . . . The reasons for this are not confined to exotic strangeness and seductively different mores and values, the attraction arises from encountering much that is revealing about ourselves and that then leads to 'something understood' at home.[8]

This 'something understood at home' means the 'irrational' of Western consciousness. This equation between Islam and unreason, albeit now recurring, has not always been the dominant discourse in European thinking, at least prior to the Enlightenment and colonial modernity. Sanjay Subrahmanyam's intellectual project of 'connected histories' offers a productive paradigm for thinking about early modern encounters between East and West, one which precisely allows historians to move beyond the 'exoticisation' of the Other.[9] His method relies on using plurivocal archives and on challenging the idea of a unilateral form of modernity brought to the East by European commerce, war and colonisation. In the Indian cases he studies, various ideas and praxis of modernity emerge that may or may not tally with European standards and which Europeans took on board for their own purposes and needs or jettisoned. In relation to the Islamicate, an excellent candidate to illustrate this idea of the relevance of connected history beyond exoticism, is Jean Bodin (1530–96), a sixteenth-century French jurist and political philosopher, religion and politics were intertwined. As he praised the unritualistic nature of

[8] Marina Warner, *Stranger Magic: Charmed States and the Arabian Nights* (Cambridge: MA, Harvard University Press, 2012), pp. 21, 23.

[9] For more on this see, Sanjay Subrahmanyam, 'Connected Histories: Notes Towards a Reconfiguration of Early Modern Eurasia', *Modern Asian Studies* 31(3) (1997): 735–62; Sanjay Subrahmanyam, *Explorations in Connected History*, 2 vols (Oxford: Oxford University Press, 2004).

Islam as theologically 'purer' in its relation to the divine, he saw its political embodiment, that is, the Ottoman Empire, as the other side of the same coin. According to Bodin, it should be emulated for being meritocratic, for knowing how to preserve law and order, for having security on its streets, for funding hospitals, schools, for using charity and centralised redistribution to the needy.[10] The Islamic polity then was a model for the French king to follow and the Ottoman Empire represented the future for Europe.

Such discourse clearly contradicts the paradigm of an Islamic golden age that is projected on the Abbasid capital of Baghdad and ends with the Mongol invasion in 1258 to begin an age of decline afterwards.[11] Outside the 'golden age' respite that prefigures the Enlightenment in Western thinking, Islam and the world literatures of Islam are presented as sitting on the side of unreason. Walter Mignolo argues that this binary division between the West and the rest, reason and unreason, repeats an epistemic separation between '*humanitas*' and '*anthropos*':

> Places of non-thought (of myth, non-western religions, folklore, underdevelopment involving regions and people) today have been waking up from the long process of westernization. The *anthropos* inhabiting non-European places discovered that s/he had been invented, as *anthropos*, by a locus of enunciations self-defined as *humanitas*.[12]

In its theorisation of the field, World Literature uses as a locus and chronotope Germany and the moment of Goethe's correspondence with Eckermann in 1827, thereby fixing the locus of enunciation in the West and its time in the early nineteenth century. World Literature existed as

[10] See Jean Bodin, *Colloquium heptaplomeres. Des secrets cachez des choses sublimes entre sept scavans qui sont de differens sentimens*, manuscrit, 1593; cited in Noel Malcolm, *Useful Enemies: Islam and the Ottoman Empire in Western Political Thought, 1450–1750* (Oxford: Oxford University Press, 2019), pp. 155–7.

[11] For a critique of neo-Hegelian reading of the Abbasid Golden Age, see Michael Cooperson, 'The Abbasid "Golden Age": An Excavation', *al-Uṣūr al-Wusṭā* 25(1) (2017): 41–65.

[12] Walter Mignolo, 'Epistemic Disobedience, Independent Thought and Decolonial Freedom', *Theory, Culture & Society* 26(7/8) (2009): 159–81 at 161.

a phenomenon and practice before, but it was presented as a Gothean moment and hence theorised as such. In other words, the way we think about World Literature in the West today dates back to this point of 'origin'. Yet that very theoretical definition of World Literature, what it is, its operative mode and functions or objectives, is based on the premise of bordered national literatures which it (World Literature), using the analogy of privileged citizens of the world with powerful passports and the English language as visa, crosses easily. This being said, there are other ways to think and theorise about World Literature that do not involve nations or the idea of the national and that clearly predate Goethe and the European definition of World Literature.

Kalila and Dimna acts as a case in point. As Beatrice Gründler maintains, the collection of animal fables '. . . was avidly read, copied, translated and rewritten in an area stretching from Spain to Malaysia in more than 40 languages until the 19th century'.[13] The tales began in India, and then entered Persia. Littérateur Ibn al-Muqaffa''s (d. 795 CE) Arabic translation is based on the Middle Persian (Pahlavi) and it is through the Arabic version that 'it became a cosmopolitan work and the most widely spread European medieval text'.[14] In reality, *Kalila wa Dimna* and *The Thousand and One Nights* are part of a larger continuum of many other literary texts that circulated (became worldly) and were translated within the structures of an Islamicate empire of letters and of the various Islamic empires. Ibn al-Muqaffa' offered a way for us to think of literature as a worldly endeavour in his translation-redaction of the famous *Kalila and Dimna* (*Kalīla wa Dimna*), a collection of animal fables that falls in the genre of wisdom literature and mirror for princes. In his preface, instead of thinking of literature as bound by a language or place, Ibn al-Muqaffa' locates the literature as circulating in various regions of the world (India, Persia, Arab lands).

[13] Beatrice Gruendler, 'Kalila wa Dimna: A Unique Work of World Literature', available at: https://www.geschkult.fu-berlin.de/en/e/kalila-wa-dimna/_inhaltselemente-rd/spotlight_anonymclassic/Gruendler-_2018__-Kalila-wa-Dimna_-a-unique-work.pdf?fbclid=IwAR3XjAMPScZ4rm8HnmWeEvUQtZsYtH06QlizZdX9GPV4IfV7s3X_bHXqYuw.

[14] Gruendler, 'Kalila wa Dimna'.

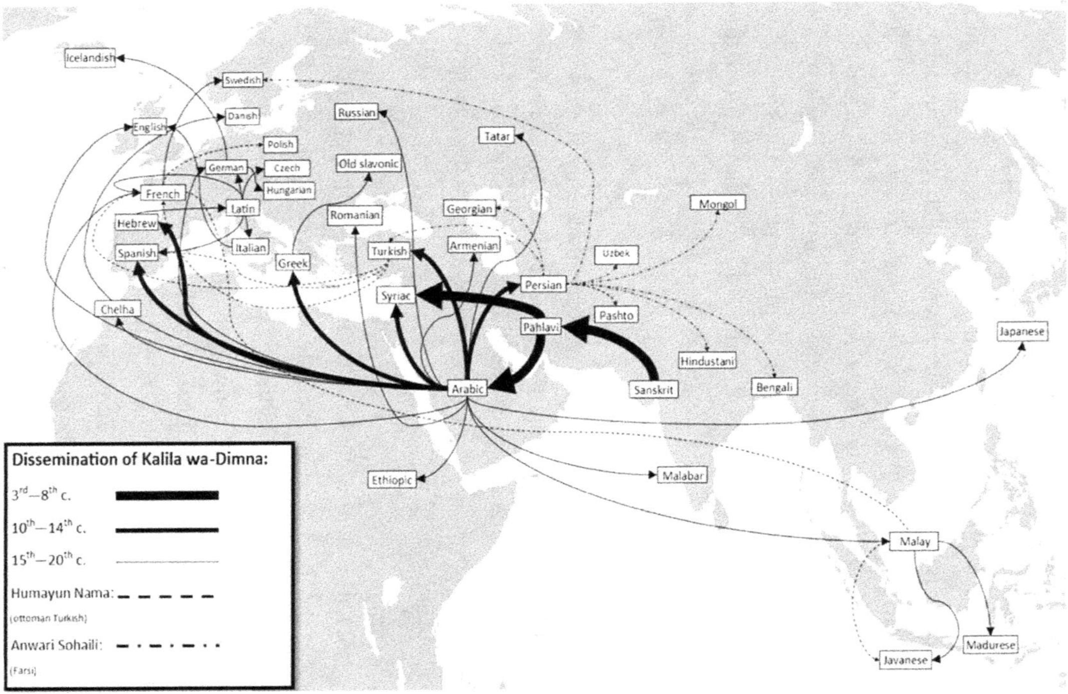

Map of *Kalila wa Dimna*'s transmission.[15]

[15] This publication has been made possible via the *Kalila and Dimna*-AnonymClassic research project at Freie Universität Berlin. The AnonymClassic project has received funding from the European Research Council (ERC) under the European Union's Horizon 2020 research and innovation programme under grant agreement no. 742 635.

It is stating the obvious that there are other types of literature that become worldly with or without the imperial frame. For instance, the literature that refugees write is a form of World Literature but generally not recognised as such, while, as Marina Warner proposed, refugees are 'bearers of stories'.[16] They become part of a World Literature complex in English or Arabic, for instance, and published in New York, London, Beirut or Cairo.

In this case, the cities mentioned above are the centres of a world publishing industry organised by a centre–periphery model. This model was delineated by Pascale Casanova in *La République mondiale des lettres* (1999) translated into English as *The World Republic of Letters* (2004). Casanova provides a chronology working in three stages and a model based on the emergence of European nation-states. Latin dominates until the emergence in the sixteenth century of a European Republic of letters based on nation-states and exchanging in vernacular languages using national literatures as 'battle-grounds':

> International literary space was formed in the sixteenth century at the very moment when literature began to figure as a source of contention in Europe, and it has not ceased to enlarge and extend itself since . . . Previously confined to regional areas that were sealed off from each other, literature now emerged as a common battleground.[17]

There are two points of contention in Casanova's description: space and time. Casanova conflates the 'European' space with the 'International' space in the narrative of the founding of the Republic of Letters later to become World Literature. The originary moment in time points back to the sixteenth century in Casanova's account of the impetus, which gave birth to World Literature. The disregard for other modes of circulation and other Republics of Letters point to both a problem and an opportunity. The problem is one of awareness of positionality. As Chen-Bar Itzhak notes, scholars of the Global

16 Marina Warner, 'Report: Bearer-Beings and Stories in Transit/Storie in Transito', *Marvels & Tales* 31(1) (2017), available at: https://digitalcommons.wayne.edu/marvels/vol31/iss1/9.

17 Pascale Casanova, *The World Republic of Letters*, trans. Malcolm C DeBevoise (Cambridge, MA: Harvard University Press, 2004), p. 11.

North have become accustomed to 'a certain theoretical tradition and are deeply rooted in the concepts, assumptions, and categories of this theoretical canon:[18]

> In acknowledging the fact that intellectual captivity exists, I am not in any way suggesting that scholars from the center should simply give up their privilege and resign from the reading of world literature, clearing the stage for scholars from marginalized traditions. What I am suggesting, however, is that scholars reading world literature should be aware of their own intellectual captivities, state them clearly and reflect upon them, as a part of their research.[19]

The results of these 'deeply rooted problems' are unequal distribution of epistemic capital and lack of self-reflexivity, which leads to reductive and unjust readings of literary texts.[20] All is not bleak. The opportunity in recognising these intellectual captivities is one that provides *New Directions* in World Literature by pluralising the field. A plurality of modes of reading and of theorising can then create the epistemic shifts needed, including the Islamicate.

Casanova's work has proven seminal; it attracted a mixture of acclaim[21] and critique.[22] Muhsin J. al-Musawi provides a welcome contribution and entry into the field of World Literature through pluralising the Republic of Letters by applying it to the Islamicate and the pre-modern period. In this respect, his conception is not a rejoinder to Casanova, but a corrective to the assumed comprehensiveness of Western literary theory in general and Casanova in particular. His conception of the Islamic Republic of Letters

[18] Chen-Bar Itzhak, 'Intellectual Captivity: Literary Theory, World Literature, and the Ethics of Interpretation', *Journal of World Literature* 5 (2020): 79–110 at 92.

[19] Itzhak, 'Intellectual Captivity', p. 101.

[20] For more on this with regard to the ethics of reading and epistemic violence, see Sarah R. Bin Tyeer, *The Qur'an and the Aesthetics of Premodern Arabic Prose* (London: Palgrave Macmillan, 2016).

[21] See, Marielle Macé, 'La critique est un sport de combat', *Acta fabula* 10(3), Essais critiques, March 2009, available at: http://www.fabula.org/revue/document4929.php, last accessed 30 August 2020.

[22] Terry Eagleton, 'The Empire Writes Back', *New Statesman* 18 (854): 50–1, 11 April 2005; Aamir R. Mufti, 'Orientalism and the Institution of World Literatures', *Critical Inquiry* 36(3) (2010): 458–93, doi:10.1086/653408.

antedates Casanova's; it complicates the idea of one centre (aligned with Paris according to Casanova[23]) acting as the 'Greenwich Meridian of literary space' centre by multiplying them (Cairo, Damascus, Aleppo, Mecca) and by revisiting the dynamics between centre and periphery. Al-Musawi avers in the *Islamic Republic of Letters* that the 'centre' description is no less applicable to Cairo and that Cairo 'stood to the postclassical Islamic world as Paris to Europe'.[24] In this Islamic Republic of Letters, '[u]nder precarious and ever-shifting politics, centers at any given time may be replaced by other centers'.[25]

Additionally, the existence of these pre-modern centres of learning and literary production debunks the idea of a period of literary decadence in the Islamicate, thereby complicating the term 'Golden Age' and by extension the idea of a 'decadent age'. This Orientalist narrative served its colonial purposes in the past and has been internalised by self-orientalising modernists. In al-Musawi's own terms:

> The modernists' disillusion with that cultural production was primarily informed by a European discourse but was also driven by a misreading of the compendious and commercial effort of the period, a misreading that could not discern the significant redirection of cultural capital to escape imitation, while simultaneously assimilating ancient and classical knowledge.[26]

Furthermore, centres are not just providers and disseminators of literature, and peripheries are not just the passive consumers. As al-Musawi argues, the

[23] 'If modernity is the sole present moment of literature, which is to say what makes it possible to institute a measure of time, the literary Greenwich meridian makes it possible to evaluate and recognize the quality of a work or, to the contrary, to dismiss a work as an anachronism or to label it "provincial". It needs to be emphasized that the relative notions of aesthetic "backwardness" and "advance", which all writers have in the back of their minds (though the structure of the literary world is never explicitly described in such terms, since one of the unwritten laws of the world republic of letters requires that literary talent and recognition be universal), are not introduced here in order to lay down some fixed and immutable definition of literature," Casanova, *The World Republic of Letters*, p. 90.

[24] Muhsin J. al-Musawi, *The Medieval Islamic Republic of Letters* (Indiana: Notre Dame University Press, 2015), p. 7.

[25] Al-Musawi, *The Medieval Islamic Republic of Letters*, pp. 1–2.

[26] Al-Musawi, *The Medieval Islamic Republic of Letters*, p. 5.

Islamicate cultural spheres go beyond territorial centres and include peripheries in a dialogical form of engagement where peripheries practice 'diversion of assets'.[27] By 'diversion of assets', it is understood that peripheries do not merely copy and regurgitate, but that they redefine relevance and repurpose the texts accordingly.

An important debunking of the centre–periphery binary and hierarchy is revealed in reading texts such as Shiblī Nuʿmānī's travelogue to the Ottoman Empire in the late nineteenth century. Not only was the Islamic scholar and educator travelling from the subcontinent to Turkey, Egypt, and Syria to seek knowledge, but he was also agreeably surprised to find his knowledge and work recognised and attractive to Beirut scholars and students of Islam:

> I usually sat at ʿAbd al-Bāsiṭ al-Unsī's shop. Many intellectuals and people of rank used to turn up there, and I would meet and be introduced to them. So much so, that when word spread throughout the city, several gentlemen even visited me where I was staying. Among them, Sheikh ʿUmar Jailī and one more gentleman whose name I no longer recall showed me great favor and regard. Sheikh ʿUmar Jailī is the owner of the famous journal *al-Ṣafā* and is extremely generous and of fine moral character. The other gentleman, who was a student, came with the intention to study logic. I excused myself for lack of time. Still, he would often come, and we would discuss literature.[28]

What the European colonial centre would consider as the (Urdu) sub-periphery to the (Arabic) periphery becomes with Shiblī a new centre for the Islamicate from where a literature in Urdu is translated in Arabic and disseminated from East (India) to West (Ottoman lands).

'Under precarious and ever-shifting politics', Muhsin J. al-Musawi maintains, 'centers at any given time may be replaced by other centers' in the Islamic Republic of Letters.[29] An Islamicate world literature would therefore function on the premise of polycentrism. The account that al-Musawi draws for us is

[27] Al-Musawi, *The Medieval Islamic Republic of Letters*, p. 5. Al-Musawi is borrowing the concept from Casanova, *The World Republic of Letters*, p. 54.

[28] Shiblī Nuʿmānī, *Turkey, Egypt, and Syria: A Travelogue*, trans. Gregory Maxwell Bruce (New York: Syracuse University Press, 2020), p. 135.

[29] Al-Musawi, *The Medieval Islamic Republic of Letters*, pp. 1–2.

one where Abbasid Baghdad and al-Andalus are replaced by Mamluk Cairo, Damascus and Aleppo, and Mecca, and so on and so forth, where peripheries of these cities are not just receiving what the centres produce but are engaged in cross-feeding interactions with them. This may also account for the fact that any given 'periphery' at any point in time may turn into a new centre. Similarly, when Baghdad-based scholar Ibn al-Nadīm (d. 990 CE) was collecting material for his *Fihrist*, he travelled across a vast territory of the Islamicate, connecting one centre to the next in order to complete the entries of his *Fihrist*.[30]

This pursuit is premised on a certain obligation of comprehensiveness on the part of the author and it is also based on a conception of 'knowledge' and 'literature' as comprehensive pursuits; a part of *adab*.[31] *Adab*, generally defined as 'literature', is more than just the literary aspect of letters. It includes an ethical dimension of erudition, scholarship, civility, conventions and observing decorum.[32] Writing in what we classify today as strictly

[30] Devin Stewart presented the new critical edition of the *Fihrist* by Ayman Fu'ād Sayyid in a lecture he gave to the Al-Furqan Institute, London, in 2015. In the various entries in the *Fihrist*, Ibn al-Nadīm informs his readers about his travels and the places he specifically visited and scholars or priests he specifically met in order to compile his *Catalogue*, tracking knowledge to the source so to speak. For more on ibn Ibn al-Nadīm's knowledge gathering practices, see 'The Fihrist of Ibn al-Nadīm and the Transmission of Knowledge in the Islamic World, Devin Stewart, 22 April 2015, Al-Furqan, London' available at: https://al-furqan.com/events/the-fihrist-of-ibn-al-nadim-and-the-transmission-of-knowledge-in-the-islamic-world-by-prof-devin-j-stewart; and the first volume of Ayman Fu'ād Sayyid's critical edition for an extensive biography of Ibn al-Nadīm: Ayman Fu'ād Sayyid (ed.), *The Fihrist of al-Nadīm (Abū al-Faraj Muḥammad Ibn Isḥāq)* (London: Al-Furqan Islamic Heritage Foundation, 2014).

[31] For more on encyclopaedism, see Elias Muhanna, *The World in a Book: Al-Nuwayri and the Islamic Encyclopedic Tradition* (Princeton, NJ: Princeton University Press, 2018), p. 12.

[32] For more on *adab*, see Seeger Adrianus Bonebakker, 'Adab and the Concept of Belles-Lettres', in Julia Ashtiany et al. (eds), *Abbasid Belles-Lettre, The Cambridge History of Arabic Literature* (Cambridge: Cambridge University Press, 1990); Wolfhart Heinrichs, 'The Classification of the Sciences and the Consolidation of Philology in Classical Islam', in Jan Willem Drijvers and Andrew Archibald MacDonald (eds), *Centres of Learning: Learning and Location in Pre-Modern Europe and the Near East* (Leiden: Brill, 1995), pp. 119–20, 16–30; Bo Holmberg, 'Adab and Arabic Literature', in *Literary History: Towards a Global Perspective* (Berlin: W. de Gruyter, 2006), 1: pp. 180–205; al-Musawi, *The Medieval Islamic Republic of Letters*; Bin Tyeer, *The Qur'an and the Aesthetics of Premodern Arabic Prose*, pp. 7–18; Michael Allan, *In the Shadow of Literature, Sites of Reading in Colonial Egypt* (Princeton, NJ: Princeton University Press, 2018).

bounded genres did not preclude the inclusion of other genres, styles and forms of writing. For instance, a book of history, or Qurʾān exegesis would include poetry, epigrams, anecdotes, etc. In the same manner, a work of *adab* would include the aforementioned literary genres (and others) of writing not for decorative purposes and showing off erudition, but it is also relying on them to pursue its own ends and needs.

This aspect of the historiographical genre was overlooked and dismissed in modern orientalism. In her book chapter on eighteenth-century edition and translation of Indo-Persian historiography, Claire Gallien analysed how British Orientalists, while curious and in need of indigenous material, treated it as non-historical non- and unreliable when insufficiently complying with their rules of history writing, which they considered as universally applicable.[33] Local traditions, when aligning the historic with the epic, the fabulous and the divine, were either excused in footnotes, modified, disparaged or discarded:

> By making room for 'other' voices, orientalism presented itself as an inclusive form of knowledge which could potentially involve the 'whole world' – However the general framework in which this process took place, and the functions it endorsed were defined in Europe. Never were the rules of European historiography challenged. This globalisation of orientalism by highlighting the inclusive capacities for European knowledge, only served to reiterate its claims to universalism.[34]

What Orientalists saw as disruptive of historical objectivity and as merely 'decorative', served an epistemic function according to indigenous standards of history writing, which relied on generic porosity and conceived of myths, fables, poetry and sacred texts as supportive of historiographical discourse. This type of generic *intercession* is also fundamental to the Islamicate World

[33] See Claire Gallien, 'British Orientalism, Indo-Persian Historiography, and the Politics of Global Knowledge', in S. Davies, D. S. Roberts, and G. Sanchez Espinoza (eds), *India and Europe in the Global Eighteenth Century*, Oxford University Studies in the Enlightenment series (Oxford: Oxford University Press, 2014), pp. 29–52 at p. 30.

[34] Gallien, 'British Orientalism, Indo-Persian Historiography, and the Politics of Global Knowledge', pp. 51–2.

Literary system. Without keeping this point in mind, we fail to understand, for instance, the inclusion of various types of classical and vernacular poetry in the corpus of tales that constitute *The Thousand and One Nights*.

By the fourteenth century, Egyptian scholar Shihāb al-Dīn al-Nuwayrī (d. 1333) was one out of many to expand the boundaries of *adab* beyond its earlier purview when writing his *Nihāyat al-arab fī funūn al-adab*.[35] His encyclopaedic work contains poetry, proverbs, parables, exemplary orations, epistles, but also medical remedies, financial accounting, theological debates and history, to name but a few of the fields mentioned by Elias Muhanna in his introduction to al-Nuwayrī's work.[36] Muhanna also indicates that a typical chapter would bring 'together a variety of materials, including verses from the Qur'ān, sayings of the Prophet Muḥammad, philological glosses, historical anecdotes, and any poetry that al-Nuwayrī was able to find on the subject'.[37] In this respect, the evolution that contributed to the breadth of *adab* cannot be captured by some restrictive definitions of 'literature'.

Even more restrictive are some conceptions of World Literature that self-define as capacious enough to encompass 'all' literatures but in reality only represent a selection. The coinage of the term itself has a well-known history, with *Weltliteratur* appearing in Goethe's letter to Eckermann in January 1827. Goethe maintained that national literatures, while still important, are becoming gradually less significant. Goethe's views might appear deceptively cosmopolitan at first, but as Damrosch maintains, the former was not the 'multiculturalist' as the coined word might indicate.[38] Goethe maintained that:

> But, while we thus value what is foreign, we must not bind ourselves to anything in particular, and regard it as a model. We must not give this value to the

[35] See Muhanna, *The World in a Book*, pp. 25–6.

[36] Elias Muhanna, 'Introduction', in *The Ultimate Ambition in the Arts of Erudition: A Compendium of Knowledge from the Classical Islamic World by Shihab al-Din al-Nuwayri*, ed. and trans. Elias Muhanna (London: Penguin Classics, 2016), p. xviii

[37] Muhanna, *The Ultimate Ambition in the Arts of Erudition,* p. xix.

[38] David Damrosch, *What is World Literature?* (Princeton, NJ: Princeton University Press, 2003), p. 12

> Chinese, or the Servian[sic], or Calderon, or the Nibelungen; but if we really want a pattern, we must always return to the ancient Greeks, in whose works the beauty of mankind is constantly represented. All the rest we must look at only historically, appropriating to ourselves what is good, so far as it goes.[39]

It seems that by the mid-nineteenth century, as Marx and Engels affirm, '[n]ational one-sidedness and narrow-mindedness become more and more impossible, and from the numerous national and local literatures, there arises a world literature'.[40] The economic metaphor and the national frame of literature lingered as Fritz Strich, in 1949, theorised world literature as a 'literary market' where 'the nations bring their intellectual treasures for exchange'.[41]

Between the mid-twentieth century and the 1990s, when World Literature was revived in US-based academia, the conception of the field shifted from an international to a global outlook. Indeed, the 1950s and 1960s saw the end of European empires in Asia and Africa. With decolonisation, new nation-states emerged eager to reclaim their identities as authentic subjects of history and to narrate, perhaps often contrapuntally, their postcolonial experiences. In the decolonial moment, national languages and literatures played a critical role, with UNESCO funding translation and publication programmes to promote 'literacy' and 'feed' markets 'hungry' for books.[42] The conception of the circulation of literatures, according to UNESCO, relied on the existence and promotion of an international book market.

But in reality, this type of literary circulation is restricted to an affluent readership, and the cultural and economic elite. The role of UNESCO

[39] Johann Wolfgang von Goethe, *Conversations of Goethe with Eckermann and Soret*, trans. from German John Oxenford, 2 vols (London: Smith, Elder 1850), vol. 1, p. 351.

[40] Karl Marx and Friedrich Engels, *Manifesto of the Communist Party*, first published 1848, Marxists Internet Archive (marxists.org) 1987, 2000, 2010, available at: https://www.marxists.org/archive/marx/works/1848/communist-manifesto/ch01.htm, last accessed 18 September 2020.

[41] Fritz Strich, *Goethe and World LIterature* (London: Routledge & Kegan Paul, 1949), p. 13.

[42] Sarah Brouilette, *UNESCO and the Fate of the Literary* (Stanford, CA: Stanford University Press, 2019), pp. 1, 2, 10–12.

programmes was to enlarge the readership on a selected list of books it subsidised,[43] on providing the Global South with the tools on how to read,[44] and via the establishment of public libraries.[45] These UNESCO efforts stem from its belief 'in the public library as a living force for popular education and for the growth of international understanding, and thereby for the promotion of peace', democracy, liberalism and modernity.[46] These endeavours unwittingly echo nineteenth-century discourses of Europe's colonial civilising mission.

In the 1990s, with the age of decolonisation now part of history, though UNESCO continues to operate in its funding and publishing activities, this impetus to support an international book market and public libraries in the Global South (the underdeveloped world in UNESCO parlance) has receded. With this, the end of the Cold War and the dominance of neoliberal ideology,[47] a new conception of world literature takes centre stage in the West, one that departs from the international and decolonial moment to become 'global'. While the international moment focused on the development of literatures and public libraries for new decolonised nations as a path from colonisation to democracy, the global moment is interested in the development of universal libraries of world literary texts.

The global moment did not find immediate resonance in the existing field of Comparative Literature, which remained centred on European literatures and languages. It required the emergence of a new field, namely, World Literature.

Indeed, Damrosch connects World Literature with this 'global moment' when he defines it as 'all literary works that circulate beyond their culture

[43] Lists such as *Books for the Developing Countries* (1965) and *Books for All: A Programme of Action* (1973) were published by UNESCO.

[44] See, for instance, *Roads to Reading* (1979) and *Teaching of Reading* (1973) by Ralph C. Staiger, executive director of the International Reading Association, funded by UNESCO.

[45] Amanda Laugesen, *UNESCO and the Globalization of the Public Library Idea, 1948 to 1965*, Library & Information History, 30(1) (2014): 1–19, doi: 10.1179/1758348913Z.00000000052.

[46] The UNESCO Public Library Manifesto, in L. R. McColvin, *The Chance to Read: Public Libraries in the World Today* (London: Phoenix Press, 1957), app. A, p. 249.

[47] For more on this point, see Joseph Massad, *Islam in Liberalism* (Chicago: University of Chicago Press, 2015).

of origin, either in translation or in their original language'.[48] In this regard, Damrosch does not consider world literature as this ineffable body of texts that constitute a canon but rather as 'a mode of circulation and reading'.[49] In *What is World Literature?* he offers a tripartite definition of world literature as: (1) an elliptical refraction of national literatures; (2) writing that gains in translation; and (3) not as a set canon of texts but as a mode of reading: a form of detached engagement with worlds beyond our own place and time.[50] With an elliptical refraction of national literatures, Damrosch suggests that national literatures circulate within a vast container called world literature and that this circulation implies the gradual erasure, what Damrosch calls 'diffusion',[51] of their original marks. While the international conception of literature acknowledges the presence of national marks and markers, the global World Literature conception implies diffusion and erasure, given that the whole point is how literatures are appropriated by the receiving cultures.

Even though Damrosch addresses loss and gain in the translation of national literatures, he maintains that it is not a question of value as one might surmise from his usage of 'loss' and 'gain'; however, he distinguishes between national literatures that lose in translation and therefore are deterministically destined to remain local, and literatures that gain in translation and turn de facto global, become de facto World Literature. And, finally, the last point about World Literature as activating a specific detached mode of reading means that readers engage with world literary texts on two levels that may intersect, contradict and supersede each other: the individual, rooted, contextual reading of the work combined with the worldly detached mode. In Damrosch's own words: 'The texts themselves exist both together and alone: when we read Dante, we are aware that we are encountering a major work of world literature, one that draws on a wealth of previous writing . . . Yet even as we register such connections, we are also immersed within Dante's singular world'.[52]

48 Damrosch, *What is World Literature?*, p. 4.

49 Damrosch, *What is World Literature?*, p. 5.

50 Damrosch, *What is World Literature?*, p. 281.

51 Damrosch, *What is World Literature?*, p. 283.

52 Damrosch, *What is World Literature?*, p. 298.

In that respect, Damrosch's conceptions chime with Moretti's theory of 'distant reading' as formulated in 'Conjectures on World Literature' where he maintains:

> . . . distance, let me repeat it, is a *condition of knowledge*: it allows you to focus on units that are much smaller or much larger than the text: devices, themes, tropes – or genres and systems. And if, between the very small and the very large, the text itself disappears, well, it is one of those cases when one can justifiably say, Less is more. If we want to understand the system in its entirety, we must accept losing something. We always pay a price for theoretical knowledge: reality is infinitely rich; concepts are abstract, are poor. But it's precisely this 'poverty' that makes it possible to handle them, and therefore to know. This is why less is actually more.[53]

According to these two modes of reading inspired by the conception of distance, Moretti proposes a distance by choice where one focuses on an aspect of the text, even at the expense of the text itself as he argues. Damrosch, on the other hand, suggested a distance due to lack of knowledge, unfamiliarity, acquaintance with the text and its literary and historical context, and uses Dante as an example of this. One can appreciate Dante, according to Damrosch, without knowing about the background. In this respect, literatures of the Islamicate, as objects, could be subjected to the same mode of reading and be placed in World Literature, along with Dante, in Damrosch's example. Replacing Dante with al-Jāḥiẓ, al-Maʿarrī, Ḥāfiẓ or Saʿdī might as well have worked? Similarly, Moretti would be reading these texts within a distant literary world system (*à la Wallerstein*), that is, 'not the sum total of the world's literary production, but rather within which literature is produced and circulates'.[54]

The present volume does not represent literatures of the Islamicate as objects to be theorised upon by scholars of World Literature but reflects on how these literatures formulate and/or enact other modes of going worldly. By 'going worldly', we mean other modes of 'being in the world' and of 'creating

[53] Franco Moretti, 'Conjectures on World Literature', *New Left Review* 1 (Jan./Feb. 2000): 56–7.

[54] Alexander Beecroft, 'World Literature without a Hyphen Towards a Typology of Literary Systems', in David Damrosch (ed.), *World Literature in Theory* (Chichester: John Wiley, 2014), pp. 180–91 at p. 181.

worlds'. In that respect our understanding complements what Edward W. Said established about texts as 'beings in the world' – 'A text in its actually *being* a text is also a being in the world; it therefore addresses anyone who reads'[55] – and 'worldly' criticism more generally: 'Most of all, criticism is worldly and in the world so long as it opposes monocentrism, a concept [Said understands] as working in conjunction with ethnocentrism, which licenses a culture to cloak itself in the particular authority of certain values over others'.[56] In rethinking world literature from the perspective of the Islamicate, our volume moves beyond monocentric tendencies of World Literature as a field that sought its originary moment in Western Europe in the nineteenth century, and now defined in the Global North and for the globalised world.

Pheng Cheah refashions World Literature as time instead of space, as temporalisation instead of cartography, and as openness to other modes of imagining and experiencing worlds, including literary worlds, that do not comply with the hegemonic understanding of time and space as defined by global capitalism:

> Instead, time itself is the force of transcendence that opens a world. Better yet, temporalization constitutes the openness of a world, the opening that is world. In situations where progressive teleological cartographies are leveled off by capitalist globalization, this openness is an unerasable normative resource for disrupting and resisting the calculations of globalization. It opens up new progressive teleological times.[57]

This notion of openness is generative as it allows us to imagine *other* modes of worlding literature than those defined by the Global North. Cheah's intervention opens a space for thinking the Islamicate as World Literature. Cheah also elaborates on the notion of 'deep time' that should be productive for our discussion. In *What is a World?*, he explains that 'the "deep time" that animates subaltern agency refers to a temporal order different from the time

[55] Edward Said, *The World, the Text, and the Critic* (Cambridge, MA: Harvard University Press, 1983), p. 33.

[56] Said, *The World, the Text, and the Critic*, p. 53.

[57] Pheng Cheah, *What is a World?* (Durham, NC: Duke University Press, 2016), p. 9.

of the clock and the calendar by which modern Westernized subjects measure our immediately appearing individual lives'.[58]

World literatures of the Islamicate also open deep time on three levels: the level of individual memory; the *longue-durée*, connecting individuals with deeper historical timelines; and, finally, transcendental time, or time of the *ākhirah* (Hereafter). In Leila Aboulela's 1999 novel, *The Translator*, the female Sudanese narrator Sammar lives in Edinburgh and works as a translator for the university. She engages with her colleagues in English and realises how certain words, such as *inshā ʾAllāh*, are missing in her sentences:

> She had enjoyed talking in Arabic, words like insha ʾAllah, fitting naturally in everything that was said, part of the sentences, the vision. How many times had she over the past days said in English 'I'm leaving on Friday', and the sentence, normal and natural as it was to the people who heard it, had sounded in her ear incomplete, untruthful without insha ʾAllah.[59]

Inshā ʾAllāh (God willing) is not only a word missing at the end of a sentence, but it opens up an experience of time that is different from what Johannes Fabian calls 'universal time' or 'secular time'.[60] For Fabian, the idea of universal/secular/Western clock time emerged during the European Renaissance, in order to respond partially to the cognitive anthropological challenges posed by the Age of Discovery. During the Age of Enlightenment, described by Fabian as 'the century that elaborated the devices of discourse that we now recognize as the foundations of modern anthropology'. It replaced the relation to teleological time as Salvation with the relation to time as Progress. The discourse of medieval religious conversions was replaced with a new form of Enlightenment conversion to universal secular time and progress, with the reification of *Others* who are denied coevalness.[61] Does a critical reading that pays attention only to this detail of *inshā ʾAllāh* deny the Muslim female protagonist coevalness and place her outside secular time through an

[58] Cheah, *What is a World?* p. 267.

[59] Leila Aboulela, *The Translator* (New York: Black Cat, 1999), p. 106.

[60] Ahmad and Turner (2015), cited in Irfan Ahmad, *Religion as Critique* (Chapel Hill: University of North Carolina Press, 2017), p. 42]).

[61] Johannes Fabian, *Time and the Other: How Anthropology Makes it Object* (New York: Columbia University Press, [1983] 2014), p. 31.

anthropological form of reading? Indeed, by paying attention to this detail and emphasising only the 'Muslimness' of the woman, one runs the risk of a literary reading that is unethical and denies coevalness of the protagonist. Or, is a critical reading that pays attention to the presence of multiple experiences of time, as the phrase *inshā ʾAllāh* opens up, more productive? There is a difference between denying coevalness and placing the Other in the past, and acknowledging the fact that the presence of *inshā ʾAllāh* at the end of a sentence does indeed change the perception of time and indicate the existence of multiple experiences of time in the world, and not just one secular progressive time.

The multiple experiences of time in the world, including the 'deep time' that *inshā ʾAllāh* conveys, connects the here and now of Samar's presence in the world with a transcendental experience of time. To further illustrate this conception of 'deep time', using a literary example form *adab* in the Islamicate would be useful. As Sarah R. Bin Tyeer maintains, the poet al-Maʿarrī's (d. 449/1058) *Epistle of Forgiveness* (*Risālat al-Ghufrān*) is structured on the premise of the existence of layers of time. In this work, often inviting comparison with its successor in the fourteenth-century, the *Divine Comedy* by Dante (d. 1321), he retrieves poets and litterateurs from distant times in the one place that could temporally and spatially allow this aesthetic gesture: the Hereafter. The Hereafter becomes a conceptual analytic category that allows al-Maʿarrī to transpose the conception of 'judgement' from the primarily religious to also the literary – they are not only judged on the basis of good deeds but also good poetry.[62] Without dispensing with the ethico-religious finality of the Hereafter, al-Maʿarrī adds a literary criticism element to this notion of finality. In other words, this is precisely because al-Maʿarrī conceptualises time as 'deep time' on the abovementioned three levels, that he can capture the Hereafter for other than Other-worldly purposes, for non-religious purposes that may be lost to an anthropological reading dispensing with these multiple experiences.

What these previous cases indicate are the limitations of reading world literatures through the lenses of a single frame, namely, that of World Literature as a post-Gothean institution operating from a homogeneous

[62] Bin Tyeer, *The Qur'an and the Aesthetics of Premodern Arabic Prose*, pp. 229–63.

perspective and time. Instead of considering World Literature as an object described through 'empirical process', one might consider what Sanjay Krishnan proposes as he encourages us to shift our approach through what he terms as 'instituted perspective'.[63] While Krishnan does not refer to World Literature in the opening pages of his book, he talks about processes of globalisation. Yet we argue that what he problematised as 'the global' and what we diagnose as understandings, paradigms and practices of World Literature resort to identical gestures of covering the world 'as a single unified entity, articulated in space and developing over (common) time'.[64] Consequently, this creates an issue related to the adequacy of the tools being used to approach, analyse, talk about the 'world' or 'world literature' – can we ethically use and defend modes of reading that resort to the same paradigms when discussing Gilgamesh and Rushdie?

Another issue salient to our discussion raised by Krishnan about 'the global' is that of 'thematisation'. In linguistics, thematisation means placing a word or phrase at the start of a sentence in order to focus attention on it. In this sense, World Literature thematises works by placing these at the beginning of the sentences in the narrative it is constructing about the worldliness of certain texts at the expense of others. To be clear, all literary critics thematise, even as they go about selecting a corpus to write an article. The problem is not in the selection per se. Rather, the issue about thematisation rests on the assumed aperspectiveness of selection and the presumed transparency of assigning relevance. The global and its concurrent selection of themes and decision on relevance is understood to refer to an 'empirical process' that takes place in what Krishnan calls 'out there' in the world.[65] We, therefore, underscore the risk of not questioning thematisation and the assumption of the *out-thereness* of certain narratives. For instance, when regarding Muslim characters, specifically women, oppression and resistance to that oppression are the default expected themes and the near-systematic repetition of the theme in works that circulate in translation for academics and students of

[63] Sanjay Krishnan, *Reading the Global: Troubling Perspectives on Britain's Empire in Asia* (New York: Columbia University Press, 2007), pp. 2–3.

[64] Krishnan, *Reading the Global,* p. 1.

[65] Krishnan, *Reading the Global,* p. 2.

World Literature corroborate the *out-thereness* or the existence of oppression and resistance. This is not to say that oppression does not exist. The point is in *it* (oppression) becoming regionalised, racialised and religionalised; what we identify and coin here as the *literary mechanics of confirmation*.

The first layer of *thematisation* is formed by focusing on certain texts, *choosing* and *naming* them as World Literature, even prior to the act of translation of these texts (translation becomes the second act), which then allow them to circulate globally. This thematisation or act of selection does not happen in a vacuum. It takes place within a larger geopolitical structure that inspires and allows thematisation or bringing to the fore certain themes and not others. For instance, the category of the dependent, oppressed Muslim woman is subsumed under the larger theme of oppression and alternatively the category of the resisting woman subsumed under the larger theme of secular liberal feminism. Both models derive their conditions of existence from or against what is fashioned as an atemporal epistemic source: religion. The thematisation relies on a classification that *produces* subjects atemporally and ahistorically. In other words, it ossifies the subject in a category, 'religion' or 'Islam', which is capable of surveying the past, of producing, and predicting her present and future conditions. The selection of themes confirms the larger narrative and the narrative calls for the themes in what we call and define as the *mechanics* and *strategies of confirmation*.

Similarly, Aamir R. Mufti criticises these strategies '[that] canonized an emphasis on the variety of ways of being human, they did so in order to establish the *same* manner of being different',[66] thereby occluding differences and dehumanising individuals. Failing to recognise the 'global', or World Literature for that matter, as instituted perspectives we risk missing the historicity of the fields and delinking them from their Orientalist and imperial genealogies. Mufti recovers the genealogy as follows:

> 'World Literature' came into being (only) when the cultural system of the modern bourgeois West had appropriated and assimilated – that is, 'discovered', absorbed, recalibrated, rearranged, revaluated, reclassified,

[66] Mufti, *Forget English!*, p. 77.

> reconstallated, compared, translated, historicized, standardized, disseminated, and, in short, *fundamentally transformed* – the widely diverse and diffuse writing practices and traditions of the societies and civilizations and of the 'East,' which extended in the Euro-Occidental imagination from the Atlantic shore of Africa to the littoral of the Sea of Japan.[67]

Mufti establishes the genealogy at two levels: first, in explaining how World Literature libraries were created in Europe via the channels of imperial expansion; and, secondly, in linking that moment of the creation of Orientalist libraries of Eastern texts with the emergence of philosophical historicism. As the British Empire was expanding eastward and into India and British Orientalists were bringing home Arabic, Persian, and Sanskrit manuscripts, a new theory of language emerged with Herder, which conceived of languages as historical and cultural formations embodying the 'spirit' of a people; what Herder called *Völksgeist*. Therefore, by learning a language and by reading from a literary corpus, the Orientalist could access the spirit of a people. The results are cultural essentialism and concomitantly cultural comparativism (not relativism) on a scale of progress defined by the Orientalists themselves, thereby creating hierarchies of nations, languages and literatures. Accordingly, the naive assumption of world literature as 'some happy-go-lucky concert of world's peoples and civilizations' betrays the complexities of the imperial nature of the Historicist–Orientalist apparatus, the material inequalities of texts as events, and the asymmetry of cultural transactions.[68]

In *What is World Literature?* (2003), Damrosch questions the origins of European Literature as strictly founded in 'the biblical and classical writings, long taken to be the originary documents of "Western" culture', and argues that the epic of *Gilgamesh* offers an older and further origin.[69] While the interest in expanding the canon of World Literature to the east and south is visible, the centre of interest remains the West and those benefiting from the cultural transactions are academics and readers of the Global North.

Since 2003 and the publication of *What is World Literature?*, the field of World Literature has evolved and is now more attuned to these issues

[67] Mufti, *Forget English!*, p. 49.

[68] Mufti, *Forget English!*, p. 29.

[69] Damrosch, *What is World Literature?*, p. 40.

of asymmetries in cultural transactions and intellectual captivity. In 2014, Damrosch wrote the introduction for a special issue of the *Journal of Qur'anic Studies*, 'The Qur'an in Modern World Literature'. In the article, he challenges a number of preconceptions that have become 'articles of faith', as he puts it, concerning 'literature'. He highlights the Qur'ān's distinctive literary qualities that 'can help to open out the restricted conception of "literature" that took hold in France in the eighteenth century and then spread through Europe and beyond'.[70] Damrosch objects to Weber and Lukács' secular and 'disenchanted' conception of literature, declaring that they understate 'the ongoing presence of religion as an active force in a number of the writers' they discussed in their theoretical writings.[71] The presentation of the Qur'ān as another mode of reading that is capable of producing different literary critical tools is coterminous to other ongoing efforts in the field of World Literature to rethink some of the limitations of its epistemic framework. Part of the solution is to work collaboratively and not 'ignore the local knowledge that specialists possess, as literary theorists of the past generation often did when developing their comprehensive theories'.[72]

One example of such collaborative work is a special issue of the *Journal of World Literature* titled 'World Literature and Postcolonial Studies', edited by Damrosch and Tiwari Bhavya in which they stated that: '[a] study of literature in translation is impossible without engaging with the politics of circulation present in the multiple iterations of the original, or of the translated in the world'.[73] Since its launch in 2016, the editors of the *Journal of World Literature* have been aware of the Eurocentric origins of the field, the debates and the shortcomings therein. The journal is responsive and welcomes all critique, as one should, for the purposes of enhancement of the field. For instance, in the inaugural volume, a special issue deals with the Chinese

[70] David Damrosch, 'Foreword: Literary Criticism and the Qur'an', *Journal of Qur'anic Studies* 16(3) (2014): 4–10 at p. 5.

[71] Damrosch, 'Foreword: Literary Criticism and the Qur'an', p. 7.

[72] Damrosch, *What is World Literature?*, p. 286.

[73] Bhavya Tiwari and David Damrosch, 'World Literature and Postcolonial Studies, Part II', *Journal of World Literature* 5(3) (2020): 321–3.

scriptworld and translation studies; in 2017, a special issue was dedicated to the question of World Literature in Arabic; and, in 2019, it published two issues on 'The Locations of (World Literature): Perspectives from Africa and South Asia'. These special issues are not mere tokenisms to widen the scope of representation of 'minor literatures', but were edited by scholars known for their methodological critique of the field, such as Francesca Orsini and Laetitia Zecchini in the two 2019 special issues.

Francesca Orsini diagnoses some of the problems in the field, namely, the opposition between the local and the global and monolingualism, and by doing so helped to think of world literature otherwise. Orsini proposes conceiving of world literature as 'situated, plural, necessarily multilingual, always-in-the-making' and to hold together 'local and cosmopolitan perspectives'.[74] Ultimately, world literatures are always conjugated in the plural since they depend for their definition on a series of literary productions that are 'significant' to the geographies of the authors and readers. Therefore, world literatures thus conceived encourage us, as Orsini writes, 'to strive for a more modest, honest, and accurate geographical depiction', producing 'world readers who, because they recognize that their own tastes are not "universal" but as conditioned and "provincial" as those of readers elsewhere, are ready to be surprised by the unexpected'.[75]

To a certain extent, Orsini is building on Sanjay Subrahmanyam's work in the field of history in the 1990s, when he specifically challenged how global history was framed and tackled the issue of the limits of expanding a corpus without fundamentally changing anything to the paradigms used. His relying on Persianate archives allowed him to rewrite colonial encounters in India and also to bring to light other-than-European modernities. The centre of his connected historiography and his epistemic framework has moved beyond Europe. Such a paradigmatic move, we argue, has not happened yet in the field of World Literature, which would allow us to construct and imagine other global literary histories.

[74] Francesca Orsini, 'The Multilingual Local in World Literature', *Comparative Literature* 67(4) (2015): 345–74 at p. 369.

[75] Orsini, 'The Multilingual Local in World Literature', p. 369.

To further elaborate on this idea, in 'The Tale of the Hunchback Cycle' (Nights 25th–32nd), in *The Thousand and One Nights*, the storyteller narrates a story set in China, with a hypothetically Chinese monarch, but the king, characters and context 'all operate in an Islamic context'.[76] The Chinese world as imagined in the tale is traversed by and interpreted through the lens of Islamic ethics.[77] China is not a *real* geography in the tale but is turned into a *significant* geography for readers from the Islamicate culture, all the more so since stretches of China were considered as a part of Islamdom, when Muslim merchants traded and controlled the Spice Routes and Silk Roads. In 'The Tale of Crafty Dalilah' (Nights 698th–708th), the Islamicate as ethical formation also serves a significant geography or point where real life persons from different places and times (ninth-century Baghdad, thirteenth-century Baghdad and fifteenth-century Cairo) are called upon to engage fictitiously with each other.[78] Ninth-century and thirteenth-century Baghdad are both spatially and temporally relevant and historically *alive* and *significant* geographies to the storyteller who narrates in a post-fifteenth-century city of the Islamicate.

Islam as a Discursive and Performative World Tradition

Islam, as it occurs in the title and throughout this volume, is used as a critical perspective. By critical perspective, we mean to think about Islam outside the box of metaphysics and faith alone, and centre on its discursive and performative traditions, namely, what type of world literary traditions it created and what effects it had on both those who shaped, invoked, deployed, celebrated and interrogated, be they Muslims or non-Muslims.[79]

[76] Muhsin J. al-Musawi, *The Islamic Context of the Thousand and One Nights* (New York: Columbia University Press, 2009), p. 152.

[77] For more on this and the tale, see Bin Tyeer, *The Qur'an and the Aesthetics of Premodern Arabic Prose*, pp. 121–46.

[78] For more on this tale, see Bin Tyeer, *The Qur'an and the Aesthetics of Premodern Arabic Prose*, pp. 169–75.

[79] We are grateful to Michael Cooperson for his generous comment on the need to further clarify the definition of Islam as used in this book and the crucial distinction between Islam as faith and metaphysics and Islam as a critical perspective.

We borrow the concept-word 'Islamicate' from Marshall G. S. Hodgson's three-volume *The Venture of Islam: Conscience and History in a World Civilization* (1974) in which he distinguished between this concept and what he calls the 'Islamic'. The latter is restricted to phenomena '"of or pertaining to" Islam in the proper, the religious, sense'.[80] On the one hand, when referring to 'Islamic literature', Hodgson looks in particular at religious texts, for instance, Qur᾿ān and *ḥādith*, but also jurisprudence, exegesis, namely, all texts pertaining to Islamic sciences. On the other hand, the adjective Islamicate is used in analogy with the 'Italianate' as in 'Italian style' to refer to not just Italy or to 'whatever is to be called properly Italian, but to something associated typically with Italian style and with the Italian manner . . . Rather similarly, "Islamicate" would refer not directly to the religion, Islam, itself, but to the social and cultural complex historically associated with Islam and the Muslims, both among Muslims themselves and even when found among non-Muslims.'[81] Added to this, Hodgson emphasises the notion that 'Islamicate culture has been expressed in many languages essentially unrelated to each other'.[82]

To further illustrate this idea, let us turn to twelfth-century Ibn Ṭufayl's famous philosophical–theological text *Ḥayy Ibn Yaqẓān*. It tells the story of a child living in complete isolation on an unnamed island but reaching philosophical and religious truths through sensorial experiments and reasoning. This tale was part of a theological debate over the ways in which a human may recognise the divine rationally and intuitively. Ibn Ṭufayl engages with al-Ghazālī's philosophy as evident in his exordium of the text, particularly *Mishkāt al-Anwār* (*The Niche of Light*), in order to correct misunderstandings of the latter's reception. Ibn Ṭufayl is believed to have been responding to Ibn Sīnā's (Avicenna) (d. 1037 CE) epistle carrying the same title *Ḥayy Ibn Yaqẓān*. Other scholars like Iraq/Syria-based al-Suhrawardī (d. 1191) and Egypt-based physician Ibn al-Nafīs (d. 1288) also responded to Ibn Ṭufayl's text within their own disciplines in admiration. In other words, there has been an ongoing engagement with Ibn Ṭufayl's text in Arabic.

80 Marshall G. S. Hodgson, *The Venture of Islam: Conscience and History in a World Civilization*, 3 vols (Chicago: University of Chicago Press, 1974), vol. 1, pp. 58–9.

81 Hodgson, *The Venture of Islam*, vol. 1, p. 59.

82 Hodgson, *The Venture of Islam*, vol. 1, p. 3.

The circulation of *Ḥayy Ibn Yaqẓān* is not restricted to Arabic. Illustrating Hodgson's point about the nature of the Islamicate as one that has distinct aesthetics, poetics and theology (although he separates the 'Islamicate' from 'Islamic') as a feature that circulates in a multiplicity of languages, we may consider how *Ḥayy Ibn Yaqẓān* was translated into Hebrew and Latin across medieval Europe, from Spain to Catalonia and into Provence. Avner Ben Zaken mentions how the text sparked local controversies in Latin between Christian theologians at the University of Paris and among the Jewish communities of Provence–Catalonia. Ben Zaken also analyses the commentary that Moses Narbonni (d. 1362 CE), a Jewish physician and philosopher, wrote in Hebrew on *Ḥayy*.[83] Not only was Narbonni writing in the Islamic tradition of commentary (*sharḥ*) and was engaging with the text's Islamic theological and philosophical arguments but also its own intertexts. Narbonni presented his commentary on *Ḥayy Ibn Yaqẓān* as *Yehiel Ben-ʿUriel* and attached to it a commentary of Ibn Bājja's (Avempace) (d. 1138 CE) *Tadbīr al-mutawaḥḥid* (*The Regime of Solitude*).[84]

The choice of these two texts *Ḥayy ibn Yaqẓān* and *Tadbīr al-mutawaḥḥid* was not serendipitous on the part of Narbonni. Indeed, while admiring Ibn Bājja, Ibn Ṭufayl was engaging with his philosophy. Narbonni was aware of this engagement and positioned his own critical thinking in relation to Ibn Bājja and Ibn Ṭufayl. Therefore, Narbonni simultaneously sits with one foot in an Islamic intellectual world and with the other in Jewish philosophy. Building on Ibn Ṭufayl and Ibn Bājja, Narbonni then invited the Jewish community of scholars to rethink its perception of philosophy and to revive the study of philosophy and reflect on the benefits of solitude for young students in the hope of 'waking up those who are asleep' as the title implies.

Narbonni's commentary and critical reappropriation of two Muslim philosophers and theologians offers an instance of what Edward W. Said called 'affiliative' thinking, as opposed to pure 'filiation'. Without denying or rejecting one's roots, Said defined affiliation as a dynamic concept that allows one to

[83] Avner Ben Zaken, *Cross-Cultural Scientific Exchanges in the Eastern Mediterranean, 1560–1660* (Baltimore, MD: Johns Hopkins University Press, 2010), pp. 43–64.

[84] Ben Zaken, *Cross-Cultural Scientific Exchanges in the Eastern Mediterranean, 1560–1660*, pp. 43–64.

transcend one's filiation, that is, the writer's or critic's natural and organic givens such as 'birth', 'tradition' and 'inherited location'. Through affiliative gestures, human beings make the conscious effort to connect with other places, other modes of thinking and of seeing the world.[85] By engaging with Ibn Bājja and Ibn Ṭufayl in their own terms, Narbonni's reappropriation is *affiliative* and connects with the wider Islamic intellectual world. Later Quaker, Anglican and Orientalist re-uses of the text *Ḥayy Ibn Yaqẓān* no longer engage with the Islamic but reappropriate it in order to undermine the role of the clergy in religion and highlight instead principles of natural connection with the divine.

The early modern European reappropriation takes us back to Damrosch's definition of World Literature constituted of texts which circulate and are read in line with the reader's own terms. This issue here is not so much about reappropriating texts, which by definition circulate whether orally or in written form, widely, globally, regionally or locally. The issue is not about uprooting, re-routing and re-rooting texts. It has always happened and always will. The problem for an academic usage of texts with recognised roots is about considering them as functioning from within a vacuum or framing them as rootless. Narbonni's mode of reading *Ḥayy ibn Yaqẓān* reappropriated the text for the Jewish audience, using Hebrew names and Jewish elements and yet it never forwent the Islamic framework of reading the text as it supplied Ibn Bājja's commentary; it is a *rooted* mode of reading. This approach is very different from the *rootless* (from the perspective of the text in discussion) approach of early modern Quakers, who dispensed with the Qur'ānic references to suit their reappropriation. In other cases, the translators felt the need to supply an explanatory preface to dismiss the 'Islamic' content and ideas present in the text, implying they are not worthy of attention and engagement. As Samar Attar maintains, Robert Barclay, a Scot and a known Quaker theologian, used *Ḥayy Ibn Yaqẓān* as a central reference in his book *An Apology for the True Christian Divinity* (1678), but in the subsequent editions of the book starting 1779 '. . . the positive reference to *Hayy Ibn Yaqzan* were dropped'.[86]

[85] Edward Said, 'Introduction: Secular Criticism', in *The World, the Text, and the Critic* (Cambridge, MA: Harvard University Press, 1983), pp. 1–30.

[86] Samar Attar, *The Vital Roots of European Enlightenment: Ibn Tufayl's Influence on Modern Western Thought* (Lanham, MD: Lexington Books, 2007), pp. xviii, 48.

In the Quaker's case, whether the Islamic references and identity are present or absent, the engagement with the text was not *affiliative*; Islam was no longer part of the discussion and neither was it circulating in 'Islamicate' literary poetics and aesthetics. This was not the case with the Quakers only. For instance, in 1686, Anglican priest George Ashwell, titled his translation, *History of Hai Eb'n Yockdan, an Indian Prince: or, the Self-Taught Philosopher*, with a much simplified narrative that erases many of the Islamic and Qur'ānic references and redacted the text, starting with the Ibn Ṭufayl's preface. Ashwell maintains, 'I have omitted two discourses in my Translation, which I conceived little or nothing pertinent to the main Design of the History'.[87] In addition to taking out the Islamic references, Ashwell also took away the philosophical debates occurring within the tales. For instance, he omitted the description of the 'self-generation' of men, one of two possible beginnings of the story and of Ḥayy's life on the island.[88] Opposed to all what he perceives as 'enthusiastick' uses of the text, the Cambridge Orientalist and Anglican vicar, Simon Ockley, who later held the Adams Professor of Arabic chair at Cambridge in 1711, did not seem to be different in his treatment of the text of *Ḥayy Ibn Yaqẓān*, which he translated in 1708. Ockley maintained that '[t]here are a great many Errors both in his *Philosophy* and *Divinity*: And it was impossible it should be otherwise, the one being altogether *Aristotelian*, the other *Mahometan*.'[89]

Shahab Ahmed has provided a critical re-reading of Hodgson's conception of the Islamicate, which we think is useful and enriching to the field and to our discussion. His redefinition stems from a dissatisfaction with the separation from the religious and the cultural, and by extension the literary, that Hodgson's binary Islamic–Islamicate implies, stating 'it is not at all clear

[87] George Ashwell, 'Preface', *The History of Hai Eb'n Yockdan, an Indian prince, or, The self-taught philosopher* (London: Printed for Richard Chiswell, 1686), p. 16

[88] For more on the Quakers', Anglicans' and Orientalists' uses of the tale, see Louisiane Ferlier and Claire Gallien, '"Enthusiastick" Uses of an Oriental Tale: The English Translations of Ibn Tufayl's *Hayy ibn Yaqdhan* in the Eighteenth Century', in Claire Gallien, and Ladan Niayesh (eds), *Eastern Resonances in Early Modern England*, Transculturalism Series, 1400–1800 (New York: Palgrave, 2019), pp. 93–114.

[89] Simon Ockley, *The Improvement of Human Reason, Exhibited in the Life of Hai ebn Yokdhan* (London: E. Powell, 1708), p. 168.

how "culture" is to be filtered out of "religion" or "religion" distilled out of "culture"'.[90] Using Ḥāfiẓ as a paradigm to think about the Islamic usage of the literary, Ahmed explains this point further:

> Ḥafiẓian discourse shows us that Muslims express themselves in literature in a *different* sense to Christians – –there is no scalar or paradigmatic equivalent to Ḥafiẓian discourse in the literary history of societies of Christians; it is *uniquely* the literary idiom of societies of Muslims. To presume that a distinction between 'secular' and 'religious' literature that might be self-defining or self-evident to us in the Christian context is necessarily and equivalently meaningful in conceptualizing and categorizing the literary discourse of Muslims serves precisely to put out of conceptual focus the crucial and distinctive con-founding or con-fusing quality of the paradigmatic literary expression of Muslims that is the very opposite of a clear-cut 'secular' versus 'religious' or 'religious' versus 'cultural' distinction.[91]

Ahmed therefore criticises the binary religious–non-religious and the Christian (namely, Catholic) lenses used by Hodgson to produce this binary. Not only is there a risk of misrepresenting Islamic relation to literature and how literature, in the Ḥafiẓian, or Ibn Ṭufaylian, or any other sense, is constitutive of Islam, but also of repeating the legal trap shared by Orientalists and Fundamentalists alike in the conceptualisation of Islam. Ahmed's larger goal is to resist the reduction of Islam to a jurisdistic discourse, to refuse the hegemonic *fiqh*-based approach to Islam, strictly conceptualised in terms of orthodoxy and orthopraxy. Indeed, one detrimental consequence of that reduction is to remove literature, also understood in Ahmed's own terms as a practice in interpretation, ambiguity, contradiction, wonder, play,[92] from the Islamic tradition, turning al-Maʿarrī, *Ikhwān al-Ṣafā* (*Brethren of Purity*), Ibn Rushd, Ibn Sīnā, etc. into sceptics, heretics and dissidents. The implication is also that 'when Muslims act and speak *exploratively* – as opposed to *prescriptively* – as they seem to have spent a great deal of their historical time doing, they are

[90] Shahab Ahmed, *What is Islam? The Importance of Being Islamic* (Princeton, NJ: Princeton University Press, 2016), p. 165.

[91] Ahmed, *What is Islam?*, p. 166.

[92] Ahmed, *What is Islam?*, p. 303.

somehow not seen to be acting and speaking in a manner and register that is representative, expressive and constitutive of Islam'.[93]

Ahmed explains and identifies the conceptual and practical production and accommodation of what he calls 'internal contradictions' as fundamental to the human and historical phenomenon of Islam. He reconnects Islam with its tradition of 'prolific *difference* and *disagreement*' and re-roots it in what he calls 'the logics of the internal contradiction'.[94] Taking this logics into account acts as pre-emptive to the excision of Muslim writers such as al-Maʿarrī and/or *Ikhwān al-Ṣafā* from the remit of Islam. Not only because they are represented in disagreement with the knowledge produced by some Orientalists,[95] but most importantly because 'when Muslims claim to be speaking and acting as *Muslims*, that is, to be speaking and acting in *Islam* we need, as an analytical and conceptual matter, to take them *at their word*'.[96]

Through Ahmed's reconnection of the religious and the literary, we move beyond the Hodgsonian separation between the religious and the non-religious and refute the divorcing of texts from their Islamic roots (aesthetics, intellectual and historical milieux). Although not a Muslim himself, Narbonni's engagement with *Ḥayy* situated itself within what Ahmed calls 'Pre-Text, Text, and Con-text'.[97] Ahmed explains these terms in the context of Revelation and the Qurʾān. The Unseen-God-Beyond-this-World (Pre-Text) is revealed, sent down through Revelation (*tanzīl*), made manifest in the World-of-the-Seen (Text).[98] Therefore by Text, Ahmed means all types of manifestation the primary objective of which is Truth-seeking; the Qurʾān being one manifestation of this hermeneutical engagement, but also the cosmos (understood as

[93] Ahmed, *What is Islam?*, p. 303.

[94] Ahmed, *What is Islam?*, p. 302.

[95] For more examples of this, see Ibrahim Haruna Hassan, 'Orientalism and Islamism: A Comparative Study of Approaches to Islamic Studies', *Arts Social Sciences Journal* 6(1) (2015): 1–3; Jasmin Zine, 'Between Orientalism and Fundamentalism: The Politics of Muslim Women's Feminist Engagement', *Muslim World Journal of Human Rights* 3(1) (2006): 1–24.

[96] Ahmed, *What is Islam?*, p. 303.

[97] Ahmed, *What is Islam?*, pp. 301–404.

[98] Ahmed, *What is Islam?*, pp. 346–7.

other 'signs' or divine idioms), and other '*dīn*-bearing' (defined by Ahmed as '*dīn*-conscious') texts (such as the *Masnavi* of Rūmī, al-Ghazālī's *Iḥyā' 'ulūm al-dīn* and *Kalīlah wa Dimnah*).[99] In other words, Ahmed's Texts are forms of emplotment for a Pre-Text that can never be entirely manifested, expressed, represented. With Con-Text, Ahmed means the accumulated layers of texts analysing, explaining, commenting on the Text, and which the new interpreter and interpretive community carry with them, consciously and unconsciously, as they write. It designates, in Ahmed's terms, 'the entire accumulated *lexicon of means and meanings of Islam* that has been historically generated and recorded up to any given moment: it is the full *historical vocabulary of Islam* at any given moment'.[100]

Although these are very useful terms, Ahmed has an expansive understanding of the term Text and does not provide a clear border to the limits of what he calls 'Text'. To what extent do texts become Texts? For instance, would *The Thousand and One Nights* register as Text, as defined by Ahmed. Surely, some tales do possess a '*dīn*-bearing' quality, and are engaged in Truth-searching, and therefore qualify for being a Text. The tale or the poem becomes Text the moment it envisages Truth-seeking as its horizon, but that gesture or that looking for signs and interpretation of signs left by the Unseen in the Seen does not have to be present throughout.

Perhaps this lack of border is a silver-lining in itself, since Ahmed is engaging with what may also be classified as literary texts, such as Rūmī's *Masnavī* as well as Jāmī's *Yūsuf and Zulaykha*, which he calls Texts. To Ahmed, these are indeed Texts in so much as they search for what he terms the Truth:

> The fact that the cosmos is the expression of the Truth/Reason of the Pre-Text of Revelation means that the Truth of the Pre-Text is accessible in and *via* the cosmos by Reason however, the multiplicity and multiplicity and multidimensionality of the cosmos renders this a difficult task. The Text is the more limited expression of Truth/Reason of Revelation in the more limited form of *discourse*[.][101]

[99] Ahmed, *What is Islam?*, pp. 310–12.
[100] Ahmed, *What is Islam?*, p. 357.
[101] Ahmed, *What is Islam?*, p. 349.

To this end, Ahmed's argument would treat *Akhlāq-i Nāṣirī* of Ṭūsī, al-Ghazālī's *Iḥyāʾ ʿulūm al-dīn* and *Kīmiyā-'i saʿādat* (*Alchemy of Happiness*), *Kalīlah wa Dimnah*, *Majnūn Laylā*, Jāmī's *Yūsuf and Zulaykha*, and the *Masnavi* of Rūmī – 'the Qurʾān in the Persian tongue', according to Jāmī – as a 'Qurʾānic exegesis by *other* means'.[102]

In this respect, going back to the example of *Ḥayy ibn Yaqẓān*, Narbonni is hermeneutically engaging with *Ḥayy* as a Text, and also his commentary, *Yehiel Ben-ʿUriel*, is partaking into a broader Con-Text, as his attaching Ibn Bājja's (Avempace) *Tadbīr al-mutawaḥḥid* (*The Regime of Solitude*) to his commentary testifies. In this sense, Narbonni's commentary, even though re-purposed for a Jewish theological–philosophical context, is embedded in the Islamic Con-Text of *Ḥayy* as Text in ways that late seventeenth–early eighteenth-century British Orientalists, such as Edward Pocoke (Elder and Younger) and Simon Ockley, Quakers, such as George Keith, and Anglicans, such George Ashwell, were not. Admittedly, their various editions and translations cannot be subsumed under and reduced to one discourse. They engaged differently with *Ḥayy ibn Yaqẓān*: Pococke's Latin translation was, in Ziad Elmarsafy's terms, fair and allowed readers to make their own judgements about the text while serving British Orientalism's interests placed in competition with other European national branches of Orientalism (Leiden, Paris, etc.).[103] Keith's retranslation in English of Pococke's Latin version used *Ḥayy ibn Yaqẓān* to support Quaker doctrine, while Ashwell, who also retranslated into English from Latin, and Ockley, who translated into English directly from the Arabic, wrapped *Ḥayy ibn Yaqẓān* with a paratext to underline what they presented as the legitimate Anglican understanding of Scripture and faith against *Ḥayy* cum Islam, and Quakers alike.

When Islam is constructed as a mere rhetorical device, as in the Quaker–Anglican–Orientalist case above, what does not fit the construction is occluded, taken out of the literal or figurative corpus (such as the erasure of

102 Ahmed, *What is Islam?*, p. 307.

103 Ziad Elmarsafy, 'Philosophy Self-Taught: Reason, Mysticism, and the Uses of Islam in the Early Enlightenment', in Bernard Heyberger et al. (eds), *L'Islam visto da Occidente: Cultura e religione del Seicento europeo di fronte all'Islam* (Genoa: Marietti, 2009), pp. 140–1; Proceedings of the Cultura E Religione del Seicento Europeo Di Fronte all'Islam (Milan: Università Degli Studi, 17–18 October 2007).

Islam in the poetry of Rūmī and Ḥāfiẓ), or is represented as not registered and belonging to Islam (such as Ibn Rushd/Averroes, for instance, often portrayed as a 'Golden boy' Prometheus, not because of Islam, but in spite of it). In *Radical Love*, Omid Safi lambasts Victorian translators and contemporary re-editions for their versions. He explains: 'In many cases, they have sought to minimize the Islamic context and cast these poems into a generic, universal globalized model of spirituality. In a few cases, such as almost all the material attributed to Rumi and Hafez online, there is no earthly historical connection between these materials and anything the mystic poets of history ever uttered.'[104] As opposed to these erasure, Safi maintains: 'The mystics of Islam see themselves as being rooted unambiguously in the word of God (the Qur᾽ān) and the very being of the Prophet. If I may be permitted a neologism, their poems and stories are "Qur᾽ān-ful", filled with both direct and indirect references to scripture.'[105]

Ibn al-Ḥajjāj is a very interesting example to further our point about what is called or presumed Islamic, who is deemed worthy of representing Islam and who is not, by whom, and for whom. Contemporary literary critic and writer Sinan Antoon produced a monograph on Ibn al-Ḥajjāj titled *The Poetics of the Obscene* (2006) in which he underlined how the poet's engagement and renewal of the *sukhf* tradition was taking place from within an Islamic environment and that there was no contradiction between Ibn al-Ḥajjāj's obscene poems and his 'Muslimness'. In fact, he was revered and praised not only by the people in the marketplace where he worked as market inspector but also by the scholars of his age.[106] In other words, Ibn al-Ḥajjāj was not a misfit of Islam and his poetry was not produced *despite* Islam. In *al-Imtā῾ wa-l-mu᾽ānasa*, littérateur al-Tawḥīdī (d. 1023 CE) recalls his first encounter with Ibn al-Ḥajjāj, telling him:

> by God I am amazed by you . . . You are indeed one of the miracles of God's creatures and the marvels of his worshippers. By God none will believe that you are the very same man who composed your dīwān and that it is yours

[104] Omid Safi, *Radical Love: Teachings from the Islamic Mystical Tradition* (Princeton, NJ: Yale University Press 2018), p. xxxvii

[105] Safi, *Radical Love*, p. xxxviii.

[106] Sinan Antoon, *The Poetics of the Obscene in Premodern Arabic Poetry Ibn al-Ḥajjāj and Sukhf* (New York: Palgrave Macmillan, 2014), pp. 7–10.

with all this contradiction which exists between your poetry and the seriousness of your person.[107]

In other words, al-Tawḥīdī, like his contemporaries and future readers, acknowledges the existence of a poetic persona of Ibn al-Ḥajjāj, and never conflates the two. Dante Alighieri's (d. 1321 CE) *Divine Comedy*, created a representation of Hell that is not found in the Scripture but one that incorporates various Greco-Roman mythopoetics and relies on apocrypha (Apocalypse of Paul) and Christian folklore; he even arguably went against Christian values by vindictively placing political opponents and people in a depiction of theological Hell,[108] without remission or salvation, and yet his Christianity was never questioned.[109] How is it that his poetic persona, or for that matter the persona that is acknowledged in literary criticism for writers across the World as well as the West, does not apply to Muslim writers and poets? By denying the poetic persona to Muslim authors, the critics and by extension readers are left with the darling daughter of colonial modernity: binaries; they could be read as either 'orthodox' or transgressive but never creative or explorative.[110]

Islam and New Directions in World Literature

To acknowledge the complex and full subjectivity of Muslims is to disrupt the categories that were created by 'colonial modernity' and that are still structuring and operating the world in which we live. Muslim subjects in general and writers in particular are denied what Shahab Ahmed called 'explorative authority'.[111] Their creative output is thus utilised and instrumentalised to confirm the 'category' of 'The Muslim' as constructed within the structure of colonial modernity. Indeed, what Magda al-Nowaihi said about the racial

[107] Quoted in Antoon, *The Poetics of the Obscene in Premodern Arabic Poetry*, p. 8.

[108] The concept of theological Hell is used here in distinction to the poetic or literary Hell that is found in al-Maʿarrī's *Risālat al-Ghufrān* (*The Epistle of Forgiveness*), where his representation of Heaven/Hell is meant as a place for poets only, whereas Dante is creating a depiction of an afterlife and judgement for everyone.

[109] For more on this, see Eileen Gardiner, *Visions of Heaven and Hell Before Dante* (New York, Italica Press, 1989), p. 43.

[110] For more on the notion of exploration, see Ahmed, *What is Islam?*, pp. 282–3.

[111] Ahmed, *What is Islam?*, p. 283.

category of the 'Arab' is also valid for the category of the 'Muslim' (and other categories that are imagined as empirical and epistemological objects of coloniality), namely, that the image corresponding to the imagined category (whether corresponding to reality or not) legitimises already held beliefs about Muslims and Islam and becomes collaborative within systems of domination or oppression.[112] The structure of colonial modernity is essential to design the world and to maintain the power relations that are constitutive of this world. The 'category' itself is already a product of this modernity:

> We can define modernity as the construction of the category of the 'category'. Modernity's 'cunning innovation' of the category resulted into 'dividing our beliefs and practices up and setting them apart from one another with analytic clarity'.[113]

Whatever disrupts that structure is occluded, including the ways in which we, as literary critics, teachers and readers, approach Islamic literatures. Nizar F. Hermes pointed to the questionable scarcity in the classroom (and by deduction publishing industry) of literary corpuses dealing with humour, food and etiquette of marital and sexual relationships, in short, literature that points to subjectivity, pleasure and living a full life – they are seen as an antinomy to the constructed category of 'Islam', 'Muslims' or the 'Muslim life' imagined by 'colonial modernity' and therefore disruptive for that imagination.[114] The Library of Arabic Literature (LAL) project at New York University started in 2012 is indeed a commendable effort to fill the aforementioned gap, making available in Arabic editions and English translations of works from the seventh to the nineteenth century that encompass a wide range of genres, including poetry, poetics, fiction, religion, philosophy, law, science, travel

[112] Magda al-Nowaihi, 'For a "Foreign" Audience: The Challenges of Teaching Arabic Literature in the American Academy', *Middle East Studies Association Bulletin* 35(1) (2001): 24–7 at 26.

[113] Ahmed, *Religion as Critique*, p. 47.

[114] Nizar F. Hermes, 'Classical and Medieval Arabic Literary Delights: Towards Teaching the Humanistic Literature of the Arabs', in Muhsin J. al-Musawi (ed.), *Arabic Literature for the Classroom: Teaching Methods, Theories, Themes and Texts* (London: Routledge, 2017), pp. 83–96.

writing, history and historiography. Indeed, the editions boast of a high quality that are geared to an academic audience and are also accessible to the common reader in paperback editions. This, and the fact that the Arabic texts are freely downloadable online, make them useful pedagogical tools, especially in Comparative Literature departments.

The present volume, born out of the arguments developed in our present introduction and each chapter by our esteemed colleagues in various fields, is an utterance of this vision. We would like to thank our contributors for their scholarship, trust, commitment to the volume during the difficult time with the onset of COVID-19 in 2020, and the collegial conversations that enriched our thinking.

This volume is conceived of as a field opener. Although the chapters taken together cover a wide geography and chronology, we do not claim that the result is all-encompassing, nor did we intend it to be so in the first place. Humble literary critics know that much happens outside the boundaries set by the frame of their fields, the locus of enunciation, and that the scholarship they produce very much depends on the channels (the theory and critical–philological tools) made available by their fields of expertise. These channels enable them to access certain literary and artistic works, and they also, by default, leave a lot behind. For instance, French scholars working on contemporary Algerian literature would know the works of authors established in the West and published by Parisian houses, but perhaps the literature produced in *fusḥa* and *darja* and published in small local publishing presses in Tlemcen or Blida may fall outside their physical nets.[115]

This is the reason why we chose not to organise our volume in geographical 'areas' precisely because it cannot be assumed that there is a possibility of 'covering' everything and because writing from the Global North renders the very gesture of 'mapping' knowledge and literatures problematic. A chronological organisation of the volume was also ruled out because the chapters, while often focusing on specific moments, are moving back and forth in time,

[115] For a sociological study of Algerian literature since the 'Black Decade' and the role of French publishing houses in consecration processes, see Tristan Leperlier, *Algérie, les écrivains de la décennie noire* (Paris: CNRS, 2018).

rendering the idea of teleological time irrelevant. In other words, the present volume does not self-define as a *comprehensive* and *totalising* companion of Islamicate literatures.

That being said, it must be mentioned that the idea of a multi-volume, multilingual anthology of Islamicate *adab* from the sixth to the nineteenth century and its literary developments in the post-colonial present would be useful to colleagues in Comparative Literatures and students across disciplines. The harrowing gaps, which such a multi-volume, multilingual anthology would fill, would interconnect with specialised academic fields (Arabic, African, Central Asian, Persian, Ottoman, Urdu Studies, and more) across periods, genres and, more importantly, place the fields in conversation with each other primarily, as well as with Comparative and World Literature. Such an endeavour remains *desideratum* and our volume is a first step in that much-needed direction. While not being oblivious to or naive about the predicaments of positionality and privilege (of scholars situated in the Global North and writing in English), about the problematic nature of anthologising desires, and about the fact that the intellectual beneficiaries of such anthologies are situated in the universities of the Global North, our volume is also motivated by an ethical drive and is not content with complacent or complicit silences.

The present volume is divided into four sections: 'Tropes of Orientalism', 'Sensory Fluctuations: Aural, Oral, Visual and Written', 'Circulation, Translation, Rereading' and 'Secular–Non-Secular'. As reflected in the titles of the sections, we did not organise the volume in a chronological or a geographical manner. The titles chosen for each of these sections articulate key concepts that relate to the concerns of the featured chapters within each section. While some chapters could find a home in other sections or share theoretical concerns with other chapters, this does not mean that their placement is arbitrary. Rather, the chapters' high reliefs provide significant connections with the titles of the sections even though their interdisciplinary resonances are shared by other sections and chapters.

The two chapters in 'Tropes of Orientalism', namely '*Los moros de la hueste*: Recovering the Islamicate in the Goths' Lament' by Gregory Hutcheson and 'Just One Word' by Gil Anidjar, are concerned with issues of European representations of Islam at various moments in history, in the context of the

Spanish Reconquista and Nazi Germany. More generally, the chapters discuss how Islam globalised in the Western imaginary based on Said's foundational reflections on Orientalism. With these chapters, we restate that the volume does not operate in a vacuum but it starts with what Said and postcolonialism have brought to the discussion on Islam as represented/fantasied and globalised in and through Western literatures to move beyond and think about how Islamic literatures work globally in the subsequent sections of the volume.

Gregory Hutcheson's chapter studies the production of a comprehensive history of Spain first conceived by Alfonso's historiographic workshop in the 1270s and titled the *Estoria de Espanna*. The *Estoria* draws liberally on previous historical and polemical works as it interpolates the rise of Islam into the history of Visigothic Spain. The chapter anchors the *Estoria* in its originary context – both its conceptual frame and its historical habitus – and gauges the degree to which it mobilises the brand of Islamophobia we routinely project onto medieval Spain. Hutcheson argues that, while in its contemporary iterations it is made to align with a universalising Islamophobic discourse, it actually emerged from and was mediated through an Islamicate textuality that supported Alfonso's colonialist agenda rather than a crusader imperative. Gil Anidjar's chapter, 'Just One Word' analyses the ways in which the word *Muselmänner* has been recorded, inscribed and translated, disseminated, and sometimes even read, though not without problems (including *literary* problems). In the chapter, Anidjar experiments with the word *Muselmänner*, a seemingly ordinary word or, rather, a word that is at once more ordinary and more literary than has otherwise appeared, and he reads from a demonstrably different grid or frame (Economy, Science, Politics, Religion and Literature).

After a necessary Saïdian foundation, the second section titled 'Sensory Fluctuations: Aural, Oral, Visual and Written' heralds the volume's conception of Islam as World Literature beginning with Walid Ghali's chapter 'Poems in Praise of the Prophet (*madīḥ*) as a Citizen of the Literary World'. Ghali interweaves performances of (*madīḥ*) poetry with the circulation of various renditions of the established genre of poems in praise of the Prophet Muḥammad (*madīḥ nabawī*), most notably the *Qaṣīdat al-Burda* by al-Būṣīrī (d. 694/1294). The chapter aims to shed light on the significance of *madīḥ* as a literary genre and its contributions to Muslim cultures, and World

Literature. Walid Ghali's chapter as well as Haiyun Ma and Brendan Newlon's chapter and his translation and analysis of Emperor Zhu Yuanzhang's (1328–98) 'Ode to the Prophet' offer an opportunity to read this genre of *madīḥ* as World Literature beyond Europe and read the figure of the Prophet as a citizen of the literary World before Goethe's own interpretation of the genre of *madīḥ* and the figure of the Prophet Muḥammad in *Mahomets Gesang* ('Song of Muḥammad') in 1772–3 and its musical rendition by Franz Schubert.

In the second section, Christiane Seydou's chapter 'The Place and Function of Imagination in Fulani Mystical Poetry (Massina, Mali)' examines Fulani mystical poetry from the eighteenth to the twentieth century, traditionally transmitted orally in the *zāwiya* or by singers during religious feasts in Mali. Seydou argues that this poetry has contributed to the diffusion of Islam in all social strata of the population, from the most literate to the most humble. By sharing with their interlocutors the emotions drawn from their intimate and personal mystical experiences, the poets inspired a spiritual communion. They also revived in believers – beyond intellectual knowledge and the reasoned application of religious Law – the depth and intensity of their faith, in other words, Seydou argues that poetry played a role of 'humanising' religious discourse with personalised and imaginative poetry.

In Musapir's (pen name) chapter 'Vanishing Islamic Art: Fluidity and Complexity of Contemporary Uyghur Sufi Storytelling Tradition', the author focuses on Uyghur oral traditions, in particular storytelling, folk literature, oral histories, *dhikr* rituals, and on Uyghur professional storytellers performing in sacred landscapes, shrines, Uyghur *muqam*, *meshrep*. The author argues that the fluidity of Uyghur storytelling, based on mentoring and creativity, has yet to be recognised within Islamic Studies, and within World Literature studies as well. Musapir focuses on the story of the Battle of Karbala, widely popular among Uyghur storytellers, as evidence of mobility and transformation in storytelling, between written form and oral performance, and within different spaces. Through these *meddah*s, we can see the interactive and living aspect of Sufi literature, beyond static books and geographies and the singular, often immobile, categorisation of cultural heritage.

Our third section, 'Circulation, Translation, Rereading', orbits around questions of circulation and various forms of translations, including literary, of course, but also cultural, of Islamic texts, themes, characters that have become part of a multilingual World Literature. The first chapter is co-written by Georges Tamer and Cüneyd Yıldırım and discusses 'Friedrich Rückert (1788–1866) and his Poetic Translation of the Qurʾān'. It offers an overview of Rückert's (pseudo-)Orientalist oeuvre as a prolific German poet, borrowing from classical Eastern literature, as in *Die Weisheit des Brahmanen*, and as a scholar of Oriental philology, translating ancient Arabic poetry and rhymed prose, such as Abū Tammām's *Diwān al-Ḥamāsa* and al-Ḥarīrī's *Maqāmāt*, as well as major parts of the Qurʾān into German rhymed prose, analysis of his translations from the Qurʾān exemplified in the *suras* of *al-ikhlāṣ*, *al-qadr* and *al-tīn* (Q. 114, Q. 97 and Q. 95, respectively). The chapter argues for a multifaceted reading of the poet's treatment of Islam and the so-called Orient and reveals his serious interest in both philologically based and aesthetic constructions of the 'Other'.

From Galland's translation of the *Arabian Nights* to Guy Ritchie's *Aladdin* produced by Disney, Muhsin J. al-Musawi presents in 'The "Islamic" *Arabian Nights* in World Imaginaries' the systematic conflation of the *Arabian Nights* with Islam as a modern concoction. Al-Musawi tracks in the prose of eminent Arabists and Orientalists a tendency to treat the *Arabian Nights* as document, a representation of manners and customs. In contemporary representations of Islam and the Arabs, al-Musawi excavates the material written as commentaries on the *Arabian Nights*, and the massive use of illustrations to represent a presumed real 'Orient'.

Finally, Hamid Dabashi's chapter 'Where is World Literature?' invites us to reconsider our conceptions of the cardinal points of the 'World', beyond the 'West' and 'East' binary, as they both have been colonially co-created. To the question of 'Where is World Literature?', Dabashi answers that it is in Manus Island refugee camp in Australia where Behrooz Boochani, a Kurdish Iranian refugee, tapped his bestselling memoir on his cell phone in Persian, had it translated into English and published to a global reception. The idea of Islam as a floating signifier plays a significant role in this redefinition of World Literature, not only by bringing to the forefront a variety of languages in which Muslims have created their poetic and literary works, such as Arabic, Persian, Turkish or Urdu, but also when similar literary works are translated across some of the languages of the Islamicate. Dabashi therefore not only argues for a revision of the 'World' but also confirms the presence of the Islamicate as World Literature.

The fourth section questions the modern preconceived boundary between secular and non-secular. Indeed, as Talal Asad reminds us, the very ideas of 'religion' and 'the secular' and the disjunction between the two concepts have a European genealogy, dating back to the post-Reformation period. It was underpinned in the Enlightenment through the philosophical proposition of a 'natural' religion as separated from the political sphere of power, and reinforced in the nineteenth-century age of positivism and evolutionary thought where 'religion was considered to be an early human condition from which modern law, science, and politics emerged and became detached'.[116] This constructed separation and the concomitant reading of Islamic traditions as political or the coupling of Islam with politics places Islam in competition with state authority. But the coupling of Islam with politics is an historical construction.

As intellectual captives of conceptual modern constructions and the ready-made couplings between Islam and politics, we may be prevented from reading the rich nuances present in the 'Ode to the Prophet' in Chinese as discussed by Haiyun Ma and Brendan Newlon in their chapter 'Praising the Prophet Muḥammad in Chinese: A New Translation and Analysis of Emperor Zhu Yuanzhang's *Ode to the Prophet*' in its own terms. A song of praise (*madīḥ*) from the fourteenth-century Chinese Emperor Zhu Yuanzhang lauding the human and moral qualities of the Prophet Muḥammad, the poem allows us to reflect prismatically on the history of maritime trade and of diplomacy, on the differences between Muslim and non-Muslim historiographical accounts of Emperor Zhu and his relationship with Islam, but as Ma and Newlon argue the poem 'represents a tipping point after which Islam may be discussed as a religion of China rather than merely as a religion practiced in China'.

Pasha M. Khan's chapter, 'A Fine Romance: Translating the *Qissah* as World Romance', further challenges inherited 'modes of reading' in the Global North, understood as an ideological location not a geographical one. That is to say, an author or a reader may be producing knowledge in Arabic, in the MENA region, for instance, using the same 'modes of reading' of the Global

[116] Talal Asad, *Genealogies of Religion:Discipline and Reasons of Power in Christianity and Islam* (Baltimore, MD: Johns Hopkins University Press, 1993), p. 27.

North thus replicating the same ideologies. Khan asks what was the 'World' assumed and conjured by the idea of the 'romance' as a world literary genre? And how did Orientalism produce the space and time of that world when translating the narrative genres of *qissah, hikāyat, dāstān, kathā* as romance. Reading *qissah, hikāyat, dāstān, kathā* as romances, European Orientalists relegated these literary genres pertaining to the Islamicate to the past, as obsolete non-secular literature, and irrelevant to the modern world. In other words, the reading of *qissah* as romance participates in a form of ongoing epistemic colonial dismissal of *qissah* as failed novel, and in what Khan describes as 'chrono-Orientalism' or 'schizochronic' condition, where Islamicate literatures are still there but do not belong to the here and now of modernity.

Nazry Bahrawi's chapter 'Indonesia's *sastera profetik* as Decolonial Literary Theory' discusses the reappropations of Islamic epistemologies as critical, dissensual and decolonial tools to rethink World Literature. Bahrawi's chapter attempts to use *sastera profetik* (prophetic literature), conceptualised by the author and academic Kuntowijoyo in the 1990s, as a critical literary lens that fulfils several objectives. Two of the most relevant are (1) to encourage a person to become more humane in their personal life so that they can affect a similar change in their environment; and (2) to urge a community to embrace spirituality as a counter to oppression and colonisation. Using this critical lens, Bahrawi reads short stories, which are part of the World Literature canon, by the Argentinian author Jorge Luis Borges and Franz Kafka's *The Metamorphosis* (1915). Bahrawi analyses these literary works, which contain little to no trace of influence by Islamic cultures, as litmus tests for the universal relevance of *sastera profetik* as critical theory. Framing Borges and Kafka in *sastera profetik* may not always prove conclusive and therefore the universal applicability of *sastera profetik* is ultimately called into question by Bahrawi. But for Bahrawi and for us, the importance of using *sastera profetik* to read Western literature lies in the very counter-hegemonic gesture of positioning *sastera profetik* as a critical literary tool to read non-Western texts.

Before concluding this introduction, some final words are due. When the call for papers went out to solicit chapters for this volume in 2018, it was our vision that the volume should attract not only excellent scholarship but gender-inclusive and diverse representations of scholarship. We aimed to have scholars not only from the Global North, but also Global South;

junior as well as senior colleagues. As women scholars, we are aware of the first glance taken at the table of contents of edited volumes that look for more participation from junior, BIPOC (Black, indigenous and people of colour), and women colleagues in the field to maintain a fuller picture and a healthy balance. We had initially achieved this; but unfortunately, along the way, COVID-19 happened in early 2020. It affected everyone; a couple of male colleagues had to withdraw their chapters, but the bulk of our female contributors dropped out even with COVID-19 extensions. As recent studies showed, the pandemic has indeed affected everyone but it was mainly women academics who took the hit: 'Our complete data on all Elsevier journals indicate that the exceptional lockdown and social distancing measures imposed by the pandemic have penalized women academics and benefited men'.[117] As a result, the geographical balance of our volume was also affected as we initially envisaged including more regions of the Islamicate world, such as the literatures of the Indian Oceanic world, Central Asia, West Africa, South America, and a greater level of representation of authors as well, including Muslim slave narratives and the literature produced by Royhinga displaced and exiled writers.

This volume was born out of a recognition of a lack in the field of World Literature for a proper discussion with other conceptions of World Literature from outside the Global North. Our goal is not to antagonise one literature against the other or repeat the claim of universalism in World Literature but to pave the way for other sites of critical engagement with World Literatures to emerge, and to create fruitful environments for discussion. It therefore fulfils a trifold aim: (a) it puts forth the argument that the literatures of the Islamicate analysed by our contributors circulate as World Literature in the Islamicate itself. In this respect, the Islamicate becomes a 'mode of reading' and World Literature in itself. These literatures also circulate beyond the Islamicate; (b) with the first claim put forth, the volume is also conceived as a critical space where a dialogue is now open between multiple fields and literatures, which are institutionally separated into area studies and are therefore disciplinarily

[117] Colleen Flaherty, 'Women are Falling Behind', *Inside HigherEd*, 20 October 2020, available at: https://www.insidehighered.com/news/2020/10/20/large-scale-study-backs-other-research-showing-relative-declines-womens-research.

not sufficiently engaging with one another as one would hope; and, finally, (c) our aim is to have these literatures of the Islamicate be engaged as World Literature, including for readers who were not cognizant of them, but who may now, we hope, be invited to rethink and retheorise their engagements with literature and the arts at large. The silver lining running through our book has been to offer a critical intervention in the form of what Sanjay Krishnan called an 'interruptive embrace'.[118]

Bibliography

Aboulela, Leila, *The Translator* (New York: Black Cat, 1999).

Ahmed, Asad Q., 'Postclassical Philosophical Commentaries: Innovation in the Margins', *Oriens* 41 (2013): 317–48.

Ahmed, Asad Q., 'Systematic Growth in Sustained Error: Dynamism of Post-Classical Rationalism', in Asad Q. Ahmed, Behnam Sadeghi and Michael Bonner (eds), *The Islamic Scholarly Tradition* (Leiden and Boston: Brill, 2011), pp. 343–78.

Ahmed, Asad Q., 'Islam's Invented Golden Age', *OpenDemocracy*, 28 October 2013, available at: https://www.opendemocracy.net/en/openindia/islams-invented-golden-age.

Ahmad, Irfan, *Religion as Critique* (Chapel Hill: University of North Carolina Press, 2017).

Ahmed, Shahab, *What is Islam? The Importance of Being Islamic* (Princeton, NJ: Princeton University Press, 2016).

Al-Musawi, Muhsin J., *The Islamic Context of the Thousand and One Nights* (New York: Columbia University Press, 2009).

Al-Musawi, Muhsin J., *The Medieval Islamic Republic of Letters* (Notre Dame, IN: Notre Dame University Press, 2015).

Al-Nowaihi, Magda. 'For a "Foreign" Audience: The Challenges of Teaching Arabic Literature in the American Academy', *Middle East Studies Association Bulletin* 35(1) (2001): 24–7.

Allan, Michael, *In the Shadow of Literature, Sites of Reading in Colonial Egypt* (Princeton, NJ: Princeton University Press, 2018).

Antoon, Sinan, 'Sinaan Antoon on the West's "Forensic Interest" in Arabic Lit, 4 March 2010, available at: https://arablit.org/2010/03/04/sinaan-antoon-on-the-wests-forensic-interest-in-the-arab-world.

[118] Krishnan, *Reading the Global*, p. 14.

Antoon, Sinan, *The Poetics of the Obscene in Premodern Arabic Poetry Ibn al-Ḥajjāj and Sukhf* (New York: Palgrave Macmillan, 2014).

Asad, Talal, *Genealogies of Religion: Discipline and Reasons of Power in Christianity and Islam* (Baltimore, MD: Johns Hopkins University Press, 1993).

Ashwell, George, *The History of Hai Eb'n Yockdan, an Indian prince, or, The self-taught philosopher* (London: Printed for Richard Chiswell, 1686).

Attar, Samar, *The Vital Roots of European Enlightenment: Ibn Tufayl's Influence on Modern Western Thought* (Lanham, MD: Lexington Books, 2007).

Beecroft, Alexander, 'World Literature without a Hyphen Towards a Typology of Literary Systems', in David Damrosch (ed.), *World Literature in Theory* (Chichester: Wiley-Blackwell, 2014), pp. 180–90.

Ben Zaken, Avner, *Cross-Cultural Scientific Exchanges in the Eastern Mediterranean, 1560–1660* (Baltimore, MD: Johns Hopkins University Press, 2010).

Bin Tyeer, Sarah R., *The Qurʾan and the Aesthetics of Premodern Arabic Prose* (London: Palgrave Macmillan, 2016).

Bonebakker, Adrianus, 'Adab and the Concept of Belles-Lettres', in Julia Ashtiany et al. (eds), *Abbasid Belles-Lettres, The Cambridge History of Arabic Literature* (Cambridge: Cambridge University Press, 1990).

Brouilette, Sarah, *UNESCO and the Fate of the Literary* (Stanford, CA: Stanford University Press, 2019).

Casanova, Pascale, *The World Republic of Letters*, trans. Malcolm C DeBevoise (Cambridge, MA: Harvard University Press, 2004).

Cheah, Pheng, *What is a World?* (Durham, NC: Duke University Press, 2016).

Cooperson, Michael, 'The Abbasid "Golden Age": An Excavation', *al-Uṣūr al-Wusṭā* 25(1) (2017): 41–65.

Damrosch, David, *What Is World Literature?* (Princeton, NJ: Princeton University Press, 2003).

Damrosch, David, 'Foreword: Literary Criticism and the Qurʾan', *Journal of Qurʾanic Studies* 16(3) (2014): 4–10.

Elmarsafy, Ziad, 'Philosophy Self-Taught. Reason, Mysticism, and the Uses of Islam in the Early Enlightenment', in Bernard Heyberger et al. (eds), *L'Islam visto da Occidente: Cultura e religione del Seicento europeo di fronte all'Islam* (Milan: Marietti, 2009), pp. 140–1.

Fabian, Johannes, *Time and the Other: How Anthropology Makes it Object* (New York: Columbia University Press, [1983] 2014).

Ferlier, Louisiane and Claire Gallien, '"Enthusiastick" Uses of an Oriental Tale: The English Translations of Ibn Tufayl's *Hayy ibn Yaqdhan* in the Eighteenth

Century', in Claire Gallien, and Ladan Niayesh (eds), *Eastern Resonances in Early Modern England*, Transculturalism Series, 1400–1800 (New York: Palgrave, 2019), pp. 93–114.

Flaherty, Colleen, 'Women are Falling Behind', *Inside HigherEd*, 20 October 2020.

Gallien, Claire, 'British Orientalism, Indo-Persian Historiography, and the Politics of Global Knowledge', in S. Davies, D. S. Roberts, and G. Sanchez Espinoza (eds), *India and Europe in the Global Eighteenth Century*, Oxford University Studies in the Enlightenment series (Oxford: Oxford University Press, 2014), pp. 29–52.

Ganguly, Debjany, 'Salman Rushdie and the World Picture of Islam', in Ken Seigneurie (ed.), *A Companion to World Literature* (Hoboken, NJ: Wiley, 2019), pp. 1–11.

Gardiner, Eileen, *Visions of Heaven and Hell Before Dante* (New York: Italica Press, 1989).

Goethe, Johann Wolfgang von, *Conversations of Goethe with Eckermann and Soret*, trans. John Oxenford, 2 vols (London: Smith, Elder, 1850).

Gruendler, Beatrice, 'Kalila wa Dimna: A Unique Work of World Literature', in Verena M. Lepper (ed.), *Arab and German Tales: Transcending Culture* (Berlin: Kultur Verlag Kadmos, 2018), pp. 67–8.

Hallaq, Wael, 'On the Origins of the Controversy about the Existence of Mujtahids and the Gate of Ijtihad', *Studia Islamica* 63 (1986): 129–41.

Hassan, Ibrahim Haruna, 'Orientalism and Islamism: A Comparative Study of Approaches to Islamic Studies', *Arts Social Sciences Journal* 6(1) (2015): 1–3.

Heinrichs, Wolfhart, 'The Classification of the Sciences and the Consolidation of Philology in Classical Islam', in Jan Willem Drijvers and Andrew Archibald MacDonald (eds), *Centres of Learning: Learning and Location in Pre-Modern Europe and the Near East* (Leiden: Brill, 1995), pp. 119–39.

Hermes, Nizar F., 'Classical and Medieval Arabic Literary Delights: Towards Teaching the Humanistic Literature of the Arabs', in by Muhsin J. al-Musawi (ed.), *Arabic Literature for the Classroom: Teaching Methods, Theories, Themes and Texts* (London: Routledge, 2017), pp. 83–96.

Hodgson, Marshall G. S., *The Venture of Islam: Conscience and History in a World Civilization*, 3 vols (Chicago: University of Chicago Press, 1974).

Holmberg, Bo, 'Adab and Arabic Literature', in *Literary History: Towards a Global Perspective* (Berlin: W. de Gruyter, 2006), vol. 1, pp. 180–205.

Ibn al-Nadīm, *The Fihrist of al-Nadīm (Abū al-Faraj Muḥammad Ibn Isḥāq)*, ed. Ayman Fu'ād Sayyid (London: Al-Furqan Islamic Heritage Foundation, 2014).

Itzhak, Chen-Bar, 'Intellectual Captivity: Literary Theory, World Literature, and the Ethics of Interpretation', *Journal of World Literature* 5(1) (2020): 79–110.

Krishnan, Sanjay, *Reading the Global: Troubling Perspectives on Britain's Empire in Asia* (New York: Columbia University Press, 2007).

Leperlier, Tristan, *Algérie, les écrivains de la décennie noire* (Paris: CNRS, 2018).

Macé, Marielle, 'La critique est un sport de combat', *Acta fabula* 10(3), Essais critiques (March 2009).

Malcolm, Noel, *Useful Enemies: Islam and the Ottoman Empire in Western Political Thought, 1450–1750* (Oxford: Oxford University Press, 2019).

Marx, Karl and Friedrich Engels, *Manifesto of the Communist Party*, Marxists Internet Archive (marxists.org) [1948] 1987, 2000, 2010.

Massad, Joseph, *Islam in Liberalism* (Chicago: University of Chicago Press, 2015).

McColvin, L. R., *The Chance to Read: Public Libraries in the World Today* (London: Phoenix Press, 1957).

Mignolo, Walter, 'Epistemic Disobedience, Independent Thought and Decolonial Freedom', *Theory, Culture & Society* 26(7/8) (2009): 159–81.

Moretti, Franco, 'Conjectures on World Literature', *New Left Review* 1 (Jan./Feb. 2000): 56–68.

Mufti, Aamir R., 'Orientalism and the Institution of World Literatures', *Critical Inquiry* 36(3) (2010): 458–93.

Mufti, Aamir, *Forget English! Orientalisms and World Literatures* (Cambridge, MA: Harvard University Press, 2016).

Muhanna, Elias, 'Introduction', in *The Ultimate Ambition in the Arts of Erudition: A Compendium of Knowledge from the Classical Islamic World by Shihab al-Din al-Nuwayri*, ed. and trans. Elias Muhanna (London: Penguin Classics, 2016).

Muhanna, Elias, *The World in a Book: Al-Nuwayri and the Islamic Encyclopedic Tradition* (Princeton, NJ: Princeton University Press, 2018).

Nuʿmānī, Shiblī, *Turkey, Egypt, and Syria: A Travelogue*, trans. Gregory Maxwell Bruce (New York: Syracuse University Press, 2020).

Ockley, Simon, *The Improvement of Human Reason, Exhibited in the Life of Hai ebn Yokdhan* (London: E. Powell, 1708).

Orsini, Francesca, 'The Multilingual Local in World Literature', *Comparative Literature* 67(4) (2015): 345–74.

Safi, Omid, *Radical Love: Teachings from the Islamic Mystical Tradition* (Princeton, NJ: Yale University Press, 2018).

Said, Edward, *The World, the Text, and the Critic* (Cambridge, MA: Harvard University Press, 1983).

Strich, Fritz, *Goethe and World Literature* (London: Routledge & Kegan Paul, 1949).

Subrahmanyam, Sanjay, 'Connected Histories: Notes Towards a Reconfiguration of Early Modern Eurasia', *Modern Asian Studies* 31(3) (1997): 735–62.

Subrahmanyam, Sanjay, *Explorations in Connected History*, 2 vols (Oxford: Oxford University Press, 2004).

Tiwari, Bhavya and David Damrosch, 'World Literature and Postcolonial Studies, Part II', *Journal of World Literature* 5(3) (2020): 321–3.

Viswanathan, Gauri, *Masks of Conquest: Literary Study and British Rule in India* (New York: Columbia University Press, 1994).

Warner, Marina, *Stranger Magic: Charmed States and the Arabian Nights* (Cambridge: MA, Harvard University Press, 2012).

Warner, Marina, 'Report: Bearer-Beings and Stories in Transit/Storie in Transito', *Marvels & Tales* 31(1) (2017), available at: https://digitalcommons.wayne.edu/marvels/vol31/iss1/9.

Zine, Jasmin, 'Between Orientalism and Fundamentalism: The Politics of Muslim Women's Feminist Engagement', *Muslim World Journal of Human Rights* 3(1) (2006): 1–24.

TROPES OF ORIENTALISM

2

LOS MOROS DE LA HUESTE: RECOVERING THE ISLAMICATE IN THE GOTHS' LAMENT

Gregory S. Hutcheson

In or around 711 CE, Arab-Berber forces crossed the Strait of Gibraltar from North Africa into Spain, overcame Visigothic resistance, and brought the great bulk of the Iberian Peninsula – al-Andalus in the Arabic – into the orbit of Dār al-Islam. Under a transplanted Umayyad dynasty, once-Roman Cordoba emerged as al-Andalus' capital city; by the tenth century, it rivalled Abbasid Baghdad as the cultural and intellectual centre of the Islamic world. New cultural hotspots sprang up in the tenth and eleventh centuries, even as the caliphate of Cordoba fragmented into dozens of petty states allied at times with each other, at times with Christian kingdoms that had begun flexing their muscles in the Iberian north. By the mid-thirteenth century, the Christian kingdom of Castile had established its ascendancy on the peninsula, so much so that when Fernando III died in 1252, he handed to his son Alfonso X the task of governing a massively expanded realm that boasted not only a coastline looking out over North Africa, but also a significant minority Muslim population.[1]

[1] For a comprehensive history of Islamic presence on the Iberian Peninsula up through the sixteenth century, see Brian A. Catlos, *Kingdoms of Faith: A New History of Islamic Spain* (New York: Hachette, 2018).

Although vexed time and again in his political ambitions, Alfonso has come down to us with the sobriquet 'the Wise' for the massive intellectual project he oversaw throughout the thirty-plus years of his rule. A cornerstone of this project was the production of a comprehensive history of Spain that attempted in no small part to make sense of Islam's centuries-long hegemony in the Iberian Peninsula. As first conceived by Alfonso's historiographic workshop in the 1270s, the *Estoria de Espanna* (*History of Spain*) draws liberally on previous historical and polemical works as it interpolates into Spanish history the rise of Islam and its expansion westward across North Africa.[2] While Islam's flashpoints with other regions are described almost dispassionately, the moment of conquest of Spain calls for a more visceral response, and here chroniclers let loose the full power of their rhetorical arsenal:

> The Moors of the host [*Los moros de la hueste*] wore silks and colourful cloths which they had taken as booty, their horses' reins were like fire, their faces were black as pitch, the handsomest among them black as a cooking-pot, and their eyes blazed like fire; their horses as swift as leopards, their horsemen more cruel and hurtful than the wolf that comes at night to the flock of sheep. The vile African people . . . was at that moment raised on high, for in a short time they speedily shattered the greatness of the Goths in a way that man has no words to express.[3]

[2] The *Estoria de Espanna* was composed in fits and starts throughout the reign of Alfonso X and well into the fourteenth century. For a general overview of scholarship on the *Estoria*'s complex manuscript tradition, see Aengus Ward (ed.), *Estoria de Espanna Digital* V.1.1 (Birmingham: University of Birmingham, 2020), available at: http://estoria.bham.ac.uk. For ease of citation, here I will use Colin Smith, *Christians and Moors in Spain*, vol. 1 (Warminster: Aris & Phillips, 1988), which draws original-language text from Ramón Menéndez Pidal (ed.), *Primera crónica general. Estoria de España que mandó componer Alfonso el Sabio y se continuaba bajo Sancho IV en 1289* (Madrid: Gredos, 1955). All translations are Smith's unless otherwise noted.

[3] Smith, *Christians and Moors in Spain*, p. 19. In the original: 'Los moros de la hueste todos uestidos del sirgo e de los pannos de color que ganaran, las riendas de los sus cauallos tales eran como de fuego, las sus caras dellos negras como la pez, el mas fremoso dellos era negro como la olla, assi luzien sus oios como candelas; el su cauallo dellos ligero como leopardo, e el su caual-lero mucho mas cruel et mas dannoso que es el lobo en la grey de las oueias en la noche. La uil gente de los affricanos . . . essora era exaltada, ca crebanto en una ora mas ayna la nobleza de los godos que lo non podrie omne dezir por lengua' (Smith, *Christians and Moors in Spain*, p. 18).

This chapter of the *Estoria*, dubbed 'Duelo de los godos' ('The Goths' Lament') by literary scholars, goes on to detail the violent acts by which Moorish armies ravaged the land, massacred its people and desecrated its sacred spaces.

While the xenophobic turns of the 'Duelo' are not original to Alfonso's chroniclers, what lends to their impact is their translation from the Latin into the vernacular at a moment when Castilian was rapidly evolving into a literary language. Both the pathos and the poetry of the 'Duelo' have made of it a fetichised text in Hispanic studies, one incorporated time and again into modern anthologies of the medieval Spanish canon, often with little introduction other than reference to its value as an exemplar of Alfonsine prose. Such uncritical readings have detached it from its conceptual frame and invited its deployment in support of wildly different political and cultural agendas. In a Europe that continues to negotiate the arrival of displaced peoples from Africa and the Middle East, it has served to justify the essentialising of Islam as a culture of violence bent on the destruction of Western values. So too has it lent support to the notion that Europe's renaissance, reliant as it was on Andalusi intellectual culture, has its deep roots in racially black Africa.

My purpose here is to apply pressure to those contemporary agendas we routinely project onto the 'Duelo' by reinserting it into the complex (con)textualities of its moment of genesis. Alfonsine chroniclers honed their craft through Alfonso's broader intellectual project – a project some have characterised as Islamicate for its proto-cosmopolitanism and the king's heavy hand in the production and dissemination of knowledge.[4] Gathering around

[4] See, for example, Maribel Fierro, 'Alfonso X "the Wise": The last Almohad caliph?', *Medieval Encounters* 15(2/4) (2009): 192–3. Fierro mobilises 'Islamicate' in its decidedly Hodgsonian sense, as (in her words) 'a common culture: not restricted to the Islamic religion, for it also embraced Jews and Christians within the Islamic sphere of influence. In this Islamicate world, ideas, doctrines, narratives, etc., existed in different religious contexts, being adapted to the specific needs of each but maintaining an essential similarity.' I hope here to push beyond this sense by exploring how Alfonso and his cohort bend an Islamicate materiality–textuality towards service to a Castilian hegemony that remains accutely aware of confessional difference, producing at times the anxious reflex of the Christian teetering on the brink of heterodoxy. David Nirenberg opened up the space for precisely this type of inquiry when he advocated in 2014 for more protracted study of 'the cultural conditions of possibility that more or less simultaneously

himself a multicultural collective of scholars, he tasked them with the compilation, translation and synthesis of a vast array of sources for the purpose of sealing his political and moral authority over the heterogeneous population that fell under his rule. The 'Duelo', I will argue, emerges from and is mediated through this bid for worldliness, even as it parrots the xenophobic formulations of its source text and so punches the alterity of Alfonso's Muslim subjects. As the ironic mobilisation of Islamophobic tropes within an Islamicate textuality, it cannot help but spin off unintended consequences that confound the too-easy parallels we might be tempted to draw between Islamophobias of the past and Islamophobias of the present.

The Arab-Berber invasion of 711 was, as historian Brian Catlos reads it, a natural extension of the Umayyads' project to wrest control of North Africa from the Byzantine empire.[5] Indeed, even as it morphed into a cautionary tale in the rest of Europe, in Iberia it played out as it had elsewhere in the expanding Islamic empire, as a political realignment that brought native populations under Muslim rule while leaving in place those localised power structures and institutions willing to enter into a contractual peace. Even the *Chronica Muzarabica*, composed by an anonymous Iberian cleric in the mid-eighth century to document the incursion of Islam into the Christian West, doubles back on its lament for the 'ruin of Spain' (*ruina Spaniae*) to concede that those cities not destroyed 'sued for peace, and the Muslims, with blandishments and mockery and guile, granted these wishes'[6] – reference, albeit backhanded, to treaties that granted Christians *dhimmi* status and lay the foundation for the community of Arabised Christians known as the Mozarabs.

Christian Iberia's greater intimacy with the Islamic world served as a check to the more fantastical representations of Muslim difference that began circulating

produced both the proudly self-conscious Alfonsine project of translation, learning and natural philosophical inquiry on the one hand, and the condemnation of that project – even by Alfonso and his collaborators themselves! – as somehow dangerously "un-Christian" on the other'. See David Nirenberg, '"Judaism", "Islam", and the Dangers of Knowledge in Christian Culture, with Special Attention to the Case of King Alfonso X, "the Wise", of Castile', in C. Burnett and P. Mantas-España (eds), *Mapping Knowledge: Cross-Pollination in Late Antiquity and the Middle Ages, Arabica Veritas*, vol. I (Cordoba: Oriens Academica, 2014), p. 274.

5 Catlos, *Kingdoms of Faith*, pp. 16–17.

6 Smith, *Christians and Moors in Spain*, pp. 12–13.

in the rest of Europe in the centuries following.[7] So too did its crusader impulse remain *in potentia* for much of the early Middle Ages as emerging Christian kingdoms in the north jostled with each other to establish their primacy on the peninsula.[8] The jumpstart for a coordinated offensive against the Muslim south came in the early thirteenth century, when the Almohads, who had half a century earlier subsumed al-Andalus into their North African empire, began making overtures towards Iberia's Christian north. Called by Pope Innocent III to crusade, a Christian alliance under the banner of Castilian king Alfonso VIII routed the Almohads at Las Navas de Tolosa in 1212 CE. This strategic victory delivered to Castile not only a ready means of access into al-Andalus and opportunities for continued expansion, but also a boost in confidence that the whole of the peninsula could be restored to Christian rule. It fell to chroniclers to invent for Spain a history that supported this manifest destiny.

Of these chroniclers, perhaps the most influential was Rodrigo Jiménez de Rada, archbishop of Toledo, who had actively campaigned for a united Christian front at Las Navas and served as chief architect of Fernando III's expansion strategy. Rodrigo expended his intellectual energy on bolstering Castilian claims to hegemony, which he configured in great part as a reset of Iberian politics to the glory days of the Visigoths.[9] To this end he composed *De rebus Hispanie sive Historia Gothica* (*On the Matters of Spain, or the History*

[7] For a comprehensive survey, see John V. Tolan, *Saracens: Islam in the Medieval European Imagination* (New York: Columbia University Press, 2002). As of the tenth century, Islam is routinely portrayed through the filter of Roman paganism, most notoriously in the *Chanson de Roland*, where Saracens are made to worship idols representing Apollo, Tervagant and Mahumet (p. 105 ff.). For the specifically Iberian context, see Kenneth Baxter Wolf, 'Christian Views of Islam in Early Medieval Spain", in John Victor Tolan (ed.), *Medieval Christian Perceptions of Islam* (New York: Routledge, 1996), pp. 85–108.

[8] See Joseph F. O'Callaghan, *Reconquest and Crusade in Medieval Spain* (Philadelphia: University of Pennsylvania Press, 2003). O'Callaghan characterises Spain's reconquest as 'a slow and intermittent advance from one river frontier to another' (p. 19) up until papal interventionism of the twelfth and thirteenth centuries transformed it into a crusade.

[9] For a comprehensive study of Rodrigo's presence in thirteenth-century politics and the complexities of his engagement with Muslims and Jews, see Lucy Pick, *Conflict and Coexistence: Archbishop Rodrigo and the Muslims and Jews of Medieval Spain* (Ann Arbor: University of Michigan Press, 2004). Pick summarises Rodrigo's political programme as 'recuperating, rebuilding, and repairing what had been lost' (p. 16).

of the Goths), a comprehensive history of Spain in which the Muslim invasion of 711 occupies the symbolic core. At this point in the historical narrative, Rodrigo hits pause to unleash his own gloss on the *ruina Spaniae* theme, a chapter-length jeremiad given the title 'Deploratio Hispanie' ('Lament for Spain') that will serve as source text for Alfonso's 'Duelo de los godos':

> The men of the army (*viri exercitus*) wear scarlet and the reins of their horses are ablaze, their countenance as blackness, their faces like the burnish of a cauldron, and their eyes like fire; their soldier is quicker than the leopard and more cruel than the wolf that comes at dusk. Indeed, the might of the Goths yields in an instant to the African people (*gens Afrorum*), who once had advanced by means of guile and riches without resorting to force.[10]

Not lost on any reader steeped in the Latin Vulgate is just how contrived the entirety of the 'Deploratio' is; in essence an admixture of Old Testament prophesies and talking points from the *Chronica Muzarabica*, it makes the Islamness of Spain's invaders a sidebar to their preternatural cruelty.[11] Enumerated are the acts of savagery visited on the populace, from the most vulnerable ('infants are crushed, adolescents overcome with beatings, young men cut down by the sword') to Spain's women ('kept for an ignoble purpose, their beauty held in scorn'). Enumerated as well are the acts of defilement and destruction of sacred spaces ('Sanctuaries are destroyed, churches demolished . . . trespassers contaminate the holy vessels').[12] Permeating the text is the theme of cultural loss, whether of language ('forgotten are the songs, now uttered by strange lips in a foreign tongue') or communal faith ('gone are the doctrine of faith and the unity of the saints') – both allusions to the historical

[10] For the Latin text, see Rodrigo Jiménez de Rada, *Historia de rebus Hispanie sive Historia gothica*, ed. Juan Fernández Valverde (Turnhout: Brepols, 1987), p. 106. Translations are my own. Rodrigo generally maintains the distinction between ethnic Arabs, who formed the governing elite in North Africa, and ethnic Berbers, called *gens Afrorum* or *Mauri*, who formed the shock troops of the first wave of invasion.

[11] Cf. The Book of Nahum, which recounts the fall of Nineveh to 'men of the army . . . clad in scarlet' (Nah. 2:3 Douay-Rheims), and the Book of Habakkuk, which prophesies the destruction of Judah by Babylonians whose 'horses are lighter than leopards, and swifter than evening wolves' (Hab. 1:8 Douay-Rheims).

[12] Jiménez de Rada, *Historia de rebus*, p. 106.

Arabisation and even Islamisation of Christians who remained under Muslim rule post-conquest.[13]

Rodrigo almost surely crafted the 'Deploratio' for his own historical moment, as a reminder to his contemporaries to remain vigilant against the threat still posed by latter-day *gens Afrorum*, the Almohads, who had only recently been repelled at Las Navas. He enunciates in the process a stereotype of the Muslim as barbarian that will resonate in Alfonso's *Estoria de España* and beyond. And yet by the time of Alfonso's accession to the throne, the explosive expansionism of his father Fernando's reign had begun yielding to a different priority: the imposition of political and moral authority over an enormously expanded and suddenly heterogeneous territory. We might read Alfonso's massive intellectual project, realised in the fields of history, science, jurisprudence and even astrology, as colonialist in its attempt to contain all available sources of knowledge within a conceptual frame that renders Christian hegemony on the Iberian Peninsula both natural and inevitable. Indeed, it derives its energy and resources in no small part from the so-called Schools of Translation that had been operating in Toledo since the mid-twelfth century – Christian Europe's effort to bend the vast wealth of Arabic intellectual culture, including commentaries on Greek classical philosophical and scientific texts, to the service of Christian exclusivism. And yet Alfonso's strategic commandeering of scholarly activity effectively side-lined the Church as sole arbiter of knowledge and activated a model of kingship that would not have been unfamiliar to the Almohads, one aligned with the sort of rationalism advanced by Maimonides and Averroes in the previous century.[14] Here the monarch is held to the Platonic ideal of a ruler who is both theoretically informed and morally invested in the physical, moral and intellectual wellbeing of his subjects.[15] Equally significant is the imposition of Castilian rather than Latin as the language of dissemination, a move that placed knowledge

[13] Jiménez de Rada, *Historia de rebus*, pp. 106, 107. Rodrigo also documents in this chapter the establishment of the Mozarab community – *Mixta-Arabes*, according to his etymology – who he alleges were duped into submission.

[14] Francisco Márquez Villanueva, *El concepto cultural alfonsí* (Barcelona: Edicions Bellaterra, 2004), p. 21. For Márquez Villanueva, Alfonso looked to Muslim models for his own sweeping interventionism in the intellectual activity of his court (p. 27).

[15] Márquez Villanueva, *El concepto cultural*, p. 216.

within reach of the broader populace. Arabist Maribel Fierro argues that only by reading Alfonso's intellectual project through the Islamicate can we make sense of the supremacy he affords to knowledge 'as a criterion of political, social or moral hierarchization . . . and an instrument to legitimize the renewal of society, a radical political transformation'.[16] Alfonsine intellectualism is expansive, pragmatic, proto-cosmopolitan in its readiness to push beyond the limits of orthodoxy in service to the universal good, even as it adheres to Christianity as the baseline for political and moral legitimacy.

As Alfonso's first attempt at a comprehensive history of Spain, the *Estoria de Espanna* already suggests the universalising features of his more mature works: 'For we composed this our *General History of the Spains* about all the kings (who have ruled) over them and all their deeds . . . as much those of Moors as those of Christians, and even of Jews if the occasion warranted it.'[17] While Rodrigo's *De rebus Hispanie* provides the backbone, the *Estoria*'s comprehensive sweep of Iberian history and its imperfect synthesis of supplementary source materials push back against a Visigothic-centred narrative and project instead what Diego Catalán has called 'the transhistorical identity of a vital dwelling space called Spain' within which 'no subject or historical events should, in principle, be excluded'.[18] To fill out the history of Arab hegemony in Iberia, Alfonso's team relies heavily on another of Rodrigo's efforts, the *Historia arabum*, a remarkably measured work for its time in that, unlike the spurious histories of Islam circulating elsewhere in the Christian West, it folds into its narrative Muslim-authored source materials, including Ibn Isḥāq's authoritative biography of Muḥammad, the eighth-century *Kitāb sīrat*

[16] Fierro, 'Alfonso X "the Wise": The Last Almohad Caliph?', p. 193.

[17] Menéndez Pidal, *Primera crónica general*, p. 653 (translation mine).

[18] Diego Catalán, *La* Estoria de España *de Alfonso X: creación y evolución* (Madrid: Castalia, 1992), p. 30 (translation mine). For a critical reading of the *Estoria*'s full Islamic narrative, see Geraldine Hazbun, *Narratives of the Islamic Conquest from Medieval Spain* (London: Palgrave Macmillan, 2015), pp. 17–61. Hazbun nuances Catalán's reading by arguing for the deliberateness with which Islamic history is interwoven with the history of the Goths: 'This opens a new vista on the linear, teleological narrative of Christian success, one that highlights cohesion and interconnection at the political level between Christian and Islamic experiences of the passage of power and the vicissitudes of rule' (p. 19).

rasūl Allāh.[19] So it is that Alfonso's team had access, via Rodrigo, to significant traditions surrounding the life of the Prophet Muḥammad, including the cleansing of his heart by two angels, his inspired intervention in the rebuilding of the Ka'bah, and both the *Isrā'* (miraculous journey to Jerusalem) and the *Mi'rāj* (ascent), rendering them for the first time in a medieval European vernacular language as part of a broader project of historical synthesis and dissemination.

While we would be tempted to read into the *Estoria*'s life of Muḥammad the stirrings of cosmopolitanism, what short-circuits such a reading are several episodes spliced into the narrative that rehearse the full roster of anti-Islamic tropes circulating in the Christian West.[20] Drawn from the *Chronicon Mundi*, a history of Spain written in Latin by Rodrigo's contemporary, the Leonese bishop Lucas de Tuy, these episodes expose the inherent transactionalism of Islam by pushing to the foreground Muḥammad's seductiveness and opportunism. Muḥammad's ministry begins, in fact, in the marketplace, where his future wife Khadīja first takes notice of his physical beauty:

> She, when she met such a tall and well-mannered young man, and one so handsome and eloquent (*mançebo tan grand et tan aguisado et fremoso et bien fablant*), fell deeply in love with him; and, in order to approach him and

[19] Matthias Maser, 'Rodrigo Jiménez de Rada and his *Historia Arabum*: An Extraordinary Example of Inter-cultural Tolerance?', in Sarah Lambert and Helen Nicholson (eds), *Languages of Love and Hate: Conflict, Communication, and Identity in the Medieval Mediterranean* (Turnhout: Brepols, 2011), p. 235. Maser warns us, though, against reading the work as evidence of inter-cultural tolerance: Islam remains for Rodrigo a *virus pestiferum*, and Muslims as partners in Muḥammad's 'savagery and disingenuousness' (p. 236).

[20] Geraldine Hazbun reads the entire of the *Estoria*'s biography of Muhammad as 'one of the less subtle portions of the chronicle' that 'in many ways deserves to be treated as a separate piece of rhetoric shaped by a wider European hostility toward the origins of Islam and its figurehead' (Hazbun, *Narratives*, p. 32). For an overview of Christian polemical treatment of the biography of Muḥammad in the pre-modern period, see Norman Daniel, *Islam and the West: The Making of an Image* (Oxford: Oneworld, [1960] 2009), pp. 100–30; Michelina Di Cesare, *The Pseudo-Historical Image of the Prophet Muḥammad in Medieval Latin Literature: A Repertory* (Berlin: De Gruyter, 2012); and Julian Yolles and Jessica Weiss (eds), *Medieval Latin Lives of Muhammad* (Cambridge, MA: Harvard University Press, 2018). For the specifically Spanish context, see Ana Echevarría, *The Fortress of Faith: The Attitude towards Muslims in Fifteenth Century Spain* (Leiden: Brill, 1999), pp. 122–9.

> be able to speak with him, she pretended that she wanted to see the goods that he was carrying. When Muhammad realized this he began, by means of charms and spells that he knew, to press and persuade her, telling her that he was the Messiah, he whom the Jews were awaiting.[21]

Dramatised here is a scene of sorcery and seduction that will serve as template for the entirety of Muḥammad's prophetic ministry as the *Estoria* tells it. Subordinating the spirit to bodily appetites, he holds his followers rapt with 'sweet and delectable speech, albeit deceptive and false' and the promise of a paradise where they will have their fill of 'everything they lust for in their hearts'. He is cast, moreover, as heresiarch, engaging in a deliberate perversion of Jewish and Christian doctrine as he brings his 'evil sect' up to the very threshold of Christian Europe:

> After this he travelled to Spain and went to Cordoba and preached there his evil sect; and he told them in his preaching that Our Lord Jesus Christ had been born of a Virgin by the work of the Holy Spirit, but that he was not God. When the good father Saint Isidore, who was just then arriving from the court in Rome, learned this, he sent his men to Cordoba to seize him and bring him to him; but the devil appeared to Muhammad and warned him to depart from that place, which he did, crossing the sea and preaching in Arabia and Africa.[22]

These Lucas-sourced passages, although discordant with the *Estoria*'s broader purpose, insert into the narrative a proto-orientalism that sets Spain, aligned through Isidore with the orthodoxy of Rome, against lands lesser equipped to resist Muhammadan heresy (Arabia and Africa). So too do they prefigure the *Estoria*'s episode of Muslim conquest of Spain. For the events of 711, Alfonso's team adheres to Rodrigo's *De rebus Hispanie*, preserving the 'Deploratio' ' or 'Duelo de los godos' in the Alfonsine translation – at its core.[23] But in contrast to the relatively literal translation of Latin source materials elsewhere in

[21] Smith, *Christians and Moors in Spain*, pp. 2–3.

[22] Smith, *Christians and Moors in Spain*, pp. 4–5.

[23] The full title of the chapter as generally recorded in the manuscript tradition is 'Concerning the lament of the Goths of Spain and the reason for which (Spain) was destroyed' (*Del duello de los godos de Espanna et de la razon por la que ella fue destroyda*). Note that here I will be using the contemporary spelling ('Duelo').

the *Estoria*, when it comes to the 'Duelo' they indulge in a wholesale *amplificatio*, beginning with Rodrigo's portrayal of the invaders (here the editorial changes are italicised):

> *The Moors of the host* (Los moros de la hueste) wore *silks and* colourful cloths *which they had taken as booty*, their horses' reins were like fire, their faces were black as pitch, *the handsomest among them* was black as a cooking pot, and their eyes blazed like fire; their horses as swift as leopards, their horsemen more cruel *and hurtful* than the wolf that comes at night *to the flock of sheep*.[24]

Lost is the archetypal language of the original (*viri exercitus*), a carry-over from Old Testament source materials. The agents here are decidedly *Moros*, a term whose semantic field in medieval Spanish had been stretched far beyond its original meaning (the historical inhabitants of Roman Mauritania) to capture the broad range of peoples of the western Mediterranean differentiated from Christians by their adherence to Islam.[25] The 'Duelo''s *Moros* are marked by a superlative degree of blackness ('the handsomest among them was black as a cooking pot') and an exoticism that draws them even closer to the Saracen stereotype long familiar to a Europe steeped in romances of chivalry.[26] Moreover, whereas Rodrigo preferred the passive voice to document atrocities, the Alfonsine text shifts the *Moros* into subject position as active agents of cruelty: '[The Moors] dashed babies at the breast against the

[24] For a comprehensive study of the *Estoria*'s translation of the 'Deploratio' as both rhetorical exercise and deliberate political messaging, see Olga Tudorica Impey, '"Del Duello de los godos de Espanna": la retórica del llanto y su motivacion', *Romance Quarterly* 33(3) (1986): 295–307. For Impey, Alfonso repurposed the 'Duelo' as a warning about the threat not only from Muslims, but also from rebellious nobles who compromised the stability of his realm.

[25] See Ross Brann, 'The Moors?', *Medieval Encounters* 15(2/4) (2009): 307–18, for a study of the semantic shifts of the term in medieval Spanish. Brann reads use of *moros* in the 'Duelo' as 'not nearly as benign as some readers have assumed' (p. 311).

[26] Black Saracens appear in abundance in European literature as of the twelfth century. See Geraldine Heng, *The Invention of Race in the European Middle Ages* (Cambridge: Cambridge University Press, 2018), p. 187. Heng issues the caveat, however, that '[d]espite their status as the international enemy par excellence . . . Saracens are not consistently nor inevitably depicted as black' (p. 189).

walls, killed the older boys with wounds, put the grown young men to the sword . . . They put the wretched women aside to dishonour them later'.[27]

The cumulative effect of these instances of artistic license is a shift of the episode's symbolic weight away from the archetypal and towards a more visceral response, or, as Olga Impey suggests, an empathic identification by thirteenth-century audiences with 'the existential anguish their ancestors felt in 711 over the loss of Spain'.[28] But what allows for an Islamophobic reading of the 'Duelo', rather than a merely catastrophic reading, is its far more immediate intertextuality with the spurious biography of Muḥammad. Muḥammad's beauty ('handsome and strong') cannot help but attach to these invading Moors ('the handsomest among them was black as a cooking pot'), producing a simulacrum of the glamour of evil, both seductive and dangerous. So too is Moorish conquest informed by Muḥammad's originary programme of deceit ('[they] achieved everything by stealth and deceit') and an overriding profit-motive ('[they] were not accustomed to help each other except by paying over great quantities of wealth').[29] Agency is confined in both sequences to the purely physical realm, within which beauty can have no transcendent value, but rather is black by its very nature. So it is that even sacred objects, inventoried at length in the Alfonsine *amplificatio*, are transformed through the act of appropriation from beauty (*beldad*) to ugliness (*laydeza*), that is, divested of their spiritual dimension:

> [The Moors] cast the crosses *and the altars* out of the churches; *the holy oils and the books and those things that were the honour of Christendom were all scattered and wasted.* Church feasts and solemnities were all forgotten; *the honour of the saints and the beauty* (beldad) *of the Church were all turned into ugliness* (laydeza) *and vileness.* The churches and the towers in which people

[27] In the original: '"Con los ninnos chicos de teta dieron a las paredes, a los moços mayores desfizieron con feridas, a los mançebos grandes metieronlos a espada . . . a las mezquinas de las mugieres guardauan las pora desonrrar las' (Smith, *Christians and Moors in Spain*, pp. 20–1).

[28] Impey, '"Del duelo"', p. 297 (translation is my own). Hazbun acknowledges this emotive response, but sees it, rather, as subsumed into the more universal themes of breakage and discord, which would have been 'of particular interest to the thirteenth-century kings who struggled against betrayal and rebellion' (Hazbun, *Narratives*, p. 41).

[29] Smith, *Christians and Moors in Spain*, pp. 2–3, 18–19.

> were wont to praise God became places in which they confessed to and called upon Muhammad. The *vestments and chalices and other* vessels of the sanctuaries *were put to evil uses (*usos de mal*), and* were fouled by the unbelievers.[30]

Enacted here is a simulacrum – this time through the conversion of sacred objects and spaces to 'evil uses' – of the master plan of perversion set in motion by the *Estoria*'s Muḥammad some sixty chapters earlier.

The 'Duelo' is no mere retweet of Rodrigo's 'Deploratio'. Rather, it functions in tandem with the *Estoria*'s Muḥammad narrative to produce a more complex poetics of abjection, one that moves beyond the rote recycling of Old Testament tropes of cruelty to infuse the invaders with both a Muslim specificity and an inherent and dangerous sensuality. Daniela Flesler sees here a 'typical orientalist gesture', one predicated on lasciviousness and violence, 'the two pillars by which the West views the East as irremediably other'.[31] Although still somewhat contrived in the *Estoria*, this stereotype has become so naturalised in our own time that Jayda Fransen, deputy leader of the ultranationalist group Britain First, found little need to gloss three baldly Islamophobic videos she posted to Twitter in 2017.[32] In the first of these videos, an Islamist mob pushes a teenage boy from a rooftop, then pummels him to death; in the second a Muslim cleric shatters a devotional image of the Virgin Mary; in the third a presumed Muslim migrant assaults a boy on crutches. Communicated by this triptych is the dual threat posed by Muslims, the first to vulnerable populations – signified by the two defenceless teenagers, one

[30] Smith, *Christians and Moors in Spain*, pp. 20–1. Here too I have italicised the *amplificatio.*

[31] Daniela Flesler, *The Return of the Moor: Spanish Responses to Contemporary Moroccan Immigration* (West Lafayette, IN: Purdue University Press, 2008), p. 75. Tolan also argues for the medieval provenance of contemporary 'Orientalist' tropes, which he traces beyond 711 to the first century of Islamic expansion: 'The negative "orientalist" portrayals of Islam that Edward Said denounces in his *Orientalism* as the ideological underpinnings of French and British colonialism in fact have their origins in the defensive reactions of Christian "orientals", unwitting subjects of the new Muslim empire' (Tolan, *Saracens*, p. 67).

[32] These videos were subsequently retweeted by then US president Donald Trump. See Elizabeth Landers and James Masters, 'Trump Retweets anti-Muslim Videos', CNN, 30 November 2017, available at: http://www.cnn.com/2017/11/29/politics/donald-trump-retweet-jayda-fransen/index.html.

on crutches – the second to the West, in particular to Euro-Christian values and notions of the sacred. Most striking, though, is the racialised pastiche produced in the second of the videos, in which a white-faced Virgin Mary, functioning as an avatar of European heritage, is subjected to the savagery of a bearded and brown-faced Muslim cleric. Reduced to a single explosive meme is the 'powerful repertoire of anti-Muslim sentiment that feeds seamlessly into contemporary Islamophobic discourse, rehearsing ideas of medieval cultures, barbarism and timeless antagonism to "the west"'.[33]

And yet just how seamless is the pipeline from medieval Islamophobias to modern? The uncritical reflex of the post-9/11 West is to read the 'Duelo' through the plethora of memes that conspire to lock in racist turns of the Orientalist impulse, that is, that mobilise an Islamophobia grounded in 'the negative conception of a racialized Muslim and an essentialized Islam both being seen as a menace to Western societies'.[34] And yet as Sharon Kinoshita has argued, by projecting onto the Middle Ages a 'monolithic and monologic orientalism', we flatten its historical complexity, 'its political, economic, and cultural practices as well as its ideological pronouncements'.[35] In the case of the Iberian Peninsula in particular, we render inert the 'experiential intercourse' of centuries of cohabitation that necessitated ongoing negotiations of identity both through and against the confessional other. Indeed, David Hanlon argues for reading the Muslim stereotype as it was articulated in post-Navas Castile as marked by a persistent ambivalence, the need to know Spain's minority Muslims, the so-called Mudejars, 'in their sameness as a subject visible to surveillance, and

[33] Claire Alexander, 'Raceing Islamophobia', in Farah Elahi and Omar Khan (eds), *Islamophobia: Still a Challenge for Us All* (London: Runnymede Trust, 2017), p. 14.

[34] Damir Skenderovic and Christina Späti, 'From Orientalism to Islamophobia: Reflections, Confirmations, and Reservations', *ReOrient* 4(2) (2019): 137. Orientalism, as Skenderovic and Späti argue, is by contrast a multilayered construct that views the East ambivalently, as an object of both prejudice and fascination: 'The signifiers of an exotic, often ambivalently perceived Other have thus transformed into a clear-cut, unfavorable perception that is fueled by prejudices and stereotypes, and which results in attitudes of undesirability, distrust, and hostility' (p. 137).

[35] Sharon Kinoshita, 'Deprovincializing the Middle Ages', in Rob Wilson and Christopher Leigh Connery (eds), *The Worlding Project: Doing Cultural Studies in the Era of Globalization* (Santa Cruz, CA: New Pacific Press, 2007), p. 89.

simultaneously as an invisible other separated by their difference'.[36] Just such an ambivalence is readily evident in the *Estoria*'s Muḥammad narrative. By casting Muḥammad as heresiarch, the *Estoria* 'genealogically locates the Prophet in a whole "family of Christian error"', that is, it preserves his knowability by confining him to a frame of Christian heterodoxy even as it strives to absolutise his otherness. So it is that his sins, including profiteering and fornication, fall in line with two practices – simony (the trade in ecclesiastic privilege) and Nicolaitism (concubinage) – that vexed Western Christendom and sparked the eleventh-century Gregorian reform. 'The net effect is therefore to represent the Prophet as a reformable subject who falls within the jurisdiction in which the church practiced inquisitorial procedure'.[37]

By punching the term *moro*, the 'Duelo' pushes deliberately into a textual field that connects Muḥammad's first community of followers, equally tainted by heresy, with the Mudejars, whose presence, together with that of Jews, compromised the unifying functions of the Christian hegemonic state.[38] The effort to police these minority communities is well documented in the *Siete partidas*, a massive compendium of law commissioned by Alfonso for the purpose of consolidating legal authority in the person of the king. Titles governing Jews ('De los judíos') and Muslims ('De los moros') are grounded, on the one hand, in Christian hegemonic entitlement and its attending phobias, and, on the other, in political expediency. In full evidence here is the very ambiguity Hanlon identifies in the *Estoria. Moros* are defined as 'a people who believe that Mohammed was the prophet and messenger of God, and for the reason that the works which he performed do not indicate the extraordinary sanctity which belongs to such a sacred calling, his religion is, as it were, an insult to God'.[39] Here the Prophet is graded on a scale of holiness that is immediately intelligible to Christians, and yet his failure to make the grade condemns his followers to invisibility:

36 David Hanlon, 'Islam and Stereotypical Discourse in Medieval Castile and Leon', *Journal of Medieval and Early Modern Studies* 30(3) (2000): 496.

37 Hanlon, 'Islam and Stereotypical Discourse', pp. 498–9.

38 For a historical analysis of the Mudejar communities of medieval Iberia, see L. P. Harvey, *Islamic Spain: 1250–1500* (Chicago: University of Chicago Press, 1990), chs 4–9.

39 *Las siete partidas*, ed. Robert I. Burns, trans. Samuel Parsons Scott (Philadelphia: University of Pennsylvania Press, 2001), p. 1438.

'the Moors should live among the Christians in the same manner as . . . the Jews, observing their own law and causing no offense to ours. But in the Christian towns the Moors may not have mosques, nor may they make public sacrifices before men'.[40] Left open, however, is the possibility of conversion: 'Christians should endeavor to convert the Moors by causing them to believe in our religion, and bring them into it by kind words and suitable discourses, and not by violence or compulsion'.[41] The *moro* here is articulated less through an intractable, ultimately racial profile, than through a colonising imperative configured at least in part as evangelisation. The racialising that will ultimately make the presence of Muslims, Jews and their descendants intolerable is the product of a later age.[42]

So it is that the *moros de la hueste*, as the nexus of complex intertextualities within the Alfonsine corpus, begin to emerge as knowable, even reformable subjects. Moreover, their representation is mediated through a material culture made familiar to post-Navas Castile through the widespread consumerism of Andalusi intellectual and cultural products. The 'silks and colourful cloths' worn by the *Estoria*'s invading Moors were in Alfonso's time a stock feature of the Castilian elite's sumptuary culture. No longer markers of difference, or 'exotic [or] incongruous elements of cultural display', Andalusi textiles were, as María Judith Feliciano argues, 'central to the formative process of the medieval Iberian aesthetic vocabulary and played a highly visible role in the development of identities through their use in ritual and daily life, outside of confrontation, in a rapidly changing cultural environment'.[43] So too are

[40] *Las siete partidas*, ed. Robert I. Burns, trans. Samuel Parsons Scott, p. 1438.

[41] *Las siete partidas*, ed. Robert I. Burns, trans. Samuel Parsons Scott, p. 1438.

[42] See Ramón Grosfoguel, 'The Multiple Faces of Islamophobia', *Islamophobia Studies Journal* 1(1) (2012): 9–33. Grosfoguel identifies the year 1492, with its multiple watershed events, including the Christian conquest of Granada, the expulsion of the Jews from Spain, and the 'discovery' of America, as the 'crucial foundational year' for a racially informed Islamophobia, grounded in 'the subalternization and inferiorization of Islam produced by the Christian-centric hierarchy of the world-system' (p. 11).

[43] María Judith Feliciano, 'Muslim Shrouds for Christian Kings? A Reassessment of Andalusi Textiles in Thirteenth-century Castilian Life and Ritual', in Cynthia Robinson and Leyla Rouhi (eds), *Under the Influence: Questioning the Comparative in Medieval Castile* (Leiden: Brill, 2005), pp. 102–3.

the invaders' horses, 'swift as leopards', marked by paradox, evoking, on the one hand, the preternatural steeds of Old Testament conquerors, and, on the other hand, the Andalusian breed, the product of a centuries-long tradition of horse-breeding in al-Andalus admired throughout Iberia for its beauty and swiftness.[44] Even the ugliness (*laydeza*) made to stick to Muslim spaces of worship – this in contrast to the beauty (*beldad*) of Christian churches – implodes as the elite of Alfonso's period occupy Muslim-built spaces, worship in mosques converted to churches, and hire Andalusi-trained craftsmen to work on new construction.[45]

Ultimately, the Islamophobia performed in the 'Duelo' squares only imperfectly with the socio-historical reality of the moment, with what Barbara Fuchs has called, drawing on Pierre Bourdieu, a 'Moorish habitus, widespread throughout Iberia'.[46] In fact, it derives wholly from an anxiety that has little to do with the historical moment of Islam's foundation or Muslim invasion of Visigothic Spain and everything to do with an emergent

[44] See Dolores Carmen Morales Muñiz, 'El caballo en la Edad Media: un estado de la cuestión', in *Homenaje al profesor Eloy Benito Ruano*, vol. 2 (Murcia: Universidad de Murcia, 2010), pp. 537–52. Significantly, a fair portion of medieval Castile's veterinary lexicon is derived from the Arabic, including the word for veterinarian – *albéitar* – from the Arabic *al-baiṯar*.

[45] See Heather Ecker, 'How to Administer a Conquered City in al-Andalus: Mosques, Parish Churches and Parishes', in Cynthia Robinson and Leyla Rouhi (eds), *Under the Influence: Questioning the Comparative in Medieval Castile* (Leiden: Brill, 2005), pp. 45–65. Ecker argues that the conquest of Toledo in 1085 served as the starting point for a centuries-long experiment in administration of conquered cities that largely preserved the urban infrastructure of al-Andalus: 'The Castilian conquests enforced intimacy and allowed for familiarity, if coerced, not only for the *ṭirāẓ*-clad archbishops and kings in the mosques and palaces, but for the surveyors, the speculators, the legions of scribes, the parish priests, the farmers, the shepherds, the artisans, the militiamen and the *hidalgos* who were enticed south; these were all Peninsular northerners who came into contact not only with the products and means of production of Muslim craftsmen but also, intimately, with their buildings and urban structures' (pp. 46–7).

[46] Barbara Fuchs, *Exotic Nation: Maurophilia and the Construction of Early Modern Spain* (Philadelphia: University of Pennsylvania Press, 2009), p. 13.

multicultural reality.[47] By foregrounding the tension between the 'Duelo''s *moros* and the Islamicate materiality–textuality through which they were articulated, we engage in the sort of deprovincialising of the Middle Ages that Sharon Kinoshita prescribes for a critical tradition that still plumbs pre-modern texts for evidence of Orientalism's *longue durée*. That is, we expose the contrivance and conditionality of the 'Duelo''s orientalism – its articulation at the convergence of competing discourses, whether political, social, cultural, intellectual or economic – and so 'make visible aspects of the premodern which in turn unsettle the unreflective construction of modernity over and against an inert medieval Other'.[48] We ultimately disrupt the continuity we would be tempted to draw between Alfonsine *moros* and the racialised Muslim subjects that inhabit contemporary Islamophobic discourse.

The 'Duelo''s provincialisation – that is, its eventual conscription by Spain as incontrovertible evidence of Islam's inert otherness – comes about primarily as a consequence of Spain's broader project of literary canon formation. Although the *Estoria* had fallen from favour as authoritative history well before the modern age,[49] in the nineteenth century it was repurposed as canonical

[47] Ana Echevarría locates anxiety principally in religious and legal texts, arguing that it derives in great part from the lingering Muslim presence in Iberia and the fear of proselytism: 'Religious and legal arguments tried to use controversy and laws to place Jews, Muslims and Christians in different spheres of everyday life while self-awareness grew on the Christian side. As it seemed that the end of Muslim power would not come as soon as expected, Christians had to be guided in order to preserve their faith and identity. The dogmas of the Church had to be explained as much as possible, and treatises became manuals for sermons. Meanwhile, Muslims and Jews had to be kept from sharing too many habits with Christians in case they might engage in proselytism' (Echevarría, *Fortress*, p. 5). Echevarría's insight would certainly explain the *Siete partidas*' comprehensive review of Christian doctrine (in the first *partida*) and its obsessive policing of interconfessional contact (in the seventh).

[48] Kinoshita, 'Deprovincializing', p. 89.

[49] As early as the fifteenth century, chronicler Alfonso de Palencia dismisses the rhetorical excess of earlier accounts of the fall of Spain, 'whose demise and horrific destruction some historians made the most wretched mention, striving to put it into words, but they failed to understand that the more they indulged in wailing and lamentation, the less they satisfied the laws of history.' See Alfonso de Palencia, *Segunda Deca de la antigüedad de España e de las fazañas de la gente española [libros XI–XX]*, ed. Francisco Javier Durán Barceló (Madrid: Javier Durán Barceló, 2016), p. 242 (translation is my own).

literary text, and the 'Duelo' was cited time and again as the privileged exemplar of Alfonsine historiographical prose. An early instance is the historian and literary critic Fermín Gonzalo Morón's high-profile series of lectures on the course of Spanish history, presented to literary societies in both Valencia and Madrid in 1840–1. Morón cannot resist inserting the 'Duelo' wholesale into his account of Muslim invasion with these words of introduction:

> Isidoro Pacense [presumed author of the *Chronica Muzarabica*] and the archbishop Don Rodrigo have painted this event with eloquent strokes, but Alfonso el Sabio surpassed them both in his general chronicle. This king's poetic numen feels profoundly moved by what he narrates, and his words are full of energy, force, and melancholy. I cannot deny myself the pleasure of reading them, because they are a true depiction, as well as a worthy monument through which to come to know the vigor, richness, and progress of our language in the thirteenth century.[50]

Notable here and elsewhere in nineteenth-century Spanish historicism is the overlap of literature and history, or, rather, the subtle ways in which deference shown to the 'Duelo' as literary masterpiece begins to legitimise its use as historical documentation ('a true depiction') for what Alejandro García Sanjuán has dubbed the 'catastrophic reading' of Muslim conquest.[51] Lending even greater impetus to the 'Duelo''s circulation in the twentieth century was preeminent philologist Ramón Menéndez Pidal's 1906 edition of the *Estoria*, titled *Primera crónica general*, a synthesis of multiple manuscript traditions into a streamlined narrative that purported to be the *Estoria* as Alfonso had intended it. In 1949, Argentine literary scholar María Rosa Lida proclaimed the 'Duelo' to be 'the first example of purely artistic Castilian prose', quoting it at length in her classic study of the prose works of fifteenth-century poet Juan de Mena.[52] Now anointed as indispensable literary touchstone and made readily available

[50] Fermín Gonzalo Morón, *Curso de historia de la civilización de España* (Madrid, 1842), vol. 2, p. 270.

[51] Alejandro García Sanjuán, *La conquista islámica de la península ibérica y la tergiversación del pasado. Del catastrofismo al negacionismo* (Madrid: Marcial Pons, 2013).

[52] María Rosa Lida, 'La prosa de Juan de Mena', *Boletín de la Academia Argentina de Letras* 18(69) (1949): 419.

through reissues of Menéndez Pidal's *Primera crónica general*, the 'Duelo' would remain as fetichised text until the turn of the twenty-first century, both in Spain and in Spanish-language and literature classrooms around the world.[53]

An inevitable consequence of the 'Duelo''s viral spread since the turn of the twentieth century has been its deployment in service to multiple and at times contradictory political and cultural agendas. Reduced to agents of sexual violence, the 'Duelo''s Moors emerge spectrally in Republican propaganda fabricated during the Spanish Civil War to denounce Franco's reliance on Moroccan mercenaries, for example, in this broadside by communist party leader and activist Dolores Ibárurri: 'Savage Moors, drunk with sensuality, that poured in horrible rapes of our girls, of our women.'[54] So too are the more recent waves of immigration from North Africa 'perversely imagined through the anachronistic and deforming lens of a confrontation with medieval Moors', as Daniela Flesler argues in *The Return of the Moor: Spanish Responses to Contemporary Moroccan Immigration*.[55] Documenting the full repertoire of tropes associated with the 'loss of Spain' that have found new life in contemporary debate on the question of immigration, Flesler argues that such tropes give strong indication of the degree to which Spaniards continue to be haunted by the 'trauma' of 711. Moreover, they feel compelled to repeat this trauma as a strategy to prevent the return of a 'repressed history of closeness between Christians and Muslims, Hispano-Romans, Visigoths, Arabs and Berbers'.[56]

The multiple phobias associated with this repressed history are nowhere more imperiously expressed than in the work of the pre-eminent twentieth-century historian and Arabist Claudio Sánchez-Albornoz, who made it his

[53] Among the more influential textbooks circulating in the English-speaking world was *Antología general de la literatura española* by Ángel del Río and Amelia A. de Del Río (New York: Dryden Press, 1954), which cites the 'Duelo' as an illustration of Alfonso's historiographic prose. As recently as 1991, Bárbara Mujica included the 'Duelo' in her *Antología de la literatura española. La edad media* (New York: John Wiley, 1991), offering little more introduction than 'Narrated in the following selection are the atrocities Christians suffered after the Arab invasion' (p. 155; translation mine).

[54] Flesler, *The Return of the Moor*, p. 78.

[55] Flesler, *The Return of the Moor*, p. 83.

[56] Flesler, *The Return of the Moor*, p. 81.

life's work to preserve for Spain the integrity of its Western identity.[57] In the foreword to a slim volume of essays he published in 1983 with the misleading title *From Islamic Andalusia to the Andalusia of Today*, he bemoans the attitude of modern-day Andalusians who deny their essential Spanishness (*españolía*) and 'allow themselves to be seduced by the Islamic past of their lands'.[58] Spain's historical *moros* were, for Sánchez-Albornoz, far more dangerous in their worldliness than in their militancy, hence, his selective documentation of the shadow side of al-Andalus in the work's appendix, an anthology of primary sources from the Arabic that reinscribe Andalusi history and culture within the dual frames of cruelty and perversion.[59] There is no pretence here at impartial analysis, only a full-throated call for resistance against both the seductiveness of the Islamic past and the duplicity of contemporary Arab interests:

> Take heed, Andalusians, forget not your centuries-old Christian past; don't squander the present, but guard yourself against the new Islamist conquerors (*los nuevos conquistadores islamistas*)! Let those Muslims arriving in Córdoba and other cities in Andalucía know that there is nothing for them to accomplish or hope for in that Spanish land (*esa tierra hispana*), despite the shameful and humiliating attitude of those who have allowed themselves to be seduced by oil magnates' dollars and have even apostacised.[60]

Lying just beneath the surface of this jeremiad are the seductive and profiteering *moros* of Alfonso's 'Duelo', embodied this time by Arab oil magnates plotting a new conquest of Spain through exorbitant funding of cultural foundations intent on recovering Spain's Islamic legacy.

57 In the more extreme turns of his scholarship, he configures medieval Spain as Europe's frontline of defence, 'the West's shield and sentinel against Islam' ('escudo y centinela de Occidente frente al Islam'). See Claudio Sánchez-Albornoz, *España. Un enigma histórico*, 2nd edn (Barcelona: Espasa-Calpe, 1981), p. 18.

58 Claudio Sánchez-Albornoz, *De la Andalucía islámica a la de hoy* (Madrid: RIALP, 1983), p. 9.

59 Sánchez-Albornoz, *De la Andalucía islámica*, pp. 79–138.

60 Sánchez-Albornoz, *De la Andalucía islámica*, pp. 33–4.

Perhaps the most original voice to rise up in protest against the reactionary historical vision propagated by Sánchez-Albornoz is author and cultural activist Juan Goytisolo, who in his experimental novel *Reivindicación del conde Don Julián* (1970) launches a full-scale assault on the cultural bulwark supporting Spanish national identity. The overall premise of the work is pseudo-autobiographical: the narrator, a Spanish expatriate, takes up residence in Tangier, from where he contemplates Spain's coastline – 'the cruel scar extending the entire length of the opposite shore'[61] – and hatches a master plan of cultural annihilation beginning with the Spanish literary canon. In a nod to the *Estoria*'s canonicity, Goytisolo deploys the 'Duelo''s iconic portrait of the invading Moors (*los moros de la hueste*) as an epigraph to the climactic episode of the work, the imagined reconquest of Spain by an 'African horde of warriors' (*africana horda de guerreros*) led by a latter-day Tariq.[62] In an evident riff on the terms of the original 'Duelo', the narrator details in a kif-driven hallucination the projected occupation of Spain's symbolic sites, reclamation of Islamic spaces, and ultimate destruction of the apparatus of Spanish nationalism:

> you will occupy churches, libraries, military barracks, the monastery of Yuste, San Lorenzo del Escorial, the Cerro de los Ángeles
> you will liberate the mosque of Cordoba, the Giralda, the Alhambra
> you will raze the palace of Charles V in Granada
> you will install your harem in the gardens of the Retiro
> you will encourage apostasy by Christians and conversion to Mohammedanism, and spread Koranic propaganda
> when the wretched Peninsula develops several focuses of infection and its physical resistance is greatly weakened, you will mount the final brutal assault
> at the head of the Moslems of your harka, armed with the keen-bladed weapons of treason[63]

In the work's most iconoclastic moment, the invading horde occupies the vagina (configured as both sacred grotto and 'cunt') of Isabel the Catholic,

[61] Juan Goytisolo, *Count Julian*, trans. Helen R. Lane (New York: Viking, 1974), p. 48.

[62] Goytisolo, *Count Julian*, pp. 108–70.

[63] Goytisolo, *Count Julian*, p. 115.

emblematic figurehead of Spain's *nacional-catolicismo*, a national identity predicated on the most reactionary values of Francoist Spain.[64] Enacted throughout this episode is the hyper-exaggeration of those Orientalist and misogynist tropes to which the 'Duelo''s *moros* had been reduced or, more rightly, the ironic recasting of cruelty and perversion as modes of recuperative and regenerative agency. Language itself is made the target as invaders 'rescue' scores of words derived from the Arabic, leaving the Spanish lexicon impoverished ('its sap sucked dry'), but also the medium for a betrayal ('oh my beautiful, noble language, the weapon of treason: a gleaming, sharp-boned scimitar') through which Spain is resurrected in an Islamicate mode, fully exposed to the transnationalism of its present and the cultural hybridities of its past.[65]

We might detect in Goytisolo's betrayal of Spanish nationalism a harbinger of Kinoshita's call for deprovincialising the Middle Ages. Through his re-enactment of Muslim conquest, he breaks the 'Duelo' free of the Orientalist overlay of two centuries of scholarship and inserts it into a post-modern Islamicate textuality that reimagines the cosmopolitanism of Alfonso's court.[66] And yet in the twenty-first century the 'Duelo' remains as a ready point of reference for cultural warriors still determined to claim for Spain a homogeneous history and identity. Arabist Serafín Fanjul includes the 'Duelo' in its entirety in *Al-Andalus contra España. La forja del mito* (2000) as documentary support for his argument that Spain was decimated by its Muslim invaders – 'The shock was brutal'

64 For an incisive critical reading of this episode, see Barbara Weissberger, *Isabel Rules: Constructing Queenship, Wielding Power* (Minneapolis: University of Minnesota Press, 2004), pp. 199–202.

65 In the full body of his critical work, Goytisolo generally aligned himself with the Américo Castro school of Hispanism, which had, by its second and third generations, committed itself to the full-scale dismantling of those binaries (Christian–Muslim/Jewish, orthodox–heterodox, pure–impure, Spain–Africa, heterosexual–homosexual) through which Spain routinely constructed its history and identity. For the best overview of Goytisolo's interventions in this cultural activism, see his collected essays in *Contra las sagradas formas* (Barcelona: Galaxia Gutenberg, 2007).

66 As Carlos Fuentes notes in his preface to a collection of Goytisolo's essays, through works such as *Don Julián* '[he] already gave indication that Spain was not Spain without the Jewish and Muslim cultures that formed language and history in the court of Alfonso el Sabio, in the *Libro de buen amor*, and in Rojas's *La Celestina*'. See Carlos Fuentes, 'Juan Goytisolo. El encuentro con el otro', preface to *Tradición y disidencia*, by Juan Goytisolo (Madrid: Fondo de Cultura Económica de España, 2003), p. 9.

(*La conmoción fue brutal*), he notes in language that deliberately configures the conquest as existential trauma – but Spaniards managed to survive the centuries-long Andalusi experience with relatively few scars and their pre-Islamic identity intact.[67] What 'Arab, Hispano-Muslim or Morisco reminiscences' persist in contemporary Spanish language, custom and cuisine, he opines, are mere pastiche, bound to fade with the passage of time.[68] Fanjul projects here a survivalist reading of Muslim conquest that is pre-packaged for export to Europe and the United States as a cautionary tale not only against Islamist terrorism, but also against immigration and the corrosive effect it stands to have on Western values.[69]

Even as Alfonso's *moros* are sublimated into the immigration debate as avatars of violence, they have begun emerging in the twenty-first century imaginary in a surprisingly different role. Already as of 1991, multiple contributors to a special issue of the *Journal of African Civilizations* (subsequently published as *Golden Age of the Moor*) had argued for reading the 'Duelo''s portrait of the *moros* as documentary evidence for the racial blackness of the invaders.[70] James E. Brunson and Runoko Rashidi note in their contribution to the volume that:

[67] Serafín Fanjul, *Al-Andalus contra España. La forja del mito* (Madrid: Siglo XXI, 2000), p. 24.

[68] Fanjul, *Al-Andalus*, p. 218.

[69] Such a reading doubtlessly informed the now infamous speech delivered by former Spanish prime minister José María Aznar at Georgetown University in 2004, in which he laid out for an American audience still processing the events of 9/11 Spain's own history of confrontation with Islam: 'You must go back no less than 1,300 years, to the early eighth century, when a Spain recently invaded by the Moors refused to become just another piece in the Islamic world and began a long battle to recover its identity.' Although his speech has become a punch-bag of sorts in progressive circles, any official record of it has long since disappeared. Still, the segment in question remains available on the YouTube channel 3diasdemarzo, available at: https://youtu.be/e7no1WObcRs, last accessed 27 February 2021.

[70] Ivan Van Sertima (ed.), *Golden Age of the Moor* (New Brunswick, NJ: Transaction, 1992); originally published in *Journal of African Civilizations*, vol. 11 (1991). The overall purpose of the volume is perhaps best summarised by Wayne B. Chandler in his contribution, titled 'The Moor: Light of Europe's Dark Age': 'It is my intent here to demonstrate that the Moorish culture was largely black in origin, bright in its achievement, and powerful in its influence on western civilization' (p. 151).

> [t]here is really no need to speculate on the ethnicity of these early invaders of the conquest period. Primary Christian sources relating to the conquest, particularly the *Primera Cronica General* of Alfonso X, make the following observation on the Moors: 'Their faces were as black as pitch, the handsomest amongst them was as black as a cooking pot'.[71]

Edward Scobie drives home a racialised reading of the episode when he stresses the 'low opinion [the Moors had] of these whites' whom they 'had beaten . . . often on the battlefield and with inferior numbers' and details the profound positive impact of the 'African (Moorish) presence' in Iberia and by extension Europe.[72] This reframing of the 'Duelo' as the staging ground for Black Africa's civilising of Europe effectively turns on its head the racist narrative perpetuated by European colonialism since the age of exploration and produces an alternate origin story for Western intellectual culture that has, with the rise of social media, gone viral within the pan-Africanist community. Scobie's citation of the 'Duelo' still circulates today as an essential plank in '15 things you did not know about the Moors of Spain', a crib sheet devised by the London-based educational outlet Black History Studies to empower Black communities by arguing for African agency in the introduction of intellectual culture and scientific innovation to Europe.[73]

While the pan-Africanist appropriation of Alfonso's *moros* relies on both an anachronistic reading of the 'Duelo' and the perpetuation of racist constructs, it nonetheless signals the ethnic and cultural complexities of the Alfonsine court in ways that Islamophobic readings do not. In this respect

[71] James E. Brunson and Runoko Rashidi, 'The Moors in Antiquity', in Ivan Van Sertima (ed.), *Golden Age of the Moor* (New Brunswick, NJ: Transaction, 1992), p. 55.

[72] Edward Scobie, 'The Moors and Portugal's Global Expansion', in Ivan Van Sertima (ed.), *Golden Age of the Moor* (New Brunswick, NJ: Transaction, 1992), p. 336. See also José V. Pimienta-Bey, 'Moorish Spain: Academic Source and Foundation for the Rise and Success of Western European Universities in the Middle Ages', in Ivan Van Sertima (ed.), *Golden Age of the Moor* (New Brunswick, NJ: Transaction, 1992), p. 184.

[73] '15 things you did not know about the Moors of Spain', Black History Studies, available at: https://blackhistorystudies.com/resources/resources/15-facts-on-the-moors-in-spain, last accessed 27 February 2021. Black History Studies is a London-based educational outlet founded in 2007 to empower Black communities in the UK 'to learn about their history from an African perspective', available at: https://blackhistorystudies.com/about.

it poses a useful challenge to those of us who have yet to make the break from aesthetic readings of the 'Duelo' that so blithely leave the Orientalist frame firmly in place. To subscribe to such readings is to hyper-simplify Alfonso's complex colonial programme, just as it is to ignore the pernicious role art can play in supporting the mechanisms of oppression. It is also to leave uncritiqued the structural racism inherent in the Spanish literary canon as constructed by nineteenth-century Hispanism, a product, ultimately, of Spain's centuries-long experience as a colonial power increasingly obsessed with matters of race as it decimated Jewish and Muslim communities on the peninsula and colonised Africa, the Americas and the Pacific. Whether the 'Duelo' should remain as exemplary text is a matter for Hispanists to debate as we contemplate the shape of the canon – or even its desirability – in a post-colonial, post-9/11 world.[74] Should we choose to keep it, the challenge will be to find ways to denaturalise the text, that is, to make its presence in the canon uncomfortable, and to acknowledge that not only at its moment of composition, but also through its insistent retweetings throughout the modern age, it has always been articulated through particular (and particularising) historical circumstances, including our own.

Bibliography

'15 things you did not know about the Moors of Spain', Black History Studies, available at: https://blackhistorystudies.com/resources/resources/15-facts-on-the-moors-in-spain, last accessed 27 February 2021.

Alexander, Claire, 'Raceing Islamophobia', in Farah Elahi and Omar Khan (eds), *Islamophobia: Still a Challenge for Us All* (London: Runnymede Trust, 2017), pp. 13–15.

Aznar, José María, 'Seven Theses on Today's Terrorism', Lecture, Georgetown University, Washington, DC, 21 September 2004.

Brann, Ross, 'The Moors?', *Medieval Encounters* 15(2/4) (2009): 307–18.

[74] Some textbook authors have made a decided break with this tradition of reading the 'Duelo' for its literary value; for example, Carmen Pereira-Muro, who walks students through a deconstruction of the *Estoria*'s ideological scaffolding by asking them to consider how Alfonso confers legitimacy to his history and how he manipulates the concepts of civilisation and barbarism. See Carmen Pereira-Muro, *Culturas de España*, 2nd edn (Stamford, CT: Cengage Learning, 2015), pp. 63–4.

Brunson, James E. and Runoko Rashidi, 'The Moors in Antiquity', in Ivan Van Sertima (ed.), *Golden Age of the Moor* (New Brunswick, NJ: Transaction, 1992), pp. 27–84.

Catalán, Diego, *La* Estoria de España *de Alfonso X: creación y evolución* (Madrid: Castalia, 1992).

Catlos, Brian A., *Kingdoms of Faith: A New History of Islamic Spain* (New York: Hachette, 2018).

Chandler, Wayne B. 'The Moor: Light of Europe's Dark Age', in Ivan Van Sertima (ed.), *Golden Age of the Moor* (New Brunswick, NJ: Transaction, 1992), pp. 151–81.

Daniel, Norman, *Islam and the West: The Making of an Image* (Oxford: Oneworld, [1960] 2009).

Del Río, Ángel and Amelia A. de Del Río, *Antología general de la literatura española* (New York: Dryden Press, 1954).

Di Cesare, Michelina, *The Pseudo-Historical Image of the Prophet Muḥammad in Medieval Latin Literature: A Repertory* (Berlin: De Gruyter, 2012).

Echevarría, Ana, *The Fortress of Faith: The Attitude towards Muslims in Fifteenth Century Spain* (Leiden: Brill, 1999).

Ecker, Heather, 'How to Administer a Conquered City in al-Andalus: Mosques, Parish Churches and Parishes', in Cynthia Robinson and Leyla Rouhi (eds), *Under the Influence: Questioning the Comparative in Medieval Castile* (Leiden: Brill, 2005), pp. 45–65.

Fanjul, Serafín, *Al-Andalus contra España. La forja del mito* (Madrid: Siglo XXI, 2000).

Feliciano, María Judith, 'Muslim Shrouds for Christian Kings? A Reassessment of Andalusi Textiles in Thirteenth-century Castilian Life and Ritual', in Cynthia Robinson and Leyla Rouhi (eds), *Under the Influence: Questioning the Comparative in Medieval Castile* (Leiden: Brill, 2005), pp. 101–31.

Fierro, Maribel, 'Alfonso X "the Wise": The Last Almohad Caliph?' *Medieval Encounters* 15(2/4) (2009): 175–98.

Flesler. Daniela, *The Return of the Moor: Spanish Responses to Contemporary Moroccan Immigration* (West Lafayette, IN: Purdue University Press, 2008).

Fuchs, Barbara, *Exotic Nation: Maurophilia and the Construction of Early Modern Spain* (Philadelphia: University of Pennsylvania Press, 2009).

Fuentes, Carlos, 'Juan Goytisolo: El encuentro con el otro', Preface to *Tradición y disidencia*, by Juan Goytisolo (Madrid: Fondo de Cultura Económica de España, 2003), pp. 9–12.

García Sanjuán, Alejandro, *La conquista islámica de la península ibérica y la tergiversación del pasado. Del catastrofismo al negacionismo* (Madrid: Marcial Pons, 2013).

Gonzalo Morón, Fermín, *Curso de historia de la civilización de España*, vol. 2 (Madrid, 1842).

Goytisolo, Juan, *Count Julian*, trans. Helen R. Lane (New York: Viking, 1974).

Goytisolo, Juan, *Contra las sagradas formas* (Barcelona: Galaxia Gutenberg, 2007).

Grosfoguel, Ramón, 'The Multiple Faces of Islamophobia', *Islamophobia Studies Journal* 1(1) (2012): 9–33.

Hanlon, David, 'Islam and Stereotypical Discourse in Medieval Castile and Leon', *Journal of Medieval and Early Modern Studies* 30(3) (2000): 479–504.

Harvey, L. P., *Islamic Spain: 1250–1500* (Chicago: University of Chicago Press, 1990).

Hazbun, Geraldine, *Narratives of the Islamic Conquest from Medieval Spain* (London: Palgrave Macmillan, 2015).

Heng, Geraldine, *The Invention of Race in the European Middle Ages* (Cambridge: Cambridge University Press, 2018).

Impey, Olga Tudorica, '"Del Duello de los godos de Espanna": la retórica del llanto y su motivacion', *Romance Quarterly* 33(3) (1986): 295–307.

Jiménez de Rada, Rodrigo, *Historia de rebus Hispanie sive Historia gothica*, ed. Juan Fernández Valverde (Turnhout: Brepols, 1987).

Kinoshita, Sharon, 'Deprovincializing the Middle Ages', in Rob Wilson and Christopher Leigh Connery (eds), *The Worlding Project: Doing Cultural Studies in the Era of Globalization* (Santa Cruz, CA: New Pacific Press, 2007), pp. 75–89.

Landers, Elizabeth and James Masters, 'Trump Retweets anti-Muslim Videos', CNN, 30 November 2017, available at: http://www.cnn.com/2017/11/29/politics/donald-trump-retweet-jayda-fransen/index.html.

Las siete partidas, ed. Robert I. Burns, trans. Samuel Parsons Scott, 5 vols (Philadelphia: University of Pennsylvania Press, 2001).

Lida, María Rosa, 'La prosa de Juan de Mena', *Boletín de la Academia Argentina de Letras* 18(69) (1949), 393–432.

Márquez Villanueva, Francisco, *El concepto cultural alfonsí* (Barcelona: Edicions Bellaterra, 2004).

Maser, Matthias, 'Rodrigo Jiménez de Rada and his *Historia Arabum*: An Extraordinary Example of Inter-cultural Tolerance?', in Sarah Lambert and Helen Nicholson (eds), *Languages of Love and Hate: Conflict, Communication, and Identity in the Medieval Mediterranean* (Turnhout: Brepols, 2011), pp. 223–38.

Menéndez Pidal, Ramón (ed.), *Primera crónica general. Estoria de España que mandó componer Alfonso el Sabio y se continuaba bajo Sancho IV en 1289* (Madrid: Gredos, 1955).

Morales Muñiz, Dolores Carmen, 'El caballo en la Edad Media: un estado de la cuestión', in *Homenaje al profesor Eloy Benito Ruano* (Murcia: Universidad de Murcia, 2010), pp. 537–52.

Mujica, Bárbara, *Antología de la literatura española. La edad media* (New York: John Wiley, 1991).

O'Callaghan, Joseph F., *Reconquest and Crusade in Medieval Spain* (Philadelphia: University of Pennsylvania Press, 2003).

Nirenberg, David, '"Judaism", "Islam", and the Dangers of Knowledge in Christian Culture, with Special Attention to the Case of King Alfonso X, "the Wise", of Castile', in C. Burnett and P. Mantas-España (eds), *Mapping Knowledge: Cross-Pollination in Late Antiquity and the Middle Ages, Arabica Veritas* (Cordoba: Oriens Academica, 2014), vol. I, pp. 253–76.

Palencia, Alfonso de, *Segunda Deca de la antigüedad de España e de las fazañas de la gente española [libros XI–XX]*, ed. Francisco Javier Durán Barceló (Madrid: Javier Durán Barceló, 2016).

Pereira-Muro, Carmen, *Culturas de España*, 2nd edn (Stamford, CT: Cengage Learning, 2015).

Pick, Lucy, *Conflict and Coexistence: Archbishop Rodrigo and the Muslims and Jews of Medieval Spain* (Ann Arbor: University of Michigan Press, 2004).

Pimienta-Bey, José V., 'Moorish Spain: Academic Source and Foundation for the Rise and Success of Western European Universities in the Middle Ages', in Ivan Van Sertima (ed.), *Golden Age of the Moor* (New Brunswick, NJ: Transaction, 1992), pp. 182–247.

Sánchez-Albornoz, Claudio, *España: Un enigma histórico*, 2nd edn (Barcelona: Espasa-Calpe, 1981).

Sánchez-Albornoz, Claudio, *De la Andalucía islámica a la de hoy* (Madrid: RIALP, 1983).

Scobie, Edward, 'The Moors and Portugal's Global Expansion', in Ivan Van Sertima (ed.), *Golden Age of the Moor* (New Brunswick, NJ: Transaction, 1992), pp. 331–59.

Skenderovic, Damir and Christina Späti, 'From Orientalism to Islamophobia: Reflections, Confirmations, and Reservations', *ReOrient* 4(2) (2019): 130–43.

Smith, Colin, *Christians and Moors in Spain, vol. 1: AD 711–1150* (Warminster: Aris & Phillips, 1988).

Tolan, John V., *Saracens: Islam in the Medieval European Imagination* (New York: Columbia University Press, 2002).

Van Sertima, Ivan (ed.), *Golden Age of the Moor* (New Brunswick, NJ: Transaction, 1992; originally published in *Journal of African Civilizations* 11 (1991)).

Ward, Aengus (ed.), *Estoria de Espanna Digital* vol. 1.1 (Birmingham: University of Birmingham, 2020), available at: http://estoria.bham.ac.uk.

Weissberger, Barbara, *Isabel Rules: Constructing Queenship, Wielding Power* (Minneapolis: University of Minnesota Press, 2004).

Wolf, Kenneth Baxter, 'Christian Views of Islam in Early Medieval Spain', in John Victor Tolan (ed.), *Medieval Christian Perceptions of Islam* (New York: Routledge, 1996), pp. 85–108.

Yolles, Julian and Jessica Weiss (eds), *Medieval Latin Lives of Muhammad* (Cambridge, MA: Harvard University Press, 2018).

3

JUST ONE WORD

Gil Anidjar

ma il loro numero è sterminato . . .

Primo Levi

Is literature guilty? Even if your object of choice is words, the numbers are hard to ignore. Regardless of content, and not unlike the expanding universe or the world population, words are proliferating. Books and journals, keywords and lexicons, multiply apace. The blogosphere balloons.

Within the literary field, expansion and growth – the rule of numbers – have made themselves dramatically, albeit controversially, felt ('billions of sentences . . . thousands of variations and permutations and approximations . . . from the 20,000 words of *Daphnis and Chloe* to the 40,000 words of Chrétien, 100,000 of Austen, 400,000 of *Don Quixote*, and over 800,000 of *The Story of the Stone*).[1] They have powered the twin engines of diversity and inclusion, a promise of 'the open-ended possibility of studying *all* literatures, with linguistic rigor and historical savvy'.[2] Distant or close, surface or depth, expertly critical

[1] Franco Moretti, *Distant Reading* (London: Verso, 2013), pp. 164–5; between words and numbers, Talal Asad interrogates the modes of representations, the constructions of experience, that are sustained by both (Talal Asad, 'Ethnographic Representation: Statistics and Modern Power', *Social Research* 51(1) (1994): 55–88).

[2] Gayatri Chakravorty Spivak, *Death of a Discipline*, The Wellek Library Lectures in Critical Theory (New York: Columbia University Press, 2003), p. 5 (emphasis added); Aamir Mufti is critical of the diversity imperative in the study of world literature (Aamir R. Mufti, 'Orientalism and the Institution of World Literatures', *Critical Inquiry* 36 (2010): 458–93).

or socio-historical, coded, branded and digito-commodified – the horizon of literary reading is governed by growth, the unmeasure of universal reach.

And so literature grows and expands, at home in the world – the whole world now – along with its locales and forms. The more it includes, the more diverse it is, the less agreement there is on what literature is. Indeed, everything is as if the less agreement there is on the *subject* of literature, the larger it swells as an *object*.

At the same time, and perhaps paradoxically, literature appears to compete less in a Darwinian universe than in a pre-Socratic one. Instead of Air, Water, Earth and Fire, one finds Economy, Science, Politics, Religion – basic and universal elements to which everything returns, to which all could be reduced.[3] And so with the fifth element. In the world historical expansion of the literary field (words, books, genres, realms, languages, regions and periods), there has been a similar reductive push. For all this expansive increase – one word and one word only.

Literature. One rigid designator, a Latin word (otherwise traced to philologically precise locations in time and space and along recognised linguistic chains, the word makes its way to its modern semantic shades in Western

[3] Each realm makes a distinct universalist claim with regard to 'the proper of man', from *homo oeconomicus* to *homo religiosus*, with *homo narrativus* never far behind; see, for example, Yuval Noah Harari, *Sapiens: A Brief History of Humankind* (London: Vintage, 2014), pp. 60–6; and compare Hayden White, for whom 'to raise the question of the nature of narrative is to invite reflection on the very nature of culture and, possibly, on the nature of humanity itself' (H. White, 'The Value of Narrativity in the Representation of Reality', *Critical Inquiry* 7(1) (1980): 5). Bruno Latour, for his part, famously recognised, refuted and later partially reinscribed, in their separateness – 'headings like Economy, Politics, Science, Books, Culture, Religion, and Local Events', although he notably gives short shrift to 'the literary supplement in which novelists delight in the adventures of a few narcissistic egos ("I love you . . . you don't")' (B. Latour, *We Have Never Been Modern*, trans. Catherine Porter (Cambridge, MA: Harvard University Press, 1993), p. 2). 'A Latourian perspective on literature' seems quite speculative, but, as Rita Felski summarises one scholar's view, it would remain intent on preserving the literary object. Indeed, in this version, what is affirmed, what must be taken seriously is 'the realness of literary objects – as residing not in their autonomy, otherness or remoteness from the world, but in their ability *to increase and multiply* connections' (R. Felski, 'Introduction to "Recomposing the Humanities — with Bruno Latour"', *New Literary History* 47(2/3 (2017): 223 (emphasis added)).

languages by the early to late modern periods), which would serve as the most accurate and the most generic label for an ever-increasing segment of the cultural – nay, human – universe that is growing still and remains even now in the process of emerging into view.[4] Enframed by an insistent 'staging of individuals', in what Yasemin Yıldız described as 'the monolingual paradigm', literature (i.e., Literature) would be the proper and appropriate noun for the plethora of oral or written record, the wealth of genres and practices, disciplines and institutions now found across historical time and planetary space.[5] In a remarkable case of wondrously accurate translation, literature – the word – would name and form a universal field of fragile but guarded specifics, filled with promise and potential (diversity and inclusiveness, knowledge, truth and – why not? – justice) while singularly distinct from other fields of human, all-too human, inventiveness (Economy, Science, Politics, Religion). Oddly absent from the *Dictionary of Untranslatables*,[6] such Greek and Latin words (ah but for 'the myriad names and powers that are not Greek, Latin, or Indo-European at all', rightly writes Donna Haraway)[7] would contain and sustain their meaning and use, they would suffice to serve their extraordinary,

[4] 'We cannot unfold here all the reasons one might insist on this Roman latinity – or on a certain *globalatinization* and, as I have tried to show elsewhere, the role the latter played, it seems to me, in what happens with what we call by another Latin word, *religion*, in the world today' (Jacques Derrida, 'Demeure: Fiction and Testimony', in Maurice Blanchot (2000), *The Instant of My Death* – Jacques Derrida, *Demeure: Fiction and Testimony*, trans. Elizabeth Rottenberg (Stanford: Stanford University Press, 2000), p. 25 and see pp. 21–3 (translation modified)); see as well Siraj Ahmed, *The Archaeology of Babel: The Colonial Foundations of the Humanities* (Stanford: Stanford University Press, 2018); Siraj quotes Derrida on p. 21; an essential and related chapter of this Latin history is described in Amnon Raz-Krakotzkin, *The Censor, the Editor, and the Text: The Catholic Church and the Shaping of the Jewish Canon in the Sixteenth Century*, trans. Jackie Feldman (Philadelphia: University of Pennsylvania Press, 2007).

[5] Yasemine Yildiz, *Beyond the Mother Tongue: The Postmonolingual Condition* (New York: Fordham University Press, 2012), pp. 17, 22.

[6] Barbara Cassin (ed.), *Dictionary of Untranslatables: A Philosophical Lexicon* (Princeton, NJ: Princeton University Press, 2014).

[7] D. J. Haraway, *Staying With the Trouble: Making Kin in the Chthulucene* (Durham, NC: Duke University Press, 2016), p. 33.

but insistently generic, purpose, in every time and place – which is to say, regardless of either.[8]

Now, there may or may not be *one* literature (or innumerable variations on *its* versions and forms), one *world literature*, but literatures surely reach to numerous other words, to multifarious other worlds. Accordingly, varying claims for the externality of alterity – text and context – have delved into and combined with Economy, Science, Politics and Religion at the limits of literature (further contingencies of translation notwithstanding, one might also refer to Law here).[9] In what follows, I mean to revisit the longstanding tradition that accords to one word, and to one word only, the capacity to sustain or index (rarely, disturb) an ever-expanding archive and its others.

[8] Describing *adab* as an institution, Sarah bin Tyeer is among the few who offer a series of arguments on the limits of translation, insisting that with regard to *adab*, at least, and to 'pre-modern Arabic prose and narrative, the modern definition of "literature" cannot be applied' (Sarah R. Bin Tyeer, *The Qur'an and the Aesthetics of Premodern Arabic Prose* (London: Palgrave Macmillan, 2016), p. 30; Bin Tyeer discusses the *Dictionary of Untranslatable* on p. 22). Michael Allan makes a related argument, though mobilising a different conception of translation (M. Allan, *In the Shadow of World Literature: Sites of Reading in Colonial Egypt* (Princeton, NJ: Princeton University Press, 2016)); and see also, in the Persianate context, Mana Kia, 'Adab as Literary Form and Social Conduct: Reading the Gulistan in Late Mughal India', in A. Korangy and D. J. Sheffield (eds), *'No Tapping Around Philology': A Festschrift in Celebration and Honor of Wheeler McIntosh Thackston Jr.'s 70th Birthday* (Wiesbaden: Harrassowitz, 2014), pp. 281–308; and Mana Kia, 'Space, Sociality, and Sources of Pleasure: A Response to Sanjay Subrahmanyam', *Journal of the Economic and Social History of the Orient* 61 (2018): 256–76.

[9] 'Religion' is no doubt a privileged other in the bibliography I have mentioned so far and Islam, of course, looms large under this heading (on which see Talal Asad's remarkable reflections on literature in Talal Asad, *Genealogies of Religion: Discipline and Reasons of Power in Christianity and Islam* (Baltimore, MD: Johns Hopkins University Press, 1993), ch. 8, and see as well Saba Mahmood, *Religious Difference in a Secular Age: A Minority Report* (Princeton, NJ: Princeton University Press, 2016), ch. 5)). Neither the broad history of philology and literature, of Orientalism and of colonialism, nor the influence and significance of Edward Said's argument for 'secular criticism', would contradict that sense. But adjudicating on that privilege, real or imagined, serves little purpose to me here.

On my way to Islam in – or out of – world literary imagination,[10] I shall experiment with another word, an ordinary word, or, rather, with a word that is at once more ordinary and more literary than has otherwise appeared. I shall proceed without assurance that I stand on the same enumerative or rhetorical ground I have just described, or indeed that I read from a demonstrably different grid or frame (Economy, Science, Politics, Religion – and the rest is Literature).[11] Just one word, then: the word *Muselmänner*, which can certainly be, and has in fact been, read and translated – Muslims.

Muslims

It is by now well known. The word *Muselmänner* has been recorded, inscribed and translated, disseminated, sometimes even read, though not without problems, of course (let us call them, for the moment, *literary* problems). It is a word that we will come to understand as both ordinary and literary, at once a rigid, or petrified, designator and a floating signifier; a word that signals and carries (and exhausts too) a certain history and a definite (or indefinite) enumeration as well, that has multiplied and proliferated, acquired a strange ubiquity, and a persistent illegibility. It has done so in a vast but specific archive – Holocaust literature – and beyond it too.

It would take too long to address, here as well, the difficulty of reading (or translating) the word 'literature' in this particular phrase ('Holocaust literature'). Suffice it to say that the invocation of an aesthetic or poetic dimension, the question of 'historical emplotment' and of rhetoric and representation,

[10] As will become clear, I wrote this chapter under a number of imperatives – the weight of words. Which means that I took it as my task to reflect on the words of the original title of the present collection, as intended by the editors: 'Islam in World Literary Imagination'. That title has now changed, yet it seemed to me important to retain its trace, if only for the significance of its appeal to the imagination, and to the literary imagination in particular. As I wrote, I adopted this phrase, indeed, subjected myself to it, and meant as well to mark it. If I do ask after 'the meaning of a word', the trajectory of the essay that follows remains nonetheless informed by the meaning of *each* word in that original title.

[11] 'What the book tries to do is to tell a story that the numbers cannot provide', writes Bruce Robbins in B. Robbins, *The Beneficiary* (Durham, NC: Duke University Press, 2017), p. 3; in what follows, this distinction should appear increasingly uncertain.

have, when it comes to the Holocaust, generated poignant and passionate discussions.[12] Referring to Nazism and the Final Solution, Hayden White notoriously broached the matter by asking the following, still pressing, questions:

> Are there any limits on the *kind* of story that can responsibly be told about these phenomena? *Can* these events be responsibly employed in *any* of the modes, symbols, plot types, and genres our culture provides for 'making sense' of such extreme events in our past? . . . In a word, do the natures of Nazism and the Final Solution set absolute limits on what can be truthfully said about them? Do they set limits on the uses that can be made of them by writers of fiction or poetry? Do they lend themselves to emplotment in a set number of ways, or is their specific meaning, like that of other historical events, infinitely interpretable and ultimately undecidable?[13]

What Sidra deKoven Ezrahi has described as 'the Holocaust in literature' – wherein she joined many others (and numerous anthologies too) in affirming, with regard to memory and meaning, the powers of art in the face of horror and trauma – might be recast as literature *against* the Holocaust (the dangers of fiction and of rhetoric), or, one might say in the present volume, the question of world literary imagination *in* the Holocaust. What each of these formulations, what the word 'literature', evokes or designates, includes,

[12] On poetry after Auschwitz, and after Adorno, see Michael Rothberg, *Traumatic Realism: The Demands of Holocaust Representation* (Minneapolis: University of Minnesota Press, 2000); on further discussions and controversies, see N. Levi and M. Rothberg (eds), *The Holocaust: Theoretical Readings* (New Brunswick, NJ: Rutgers University Press, 2003), pp. 273–367; and see Karyn Ball's indispensable study, K. Ball, *Disciplining the Holocaust* (Albany: State University of New York Press, 2008), as well as Marc Nichanian, *The Historiographic Perversion*, trans. Gil Anidjar (New York: Columbia University Press, 2010).

[13] H. White, 'Historical Employment and the Problem of Truth', in S. Friedländer (ed.), *Probing the Limits of Representation: Nazism and the 'Final Solution'* (Cambridge, MA: Harvard University Press, 1992), pp. 37–53; the entire volume is an explicit rebuttal of White's very questions. Nichanian rightly underscores the significance of Carlo Ginzburg's contribution, which also raises the question of numbers, and is titled 'Just One Witness' (in *Probing the Limits*, pp. 82–96; and see Nichanian, *The Historiographic Perversion*, pp. 60–86). I draw inspiration from Ginzburg's for my own title.

as I will try to show, Muslims.[14] For now, I merely wish to register the problem raised by, as well as the proliferation of, each time and once again, one word (literature, Muslims) in the context of the Holocaust.[15]

The archive to which I am referring is also growing. It includes testimony – often in the form of novels – but also films and works of art, as well as multifarious scholarly publications (historical, literary critical, philosophical, etc.).[16] What this vast corpus shares is without a doubt a *literary* fact, by which I mean the repeated, literal inscription of a word thereby made available (one might say: made ordinary, if it were not already so), but also resistant, to reading – of whatever kind. Though not always translated, nor transliterated according to established or recognisable rules, the word *Muselmänner* (sing. *Muselmann*) is – let us say, sufficiently, even plentifully – there to-be-read on the countless pages of Holocaust literature (in German, Italian, English, French, Polish, Hebrew, Russian and more). The word belongs to the German language, though it is documented in English as well, according to Ngram at least (not the OED, unless one thinks of consulting the entry for 'Mussulman'), since 1866 (with noticeable, indeed, remarkable spikes in the 1940s and since *c.* 2000).[17] Now listed as 'archaic'

[14] Sidra DeKoven Ezrahi, *By Words Alone: The Holocaust in Literature* (Chicago: University of Chicago Press, 1980); and see the important perspective introduced by Pascale Bos with regard to (gendered) literature in P. R. Bos, *German-Jewish Literature in the Wake of the Holocaust: Grete Weil, Ruth Klüger and the Politics of Address* (New York: Palgrave Macmillan, 2005).

[15] One envisions here a Wittgensteinian exploration, where the uses – to be distinguished from the senses – of the word 'literature' are described, counted and accounted for, revealing the impossibility, perhaps the futility, of semantic or conceptual, much less scholarly, institution, policing, inflations or confinements.

[16] I have previously attended to this archive and proposed a broad, theologico-political frame towards an understanding of the *Muselmänner* in G. Anidjar, *The Jew, the Arab: A History of the Enemy* (Stanford: Stanford University Press, 2003); and see as well my 'Muslims (*Shoah, Nakba*)', in Bashir Bashir and Amos Goldberg (eds), *The Holocaust and the Nakba: A New Grammar of Trauma and History* (New York: Columbia University Press, 2019), pp. 66–78. A recent study lists a voluminous bibliography (P. Bernard-Nouraud, *Figurer l'autre. Essay sur la figure du « musulman » dans les camps de concentration nazis* (Paris: Kimé, 2013)).

[17] See at: https://books.google.com/ngrams/graph?content=Muselmann&case_insensitive=on&year_start=1800&year_end=2000&corpus=15&smoothing=3&share=&direct_url=t4%3B%2CMuselmann%3B%2Cc0%3B%2Cs0%3B%3BMuselmann%3B%2Cc0%3B%3Bmuselmann%3B%2Cc0, last accessed 4 July 2019.

in German etymological dictionaries, use of the word in the German language has generally declined, while showing increases (parallel to those in the English language) in the 1940s and the late 1990s and after.[18] The word appears in songs that are still sung to children and performed in public.[19] As the dictionaries make clear, the word is accurately translated as 'Muslim'.

One of the earliest and no doubt most notorious inscriptions of the term in – dare I call it – *world literature* can be found in Primo Levi's *If This Is a Man* (later translated as *Survival in Auschwitz*).[20] In the Italian original, the word Levi uses is *mussulmani.* But the German also appears in Levi's text as it does in countless other writings and testimonies, in its plural and singular forms (English editions offer transliterations and/or inconsistent spellings like 'mussulmans' or 'musselmans' or revert, in a newer edition, to the untranslated German *Muselmänner*, even where the Italian has *Mussulmani*). Levi uses the term early on, in a chapter called 'The Drowned and the Saved' (later the title of another one of his books). Here is how Levi describes

[18] See at: https://www.dwds.de/wb/Muselmann, last accessed 4 July 2019 – but the entry remarkably says nothing of Auschwitz – and see at: https://books.google.com/ngrams/graph?content=Muselmann&case_insensitive=on&year_start=1800&year_end=2000&corpus=20&smoothing=3&share=&direct_url=t1%3B%2CMuselmann%3B%2Cc0#t1%3B%2CMuselmann%3B%2Cc0, last accessed 4 July 2019.

[19] See at: https://www.youtube.com/watch?v=MEhtaGMGixE], last accessed 5 July 2019); I quote this old song, though not its latest performance, in Anidjar, *The Jew, the Arab*, p. 142.

[20] 'We need to prepare ourselves to read different works with different expectations', writes David Damrosch in a truly puzzling moment of boundary policing, hypothetical history and even speculative fiction with regards to the ethics of reading. 'Primo Levi's haunting *Survival in Auschwitz* would lose much of its force if it ever turned out that Auschwitz had never existed, or that Levi had not been interned there, whereas for readers of Boccaccio's *Decameron* it hardly matters whether there was an actual plague in Florence that forced people to flee the city and start telling each other ribald stories in the countryside' (D. Damrosch, *How to Read World Literature?* (Malden, MA: Wiley-Blackwell, 2009), p. 7; and see, as I finish writing this chapter, Sam Jordison, 'Primo Levi brings readers as close as prose can to the horror of Auschwitz', *The Guardian*, 9 July 2019). Levi cuts an iconic figure, of course. As a survivor, writer and thinker of the Holocaust, as a user of the word 'Muslims', Levi is also one among many. Representative? Exemplary? No two accounts are similar, not even Levi's, much less identical.

and names, here is how he counts, the drowned, the Muslims: 'Their life is short, but their number is endless [*ma il loro numero è sterminato*]; they, the *Muselmänner*, the drowned, form the backbone of the camp, an anonymous mass, continually renewed and always identical [*continuamente rinnovata e sempre identica*] . . .'[21] As I read this terrifying passage again, I am struck by the force of the name, the devastating power of the generic, as well as by the endless insistence of numbers (*sterminato*, without term or limit, endless, yes, but also – this seems hard to ignore – exterminated), the proximate inscription of mass and growth ('continually renewed'), of undifferentiated proliferation ('always identical') and (destructive) enumeration, to which Levi testifies.

Otherwise significant is Levi's association – or rather, dissociation – of the Muslims with narrative ('All the mussulmans who finished in the gas chambers have the same story, or, more exactly, have no story [*Tutti i mussulmani che vanno in gas hanno la stessa storia, o, per meglio dire, non hanno storia*]', and, as Levi goes on to write, with memory and an emblematic image: 'They crowd my memory with their faceless [*senza volto*] presence, and if I could encompass all the evil of our time in one image, I would choose this image, which is familiar to me: an emaciated man, head bowed and shoulders bent, on whose face [*suil cui volto*] and in whose eyes no trace of thought can be seen.' One familiar image, one thoughtless face, for all the innumerable faceless faces, and for all the evil of our time. A face, nonetheless, just one thoughtless face and one image, a memory; a figure that is and is not a figure, a trope or a turn (Levi did not use the words *tropo*, *volta*) of oneness and of endlessness, a number without count, a number without number, perhaps a fiction, one in any case void of narrative. The Muslim marks at once the strange irruption of a literary and rhetorical lexicon (the wish for the ultimate synecdoche, the substitution of one or the other, for the other, without difference, always identical, the

[21] Primo Levi, *If This Is a Man*, trans. Stuart Woolf (New York: Orion Press, 1959), p. 103; a few paragraphs earlier, Levi confesses his ignorance about the term, which he nevertheless translates in the same pages: 'This word, *Muselmann*, was used, although I do not know why, by the old hands of the camp to describe the weak, the inept, those doomed to selection' (p. 101n1).

same story) and the end of all stories, the endlessness of numbers and possibly the end of literature.[22]

In *The Drowned and the Saved*, Levi goes on, in an apophatic register, to elaborate on the language of the camps ('Auschwitz-language', LTI), and returns, in the process, to the word *Muselmann*, offering explanations – explanations which he immediately takes back and renounces (*apophasis*):

> Common to all the Lagers was the term *Muselmann*, Muslim, to describe prisoners who were irreversibly exhausted, emaciated, and close to death. Two equally unconvincing explanations for its origin have been proposed: fatalism, and the turban-like dressing of head wounds. This is perfectly mirrored, even in its cynical irony [*cinica ironia*], by the Russian term *dochodjaga*, literally 'come to the end', 'concluded'. In the Ravensbrück Lager (the only all-female camp) the same concept was expressed, Lidia Rolfi tells me, by the two specular nouns *Schmutzstück* and *Schmuckstück*, 'garbage' and 'jewel', which in German are almost homophones, one a parody of the other.[23]

Whatever one makes of these and other explanations, from Levi's conception of 'Auschwitz-language', or from the fact that the term 'Muslims' was obviously not 'common to all the Lagers', there is no doubt that the word *Muselmann* – the explanations it occasions, the remarkable dissemination and 'reception' it has gained since the liberation of the camps – unsettles any simple (or even complex) notion of referentiality, any straightforward semantics and hermeneutics, any reading of the literary kind. It is an ordinary word, which undoubtedly belongs to a history of tropes and figures, and can surely be described as a slur and a popular stereotype as well, a generic generalisation

[22] The language of fiction obtains to the extent that one might want to claim that there were no 'real' Muslims in the camps. For a more serious treatment of the question, see Gerhard Höpp, '"Gefährdungen der Erinnerung": Arabische Häftlinge in Nationalsozialistischen Konzentrationslagern', *Asien afrika lateinamerika* 30 (2002): 373–86; and G. Höpp, 'Im Schatten des Mondes. Arabische Opfer des Nationalsozialismus', *Sozial Geschichte Zeitschrift für historische Analyse des 20. Jahrhunderts* 2 (2002); and see David Motadel, *Islam and Nazi Germany's War* (Cambridge, MA: Harvard University Press, 2014), pp. 242–3.

[23] Primo Levi, *The Drowned and the Saved*, trans. Michael F. Moore, in Primo Levi, *The Complete Works of Primo Levi*, ed. Ann Goldstein (New York: Liveright Publishing/W. W. Norton, 2015). I quote from the Apple Books electronic edition.

and an abstraction (the history of Orientalism, of religion and race, as well as, I explained elsewhere, the history of philosophy).[24] Rightly or wrongly, but dreadfully enough, the word also evokes literature; it functions as a rhetorical figure (synecdoche, metonymy, parody and, as we shall soon see, irony) that presents as 'a special case of a more general pattern of substitution that all tropes have in common. It is the result of an exchange of properties made possible by a proximity or an analogy so close and intimate that it allows the one to substitute for the other without revealing the difference necessarily introduced by the substitution.'[25] One – *un numero sterminato* – is called a Muslim, each one substituting for any other, *sempre identico*, the one name substituting, indicating an exchange of (many) properties, a proximity or an analogy, the identical intimacy of which has only grown thicker over the years and the publications. The word stands for the many, uncounted, innumerable (continually renewed, always identical). Endless, it swells as an anonymous mass. And a vanishing one into none. It substitutes for itself, as it were, and for other monikers, other designators, without revealing the difference it introduces, if any, without revealing the nature of the substitution, or of the enumeration.

[24] I traced the emerging figures – association and dissociation – of Jews and Muslims in Kant, Montesquieu and Hegel as they become 'slaves' to the one God of the 'religions of the Sublime' and later 'Semites' (see Anidjar, *The Jew, the Arab*, esp. ch. 5), but philosophy is only one generic marker in the long history of Orientalism and – but it is the same story and history – of anti-Semitism; for more on Jews and Arabs, Jews and Muslims, and on religion and race in this context, see G. Anidjar, *Semites: Race, Religion, Literature* (Stanford: Stanford University Press, 2008).

[25] Paul de Man, *Allegories of Reading: Figural Language in Rousseau, Nietzsche, Rilke, and Proust* (New Haven, CT: Yale University Press, 1979), p. 61; 'tropes are transformational systems', de Man goes on to add (p. 63n8). Indeed, as he reflects in the same passage on what he calls 'the most impossible sentence conceivable', de Man makes a comment that, even if perhaps too general, seems to me of great pertinence in attempting to read or account for the word *Muselmann*. 'Its absurdity', de Man writes, 'not only denies the intelligibility of natural metaphors but of all tropes; it is the figure of the unreadability of figures and therefore no longer, strictly speaking, a figure' (p. 61n5). And recall that, for de Man, the 'critique of metaphysics, which is itself a recurrent gesture throughout the history of thought, is the rhetorical model of the trope or, if one prefers to call it that, literature' (p. 15).

By the time Giorgio Agamben initiates his own inquiries into the Holocaust, putting the *Muselmann* at the centre of his reflections and bringing the word the unprecedented attention it surely deserves, he does so by foregrounding the tropology and tropicality of the term.[26] Acknowledging 'the deprecatory sense of the term . . . in European languages', Agamben also describes it in words that his English translator rendered as 'a kind of ferocious irony'.[27] Yet Agamben's Italian suggests something slightly different, ascribing agency and reflexivity to the users or speakers of the word. Agamben writes of '*una sorta di feroce autoironia*' (*a kind of ferocious self-irony*), as if the speakers were themselves the authors of a word, of a rhetorical gesture that, always already reflexive and self-directed, constituted a strange – and ferocious – instance of self-ascription. Which transports us, in yet another tropic turn perhaps, towards another literary issue, the matter of authorship.

Did the Jews call themselves Muslims? What would these Jews be, these Muslims, in world literary imagination? Did they write the story of the end of all stories, while no longer making their own history?[28] Can a slur or a trope,

[26] Agamben is not beyond criticism, obviously, yet it is undeniable that – for better or for worse – his work, and its timeliness, is owed a crucial debt for having brought the term *Muselmann* a remarkable measure of critical attention, an attention that was simply inexistent beforehand.

[27] The full sentence reads: 'In any case, it is certain that, with a kind of ferocious irony, the Jews knew that they would not die at Auschwitz as Jews' (G. Agamben, *Remnants of Auschwitz: The Witness and the Archive (Homo Sacer III)*, trans. Daniel Heller-Roazen (New York: Zone Books, 1999), p. 45; for Agamben, who here deviates from Levi's opinion, 'the most likely explanation of the term can be found in the literal meaning of the Arabic word muslim [the term, rendered *muslim*, in Italian is not italicised in the English translation – GA]: the one who submits unconditionally to the will of God. It is this meaning that lies at the origin of the legends concerning Islam's supposed fatalism, legends which are found in European culture starting with the Middle Ages (this deprecatory sense of the term is present in European languages, particularly in Italian). But while the muslim's resignation consists in the conviction that the will of Allah [the name of God is here left untranslated with no explanation – GA] is at work every moment and in even the smallest events, the *Muselmann* of Auschwitz [*il musulmano di Auschwitz*, i.e., the Muslim of Auschwitz] is instead defined by a loss of all will and consciousness' (ibid.).

[28] Discussing authorship and agency, and the making of history, Talal Asad writes that 'even the inmates of a concentration camp are able, in this sense, to live by their own cultural logic. But one may be forgiven for doubting that they are *therefore* "making their own history"' (Asad, *Genealogies of Religion*, p. 4).

can literature, have more than one author? No author at all? Can it be one and author-less?[29] Subjectless? How to account for a strangely ritualised gesture, the repeated inscription of a word without intent, included and excluded from 'its' languages, at once full and void of its meaning and with hardly a secure referent (living or dead, Jew and Muslim, etc.)? How to read one word as many? Many into none? A figure (of speech) that is less a dead metaphor than a living, killing (yet unknowing) letter? Recurring claims that the term was wielded *nolens volens* but always *malevolens* by camp inmates (rather than by the guards, by official and literary discourse; really by any German speaker, inmate or not, and by countless non-German ones too), that it was hurled by Jews – such claims ignore the well-documented use of the word in the German language long before the Nazi regime. These claims also ignore the (to me much more remarkable) dissemination, the *endless* proliferation of the term in multiple publications, across multiple languages *since the end of the war*. The term does not annul, but it does undermine, the attempt to anchor it in its 'original' context, to identify or determine authorial intent or control as opposed to the uncontrolled propagation, the cacophony of voices that confirm, while denying, the ordinariness of its use, iteration and reception. The word *Muselmann* circulates and proliferates. It spreads, it continues to be used, in a global landscape of *ignorance* (recall that Levi wrote that 'This word, *Muselmann*, was used, although I do not know why').

The Meaning of a Word and the End of Literature

In the Beginning Was the Word.

It might seem strange to wrap up my contribution to the topic of 'Islam in World Literary Imagination' with the famous prologue of the *Gospel of John*. Yet the phrase might help in calling attention to the force (or weakness) of a word. Not merely the *meaning* of a word, as the admittedly less notorious question has it, which I have attempted to address nonetheless.[30] It is after all

[29] Abdelfattah Kilito, *The Author and His Doubles: Essays on Classical Arabic Culture*, trans. Michael Cooperson (Syracuse, NY: Syracuse University Press, 2001).

[30] 'The Meaning of a Word' is the title of a lecture by J. L. Austin (in J. L. Austin, *Philosophical Papers*, ed. J. O. Urmson and G. J. Warnock (Oxford: Oxford University Press, 1970), pp. 55–75), and the subject of recurring explorations by Ludwig Wittgenstein.

remarkable that both phrases, the biblical and the philosophical, tentatively invoke just one word (the word, a word). Each mobilises that is, a peculiar grammatical singular (the word, a word) that introduces, from the beginning, a familiar tension between the one and the many. What could it mean to begin (anything, everything) with one word?[31] Could one word – in and at the beginning, but in other times and other places too – command, hold and organise meaning? Could one word *end* it?

Whatever translational and exegetical difficulties, whatever theological disputes and conundrums, are evoked and provoked by the word, by the word for word (*logos*, *verbum*), in the beginning, the force and power of a number (one) does seem to rule in it, by it, and over it.[32] We find ourselves, in other words (for there *are* other words), in the vicinity of what Yasemin Yildiz described, we saw, as 'the monolingual paradigm', an insistent 'staging of individuals', where single words perform the work of single languages, as if in their homogeneous entirety.[33] In the beginning was *the* word. One word and/or one language. And who would dispute it? No doubt, and to begin with, translators, exegetes and theologians. Philosophers, too, who have also found numerous reasons to interrogate the oneness of the word, here the

[31] Yitzhak Lewis reminded me of Jorge Luis Borges, who, in 'The Writing of the God', has the priest Tzinacan explain that 'a god . . . must speak but a single word, and in that word there must be *absolute plenitude.* No word uttered by a god could be less than the universe, or briefer than the sum of time. The ambitions and poverty of human words – *all, world, universe* – are but shadows or simulacra of the Word which is the equivalent of a language and all that can be comprehended within a language' (J. L. Borges, *Collected Fictions*, trans. Andrew Hurley (New York: Penguin, 1999), p. 252).

[32] The question of numbers is obviously crucial to any reading of the opening sentence (and of the word *logos*) of the Gospel of John, one literary-minded scholar going so far as to write that 'perhaps the main difficulty for gentile readers would be the monotheism of the prologue and the understanding of two divine personal entities as one and the same God' (Christos Karakolis, 'The Logos-Concept and Dramatic Irony in the Johannine Prologue and Narrative', in Jan G. van der Watt, R. A. Culpepper and U. Schnelle, U. (eds), *The Prologue of the Gospel of John* (Tübingen: Mohr Siebeck, 2016), p. 152n65). But numbers cannot be confronted *more theologico* exclusively, unless theology is more broadly recognised, after Wittgenstein, as grammatical.

[33] Yildiz, *Beyond the Mother Tongue*, pp. 17, 22.

word for word, according at least to some well-documented translations.[34] But the word in its oneness persists.

It is not always the word for word that so insists, of course, nor is it *every* word. Elias Canetti powerfully wrote of 'the conscience of words', but he may have exaggerated when he confidently asserted, as if about *all* words, that they 'are charged with a special kind of passion [*mit einer besonderen Art von Leidenschaft geladen sind*]. They are really like human beings [*wie Menschen*], they refuse to be neglected or forgotten. However they may be preserved, they maintain their life; they suddenly spring forth and demand their rights [*ihr Recht*].'[35] The staging of individuals. Indeed, it is only *some* words that are so staged, that sometimes serve as privileged occasions for attachment (or aversion). Only some that are so burdened and charged, that act or function as if they were invested in a particular way. Under certain regimes of iteration, they operate, one might say, as *keywords*. And yet no word (nor keyword) is in fact one, nor is it ever alone (even if other words, not to mention, grammar, remain implicit or hidden). No word is an island, not even the word that – inevitably framed by one sentence or more – was in (and possibly at) the beginning. And this is true with regard to use and to force (Canetti's 'passion'), and true, too, with regard to meaning, however we understand *those* words.

Stanley Cavell further clarifies the matter as he expresses the wish to put 'pressure on philosophical language that is not unlike a literary pressure'.[36] Cavell wants to encourage 'a freedom of responsiveness to the fact that philosophy continuously finds itself averse to various ordinary words it seems

[34] See the entries for 'Logos' and 'Word' in Cassin, *Dictionary of Untranslatables*.

[35] E. Canetti, *The Conscience of Words*, trans. Joachim Neugroschel (New York: Farrar, Straus and Giroux, 1984), p. 142 (there is nothing irenic about Canetti's words here: he called this speech 'Word attacks [*Wortanfälle*]'). Acknowledging, with William James, that there are feelings and sensations associated with certain words (in this case the words *and*, *if*, *or* and *not*), Ludwig Wittgenstein insists that 'these sensations do no accompany every use' of these words, and certainly not *every* word. 'Ask yourself', he goes on, 'what means we have of finding out the feelings which they produce in different people and on different occasions' (L. Wittgenstein, *The Blue and Brown Books: Preliminary Studies for the 'Philosophical Investigations'* (Oxford: Blackwell, 1958), p. 79).

[36] S. Cavell, *The Claim of Reason: Wittgenstein, Skepticism, Morality, and Tragedy* (New York: Oxford University Press, 1999), p. xii.

unable to do without'.[37] It is as if, Cavell continues, 'philosophy's desire for words knows no bounds and yet would shun every word it craves'.[38] One might wish for a similar pressure on literature – writ small or large. Could literature ever find itself averse to a word – perhaps a concept – it seems unable to do without? 'But the greater the attachment to a concept (as to a person, or to a god)', Cavell goes on to write, 'the harder it may be to explain either the attachment or the concept; or perhaps it should be said that everything one does is, or could be, the only explanation of it'.[39] Is literature, is Muslims, a word or a concept? And are these sites of attachment – or of aversion? How many things can one do with just one word?

Each of the words that the editors of this volume on 'Islam in World Literary Imagination' have invited us to reflect and elaborate upon – to respond to – is undoubtedly 'charged with a special kind of passion'. Each provides a credible ground, upon which the others might be said to rest; a beginning from which they might depart, in distinct narrations or configurations. Each could serve as a frame or as a container of sorts for the others, with various degrees of plausibility or felicity (the word 'in' in its specific placement limits but also provokes this logic or strategy of containment). Each carry a claim, a refusal to be neglected or forgotten. Each springs forth and demands its rights. For my part, I have left the world as it is, or alluded to it only in passing. I have only attended to the word 'Muslims'.

What of the word 'literature' then? As I have already suggested, a number of compelling arguments were made for the historical novelty, the emergence, of both the word and the practices and institutions to which it refers. Raymond Williams, for instance, describes this keyword, this 'difficult word', and traces its English usage to the fourteenth century, underscoring the novelty of a specialised practice, which he dates to the late eighteenth and even nineteenth century.[40] Among those who concern themselves with broader world geographies, Michael Allan confirms, and

[37] Cavell, *The Claim of Reason,* p. xii.

[38] Cavell, *The Claim of Reason,* p. xii.

[39] Cavell, *The Claim of Reason,* p. 6.

[40] Raymond Williams, *Keywords: A Vocabulary of Culture and Society* (Oxford: Oxford University Press, 2015), pp. 134–8; and see Derrida, 'Demeure'.

proposes 'to consider transformations that both create the modern literary disciplines and define the contours of a reading public', to address 'the emergence of literature for the cultivation of aesthetic sensibilities and the development of character'.[41] Accordingly, such wide-ranging transformations, which involve the massive recasting of linguistic archives and the mobilisation of specific arrays of texts and technologies in aesthetic (or civilisational) education, have been interpreted under the distinct headings of modernity,[42] the printing revolution, later the philological revolution, in their links to capitalism and to national-aestheticism,[43] colonialism and secularism.[44] The word 'literature', then certainly corresponds to one of the new divisions of spheres associated with the modern, as well as to the formation of new subjectivities.[45]

Of a different nature is the word 'Muslims'. Yet I have tried to show that *it might translate literature*. Which is to say that it constitutes and is constituted by ordinary and literary questions of great magnitude in the corpus we call 'Holocaust literature' and more broadly through representations of the Holocaust – and well beyond these. Yet the word – now even a movie[46] – exceeds the genres and genealogies, the languages and the disciplines, and the archives too, within which it nonetheless appears and operates, disappears and ceases to operate, and to which it might be confined, however uneasily. The word 'Muslims' is itself a heading, and an archive of sorts. Has the archive turned

41 Allan, *In the Shadow of World Literature*, p. 3.

42 Philippe Lacoue-Labarthe and Jean-Luc Nancy, *The Literary Absolute: The Theory of Literature in German Romanticism*, trans. Philip Barnard and Cheryl Lester (Albany: State University of New York Press, 1988).

43 Benedict Anderson, *Imagined Communities: Reflections on the Origin and Spread of Nationalism* (London: Verso, 2006); Friedrich Kittler, *Discourse Networks 1800/1900*, trans. Michael Metteer and Chris Cullens (Stanford: Stanford University Press, 1990); Marc Nichanian, *Mourning Philology: Art and Religion at the Margins of the Ottoman Empire*, trans. G. M. Goshgarian and Jeff Fort (New York: Fordham University Press, 2014).

44 Gauri Viswanathan, *Masks of Conquest: Literary Study and British Rule in India* (New York: Columbia University Press, 1992); Tracy Fessenden, *Culture and Redemption: Religion, the Secular, and American Literature* (Princeton, NJ: Princeton University Press, 2007).

45 Sudipta Kaviraj, *The Invention of Private Life: Literature and Ideas* (New York: Columbia University Press, 2015).

46 See at: https://www.imdb.com/title/tt3182898, last accessed 16 July 2019.

into a crypt? An illegible sign or cypher? Has it shed its history, its senses, its literality or literarity? Has it not accumulated layers and senses, baggage and cathexes, texts and contexts, in ways that challenge, still, our reading *and* enumerative and even computational practices?[47] Our literary ones? Are *these* literary questions?

The word 'Muslims' provokes and disturbs the imagination. It also fails to do so (did not Levi dismiss the 'explanations' that he himself volunteered?). Some might suggest, after all, that there is no such thing as 'Islam in world literary imagination', others that it is a 'religious' question, not a literary one.[48] As we have seen, the word also signals (figures, names) the end of stories, the end of world and of world-making, the end of literature. The end.

Incidentally, when asking whether one can speak of Muslims, whether one can 'speak of a unified Muslim identity', Salman Sayyid proposes that Muslims 'share the possibility of telling stories about themselves; stories that begin with the revelations received by the Prophet (pbuh) and continue with the addition of many discursive threads through time to create a tapestry that can be signified as being distinct, with its own system of

[47] Dennis Tenen eloquently writes that 'literary scholarship cannot survive without awareness of its computational present' (D. Tenen, *Plain Text: The Poetics of Computation* (Stanford: Stanford University Press, 2017), p. 7), guiding readers towards those 'surfaces that are not available for immediate scrutiny', towards the possibility of 'an illegible sign . . . that never enters the hermeneutic circuit' (p. 8). But whereas Tenen advocates a humanism, a literary humanism, that resists the distraction of 'things powerless, inarticulate, and indifferent to our protestations' and wishes thereby to counter 'the systematic erasure of the human from the literary process' (p. 11), I have been trying to read the illegible erasure of the (powerless, inarticulate and indifferent) Muslim *in and as* the literary (and non-literary, ordinary) process.

[48] I would venture that it is not only the secularity of 'literature' that leaves so little room to Islam in discussions of world literature. Take the example of a hefty anthology, which, under the heading of 'the geographical dimension' (rather than the historical or theoretical dimensions it also singles out) treats Islam explicitly in one chapter only ('World Literature and Muslim Southeast Asia'), while mentioning it, as if in passing, in chapters on Africa and on *The Thousand and One Nights* (where the distinction between Arabic and Islamic is more or less collapsed, not necessarily wrongly) (T. D'haen, D. Damrosch and D. Kadir (eds), *The Routledge Companion to World Literature* (New York: Routledge, 2012). But more illustrations (or the lack thereof) could be gleaned from any number of discussions of world literature since Goethe's love of Ḥāfiẓ and all the way to Pascale Casanova.

signifying practices'.[49] And consider how Shahab Ahmed claimed to 'very much doubt that there is any community of discourse in the history of the world whose individual and collective language of self-exploration, self-expression and social communication – that is, whose language of individual and collective meaning-making – is as extensively, prolongedly, pervasively and routinely *metaphorized and paradoxical* as the literary idiom of Muslims; especially the prodigious Persian, Ottoman, Urdu, and Arabic literatures of the Muslims of the half-half-millennium and half-world of the Balkans-to-Bengal complex.'[50] Whereas it used to be difficult to call Islam a 'religion' (the novelty of the religions of the sublime, to which I alluded above), one is led to wonder about the possibility of calling it *literature* – Islam's overwhelming absence from discussions of world literature notwithstanding (give or take few exceptions, which the present volume seeks to correct).

We do need imagination – yet another word whose translations might require *imagination* and a few more things. But it would be presumptuous, it seems to me, to anticipate (not to say, restrict and confine) the imagination we need to a specific kind, however expansive or capacious. We simply cannot know the kind of imagination – the kinds of imagination – we need. Derrida early on suggested that 'the future can only be anticipated in the form of an absolute danger. It is that which breaks absolutely with constituted normality and can only be proclaimed, presented, as a sort of monstrosity. For that future world,' Derrida continued (though he could have mentioned the past as well), signalling towards the literary and toward its limits, 'and for that within it which will have put into question

[49] S. Sayyid, *Recalling the Caliphate: Decolonization and World Order* (London: Hurst, 2014), pp. 41–2; Sayyid had earlier raised the question of names ('Islam is the name that gives Muslims a name', he writes (p. 1) and goes on to invoke the *Muselmann* as well (pp. 4–5)), which opens or suspends the question of 'literal' or 'historical' Muslims versus 'metaphorical' and 'literary' Muslims. This is a distinction we have already encountered (like the distinction between literature and religion) and the fragility of which goes to the heart of the question of 'Islam in world literary imagination' as I address it here.

[50] Shahab Ahmed, *What is Islam? The Importance of Being Islamic* (Princeton, NJ: Princeton University Press, 2016), p. 389.

the values of sign, word, and writing, for that which guides our future anterior, there is as yet no exergue'.[51] The word *exergue* (originally used in numismatics) also comes from the Latin, *ex ergo*. It refers to a space that, in the work, is also outside the work. An epigraph, heading or a title, for example, perhaps just a word. There is no meta-language, Derrida would be saying for the nth time. And counting. Any word that marks an exterior place ('Islam in world literary imagination') already does so, as it were, on the inside. There is no outside here, no outside and no limits, no *hors-texte*, for this (endless, *sterminato*) text, no word that would enable naming it, confining it, with certainty – literature, for instance. The future, or the monstrous past.

Still, the literary imagination has surely proven creative.[52] One might now say: monstrously so (and recall Georges Bataille arguing about literature and evil).[53] And it is no doubt worth preserving and pursuing, growing and developing. Other forms of imagination, too (economic, scientific, political, religious, to return to our Pre-Socratic elements), have been and will surely be no less active – and no less destructive – in shaping and reshaping the world. Ending and destroying worlds as well. They will have done their work, and failed to do so, with words and with practices, with peoples and with institutions. But whatever creation (or de-creation) will be required,[54] or simply,

[51] J. Derrida, *Of Grammatology*, trans. Gayatri Chakravorty Spivak (Baltimore, MD: Johns Hopkins University Press, 1997), p. 5.

[52] For an expansive and pertinent deployment of the imagination – formative, creative, *worldly* (*cālam al-khayāl, cālam al-mithāl*), which is to say, also cosmic and prophetic – see Stefania Pandolfo, *Knot of the Soul: Madness, Psychoanalysis, Islam* (Chicago: University of Chicago Press, 2018); and see William C. Chittick, *The Sufi Path of Knowledge: Ibn al-ʿArabi's Metaphysics of Imagination* (Albany: State University of New York Press, 1989); and Norman O. Brown, *The Challenge of Islam: The Prophetic Tradition. Lectures, 1981*, ed. Jerome Neu (Santa Cruz, CA: New Pacific Press, 2009).

[53] Georges Bataille, *Literature and Evil*, trans. Alastair Hamilton (London: Penguin, 2012).

[54] On 'decreation', a term deployed by Simone Weil, see Beatrice Marovich, 'Simone Weil', in A. Kotsko and C. Salzani (eds), *Agamben's Philosophical Lineage* (Edinburgh: Edinburgh University Press, 2017), p. 295; and see B. Marovich, 'Recreating the Creature: Weil, Agamben, Animality and the Unsaveable', in R. A. Rozelle-Stone (ed.), *Simone Weil and Continental Philosophy* (New York: Rowman & Littlefield, 2017), pp. 164–202.

brought about, by that which is to come, in one word or more (and perhaps much less), remains indeed to be imagined.

For Talal Asad

Bibliography

Agamben, Giorgio, *Remnants of Auschwitz: The Witness and the Archive (Homo Sacer III)*, trans. Daniel Heller-Roazen (New York: Zone Books, 1999).

Ahmed, Shahab, *What is Islam? The Importance of Being Islamic* (Princeton, NJ: Princeton University Press, 2015).

Ahmed, Siraj, *The Archaeology of Babel: The Colonial Foundations of the Humanities* (Stanford: Stanford University Press, 2018).

Allan, Michael, *In the Shadow of World Literature: Sites of Reading in Colonial Egypt* (Princeton, NJ: Princeton University Press, 2016).

Anderson, Benedict, *Imagined Communities: Reflections on the Origin and Spread of Nationalism* (London: Verso, 2006).

Anidjar, Gil, *The Jew, the Arab: A History of the Enemy* (Stanford: Stanford University Press, 2003).

Anidjar, Gil, *Semites: Race, Religion, Literature* (Stanford: Stanford University Press, 2008).

Anidjar, Gil, 'Muslims (*Shoah, Nakba*)', in Bashir Bashir and Amos Goldberg (eds), *The Holocaust and the Nakba: A New Grammar of Trauma and History* (New York: Columbia University Press, 2019), pp. 66–78.

Asad, Talal, *Genealogies of Religion: Discipline and Reasons of Power in Christianity and Islam* (Baltimore, MD: Johns Hopkins University Press, 1993).

Asad, Talal, 'Ethnographic Representation: Statistics and Modern Power', *Social Research* 51(1) (1994): 55–88.

Austin, J. L., *Philosophical Papers*, ed. J. O. Urmson and G. J. Warnock (Oxford: Oxford University Press, 1970).

Bataille, Georges, *Literature and Evil*, trans. Alastair Hamilton (London: Penguin, 2012).

Ball, Karyn, *Disciplining the Holocaust* (Albany: State University of New York Press, 2008).

Bernard-Nouraud, P., *Figurer l'autre. Essay sur la figure du 'musulman' dans les camps de concentration nazis* (Paris: Kimé, 2013).

Bin Tyeer, Sarah R., *The Qur'an and the Aesthetics of Premodern Arabic Prose* (London: Palgrave Macmillan, 2016).

Borges, Jorge L., *Collected Fictions*, trans. Andrew Hurley (New York: Penguin, 1999).

Bos, Pascale R., *German-Jewish Literature in the Wake of the Holocaust: Grete Weil, Ruth Klüger and the Politics of Address* (New York: Palgrave Macmillan, 2005).

Brown, Norman O., *The Challenge of Islam: The Prophetic Tradition. Lectures, 1981*, ed. Jerome Neu (Santa Cruz, CA: New Pacific Press, 2009).

Canetti, Elias, *The Conscience of Words*, trans. Joachim Neugroschel (New York: Farrar, Straus and Giroux, 1984).

Cassin, Barbara (ed.), *Dictionary of Untranslatables: A Philosophical Lexicon* (Princeton, NJ: Princeton University Press, 2014).

Cavell, Stanley, *The Claim of Reason: Wittgenstein, Skepticism, Morality, and Tragedy* (New York: Oxford University Press, 1999).

Chittick, William C., *The Sufi Path of Knowledge: Ibn al-ʿArabi's Metaphysics of Imagination* (Albany: State University of New York Press, 1989).

D'haen, T., D. Damrosch and Kadir, D. (eds), *The Routledge Companion to World Literature* (New York: Routledge, 2012).

Damrosch, David, *How to Read World Literature?* (Malden, MA: Wiley-Blackwell, 2009).

DeKoven Ezrahi, Sidra, *By Words Alone: The Holocaust in Literature* (Chicago: University of Chicago Press, 1980).

De Man, Paul, *Allegories of Reading: Figural Language in Rousseau, Nietzsche, Rilke, and Proust* (New Haven, CT: Yale University Press, 1979).

Derrida, Jacques, *Of Grammatology*, trans. Gayatri Chakravorty Spivak (Baltimore, MD: Johns Hopkins University Press, 1997).

Derrida, Jacques, 'Demeure: Fiction and Testimony' in Blanchot, Maurice. *The Instant of My Death*/Jacques Derrida. *Demeure: Fiction and Testimony*, trans. Elizabeth Rottenberg (Stanford: Stanford University Press, 2000).

Felski, Rita, 'Introduction to "Recomposing the Humanities – with Bruno Latour"', *New Literary History* 47(2/3) (2016): 215–29.

Fessenden, Tracy, *Culture and Redemption: Religion, the Secular, and American Literature* (Princeton, NJ: Princeton University Press, 2007).

Ginzburg, Carlo, 'Just One Witness', in S. Friedländer (ed.), *Probing the Limits of Representation: Nazism and the 'Final Solution'* (Cambridge, MA: Harvard University Press, 1992), pp. 82–96.

Harari, Yuval N., *Sapiens: A Brief History of Humankind* (London: Vintage, 2014).

Haraway, Donna, J., *Staying With the Trouble: Making Kin in the Chthulucene* (Durham, NC: Duke University Press, 2016).

Höpp, Gerhard, '"Gefährdungen der Erinnerung": Arabische Häftlinge in Nationalsozialistischen Konzentrationslagern', *Asien afrika lateinamerika* 30 (2002): 373–86.

Höpp, Gerhard, 'Im Schatten des Mondes. Arabische Opfer des Nationalsozialismus', *Sozial Geschichte Zeitschriftt für historische Analyse des 20. Jahrhunderts* 2 (2002).

Karakolis, Christos, 'The Logos-Concept and Dramatic Irony in the Johannine Prologue and Narrative', in Jan G. van der Watt, R. A. Culpepper and U. Schnelle (eds), *The Prologue of the Gospel of John* (Tübingen: Mohr Siebeck, 2016), pp. 139–56.

Kaviraj, Sudipta, *The Invention of Private Life: Literature and Ideas* (New York: Columbia University Press, 2015).

Kia, Mana, 'Adab as Literary Form and Social Conduct: Reading the Gulistan in Late Mughal India', in A. Korangy and D. J. Sheffield (eds), *'No Tapping Around Philology': A Festschrift in celebration and honor of Wheeler McIntosh Thackston Jr.'s 70th Birthday* (Wiesbaden: Harrassowitz, 2014), pp. 281–308.

Kia, Mana, 'Space, Sociality, and Sources of Pleasure: A Response to Sanjay Subrahmanyam', *Journal of the Economic and Social History of the Orient* 61 (2018): 256–76.

Kilito, Abdelfattah, *The Author and His Doubles: Essays on Classical Arabic Culture*, trans. Michael Cooperson (Syracuse, NY: Syracuse University Press, 2001).

Kittler, Friedrich, *Discourse Networks 1800/1900*, trans. Michael Metteer and Chris Cullens (Stanford: Stanford University Press, 1990).

Lacoue-Labarthe, Philippe and Jean-Luc Nancy, *The Literary Absolute: The Theory of Literature in German Romanticism*, trans. Philip Barnard and Cheryl Lester (Albany: State University of New York Press, 1988).

Latour, Bruno, *We Have Never Been Modern*, trans. Catherine Porter (Cambridge, MA: Harvard University Press, 1993).

Levi, N. and M. Rothberg (eds), *The Holocaust: Theoretical Readings* (New Brunswick, NJ: Rutgers University Press, 2003).

Levi, Primo, *If This Is a Man*, trans. Stuart Woolf (New York: Orion Press, 1959).

Levi, Primo, *The Complete Works of Primo Levi*, ed. Ann Goldstein (New York: Liveright Publishing/W. W. Norton, 2015).

Mahmood, Saba, *Religious Difference in a Secular Age: A Minority Report* (Princeton, NJ: Princeton University Press, 2016).

Marovich, Beatrice, 'Simone Weil', in A. Kotsko and C. Salzani (eds), *Agamben's Philosophical Lineage* (Edinburgh: Edinburgh University Press, 2017), pp. 292–301.

Marovich, Beatrice, 'Recreating the Creature: Weil, Agamben, Animality and the Unsaveable', in R. A. Rozelle-Stone (ed.), *Simone Weil and Continental Philosophy* (New York: Rowman & Littlefield, 2017), pp. 69–86.

Moretti, Franco, *Distant Reading* (London: Verso, 2013).

Motadel, David, *Islam and Nazi Germany's War* (Cambridge, MA: Harvard University Press, 2014).

Mufti, Aamir R., 'Orientalism and the Institution of World Literatures', *Critical Inquiry* 36(3) (2010): 458–93.

Nichanian, Marc, *The Historiographic Perversion*, trans. Gil Anidjar (New York: Columbia University Press, 2010).

Nichanian, Marc, *Mourning Philology: Art and Religion at the Margins of the Ottoman Empire*, trans. G. M. Goshgarian and Jeff Fort (New York: Fordham University Press, 2014).

Pandolfo, Stefania, *Knot of the Soul: Madness, Psychoanalysis, Islam* (Chicago: University of Chicago Press, 2018).

Raz-Krakotzkin, Amnon, *The Censor, the Editor, and the Text: The Catholic Church and the Shaping of the Jewish Canon in the Sixteenth Century*, trans. Jackie Feldman (Philadelphia: University of Pennsylvania Press, 2007).

Robbins, Bruce, *The Beneficiary* (Durham, NC: Duke University Press, 2017).

Rothberg, Michael, *Traumatic Realism: The Demands of Holocaust Representation* (Minneapolis: University of Minnesota Press, 2000).

Sayyid, S., *Recalling the Caliphate: Decolonization and World Order* (London: Hurst, 2014).

Spivak, Gayatri Chakravorty, *Death of a Discipline*, The Wellek Library Lectures in Critical Theory (New York: Columbia University Press, 2003).

Tenen, Denis, *Plain Text: The Poetics of Computation* (Stanford: Stanford University Press, 2017).

Viswanathan, Gauri, *Masks of Conquest: Literary Study and British Rule in India* (New York: Columbia University Press, 1992).

White, Hayden, 'The Value of Narrativity in the Representation of Reality', *Critical Inquiry* 7(1) (1980): 5–27.

White, Hayden, 'Historical Employment and the Problem of Truth', in Saul Friedländer (ed.), *Probing the Limits of Representation: Nazism and the 'Final Solution'* (Cambridge, MA: Harvard University Press, 1992), pp. 37–53.

Williams, Raymond, *Keywords: A Vocabulary of Culture and Society* (Oxford: Oxford University Press, 2015).

Wittgenstein, Ludwig, *The Blue and Brown Books: Preliminary Studies for the 'Philosophical Investigations'* (Oxford: Blackwell, 1958).

Yildiz, Yasemin, *Beyond the Mother Tongue: The Postmonolingual Condition* (New York: Fordham University Press, 2012).

SENSORY FLUCTUATIONS: AURAL, ORAL, VISUAL AND WRITTEN

4

POEMS IN PRAISE OF THE PROPHET (*MADĪḤ*) AS A CITIZEN OF THE LITERARY WORLD

Walid Ghali

Across Muslim cultures, many Muslims celebrate the Prophet Muḥammad's birthday, on the twelfth day of the third month of the Hijrī calendar, Rabīʿ al-Awwal, in a ceremony known as *Mawlid*. The festival, a public holiday in some countries, is taken as a means to teach Muslims about Muḥammad's way of life, which they all seek to emulate. There are various expressions for this ceremony's observance, including sharing food, attending lectures, participating in parades, and reading and reciting the Qurʾān and devotional poetry. Reciting praise poetry, *al-madāʾiḥ al-nabawīyya*, remains an essential part of the ceremony and the popular culture of Muslims.

Panegyric poetry or (*madīḥ*) has its roots in pre-Islamic literature. It had a particular style and function connected to life in the Arabian Peninsula before the emergence of Islam. After the advent of Islam, the panegyric genre did not disappear and remained a tool used by poets and rulers. Poems in praise of the Prophet appeared during his lifetime, starting with works by Ḥassān ibn Thābit (d. 674) and the famous *Bānat Suʿād* by Kaʿb ibn Zuhayr (*c.* 670). The genre continued to develop, reaching a level of maturity in the thirteenth century with *Qaṣīdat al-Burda* by Sharaf al-Dīn Muḥammad ibn Saʿīd al-Buṣīrī (c. 1295).[1] Thereafter, *al-Burda* became

[1] The *Qaṣīdat al-Burda*, commonly known as the 'Poem of the Mantle', is al-Buṣīrī's most famous poem in praise of the Prophet, and is about 160 to 165 lines long. Its appellation '*al-Burda*', meaning a mantle of woollen cloth in Arabic, refers to another highly esteemed

pivotal in the developing stream of *madīḥ* poetry in different cultures and languages. This happened through numerous translations, imitations or *muʿāraḍāt* (pastiche) that allowed new poems to emerge. Several studies have focused on various religious and literary aspects of *madīḥ* in general and *al-Burda* in particular since its inception; only a few studies have dealt with it as a popular masterpiece but none have done so as a World Literature.

Goethe was one of the first scholars to speak about World Literature and poetry as a universal possession of humankind. His direct interaction with Arabic and Persian poetry is evident in his poem titled *Mahomets Gesang* (1774) and his collection titled *West-östlicher Divan* (1819).[2] Recently, there have been several studies problematising the theorisation and the euro-centrism of World Literature. For instance, Thomas Bauer and Angelika Neuwirth's work *Transformations of a Literary Genre* (2005), advocating the acceptance of *ghazal* as World Literature, and Hamid Dabashi's work on the Persian Epic, *Shahnameh*, are examples of this recent approach. As far as praise poetry is concerned, the work of Oludamini Ogunnaike (2020) on *madīḥ* poetry in West Africa is an essential reference.[3] These studies and how they introduce a critical approach towards World Literature as defined by Western academia are an open invitation to further studies on non-Western traditions of World Literature. This chapter takes the same line of argument that *madīḥ nabawī* represents a concrete example of World

poem in praise of Muḥammad, which is known after its opening words as '*Bānat Suʿād*' and was composed by Kaʿb b. Zuhayr. After the recitation, Kaʿb received, as a reward for his poem, the Prophet's mantle. When al-Buṣīrī, some 650 years later, suffered a stroke and remained semi-paralysed, the Prophet appeared to him in dream guise, touched him with his hand and threw his mantle over his shoulders. Al-Buṣīrī was instantly cured and set about composing his poem titled in reference to this miraculous healing. (*Qasida Burda*, p. 8).The actual title of *al-Burda* is *al-Kawākib al-Durrīya fi Madḥ Khayr al-Barīya*, which, in Jan Knappert's translation reads 'The Scintillating Stars in Praise of the Best of Mankind'.

[2] This collection has been recently republished in the original German with an outstanding introduction and translation by Eric Ormsby in *West-Eastern Divan: Complete, Annotated New Translation, Including Goethe's 'Notes And Essays' & The Unpublished Poems* (London: Gingko Library, 2019).

[3] Oludamini Ogunnaike, *Poetry in Praise of Prophetic Perfection: A Study of West African Arabic Madīḥ Poetry and Its Precedents* (Cambridge: Islamic Texts Society, 2020).

Literature. Thus, the study will demonstrate the development of *madīḥ* as a literary genre and its significance in Muslim cultures with a focus on *al-Burda* of al-Būṣīrī as a potential citizen of World Literature.

Setting the Scene

Panegyric or *madīḥ* was and still is a widespread genre in Arabic literature. It goes back to the pre-Islamic period when it was connected to other poetic genres such as *fakhr* (boasting), *rithā*ʾ (elegy or lament) and *hijā*ʾ (lampooning, satire). It also appears from written records that the *madīḥ* genre was a pervasive feature in other non-Arab Muslim cultures.[4] However, the term was used to designate a diversity of manifestations, and it is nearly impossible to find an exact definition that encompasses all its different meanings. Nevertheless, *madīḥ* can be defined as the poems or a section in a poem devoted to praising God, the Prophet, the sultan or any well-known figure.

On the other hand, the term *al-madāʾiḥ al-nabawīyya* is often used to refer to the lyrics of poems sung in praise of the Prophet Muḥammad and his family. It is still hard to pinpoint when these lyrics or poems of praise started to appear widely. For instance, the first chapter in Ibn Ḥajar al-ʿAsqalānī's (1372–1449) *Dīwān* is dedicated to *nabawiyyāt*, which consist of seven poems in praise of the Prophet.[5] This might be interpreted as showing that this genre enjoyed great popularity after the thirteenth century, as this chapter will argue, and as Bauer also claims: 'By the time of Ibn Ḥajar [*madīḥ nabawī* was] considered [a] more or less indispensable part of all poetry.'[6]

Schimmel, however, argues that the genre of *madīḥ* emerged in the early eleventh century. She cites expressions like those collected by al-Thaʿālibī (d. 1038), in his most celebrated work *Yatīmat al-Dahr fī Maḥāsin Ahl al-ʿAṣr*,

[4] G. M. Wickens, J. W. Clinton, J. Stewart Robinson, J. A. Haywood and J. Knappert, 'Madīḥ, Madḥ', in P. Bearman et al. (eds), *Encyclopaedia of Islam*, 2nd edn, Brill online, last accessed 27 November 2020.

[5] Ibn Ḥajar al-ʿAsqalānī, Aḥmad ibn ʿAlī and Syed Abul Fazl, *Dīwān Ibn Hajar al-ʿAsqalānī* (Ḥaydarābād al-Dakkan: Jāmiʿat al-ʿUthmānīyah, 1962).

[6] Thomas Bauer, 'Ibn Ḥajar and the Arabic Ghazal of the Mamluk Age', in Thomas Bauer and Angelika Neuwirth (eds), *Ghazal As World Literature: Transformations of a Literary Genre* (Beirut: Orient-Institut, 2005), vol. 2, p. 37.

and it was Sanā'ī (d. 1131) who was the first advocate of the genre in Persia.[7] Nevertheless, it is evidenced that the first praise poem was written during the Prophet's life. Moreover, poets were part of the Prophet's entourage, and their verses likewise contained some source material for the first period of Islam. According to Schimmel, 'Hassān ibn Thābit [d. 674] served [the Prophet] as a poet in Medina. His duty was in a certain sense that of a journalist to note down poetically the important events that happened in the young Islamic community.'[8] In addition to Hassān, there were Ka'b ibn Zuhayr, who wrote the famous poem *Bānat Su'ād*, Ka'b ibn Mālik (d. *c.* 670), and 'Abd Allāh ibn Rawāḥa (d. 629). The latter is barely mentioned in the later non-Arabic tradition.

In the Iranian court, the most highly-developed vehicle for *madīḥ* was the panegyric ode, or *qaṣīda-yi madīḥ*, a genre that was already fully articulated by the time of Rūdakī (d. 941). Among the Muslim Turks, especially the Ottoman Turks in the nineteenth century, the collective abstract form, *madīḥ*, used in precisely the same sense, was preferred. The same term designates any poem composed to extoll an individual.[9] *Na'at* is the name for *madīḥ* in Urdu, although the term is derived from Persian, like other poetic genres. In Swahili, the word *qaṣīda* (ode) typically refers to a poem praising the Prophet. The two well-known Arabic *qaṣīdas*, both of which have been translated into Swahili are the *Burda* and *Hamzīyya*, by al-Būṣīrī, which are still recited during Swahili ceremonies.[10]

Suzanne Stetkevych argues that 'the term *madīḥ nabawī* as a term [that] came in retrospect. Although it started in the Prophet's lifetime, the genre itself did not crystalise until the post-classical period.' She also opines that

[7] Schimmel argues that it was with Sanā'ī of Ghazna in eastern Afghanistan, around 1100, that the tradition of praise poetry began. Sanā'ī renounced his former activities as a court panegyrist and shifted his interest to religious, more specifically, ascetic poetry to become the founder of the ascetic mystical *mathnawī* tradition in Persian. But at the same time he appears as the first and greatest panegyrist of the Prophet. Annemarie Schimmel, *And Muhammad is His Messenger: The Veneration of the Prophet in Islamic Piety* (Chapel Hill: University of North Carolina Press, 1985), p. 181.

[8] Schimmel, *And Muhammad is His Messenger*, p. 179.

[9] Wickens et al., *Madīḥ*, p. 2.

[10] Ogunnaike, *Poetry in Praise of Prophetic Perfection*, p. 90.

the development of the poetic genre, *madīḥ nabawī*, deserves further study, with its rich history of development from the first until the thirteenth century, when al-Būṣīrī's *al-Burda* become a genre-defining paradigm for *madīḥ nabawī*, which clearly confirms the extent of influence of *al-Burda* on the genre of *madīḥ*.[11] The Mamluk period (1250–1517) was seemingly a turning point in the *madīḥ* genre as evidenced in works by al-Būṣīrī, Ibn al-Fāriḍ, al-Ḥillī and Ibn Ḥajar al-ʿAsqalānī. Following this period, there emerged a rich corpus of commentaries,[12] translations and imitations of *Burda*-like works. Even with the early translations of *al-Burda* in the nineteenth century by Redhouse and others, as will be discussed, it was still not seen as World Literature.

Ironically, World Literature is a field that is still in the ascendant, and it might be challenging to provide a standard accepted definition. For instance, Goethe sees poetry as the universal possession of humankind, revealing itself everywhere and at all times in hundreds and hundreds of men.[13] This is also supported by Vinay Dharwadker, who described World Literature as 'a montage of overlapping maps in motion'.[14] David Damrosch provides a more flexible definition of World Literature as 'writing that gains in translation', writing that functions as an 'elliptical refraction of national literature' and 'a mode of reading: a form of engagement with worlds beyond our place and time'.[15] He opines three definitions of literary contributions: an established body of classics; an evolving canon of masterpieces; or multiple windows on the world.

One of his key concepts is that 'World Literature is not an infinite, ungraspable canon of works, but rather a mode of circulation and reading, a mode that is as applicable to individual works as to bodies of material, available for reading established classics and discoveries alike'.[16] This definition

[11] Suzanne Stetkevych, *The Mantle Odes: Arabic Praise Poems to the Prophet Muḥammad* (Bloomington: Indiana University Press, 2010), pp. 71–2.

[12] Charles Brockelmann, *Geschichte der Arabischen Litteratur* (Weimar, 1898), vol. 1, pp. 264–7.

[13] David Damrosch, *What is World Literature?* (Princeton, NJ: Princeton University Press, 2003), p. 5.

[14] Vinay Dharwadker (ed.), *Cosmopolitan Geographies: New Locations in Literature and Culture* (New York: Routledge, 2001), p. 3.

[15] Damrosch, *What is World Literature?*, p. 5.

[16] Damrosch, *What is World Literature?*, p. 5.

could be easily applied to *madīḥ* as a literary form and its richness of meaning and cultural values, as will be discussed. The World Literature in this chapter is defined as the work that can contribute to the intellectual and social lives of many communities and remain a tool for different kinds of expression (emotional and literary) that stand the test of time and space. It is believed that through *madā'iḥ nabawīyya* one could really understand the global and multilingual scope of the Islamicate literary body.

Contribution to Muslim Cultures

World Literature is as much about the host culture's values and needs as it is about a work's source culture. The receiving culture (non-Arabic-speaking Muslims and non-Muslims) can use the foreign material (*madīḥ* poetry in Arabic) in all sorts of ways: as a positive model for the future development of the receiving culture's own tradition; as a negative case of any primitive or decadent behaviour that must be avoided or rooted out at home; or, as an image of radical otherness against which the home tradition can be more clearly defined.[17]

The influence of devotional literature in the spread of Islam is unquestionable through the Sufis' role, who provided a bridge between the beliefs of non-Muslim and Muslim worship. Ronit Ricci argues that literary texts of various kinds magnified, enhanced and shaped this process by introducing those who converted to Islam to their newly acquired faith, its history, practices and genealogies. So, a sense of common ground with a particular vocabulary, idiom and belief system was enriched, and, moreover, they also inspired local creativity and provided a means to address local concerns and agendas.[18]

The love of the Prophet Muḥammad lies at the heart of this devotional literature, particularly *madīḥ*. Jan Knappart remarks that Swahili religious literature breathes with the spirit of great love and devotion to the Prophet.[19] Moreover, Ogunnaike argues that *madīḥ* poetry in West Africa shapes a kind of living history because it exists together in the books, ears, tongues and

[17] Damrosch, '*World Literature, National Contexts*', p. 514.

[18] Ronit Ricci, 'Islamic Literary Networks in South and Southeast Asia', *Journal of Islamic Studies* 21(1) (2010): 3.

[19] Schimmel, *And Muhammad is His Messenger*, p. 212.

hearts of the many poets and patrons of the tradition with adaptations and changes. So, the positive influence of *madīḥ* was beyond the process of introducing Islam. It also assisted in the process of assimilation to the model of the Prophet.[20]

The spirit of Islam transmitted by Sufis worked as a catalyst in making the new Muslim communities' identity. Kutty argues, 'this particular state, which is termed as Arabic *cosmopolis*, represents the concept of a global Muslim, who shares the same culture, same notion, and same spirit'.[21] For instance, *madīḥ* poetry has become part of the celebration of the Prophet's birthday, known as a *mawlid*, since the inception of this festival. The term *mawlid* (pl. *mawālid*) may semantically refer to the place of birth, the date of birth and the event of the birth of any individual. In modern times, however, it refers to the celebration of the Prophet's birthday. In West Africa, for example, the term *mawlid* means a *madīḥ* poem in honour of the Prophet.

Thus, singing *madīḥ* while marching in the streets has become a tradition that continues generation after generation. More specifically, singing *al-Burda* or other poems modelled on *al-Burda* is the common feature of these marches, performed both with or without music, and this tradition has become more robust in non-Arabic than in Arabic Muslim cultures. Schimmel confirms that in a region such as East Africa, the desire to preserve the communal rituals and devotional ceremonies – of which the *mawlid* is the most popular celebration – is often more widespread and practised than in the heartlands of Islam. Numerous popular tales and poems elevate the Prophet to an almost superhuman level, and these form the basis for much *mawlid* material.[22]

In addition to *madīḥ* contributing to the spread of Islam, it has also become integrated into the new cultures, and this also highlights how these cultures have become connected. For instance, when I was a child, I participated in the *mawlid* celebration in a remote village in the western desert

20 Ogunnaike, *Poetry in Praise of Prophetic Perfection*, pp. 73–4.

21 P. Moyin Kutty, 'The Role of Devotional Literature in the Enlightenment of Kerala Muslims', *Research Ambition* 1(II) (2016): 35.

22 Annemarie Schimmel, *Mystical Dimensions of Islam* (Chapel Hill: University of North Carolina Press, 1976), pp. 216–17.

of Egypt (Hindāw).[23] The festival always started with participants carrying green flags and marching in the narrow alleys of the village. The most memorable part was the musical recitation of *al-Burda* and other *madīḥ* poems to musical accompaniment. I could not have imagined that similar celebrations are taking place on the same day in other places, thousands of miles away from the village, such as in East Africa, and South and Southeast Asia, despite the different manifestations it displays.

Amongst these different manifestations, the part common to all is the chanting of al-Būṣīrī's *al-Burda* either in Arabic or the translation into local languages, such as Swahili. The celebrations' visibility proves the universality of *madīḥ nabawī* in Muslim cultures and their role in connecting them. One reason could be the spiritual gravity that *madīḥ* poetry offers to Muslims because it focuses on love for the Prophet. Karić argues that '[d]evotional poetry is often composed for purposes of supplication, intercession, admiration, pleas for forgiveness, or even personal encounters with God, and, in a more pragmatic sense, it is used as an accompaniment to religious rituals or performances'.[24]

Muslims also believe that there are psychological, spiritual and medicinal properties attached to *madīḥ* poetry, especially to *al-Burda*. Perhaps this is connected to the story of composing *al-Burda* itself, on the one hand, and the Prophet's central position as an intercessor, on the other. To this end, Schimmel argues that *al-Burda* comprises all these notions that Muslims loved and accepted, and has therefore contributed substantially to the formation of the Prophet's ideal picture in Arabic and subsequently in the translated poetry.[25]

Thus, the quality of *madīḥ* is not judged by its distinctiveness or innovation, but by its ability to deploy the common elements of the Muslim tradition to effectively convey and cultivate particular psycho-spiritual aesthetic states.[26] Schimmel argues that *madīḥ* goes much further than simply

[23] A village on al-Dākhla Oasis (the New Valley Governorate) approximately 850 km south of Cairo. Dākhla Oasis is one of the five oasis in the Western Desert of Egypt; it has strong tradition/folklore that is linked to other cultures such as North Africa.

[24] Dženita Karić, 'Devotional Poetry', in *The Oxford Encyclopaedia of Islam and Women*, Oxford Islamic Studies Online, available at: http://www.oxfordislamicstudies.com.iij.idm.oclc.org/article/opr/t355/e0239, last accessed 27 December 2020.

[25] Schimmel, *And Muhammad is His Messenger*, p. 187.

[26] Ougannaiki, *In Praise of Prophetic Perfection*, p. 75.

expressing veneration for the Prophet. It, however, excels by its 'character-building power' and stimulates a 'longing for the perfect man'.[27]

The concept of Perfect Man, or *al-insān al-Kāmil*, was first featured in the writing of the great scholar and Sufi Muḥyīddīn ibn ʿArabī (d. 1240) and his disciple Ṣadr al-Dīn Qunawī (d. 1274). In his *al-ʿUmda fī Sharḥ al-Burda* (The Mainstay: a Commentary on Qaṣīdat al-Burda), Moroccan Ṣūfī Ibn ʿAjība (d. 1809) connects the meanings of the references in *al-Burda* to events in the Prophet's biography 'Al-Būṣīrī narrates incidents of the Prophet protecting others in time of need, giving relief to the desperate and how he hopes for his presence and protecting care.'[28]

It is worth concluding by confirming that *al-Burda* is a poetic portrait of the Prophet produced when Cairo stood to the post-classical Islamic world as Paris to Europe.[29] It played a role in enhancing people's intellectual and creative lives and included historically, geographically and culturally diverse audiences into a coherent Islamicate literary body. This integration gives the audience access to cultures and stories from corners of the world that are unknown and beyond the reader's time or place.[30]

Between *al-Burda* and *Nahj al-Burda*

Literature produced within local Muslim communities and the literary networks that extended across and beyond the local – mainly when studied comparatively – provide new insights into Islam's history in these regions.[31] As discussed in the previous section, *madīḥ* played a significant role in connecting different Muslim cultures. This section, however, focuses on the impact of *madīḥ* on literary traditions either through the emergence of new literary subgenres and the countless imitations and translations of *madīḥ*, with a focus on al-Būṣīrī's *al-Burda*.

[27] Schimmel, *And Muhammad is His Messenger*, p. 178.

[28] Yunus Khamissa, *The Meaning of Qaṣīda Burda of Imām Buṣīrī*, available online, p. 10.

[29] Muhsin al-Musawi, *The Medieval Islamic Republic of Letters: The Arabic Knowledge Construction*. (Notre Dame, IN: University of Notre Dame Press, 2015), p. 5.

[30] Kevin Brooks, 'Dave Eggers's "What Is the What" as World Literature', *World Literature Today* 84(2) (2010): 36–40, available at: http://www.jstor.org/stable/27871023, last accessed 19 December 2020.

[31] Ricci, 'Islamic Literary Networks in South and Southeast Asia', p. 439.

In his study on *madīḥ* in the Mamluk period, ʿIzzat Ibrāhīmī argues that *madīḥ* had a direct impact on people's lives and poetry. Speaking of the latter, he explains that the significant effect is that '[*madīḥ*] has become an established literary genre' and had an impact on the creativity of poets, and in the emergence of new subgenres such as the rhetorical *madīḥ*.[32]

The emergence of new interconnected subgenres of *madīḥ nabawī* strengthens the impact of *madīḥ*. Two forms have become the subject of many studies, the *badīʿiyyāt*, the rhetorical poems, and *muʿāraḍāt* (poems following/imitating themes and forms of earlier poems). The purpose of the *badīʿiyyāt* was to praise the Prophet Muḥammad, but at the same time, they incorporated rhetorical embellishments, with each line typically illustrating a different rhetorical device. It is believed that *badīʿiyyāt* was first developed by Ṣafī al-Dīn al-Ḥillī (d. 1349). While some believe that the *badīʿiyyāt* is a mere educational device used in teaching Arabic rhetoric, others elevate them to the genre of pure *madīḥ nabawī*. Regardless, it is worth noting that the proportion of *badīʿīyyāt* in Arabic literature is immense. Also, the story of al-Ḥillī's work *al-Kāfiya al-Badīʿiyya fī al-Madāʾiḥ al-Nabawīyya* is almost identical to the story of al-Būṣīrī's *al-Burda*. It is noteworthy that scholars such as al-Suyūṭī (d. 1505) and ʿĀʾisha al-Bāʿūniyya (d. 1516) also contributed to this new form. Musa argues that similar poems continued to be produced in the modern era.[33]

The second subgenre is *muʿāraḍāt*, where poets imitate the rhyme and meter of a *madīḥ* poem. Suzanne Stetkevych argues that the *al-Burda* was used in the nineteenth century's broader literary and cultural reform movement. For example, in Shawqī's *Nahj al-Burda* (*The Path of the Mantle*, 1903), he uses the pastiches as a tool to support his approach towards reform, as reform suggests a return to the past. She adds, 'We must not forget that this literary movement was part of the broader movement of *Nahdah* (renaissance), re-birth

[32] ʿIzzat Mulla Ibrāhīmī, 'Tadāʿiyyāt al-Madāʾih al-Nabawiyya ʿala al-Biʾah fī al-ʿAsr al-Mamlūkī', *Majallat Kullīyyat al-Tarbiya al-Asāsīyya lil-ʿulūm al-Tarbawīyya wa-al-Insānīyya* (Jāmiʿat Bābil), No. 34 (2017): 37.

[33] Mashārī Musa, '*Badiʿiyyāt* in Praise of the Prophet: Gift Exchange Theory', *Journal of King Abdulaziz University Arts and Humanities* 28 (2020): 236–55.

and reform of Arab and more generally Islamic culture under the influence of European liberal thought and scientific progress.'[34]

Aḥmad Shawqī (d. 1932) provided more works on *mawlid* poetry using al-Būṣīrī's *al-Burda* and *Hamziyya* as vehicles in his literary reform movement, which shows the strong tradition of *madīḥ* that found its way into the early twentieth century. Before Shawqī, Maḥmūd Sāmī al-Bārūdī (d. 1904), who was recognised as a figure of most significant importance in the development of modern Arabic literature, produced a *mu'āraḍa* of the *al-Burda*, but it is less famous than the one by Shawqī, due to the length of the poem and the subject it covers, as well as its tendency towards *fakhr* (self-exaltation), not *madīḥ*.

I encountered another example, yet less famous, from Egypt. A poem called, *Manẓūmat Ahl al-Bayt wa-al-Ṣaliḥīn* (Poem of the Prophet's Family and the Virtuous) by 'Abd al-Maqṣūd Sālim (d. 1977).[35] The poem is in praise of the Prophet, his family, companions and scholars. In my conversation with one of the *munshids* (performers) of this poem, he confirmed that it is part of *al-Burda*. This is possibly because the rhyme is similar to *al-Burda*'s meter, and the oral transmission confused ordinary people.

Another phenomenon that is strongly visible in *madīḥ* and particularly with *al-Burda* is the insertion of blessings and praises of the Prophet (*ṣalawāt*), and often the interpolation of additional poetic lines matching the original. These insertions or expansions took many forms (*tashṭīr*, *takhmīs*, especially, and *tasbī'*).[36] One example that shows the impact of this phenomenon is that the renowned Egyptian reciter 'Abd al-'Azīm al-'Aṭwānī, recorded the entire *al-Burda* using the expanded *tashṭīr* on a series of cassettes, as a vocal solo with a chorus.[37]

[34] Suzanne Stetkevych, *The Mantle Odes: Arabic Praise Poems to the Prophet Muḥammad*. Bloomington: Indiana University Press. 2010), p. 154.

[35] 'Abd al-Maqṣūd Muḥammad Sālim (1899–1977): he was the leader of a Sufi group in Egypt and provided many lyrics used in Sufi *dhikr*. His works were criticised because of the repetitive formula that makes it a mere copy of famous poems such as *al-Burda*.

[36] *Takhmīs*, *tathlīth* and *tashṭīr* indicate the addition of five, three or one and two hemistichs, respectively; see Azartash Azarnoush, 'Burda', *Encyclopaedia Islamica*, Brill online, vol. 5, p. 169.

[37] Micheal Frishkopf, 'Inshād Dīnī and Aghānī Dīnīyya in Twentieth-Century Egypt: A Review of Styles, Genres, and Available Recordings', *Middle East Studies Association Bulletin* 34 (2000): 167–83.

Another literary strength of *madīḥ* is the textual relations that can help one better understand this poetry. Michael Frishkopf argues that '[a]t the same time, the best Sufi authors draw near to each other even merging, textually and authorially, due both to their joint proximity to a common origin and their influence on each other, via the spiritual–social network linking them together'.[38] If this phenomenon is widespread in Arabic literature, it is more visible in *madīḥ*, because of the main subject (Prophet Muḥammad) that make themes, motifs and stylistic features of this poetry almost identical. The Moroccan poet, Abdellatif La'abī, argues that poetry is a 'laboratory of literature. Language moves there, it transforms itself, and as a result, it has an impact on other literary genres.'[39]

In summary, it has been shown in this section that *madīḥ nabawī* has a direct impact on the development of the panegyric genre and other literary phenomena such as *badī'iyyāt*. This confirms the universality of the genre from the literary perspective. Another significant aspect of World Literature is the cultural and literary transformation of the work(s) to become recognised globally. Therefore, the following section will shed light on the channels through which *madīḥ nabawī* achieved its cultural and literary transformation.

The Classics and Circulation of *madīḥ*

Some *madīḥ* works have received much attention in Muslim scholarship and have become classics. *Al-Burda* of Ka'b ibn Zuhayr, and the two famous poems by al-Būṣīrī (the *Hamziyya* and *al-Burda*), and Ibn al-Fāriḍ's *Khamriyya* are the prominent examples, although one must also mention the hundreds of poems produced in the subgenre of *badī'iyyāt*, as will be discussed later. North Africa was incredibly fertile in producing poetic eulogies and prayers for the Prophet. Some of them have become classics in their own right, among them the blessing formulas composed by Ibn Mashīsh (d. 1227/8) and, somewhat later, al-Jazūlī's (d. 1465) *Dalā'il al-Khayrāt.*

[38] Micheal Frishkopf, 'Authorship in Sufi Poetry', *Alif: Journal of Comparative Poetics* 23 (2003): 98.

[39] Interview with Christopher Schaefer, *The Quarterly Conversation* 32 (June 2013), available at: http://laabi.net/index.php/en/2018/06/30/with-christopher-schaefer-interview, last accessed 22 December 2020.

According to Damrosch, the global circulation of literature beyond its original environment is vital for its consideration as World Literature.[40] *Madīḥ* poetry was circulated through many channels to reach readers across the world. These channels vary from one culture to another, but translation is still the popular channel for any literature's circulation amongst all cultures. Zhang Longxi argues that there is nothing wrong with using translation in World Literature study because no one can read all works in the original.[41] Even though translation is vital in literary studies, the limitation of Longxi's principle is that it does not explain how the translated works can be judged. As for *madīḥ*, it is essential to examine it in its original language, culture and the time when it was developed. For instance, *al-Burda* has been translated into most of the languages spoken by Muslims, including local dialects in Africa, Southeast Asia and the Balkans.[42] Moreover, in certain parts of the Islamic world, some of the translations have become much more famous than *al-Burda* itself, such as the Persian translation by ʿAbd al-Raḥmān Jāmī (d. 1492) and an anonymous Malaysian translation. Also, the interpretations of the poem by ʿĀʾisha bint Yūsuf al-Bāʿūniyya from Damascus (d. 1517) gained significant popularity.[43]

In non-Arabic-speaking countries, people liked to copy, and later print copies of *al-Burda* in Arabic alongside one or two translations. Also, interlinear

[40] David Damrosch (ed.), *World Literature in Theory* (Chichester: Wiley-Blackwell, 2014), p. 180.

[41] Zhang Longxi, 'World Literature, Canon, and Literary Criticism', in Weigui Fang (ed.), *Tensions in World Literature: Between the Local and the Universal* (Singapore: Palgrave Macmillan, 2018), p. 181.

[42] Mubārak, *Al-Madāʾiḥ al-Nabawīyya*, pp. 148–50; Ḥajji Khalīfa, *Kashf al- Ẓunūn*, 2:1331–6, and n. 1, p. 1331; Jan Knappert, *Swahili Islamic Poetry* (Leiden: Brill, 1971), p. 168; al-Būṣīrī, *Dīwān al-Būṣīrī*, ed. Muḥammad Sayyid Kilānī, 2nd edn (Cairo: Muṣṭafa al-Bābī al-Ḥalabī, 1972), pp. 29–30; ʿAbd al-ʿAlīm al-Qabbāni, *Al-Būṣīrī: Hayātuh wa-Shiʿruh* (Cairo: Dār al-Maʿārif, 1968), pp. 3–5, 131–2. For a broad overview in English, see Schimmel, *And Muhammad is His Messenger*, ch. 10, 'Poetry in Honor of the Prophet', pp. 176–215, esp. pp. 178–87. See also Stefan Sperl, *Mannerism in Arabic Poetry: A Structural Analysis of Selected Texts (3rd Century AH/9th Century AD–5th Century AH/11th Century AD)* (Cambridge: Cambridge University Press, 2004); and S. Sperl, C. Shackle and N. Awde, *Qasida Poetry in Islamic Asia and Africa* (Leiden: Brill, 1996), vol. 1: Index, al-Buṣīrī.

[43] Karić, 'Devotional Poetry'.

versions of *al-Burda* are widely available in Lahore, Delhi and elsewhere.[44] It may be that al-Būṣīrī's *al-Burda*, which was translated into Dakni Urdu by Muḥammad b. Riḍā, around the turn of the eighteenth century, was often mentioned by poets and critics to justify the inclusion of an explicitly erotic prelude in *na't* odes.[45]

European scholars also became interested in the poem at a very early stage in publishing Arabic literary texts in the West. Following a Latin translation in 1761, many translations into different languages appeared, for example, Rosenzweig-Schwannau's poetic rendering in 1824, C. A. Ralfs edited the work (Vienna, 1860), along with a Turkish and Persian poetic version, translated into German prose. The French orientalist Silvestre de Sacy translated *al-Burda* for Garcin de Tassy's *Exposition de la Foi Musulmane* (1822). Still frequently cited is the French scholar René Basset (Paris, 1849), who despite his aversion to mystical poetry, gives a useful commentary that explains many of the allusions with which *al-Burda* is replete.[46]

The British scholar J. W. Redhouse published his version in a privately printed book titled *Arabian Poetry for English Readers*, edited by W. A. Clouston (Glasgow, 1881). Versions by Faizlullah-Bhai (Bombay, 1893), and by Arthur Jefferey (1962) followed. According to Schimmel, Arthur Jefferey's is 'the handiest and reliable modern translation for [the English- speaking world]'.[47] Sheikh Abdal Hakim's translation renders the poem in beautiful and moving English in a parallel text alongside the original Arabic.[48] Each verse is followed by lines from other poets – classical and modern, and from many parts of the world – echoing and amplifying its theme, encouraging the reader to reflect on its meanings more fully. It is worth mentioning that many other less popular versions are translated either by believers or by contemporary Sufis.

In sum, the classical form of the laudatory ode has remained alive in Arabic and other languages used in Muslim cultures. The main structure of the Arabic *qaṣīda* was preserved in Muslim lands as poets continued to write in the same

44 Schimmel, *And Muhammad is His Messenger*, p. 183.

45 Wickens, *Madīḥ*, p. 9.

46 Schimmel, *And Muhammad is His Messenger*, p. 185.

47 Schimmel, *And Muhammad is His Messenger*, p. 185.

48 Al-Būṣīrī, *The Mantle Adorned: Imam al-Busiri's Burda*, trans. Abdal Hakim Murad (London: Quilliam Press, 2009).

style as the pre-modern poets, for Arabic was the commonly used language of theology.[49] *Al-Burda* is a significant example of the continuation of *madīḥ* poetry. It has become the model, which is in itself based on an early Islamic poetry poem (*al-Burda* of Kaʿb); the latter is based on pre-Islamic praise poetry. It is 'by far, the most studied, imitated, quoted, memorised, recited and quatrained or quintained sources of West African *Madīḥ* tradition'[50] and is considered 'very probably the most influential and the most popular single poem in the history of any language'.[51]

Muslims have treasured *al-Burda* because of its beauty, its lessons on spirituality, morality and history, and its literary refinement. As a result of this cultural and religious prestige, it gained a degree of protection from change brought about by design or by the keen transmission. It became the subject of a hundred commentaries and many translations, with lines of *al-Burda* adorning tombs, palaces and religious buildings, making it arguably the second most-used Arabic calligraphy text in Islamic architecture after the Qurʾān.

Why did World Literature Ignore *madīḥ*?

With all the cultural, religious, spiritual and literary fame of *madīḥ* exemplified in one great classics poem, there is no sound explanation as to why World Literature has ignored it. It may be useful to provide some hypotheses about why this has been the case, and the next section attempts to analyse this issue by discussing two factors: the first is related to *madīḥ* criticism, and the second is related to the field of World Literature.

It is worth noting that *madīḥ* was criticised in the earliest manuals of poetry criticism. For example, Qudāma ibn Jaʿfar (d. 948) provided very narrow criteria for acceptable *madīḥ* based on its purpose, which he restricted it to the intellect, bravery, justice and dignity.[52] In the early twentieth century, Shiblī Nuʿmānī tried to lay down conditions for acceptable panegyrics, such as that the person praised must be praiseworthy, the qualities commended in

[49] Al-Būṣīrī, *The Mantle Adorned*, p. 189.

[50] Ogunnaike, *Poetry in Praise of Prophetic Perfection*, p. 90.

[51] The Celestial Lights in Praise of the Best of Creation, available at: https://www.wdl.org/en/item/11229, last accessed 6 September 2020.

[52] Qudāma Ibn Jaʿfar, *Naqd al-Shiʿr*, ed. Muḥammad ʿĪsa Mannūn (Cairo, 1934), p. 39.

him must be genuine and, finally, the poet must describe them convincingly. Although he admitted that no Persian poet ever fulfilled all these three conditions, it is fair to say that scholars have endeavoured to provide some critical criteria for an acceptable panegyric.[53]

Ogunnaike explains that the prejudices against devotional poetry have led some Islamic literature scholars to neglect and mischaracterise it as mere 'pious flattery' that lacks significant literary quality or intellectual content. The marginalisation of *madīḥ* poetry in literary studies in Europe would seem to be connected to these preconceptions. However, the content and intentions of *madīḥ nabawī* is commended for being profoundly philosophical and sincerely devotional, also because of its contents that are much more than empty mannerism. The closest parallel is the Christian hymns extolling Jesus[54] and the worshippers' love for him.[55] *Madīḥ nabawī* also enjoys popular reception amongst all Muslims, making it a world literature phenomenon despite the dismissive approach in scholarship. There is a gap between the popularity of devotional poetry, including *madīḥ nabawī*, and the scholarship resulting from European literature's tendency to separate the devotional and the literary; the sincere and the ritually formal.[56]

The high volume of panegyric in Arabic poetry is another reason that affected the full appreciation of this genre by the average Western reader. Perhaps the high proportion is linked to the lack of sincerity as a criterion for good poetry. Wicken's counterargument is that virtually all pre-modern Arabic poetry was composed for a patron for socio-economic reasons.[57] However,

[53] Shiblī Nuʿmānī and Muḥammad Taqī Fakhr Dāʿī Gīlānī, *Shiʿr al-ʿAjam* (Tehrān: Dunyā-yi Kitāb, 1984), vol. 21, p. 6.

[54] The metaphors in these hymns centre on Jesus as Light of the World, Sun of Righteousness, Dayspring, Morning Star. In a song written by Robin Mark (Northern Irish Christian singer, songwriter, worship leader), he says 'Behold He comes, riding on the clouds Shining like the sun at the trumpet's call' ('Day of Elijah', Robin Mark (© 1996 Song Solutions Daybreak). The Prophet Muḥammad in *al-Burda* is also described as the sun of virtue (verse 25): 'For verily, he is the sun of virtue, and they (all other prophets) are its stars which show the people their lights in the dark.'

[55] Ogunnaike, *Poetry in Praise of Prophetic Perfection*, pp. 2–4.

[56] Ogunnaike, *Poetry in Praise of Prophetic Perfection*, p. 117.

[57] Wickens, *Madīḥ*, p. 1.

to my mind, there is another crucial fact about religious poetry that makes the issue of sincerity/intentions less convincing; devotional poetry is rarely commissioned. *Madīḥ nabawī*, in particular, is dedicated to the Prophet Muḥammad as the primary benefactor. The poet expects no rewards except in a few instances, such as Kaʿb ibn Zuhayr asking for the Prophet's forgiveness.

Related to the sincerity point, Schimmel argues that religious poetry was artificial to a great extent and that this almost suffocates the real concerns of the poets. The reason is that those poets competed with each other, so their style was often overburdened with rhetorical devices and puns.[58] While this criticism rings true, especially regarding the poetry of the thirteenth century, one should not ignore that those poets were seeking perfection and applying the best of their intellect in the form of praise or descriptions of the Prophet. It suffices to say that some studies undermine the cultural and religious factors of *madīḥ* poetry.

Frishkopf noted that, for a Sufi poet or performer, 'originality' lies in his/her connection to the Divine origin, not in the individual, idiosyncratic innovation or distinction that constitutes originality for the modern author. This is the reason for the highly repetitive formulaic and intertextual nature of Sufi poetry. Not understanding these crucial points has led many modern literary scholars to dismiss Sufi poetry written after the thirteenth century as decadent or lacking originality or inspiration. They judge it by modern standards exogenous to the tradition itself.[59]

Comparing the fame that *ghazal* as a literary form has received in Western scholarship to the neglect of the *madīḥ* genre raises many questions. Bauer and Neuwirth argue that the power of the *ghazal* itself inspired them to turn to this universal genre and discuss its complex aesthetic manifestations, the eloquence of its refined language and musicality that radiate forms from within its poetic form.[60] One can argue that *ghazal*, *fakhr* and *madīḥ* are already connected, and there is no apparent reason why it has been excluded from or overlooked in these studies. *Ghazal* is all about love, which is a universal language, and so is *madīḥ nabawī*, which is an expression of unquestioned love to the Prophet

[58] Schimmel, *And Muhammad is His Messenger*, p. 187.

[59] Frishkropf, *Authorship in Sufi Poetry*, p. 93.

[60] Bauer and Neuwirth, *Ghazal as World Literature.*

Muḥammad. Also, *madīḥ* and *fakhr* go hand in hand; ʿAmr ibn Kulthūm (d. 584) praised his tribe and their qualities in his famous *fakhr* ode.[61]

Despite its impact on the literary and religious spheres, the famed *al-Burda* enjoys no particular protection from criticism and objections. *Al-Burda* lies at the cross-point of three controversial elements in Muslim cultures: poetry, Sufism and *mawlid* celebrations, but these are not the concern of the current study, and it suffices to say that detractors of *al-Burda* base their opposition to it on the criticism of poets in the Qurʾān (Q. 26:224–227).[62] Nevertheless, this criticism based on misunderstanding has not prevented Muslims promoting poetry as an artistic tool for expressing and conveying the religious message. In the centuries following the Prophet's death and the subsequent rise of Islamic empires, poetry witnessed significant developments in terms of themes and topics, which gave rise to poetry written in praise of God (*ḥamd*), of the Prophet Muḥammad for his intercession (*madīḥ*), and critical religious personages (*manāqib*).[63]

Notwithstanding all the debates and argumentation, *al-Burda* remains the most recited devotional poem in the Muslim world and still attracts scholars globally to study its literary, folkloric and anthropological manifestations, even though the poem itself is not featured in discussions around World Literature. This is also the case with other literary traditions from the non-Western world. World Literature has been criticised for its bias and non-inclusiveness. The following section will shed light on this problem before demonstrating the suitability of *madīḥ* to be considered a part of World Literature.

The second reason for the undeserved negligence of *madīḥ* in World Literature is related to the field of World Literature itself. A very Eurocentric

[61] Muʿallaqat ʿAmr ibn Kulthūm.

[62] Ghāzī al-Quṣaybī provided significant evidence from the Qurʾān, *ḥadīth* and *sīra* that Islam is not against poetry, and that the Prophet Muḥammad enjoyed listening to poets like Ḥassān ibn Thābit and ʿAbd Allah ibn Rawāḥah. He also analyses different Qurʾān commentaries where most of them agree that poetry is not prohibited and the three verses were mainly about pre-Islamic poets. (Quṣaybī, *Man hum al-shuʿarāʾ alladhīna yattabaʿuhum al-ghāwūn?*, p. 27). See also Michael Zwettler, 'Mantic Manifesto: The Sura of "The Poets" and the Qur'anic Foundations of Prophetic Authority', in James L. Kugel (ed.), *Poetry and Prophecy: The Beginnings of a Literary Tradition* (Ithaca, NY: Cornell University Press, 1990), pp. 75–119.

[63] Karić, *Devotional Poetry.*

approach forms the essential background for interest in the non-Western world in the revival of Goethe's concept of World Literature. Goethe theorised about which serious works should be considered World Literature. He expressed hopes that the coming era would be based on an international exchange which would lead to mutual refinement.[64] In addition to the Eurocentric foundations of the field, Moretti considers World Literature to be an unequal system because the current practice contradicts the unified system of *Weltliteratur* that Goethe wished for.[65] Damrosch comments on that by inviting scholarship to 'open the field of World Literature to an unprecedented, even vertiginous variety of authors and countries'.[66]

Judith Pfeiffer connects Persian poetry's negligence, for example, that of Ḥāfiẓ, by Western scholarship to the reductionist movement in the twentieth century. She refers to 'the latent cultural chauvinism that favours Greek, Latin, and Christian sources as sources of western literary genius and inspiration over oriental ones'.[67] This can easily be applied to *madīḥ* in general and to the epic *al-Burda* in particular; and it is likely linked to the assumption that the non-Western world cannot produce any independent form of abstract thought.[68]

Edward W. Said's contribution to World Literature as a discipline also had an enormous impact, as it both reformed comparative literature and initiated post-colonial studies. He introduced the terms worldly and worldliness, which mean writing or knowing in a specific way linked to humanism. It is all-inclusive and thereby not meant to identify specific categories, such as ethnic or religious groups. This is very similar to Goethe's notion of World Literature and humankind.[69]

[64] John Pizer, 'Goethe's "World Literature" Paradigm and Contemporary Cultural Globalization', *Comparative Literature* 52(3) (2000): 213–27.

[65] Franco Moretti, 'Conjectures on World Literature', *New Left Review* 1(4) (2014): 56.

[66] Damrosch, *What is World Literature?*, p. 1.

[67] Judth Pfeiffer, 'Goethe and Saʿdī: Christian Wurm's Interpretation of Selige Sehnsucht Revisited', in Thomas Bauer and Angelika Neuwirth (eds), *Ghazal As World Literature: Transformations of a Literary Genre* (Beirut: Orient-Institut, 2005), p. 281.

[68] Krishnaswamy, 'Toward World Literary Knowledges', p. 141.

[69] Edward W. Said, 'Travelling Theory', in David Damrosch (ed.), *World Literature in Theory* (Chichester: Wiley-Blackwell, 2014), p. 115.

In proposing the category of 'world literary knowledge' as a new component to global literary studies, Revathi Krishnaswamy explains that the purpose of this category is to open up the canon of literary theory and criticism to alternative ways of conceptualising and analysing literary production. This means that regional, subaltern and popular traditions, whether latent or emergent, may be studied, analysed and evaluated as epistemologies of literature and literariness alongside the traditions of poetics that currently constitute both the canon (Euro-American) and the counter-canon (Arabic, Sanskrit, Chinese, Japanese) of literary theory.[70]

Ostensibly, there has been a paradigm shift in the field of World Literature to make it more inclusive. 'We now must take the "world" in "World Literature" seriously.'[71] As a result, the study of World Literature in recent years covers a large and multi-regional area and considers literary works from different continents. It may be argued that the criticism of World Literature and the 'reform' movement has paved the way for studies and literary classics to claim their rights to be included in World Literature.

For instance, in his work to position the Persian epic, the *Shahnameh*, in World Literature, Hamid Dabashi first challenges the principles of World Literature by questioning whether the word 'world' implies 'from the Eurocentric point of view, or perhaps according to the imagination of European cartographers, philosophers, conquerors, and enlightened thinkers and their North American descendants'. He also criticises the theorisation of the claim that 'what Goethe and his followers have theorised is not World Literature, it was their world'. He then criticises how a literary work from 'the real world' must first ask permission from 'a fictive white European literary critic'. Before imagining works like the *Shahnameh*, Dabashi invites scholarship to reassess the theories of World Literature and 'the world in the World Literature, as we use it today, is a fictional (Western) world'.[72]

Moreover, Revathi Krishnaswamy proposes the decolonisation of the literary theory itself, through new attention to local knowledge and the theories

[70] Krishnaswamy, 'Toward World Literary Knowledges', p. 143.

[71] Longxi, 'World Literature, Canon, and Literary Criticism', p. 179.

[72] Hamid Dabashi, *The Shahnameh: The Persian Epic as World Literature* (New York: Columbia University Press, 2019), p. 2.

derivable from various literary traditions.[73] The above criticism urges us to return to reading World Literature on a much larger scale than ever before. It helps to remind literary scholars that their business is, or should be, primarily, to make sense of literary works, such as *madīḥ*, from different traditions, in a global perspective, beyond any narrowly defined linguistic or national boundaries.[74]

Conclusion: World Literature or Not?

An analysis of the development of *madīḥ* as a literary genre and its impact on cultural and literary history in Islam's history proves its positive contribution to Muslim communities' intellectual and social lives and scholarship. It remains a tool for different kinds of expression (emotional and literary) that stand the test of time and space. Playing loosely with David Damrosch's provocative and flexible definition of world literature as: (1) 'writing that gains in translation', (2) writing that functions as an 'elliptical refraction of national literature', and (3) 'a mode of reading: a form of engagement with worlds beyond our place and time',[75] I build my case to position the poetry in praise of the Prophet Muḥammad to be regarded in the World Literature.

Works in praise of the Prophet (*madīḥ*) are a popular literary genre that has made a worldwide contribution. Worldwide here means the impact on almost 1.8 billion Muslims across a geographically and culturally diverse spectrum. It might be hard to find a literary genre that had the same cultural, emotional and poetic impact, not even eloquent pre-Islamic poetry. Worldwide also refers to the multidisciplinary fields of scholarship that connect Arabic literature, devotional poetry, ethnographical studies and Sufism, to mention but a few. Among its many contributions, *madīḥ* also provides a window into the history of Islam and the Prophet's character. It is not mere emotional poetry that describes one character.

This chapter argued that *madīḥ nabawī* influenced the lives, cultures and literature of the Islamicate world. The performance of the annual celebration and festivities connected with the birth of the Prophet are cultural phenomena that

[73] Krishnaswamy, 'Toward World Literary Knowledges', p. 137.

[74] Longxi, 'World Literature, Canon, and Literary Criticism', p. 174.

[75] Damrosch, *What is World Literature?*, p. 5.

have been widely covered in many studies. Although *al-Burda* of al-Būṣīrī is a classic of *madīḥ* poetry, the poetry recited in these ceremonies, however, remain understudied as a poetic phenomenon in the Global North. The widespread, as well as the different manifestations, make *al-Burda* a concrete example of World Literature. When al-Būṣīrī composed his ode, he would probably not have expected his poem to reach every corner of the Muslim world or to become the subject of a plethora of academic studies, translations and imitations.

After *al-Burda* was developed, the genre of *madāʾiḥ nabawīyya* became very popular, starting from the Mamluk period. Moreover, new literary sub-genres were introduced and positively affected the literary history not only in Arabic, but also in vernacular languages in West and East Africa, and South and Southeast Asia. *Al-Burda* inspired other poets to provide their local traditions of praise poetry and commence a great movement of translation and interpretation, and, finally, leading to a significant response from Sufi poets who tried to imitate its structure.

In conclusion, it can be said that *madīḥ* poetry started as a local practice, and then developed and expanded as a religious and literary practice. The turning point in this tradition came about with *al-Burda* by al-Būṣīrī that connected pre-Islamic panegyrics to early Islamic praise poetry until it became a widespread literary tradition after the Mamluk period. This type of devotional literature can be a concrete example of the phenomenon of World Literature outside the remit of World Literature.

Bibliography

Al-ʿAsqalānī, Ibn Ḥajar, Aḥmad ibn ʿAlī and Syed Abul Fazl, *Dīwān Ibn Hajar al-ʿAsqalānī* (Ḥaydarābād al-Dakkan: Jāmiʿat al-ʿUthmānīyah, 1962).

Al-Būṣīrī, Sharaf al-Dīn Muḥammad ibn Saʿīd, *Dīwān al-Būṣīrī*, ed. Muḥammad Sayyid Kilānī, 2nd edn (Cairo: Muṣṭafa al-Bābī al-Ḥalabī, 1972).

Al-Būṣīrī-al, Sharaf al-Dīn Muḥammad ibn Saʿīd, *The Mantle Adorned: Imam al-Busiri's Burda*, trans. Abdal Hakim Murad (London: Quilliam Press, 2009).

Al-Musā, Mashārī ʿAbd al-ʿAzīz, '*Badīʿīyyāt* in Praise of the Prophet: Gift Exchange Theory/ البديعيات في المديح النبوي: مقاربة على ضوء نظرية تبادل الهدايا.' *Majallat Jāmiʿat al-Malik ʿAbd al-ʿAzīz* 28(13) (2020): 225–36.

Al-Musawi, Muhsin, *The Medieval Islamic Republic of Letters: The Arabic Knowledge Construction* (Notre Dame, IN: University of Notre Dame Press, 2015).

Al-Qabbāni, ʿAbd al-ʿAlīm, *Al-Būṣīrī: Hayātuh wa-Shiʿruh* (Cairo: Dār al-Maʿārif, 1968).

Asani, Ali Sultan Ali, Kamal Abdel-Malek and Annemarie Schimmel, *Celebrating Muḥammad: Images of the Prophet in Popular Muslim Poetry*, Studies in Comparative Religion. (Columbia, SC: University of South Carolina Press, 1995).

Atkinson, William. 'The Perils of World Literature', *World Literature Today* 80(5) (2006): 43–7.

Bauer, Thomas, 'Ibn Ḥajar and the Arabic Ghazal of the Mamluk Age', in Thomas Bauer and Angelika Neuwirth (eds), *Ghazal As World Literature: Transformations of a Literary Genre* (Beirut: Orient-Institut, 2005), vol. 2.

Bauer, Thomas and Angelika Neuwirth (eds), *Ghazal as World Literature: Transformations of a Literary Genre*, Beiruter Texte Und Studien: Bd. 89 (Beirut: Orient-Institut, 2005).

Brooks, Kevin, 'Dave Eggers's "What Is the What" as World Literature', *World Literature Today* 84(2) (2010): 36–40.

Conversations with Moroccan Poet and Writer Abdellatif Laʿabī, 20–21 February 2020, available at: https://www.ertegun.ox.ac.uk/article/conversations-moroccan-poet-and-writer-abdellatif-laabi-0.

Dabashi, Hamid, *The Shahnameh: The Persian Epic as World Literature* (New York: Columbia University Press, 2019).

D'Haen, Theo, César Domínguez and Mads Rosendahl Thomsen, *World Literature: A Reader* (London: Routledge, 2013).

Damrosch, D., 'World Literature, National Contexts', *Modern Philology* 100(4) (2003): 512–31.

Damrosch, David, *What is World Literature?* (Princeton, NJ: Princeton University Press, 2003).

Damrosch, David (ed.), *World Literature in Theory* (Chichester: Wiley-Blackwell, 2014).

Dharwadker, Vinay (ed.), *Cosmopolitan Geographies: New Locations in Literature and Culture* (New York: Routledge, 2001).

Dharwadker, Vinay, 'Translating the Millennium: Indian Literature in the Global Market', *Indian Literature* 52(4) (2008): 133–46.

Ernst, Carl W. and Bruce B. Lawrence, *Sufi Martyrs of Love: The Chishti Order in South Asia and Beyond* (London: Palgrave Macmillan, 2002).

Frishkopf, Michael, 'Inshād Dīnī and Aghānī Dīnīyya in Twentieth-Century Egypt: A Review of Styles, Genres, and Available Recordings', *Middle East Studies Association Bulletin* 34(2) (2000): 167–83.

Frishkopf, Michael, 'Authorship in Sufi Poetry/ مفهوم المؤلف في الشعر الصوفي.' *Alif: Journal of Comparative Poetics* 23 (2003): 78–108.

Hamsa Stainton, 'Poetry as Prayer: The Śaiva Hymns of Jagaddhara Bhaṭṭa of Kashmir', *International Journal of Hindu Studies* 20(3) (2016): 339–54.

Ibn, Ḥajar and Firdaws N. A. Ḥusayn, *Dīwān Shaykh Al-Islām Ibn Ḥajar Al-ʿAsqalānī* (Cairo: Dār al-Fikr al-ʿArabī, 1996).

Ibrāhīmī, ʿIzzat Mulla and ʿAlī Rasūlī, 'Tadāʿīyāt al-Madāʾiḥ al-Nabawīyya ʿala al-Bīʾah fī al-ʿAṣr al-Mamlūkī', *Majallat Kullīyyat al-Tarbiya al-Asāsīyya lil-ʿulūm al-Tarbawīyya wa-al-Insānīyya* 34 (2017): 30–45.

Karić, Dženita, 'Devotional Poetry', in *The Oxford Encyclopaedia of Islam and Women*, Oxford: Oxford University Press, 2013, available at: https://www.oxfordreference.com/view/10.1093/acref:oiso/9780199764464.001.0001/acref-9780199764464-e-0239.

Khamissa, Yunus, *The Meaning of Qaṣīda Burda of Imam Busiri*, online, 2019, available at: https://www.academia.edu/40375973/The_meaning_of_Imam_al_Busiris_Qasida_Burda.

Kim, Youngmin, 'Introduction: Ethics of Reading in World Literature and Ethical Literary Criticism', *The Free Library* (1 June 2016), available at: https://www.thefreelibrary.com/Introduction: ethics of reading in world literature and ethical...-a0461068377.

Knappert, Jan, *Swahili Islamic Poetry* (Leiden: Brill, 1971).

Krishnaswamy, Revathi, 'Toward World Literary Knowledges: Theory in the Age of Globalization', in David Damrosch (ed.), *World Literature in Theory* (Chichester: Wiley-Blackwell, 2014), pp. 134–58.

Kutty, P. Moyin, 'Role of Devotional Literature in the Enlightenment of Kerala Muslims', *Research Ambition* 1(II) (2016): 35–46.

Lings, Martin, *A Sufi Saint of the Twentieth Century: Shaikh Aḥmad al-Alawī – His Spiritual Heritage and Legacy* (Cambridge: Islamic Texts Society, 1993).

Longxi, Zhang, 'World Literature, Canon, and Literary Criticism', in Weigui Fang (ed.), *Tensions in World Literature: Between the Local and the Universal* (Singapore: Palgrave Macmillan, 2018), pp. 171–90.

Metcalf, Barbara Daly, *Islam in South Asia in Practice* (Princeton, NJ: Princeton University Press, 2009).

Moretti, Franco, 'Conjectures on World Literature', *New Left Review* 1(4) (2014): 54–68.

Nuʿmānī, Shiblī and Muḥammad Taqī Fakhr Dāʿī Gīlānī, *Shiʿr al-ʿAjam* (Tehrān: Dunyā-yi Kitāb, 1984).

Ogunnaike, Oludamini, *Poetry in Praise of Prophetic Perfection: A Study of West African Arabic Madīḥ Poetry and Its Precedents* (Cambridge: Islamic Texts Society, 2020).

Ormsby, Eric (trans.), *West-Eastern Divan: Complete, Annotated New Translation, Including Goethe's 'Notes And Essays' & The Unpublished Poems* (London: Gingko Library, 2019).

Qudāma Ibn Jaʿfar, *Naqd al-Shiʿr/tahqiq Muhammad Isa Mamnun* (Cairo: Maṭbaʿah al-Malījīyah, 1934).

Pfeiffer, Judith, 'Goethe and Sa'di: Chrisian Wurm's Interpretation of Selige Sehnsucht Revisited', in Thomas Bauer and Angelika Neuwirth (eds), *Ghazal as World Literature: Transformations of a Literary Genre* (Beirut: Orient-Institut, 2005), pp. 259–84.

Pizer, John, 'Goethe's "World Literature" Paradigm and Contemporary Cultural Globalization', *Comparative Literature* 52(3) (2000): 213–27.

Ricci, Ronit, 'Islamic Literary Networks in South and Southeast Asia', *Journal of Islamic Studies* 21(1) (2010): 1–28.

Said, Edward W., 'Travelling Theory', in David Damrosch (ed.), *World Literature in Theory* (Chichester: Wiley-Blackwell, 2014), pp. 114–33.

Sālim, Muḥammad al-Hādī, Interview, conducted by Walid Ghali, 9 March 2021.

Schimmel, Annemarie, *Mystical Dimensions of Islam* (Chapel Hill: University of North Carolina Press, 1976).

Schimmel, Annemarie, *And Muhammad is His Messenger: The Veneration of the Prophet in Islamic Piety* (Chapel Hill: University of North Carolina Press, 1985).

Schimmel, Annemarie, *My Soul is a Woman: The Feminine in Islam*, trans. Susan. H. Ray (New York: Continuum, 2003).

Smith, Margaret, *Rabiʿa the Mystic and Her Fellow-Saints in Islam* (Cambridge: Cambridge University Press, [1928] 2010).

Sperl, Stefan, *Mannerism in Arabic Poetry: A Structural Analysis of Selected Texts (3rd Century AH/9th Century AD–5th Century AH/11th Century AD)* (Cambridge: Cambridge University Press, 2004).

Sperl, S., C. Shackle and N. Awde, *Qasida Poetry in Islamic Asia and Africa* (Leiden: Brill, 1996).

Stetkevych, Suzanne, *The Mantle Odes: Arabic Praise Poems to the Prophet Muḥammad* (Bloomington: Indiana University Press, 2010).

Wickens, G. M., J. W. Clinton, J. Stewart Robinson, J. A. Haywood and J. Knappert, 'Madīḥ, Madḥ', in P. Bearman et al. (eds), *Encyclopaedia of Islam*, 2nd edn., Brill Reference online, 2012.

Zwettler, Michael, 'Mantic Manifesto: The Sura of "The Poets" and the Qur'anic Foundations of Prophetic Authority', in James L. Kugel (ed.), *Poetry and Prophecy: The Beginnings of a Literary Tradition* (Ithaca, NY: Cornell University Press, 1990), pp. 75–119.

5

THE PLACE AND FUNCTION OF IMAGINATION IN FULANI MYSTICAL POETRY (MASSINA, MALI)[1]

Christiane Seydou

Islam, which was introduced to Sub-Saharan Africa more than a millennium ago, spread outward from the various points of entry that formed its base. It progressively impacted, more or less decisively, the social and historical organisation of numerous populations.[2]

The Fulani, originally nomadic herders present in the entire Sahelian zone, were among Islam's most active disseminators. By combining political domination and religious conquest, they distinguished themselves as

[1] Translated from the French by Brunhilde Biebuyck in collaboration with Anouk Allart and Krista Faurie. May they receive my sincere thanks.

[2] See Joseph M. Cuoq, *Les musulmans en Afrique* (Paris: Maisonneuve et Larose, 1975); Joseph M. Cuoq, *Histoire de l'islamisation de l'Afrique de l'Ouest, des origines à la fin du XVIe siècle* (Paris: Geuthner, 1984); Ousmane Kane and Jean-Louis Triaud, *Islam et islamismes au sud du Sahara* (Paris: IREMAN-Karthala-MSH, 1998); Nehemia Levtzion, *Islam in West Africa: Religion, Society and Politics to 1800* (Aldershot: Variorum, 1994); Adriana Piga, *Les voies du soufisme au sud du Sahara*, Parcours historiques et anthropologiques, Préface Louis Triaud (Paris: les Éditions Karthala, 2006); David Robinson and Jean-Louis Triaud (eds), *Le temps des marabouts. Itinéraires et stratégies islamiques en Afrique occidentale française, 1880–1960* (Paris: Karthala,1997); J. Spencer Trimingham, *A History of Islam in West Africa* (Oxford: Oxford University Press, 1974).

founders of considerable states, from Senegal and Guinea to Nigeria and Cameroon.[3]

From the fourteenth century onward, Mali was especially affected by the influence of Timbuktu and Djenné and by the founding of the Dīna, a theocratic state known as the Fulani Empire of Massina (1818–62). In this context and through historical coincidences, Islam blended the orthodoxy of Mālikī theology with the *ṭarā'iq* (path, way) of the Qādiriyya and Tijāniyya brotherhoods.

Among the Fulani, Islam became a fundamental part of their culture; it permeated their literary production, based on the history of each region where the Fulani established political and religious domination between the seventeenth and nineteenth centuries.[4] Spoken and written Arabic spread with the advent of Islam, but it was mainly used for *tarikh*s (history) and theological or legal texts. However, in order to communicate religious messages to the population

[3] Futa-Toro, in Senegal, and Futa-Jallon, in Guinea (starting in the seventeenth century), Sokoto Empire in Nigeria, and Adamawa Empire in Cameroon (during the nineteenth century), and, finally, the jihad of Al-Hajj Umar (1848–64). See Michel Abitbol, *Tombouctou et les Arma. De la conquête marocaine du Soudan nigérien en 1591 à l'hégémonie de l'empire peul du Macina en 1833* (Paris: Maisonneuve et Larose, 1979); Mervyn Hiskett, *The Sword of Truth: The Life and Times of the Shehu Usuman Dan Fodio* (New York: Oxford University Press, 1973); David Robinson, *La guerre sainte d'al-Hajj Umar* (Paris: Karthala, 1988); Bintou Sanankoua, *Un empire peul au XIXe siècle. La Diina du Maasina* (Paris: Karthala, 1990).

[4] See Amadou Hampâté Bâ and Marcel Cardaire, *Tierno Bokar, le sage de Bandiagara* (Paris: Présence africaine, 1957); Louis Brenner, *West African Sufi: The Religious Heritage and Spiritual Search of Cerno Bokar Saalif Taal* (London: Hurst, 1984); Paul K. Eguchi (trans.), *Poem of Repentance*, African Languages and ethnography IV (Tokyo: ILCAA, 1976); Henri Gaden, *Tyam Mohammadou Aliou, La Vie d'El Hadj Omar. Qacida en poular* (Paris: Institut d'ethnologie, 1935); Johannes Haafkens, *Chants musulmans en peul. Textes de l'héritage religieux de la communauté musulmane de Maroua. Cameroun* (Leiden: Brill, 1983); Alfâ Ibrâhîm Sow, *La Femme, la Vache, la Foi*, Classiques africains 5 (Paris: Julliard, distribué par Karthala, 1966); Alfâ Ibrâhîm Sow, *Le Filon du bonheur éternel* par Mouhammadou-Samba Mombéyâ, Classiques africains 10 (Paris: Armand Colin, distribué par Karthala, 1971); Jean-Louis Triaud and David Robinson (eds), *La Tijâniyya. Une confrérie musulmane à la conquête de l'Afrique* (Paris: Karthala, 2000); John Ralph Willis (ed.), *Studies in West African Islamic History, vol. 1: The Cultivators of Islam* (London: Frank Cass, 1979).

at large, local African languages were also used; poetry was especially recommended since it facilitated the memorisation of texts.[5]

The Fulani opted for their own language because 'to each one, indeed, only one's own language makes it possible to grasp what the Authentics are saying'.[6] Thus, in addition to interlinear translations of the Qur'ān and the production of scholarly and academic literature by erudite intellectuals trained in Arabic theological and literary classics, a rich poetic diversity was born. This poetry ranged from an austere and didactic presentation of the articles of faith and ethics, which can bond a community, to a more original form of expression, borrowed from two opposing orientations. The first orientation, emerging from modest marabouts and addressing a general public with little instruction, gave poetic form to sermons on the most varied subjects, from the ordinary (against tobacco,[7] taxes[8] and so on) to the most fervent (descriptions of infernal agonies),[9] both lending themselves to a fecund imagination. The second orientation, destined for pure spiritual elevation and the revelation of truths, took on a form of refined poetry, a reflection of the most personal mystical inspiration.[10] It is this literary production of mystical inspiration, linked to Sufi influence – more or less important depending on the involvement of the brotherhoods in each region – that was the most developed and widespread in the *zāwiya*.[11]

[5] Jean-Michel Djian, *Les manuscrits de Tombouctou. Secrets, mythes et réalités* (Paris: JC Lattès, 2012), p. 115.

[6] Alfâ Ibrâhîm Sow, *Le Filon du bonheur éternel* par Mouhammadou-Samba Mombéyâ, Classiques africains 10 (Paris: Armand Colin, distribué par Karthala, 1971), p. 43.

[7] Christiane Seydou, 'Prône contre le tabac. Un manuscrit peul du fonds Vieillard', in Pascal Boyeldieu and Pierre Nougayrol (eds), *Langues et cultures. Terrains d'Afrique*, hommage à France Cloarec-Heiss, Collection Afrique et Langage, No. 7 (Louvain and Paris: Peeters, 2004), pp. 147–53. See also Christiane Seydou, 'Poésie religieuse et inspiration populaire chez les Peuls du Foûta-Djalon', *Journal of African Cultural Studies* 14(1) (2001): 23–47.

[8] For Guinea, see Sow, *La Femme, la Vache, la Foi*, pp. 118–25.

[9] Christiane Seydou, '*Majjaado Alla gaynaali*, poème en langue peule du Foûta-Djalon', *Cahiers d'Études Africaines* 24(6) (1966): 643–81.

[10] African poets were especially inspired by the works of al-Būṣīrī (1213–96): *Al-Hamziyya* and especially *Al-Burda*.

[11] Religious institutions gathering students or disciples studying religious texts under the direction and authority of a master affiliated to a brotherhood; a.k.a. 'Sufi lodges'.

In the following pages, we will examine this poetry based on a body of texts collected in Mali. Comprising the works of four renowned poets (from the eighteenth to the twentieth centuries), this poetry was traditionally transmitted orally in the *zāwiya* or by faithful, often blind singers[12] during religious festivals, and after the Friday mosque prayers.

Some of these poems were recorded in 1970 in Sévaré, near Mopti. They were sung in chorus by the *talibés* of master Âmadou Abbas Sinna, who ensured the continued existence of the repertoire of Mouhammadou Abdoullâye Sou'âdou (1819–57). Other poems were recorded in 1977 in Bandiagara. They were sung by a blind, elderly cantor, Âmadoun Koundié. Also known as Missi, he was a former student of Tierno Bôkar Sâlif (known as 'the sage of Bandiagara'), and an interpreter of the poems of Âmadoun Fôdiya Moussa (end of the eighteenth century–beginning of the nineteenth century) and Alfâ Bôkari Mahmoûdou (d. *c.* 1932).

Although one can find manuscript transcriptions in *ajami*, i.e. West-African languages using the Arabic script, this literature was usually transmitted and kept alive orally.[13] The accuracy assured through oral transmission is likely attributable to the fact that song and scansion are conducive to memorisation. This poetic production extended across the entire Fulani region, meaning eighteen countries from Nigeria to Sudan, with poets possessing respective local zones of influence while at the same time sharing significant repertoires and borrowing from each other.[14]

[12] Examples borrowed from collected and published texts; cf. Christiane Seydou, *La poésie mystique peule du Mali*, Introduction Louis Brenner (Paris: Karthala, 2008).

[13] We can find written copies written in Arabic characters known as *ajamiyya*, which are carefully preserved but rarely consulted. These texts were primarily transmitted orally, but, accompanied by song, which combined with rhyme and scansion, contribute to their memorisation.

[14] Written texts in Arabic concerning creed, law and political problems circulated much more widely within learned circles. See, for example, Djian, *Les manuscrits de Tombouctou*; John. O. Hunwick, *Arabic Literature of Africa: The Writings of Western Sudanic Africa*, vol. 4, compiled by John O. Hunwick with the assistance of Ousmane Kane, Bernard Salvaing, Rüdiger Seesemann, Mark Sey and Ivor Wilks (Leiden: Brill, 2003). See, for example, the very important literary production of an author like Ousman dan Fodio (1817–1854) in Nigeria (and that of his brother and his son), was widely circulated in writing, mainly because of the historical and religious significance of this intellectual and political figure but also because a large number of his works were written in Arabic. See M. Kensdale, *Catalogue of the Arabic*

This poetry follows the usual rules of prosody, using the aesthetic aspect of speech in its two qualities: rhythmic and melodic. It also associates the metric system borrowed from classical Arabic poetry with the rules of its traditional poetic stylistics, mainly centred on phonic interplays.[15] In addition, it adopts not only a learned register – the use of numerous words borrowed from Arabic – but also a figurative style that draws from an ordinary and realistic lexicon often at the service of allegorical formulations, the fruit of an inspired imagination. Since this poetry is always sung,[16] the sound effects of language are complemented by those of the voice. Indeed, as the product of a human instrument created by God, vocal music is the only expression allowed.[17] In these poems, symbolic imagery and musical interpretation must be combined in order to accompany the souls to the threshold of the truths evoked therein.

Singing is inherent to religious poetry.[18] Indeed, in order to commit a poem to memory before interpreting it, the reciter will often begin by humming the tune. To select the meter for composing his poem, the author will, for his part, sing the musical phrase serving as the rhythmic and melodic matrix to which he applies his words. The verse will thus be phrased according to the textual

Manuscripts preserved in the University Library, Ibadan, Nigeria (Ibadan: AN 1955–8); Norbert Tapiéro, 'The Great Fulani Shaykh 'Uthman Ibn Fudi (Othman Dan Fodio, who died in 1232 H.=1816–17 J.C.) and certain documents concerning his doctrinal Islam', *Revue des Études Islamiques* (1963): 49–88. He translated much of his Arabic poetry into Fulani and Hausa, thus promoting its distribution but also restricting it only to the speakers of these languages.

15 See Christiane Seydou, *Bergers des mots, poésie peule du Massina*, Classiques africains 24 (Paris: Les Belles Lettres, distribué par Karthala, 1991), p. 360. The golden rule of this poetry is to ensure a phonic continuum by a game of sonic echoes and alliterations that are linked to each other in a potentially indefinite way.

16 The name of this kind of poetry, *yimre*, actually confirms this (root *yim-* : 'to sing'). We know the interest in the cantillation of the Qur'ānic text, contrary to the rejection of instrumental music in the domain of the profane.

17 See Navid Kermani, *God is Beautiful: The Aesthetic Experience of Quran*, trans. Tony Crawford (Malden, MA: Polity, 2015).

18 We can find written copies written in Arabic characters known as *ajamiyya*, which are carefully preserved but rarely consulted. These texts were primarily transmitted orally, but, accompanied by song, which combined with rhyme and scansion, contribute to their memorisation.

and musical parameters of the rhyme – the same throughout the poem – usually marked by a more or less accentuated modulation or melisma.

This poetry falls under several genres: *yettoore* (action of grace), *mantoore* (praises), *waajoore* (sermon, exhortation), *waynorde* (eulogy), *jaaroore* (religious hymn), *beegoore* (mystical love song). The poems discussed here mainly belong to the last two categories. The religious poetry that permeates teachings in the *zāwiya* of Massina in Mali is profoundly marked by mystical interpretation and Sufi influence, as is reflected at two levels: the level of the signified where the recurrence of the word 'I' can be found in all of these poems. Indeed, they oscillate between the author's recollection of his personal mystical experience and his address to a sublime 'You' – the object of his prayers or his spiritual love and engaged appeals to another fraternal 'You', to whom he wants to transmit the revelation of Truth. The level of the signifier, which relies on a dominant expression full of imagery, from the most conventional metaphors to an entirely figurative narrative that can follow an extended '*mise en scène*', the only medium, or so it seems, through which the unspeakable, the ineffable aspect of this Truth can be conveyed in human terms.

The Personalisation of Expression

What stands out in this poetry is the predominance of, on the one hand, a confidential discourse on the part of the author, and, on the other hand, a direct one-way dialogue between the poet and his interlocutors – be they God, the Prophet or his fellow humans. Throughout these poems, this self-presentation and personal address constantly shift from the 'I/We' to the 'You (sing.)/You (plural)'. From the outset, this shift designates the texts as messages both 'revealed' and 'to be revealed', and their author as the voice/path of this revelation. This justifies numerous intimate verses that evoke the preacher's mystical experience and his role as 'messenger'; thus, the poet Alfâ Bôkari Mammoûdou, in his long poem, '*Tifal*' ('A Long Voyage'), says:

> The lightning bolt of the Lord-of-the-two-Worlds passes through me
> and I am so overwhelmed that it makes me lose my mind, as if I were
> inebriated,

and my eyes penetrate his mystery, which I distill within me and with which
I fill myself . . .
then I come back to my senses, and the truths of Aḥmad pour out of me![19]

In this poetry, the distinction between God and his Prophet is often ambiguous, as one can see in the author's rendering of his mystical experience, where the shift from one to the other is often imperceptible. An example is the shifting from 'the Lord-of-the-two-worlds' (God) at the beginning of the verse, to the 'truths of Aḥmad', at the end this [con]fusion takes place within the one, the mediator, who pronounces this eminently confidential discourse.

In his poem III, Mouhammadou Abdoullâye Sou'âdou, also develops this same ambiguity between his 'Prophet' and his 'Master' ('He who remains concealed in his secrets'), and uses the same expressions to describe his state of being:

By the grace of my Prophet, the Excellent,
I am so intoxicated by his light that,
once I have recovered my senses, I exult in a pledge
proclaiming the truth of religion.

I had the pleasure of having an intimate exchange with my Master
its sweetness penetrated my entire body
and the marrow in my bones melted when I felt
the sweetness of He who remains concealed in his secrets.

I had the pleasure of encountering Truth . . .[20]

For both poets, the spiritual reality that is impossible to describe can be conveyed only through experienced emotions, which are so intense that only expressions verging on indecorousness can communicate them:

I groan in my fervent love for Aḥmad
seized by tremors for having accessed the sweetness of Aḥmad's love.
/ . . . /

[19] Seydou, *La poésie mystique peule du Mali*, p. 88, v. 38

[20] Seydou, *La poésie mystique peule du Mali*, p. 272, vv. 19–21.

Am quenched by a deep cup filled with the Truth
and the knowledge emanating from within Aḥmad!
I fill my lungs and bowels, and my entire belly
And, seized by hiccups, I pour out Muḥammad's light![21]

When he implores his audience, here again, his tone can shift from the solemn to the familiar:

Fear the Lord who is filled with kindness!
/ . . . / in order to follow the Law of He who will establish Tradition![22]

But when the plea becomes more pressing, the vocabulary becomes more harsh:

You were stubborn in evil, think, lament, to the point of rolling on the floor
lying there, beaten down by terror, and moaning to death!

Each night you succumb to sleeplessness at the thought of your tomb!
Tremble and let yourself be stricken by the fear of your Lord in order to free yourself from it![23]

In his edifying attempt at persuasion and his call for loyalty to the Prophet, the poet seals his discourse in this spiritual intimacy. At times, it confronts him with divine authorities through imploration, or, conversely, in an expression of gratitude for the gift of a sublime revelation. At other times, it confronts him with his human brothers when he recalls their destiny in this world, and the remedies he must provide so they can reach the Truth that will save them.

Thus, in three of his poems,[24] Alfâ Bôkari Mahmoudou expresses himself as follows: in the first, he addresses himself to the Prophet ('Oh, Chosen-one,

[21] Seydou, *La poésie mystique peule du Mali*, p. 396, vv. 13–16.

[22] Seydou, *La poésie mystique peule du Mali*, p. 274, v. 25; the Gathering at the Last Judgement.

[23] Seydou, *La poésie mystique peule du Mali*, p. 388, vv. 27–8.

[24] Seydou, *La poésie mystique peule du Mali*, pp. 132–71.

in you I have found support . . .'), and in the second, to God himself ('My Master . . . You are the epitome of all wisdom! . . . Grant me knowledge, Oh, Knowledgeable-one!'). In the third poem, he shifts from confidential declarations with a mediating 'I' aimed at disseminating the truth ('I moan in order to expel the truth lodged in my heart . . . I have orders to repeat the Truth, understand my brothers . . .') to moralising injunctions ('My brothers, come, let us follow the path of Truth and leave the lies behind!'),[25] with the last verses returning to the intimacy of 'I':

> I beg my Master to plant the seeds of truth in my heart,
> so I can instill it in the heart of my brothers, so truth will revive them![26]

In his poem, 'A Long Voyage', dedicated to Aḥmad (as evidenced by this single rhyme throughout the poem), the poet beckons his interlocutor from the initial verse:

> Now is not the time for you to stop! You have not reached the end!
> / . . . / Friend, courage! Walk in the footsteps of the precursors and be their reflection!
> / . . . / Friend, beware of this world . . . / . . . / Friend, beware of your steps . . .
> / . . . / Emulate the men of Aḥmad . . . (vv. 1–7)

then, he addresses God and the Prophet directly:

> Dear God, ensure that my ultimate paradise is a vision of Aḥmad!! (v. 81)

> My Messenger! Fill me entirely with your being and grant me the wisdom, (v. 83)
> energy, and zeal needed to devote freely to the celebration of Aḥmad . . .

and, finally, follows with a long oration on the glory of the Prophet in which ten verses all begin with *Nulaado heyli*:

[25] Seydou, *La poésie mystique peule du Mali*, poem I, p. 140, v. 35; poem II, p. 150, vv. 17 and 24; poem III, p. 62, vv. 6–7, p. 168, vv. 34–6.

[26] Seydou, *La poésie mystique peule du Mali*, p. 168, v. 43.

The Messenger[27] is the utmost eternal origin, the seed of all things!
The Messenger is himself the infinity of the end of all things! (v. 120)

The poet's role as mediator appears clearly in these dialogues, of which he is the pivot, shifting from orations, prayers and celebrations addressed to God and his Messenger, to advice, admonitions and encouragements addressed to the believers.

The purpose of this poetry does not, however, prevent the poet from using the third person, which is more objective but not any less effective, in long, descriptive passages that are especially evocative. In this poetic production, devotion to the Prophet takes the upper hand, and the poet[28] can deliver an energetic and detailed description of Muḥammad, with each verse beginning as follows: 'He was a splendid young man . . .' (vv. 11–24), and then referring to his companions using the same terms: 'They were youths . . . brothers . . . men who . . . (vv. 26–42). In another text, the same poet[29] narrates at length the deeds of the Chosen-one, such as his ascent (*miʿrāj*); but, by v. 17, he declares his fervent love for Aḥmad and adopts his usual role of mediator, returning to 'I' and continuing with long, repetitive litanies: 'I implore my Master to let me see Aḥmad . . .' (vv. 26–9); then: 'I implore Aḥmad . . . to guide my heart so I may see the Truth . . .' (vv. 37–43); and, finally, addressing the prophet directly: '"Quench" my disciples for me so that . . .' (vv. 44–50).

There are many examples of this adjustment of objective expression with a return to personal discourse or dialogue. Thus, in most cases, the distancing imposed by the representation of a scene is 'adjusted' by introducing an invocation or an injunction in the first person, ending the verse. Âmadoun Fôdiya Moussa (end of the eighteenth and beginning of the nineteenth century) offers a particularly telling example in one of his famous poems,

27 'The Messenger': this is the epithet typically used in these religious poems to refer to the Prophet Muḥammad.

28 Seydou, *La poésie mystique peule du Mali*, Mouhammadou Abdoulâye Sou'âdou, poem IX, pp. 370–9.

29 Seydou, *La poésie mystique peule du Mali*, Mouhammadou Abdoulâye Sou'âdou, poem VIII, pp. 354–67.

Geloobal,[30] dedicated to the Prophet. This *qaṣīda* is based on a theme of pre-Islamic Bedouin poetry: the long nostalgic march of a camel-rider towards his beloved's encampment, which is transposed here into a pilgrim's march towards the Prophet's tomb. While the poet's central theme is his devotion to Aḥmad, he does not fail in praising his mount: thus, in sixteen of the twenty-eight *takhmīs* (pentastich, or verses made up of five *bayt*), the first four *bayt* describe and praise the camel;[31] only the last one, which rhymes with 'Aḥmad' or 'Muḥammad', centres on the real subject of the poem and shifts from the 'third person' to the 'first' – 'I or Us'– recalling the poet's personal involvement in the action:

> She will rise over the sandy dunes, looking like a young wild beast
> she will hurtle down the grassy banks with the speed of a leveret
> she will make good progress through stony mounds like a Lycaon's last born
> she will shine on the Hamadas like a female turtledove
> she will trigger a flight of sparrows and I will have high hopes of reaching Aḥmad!
> / . . . /
> Her leg resembles the posts of a weaver's shed
> her cushion-like pad resembles one of those potteries called lids
> her small ears are short and pointy whereas her legs resemble a wooden bedstead
> her large bulging eyes and her lips, they look just like leather!
> May she carry me high so I that I can recite at the tomb of Muḥammad![32]

Despite the profoundly religious orientation of his poetry, this poet remains visibly influenced by pre-Islamic poetry. In the two other poems of his trilogy – both using the same metrical system and rhyme 'Aḥmad/Muḥammad' – he proceeds as before. In 'The Equestrians', we recognise the epic spirit and the horse motif,

[30] 'Camel' (more precisely dromedary and a female); see Seydou, *La poésie mystique peule du Mali*, pp. 178–89; Christiane Seydou, '"Le Chameau": poème mystique ou . . . pastoral?' in *Itinérances en pays peul et ailleurs*, Mélanges à la mémoire de Pierre-Francis Lacroix, vol. 2 (Paris: Mémoires de la Société des Africanistes, 1981), pp. 25–52.

[31] Here we recognise the tenor of the *mu'allaqāt* of the pre-Islamic poet Ṭurfa Ibn al-'Abd b. Sufyān (543–569), whose verses 11–44 centre on a description of his female camel, and 'Antara (525–615), verses 20–33; see Jean-Jacques Schmidt, *Les Mou'allaqât, poésie arabe préislamique* (Paris: Seghers, 1978), pp. 80–95 and 164–5.

[32] Seydou, *La poésie mystique peule du Mali*, pp. 182–4, vv. 11 and 14.

with the vigorous galloping recalling the tribal odes of ʿAntara.[33] In 'The Gazelle', which borrows its subject matter from hagiographic narratives, he attempts to transform the tenor of a folktale into that of a parable, but the first ten of twenty-five verses focus on a description, rich in imagery, of a stormy downpour over *Thamūd*[34] land scorched by drought, the cloud is personified and drawn into an animated sequence:

> The Messenger invoked God and the Orient rumbled silently without a clap of thunder,
> a dark cloud, where manes and tails wound the orbit of their race
> finally releasing the Lord-of-the-stars-Fargad in his pure brightness,[35]
> spread its wings and, in a muffled rumble, licked the sky with bolts of lightning,
> and the spirited chargers of the water headed directly to the city of Aḥmad!
>
> A few wind gusts, and suddenly the dark cloud was freed of all its veils,
> it drummed down rain and, in a gay tumult, covered its brightness,
> it extended a thousand arms toward the flasks suspended from the sky, spilled them over,
> then, setting down its loads, it opened the waterskins that spread out
> and, knees to the ground, it bowed down before the Prophet Muḥammad.
>
> / . . . / The rain fell for seven days! They told the Prophet that their thirst was quenched.
> He ordered: 'Cloud, retire thyself!' And the cloud said: 'Very well, Muḥammad!'[36]

[33] Poet and hero of the epic *Sirā ʿAntar*, among the classics of pre-Islamic literature. Cf. *Les Aventures d'Antar, fils de Cheddad. Roman Arabe des temps Anté-Islamiques*, trans. L. Marcel Devic (Paris: Ernest Leroux editor, 1878).

[34] Name of an ancient pre-Islamic tribe of Arabia, often cited in the Qur'ān; also the name of the region occupied by this tribe in northwest Arabia.

[35] Epithet for the sun; Fargad is the name of two neighbouring stars of the North Pole.

[36] Seydou, *La poésie mystique peule du Mali*, p. 206, vv. 3 and 4. This description inspired Âmadou Hampâté Bâ for his description of the storm that takes place during the initiation journey as the cause of the wiseman Hammadi's separation. He respects the advice given by a mysterious elder and will have the mysteries revealed to him. His disobedient companions, however, will die; see Amadou Hampâté Bâ and Lilyan Kesteloot, *Kaïdara. Récit initiatique peul*, Classiques africains No. 7 (Paris: Julliard, distribué par Karthala, 1969), pp. 102–7, vv. 1240–1320.

Even though the evocative power of their style – the fruit of vivid imaginations – could overshadow the spiritual assertions of these poets, it still serves to further edify their audiences.

Allegorical and Metaphorical Expression

As we can see in all of these examples, the inspiration underlying this poetry springs from a mystical event experienced by the authors. Despite the intimate involvement of the poets, both in feeling and expression, these experiences can be revealed and transmitted only through the mediation of an allegorical language sealed by very inventive imaginations.

Certainly, emphasis is always placed on the relationship to the Prophet, who intercedes in the search for the ultimate experience, and as such becomes the recipient of praise from the poet. At the same time, one finds in the poetry a more personal and direct relation to God. Within Sufi praxis references to asceticism and subjective religious experience serve as prologues to a mystical union based on the notion of love, about which the tenth-century poet al-Ḥallāj was the most inspired.[37]

However, this mystical repertoire also shares a certain number of required themes with other poetic genres, which are more didactic. These themes evoke man's mortal destiny and the Hereafter, whose punishments and rewards are impressively depicted in great detail, depict the miserable human condition, deprecate the mundane world where dangers threaten the spiritual state of believers, in this world and the Hereafter. These themes lend themselves, more or less, to allegorical interpretation. Thus, references to the human condition remaining trapped in the mundane, as, for example, when various parts of the human body are depicted as sites of punishment.[38] As for

[37] See Abū Ḥāmid Muḥammad al-Ghazālī, *Al-durra al-fākhira*, trans. L. Gauthier (Leipzig: Otto Harrassowitz, 1925); Akhbār al-Ḥallāj, *Recueil d'oraisons et d'exhortations du martyr mystique de l'islam Husayn Ibn Mansur Hallaj*, trans et annotation Louis Massignon and Paul Kraus (Paris: Éditions J. Vrin, collection 'Études musulmanes', [1957] 1975). Édition bilingue. Ibn ʿArabi, *Traité de l'amour*, traduit et présenté par Maurice Gloton (Paris: Albin Michel, 2013).

[38] Seydou, *La poésie mystique peule du Mali*, pp. 308–11, vv. 10–23, pp. 312–14, vv. 26–38, pp. 328–31, vv. 30–9.

the Otherworld, the poet projects his vision, inspired by descriptions from the Qurʾān, through highly realistic situations, be they about Hell:

> the roaring Jahannam ablaze . . .
> Furious, the fire begins its chase to capture people,
> harassing their gatherings until they are surrounded . . .[39]

or about Paradise:

> Pearls and corals adorn the residences in Paradise
> jewels and saffron decorate the wedding beds of Paradise
> camphor, amber, and musk perfume them
> softened silk renders the gold even smoother!
> Resting on cushions, here they are giving thanks to Aḥmad![40]

The poet, eager to convince, uses disquieting images for the torments reserved for the sinner, and the most sensual evocations for the pleasures promised to the believer: pleasures of hearing, seeing, smelling, tasting, touching . . . The poet takes themes and phrases from *ayah*s in the Qurʾān and expands on them creatively to produce his own poetic lines:

> City of splendour and beauty
> filled with elegant women and perfumed all around.
> / . . . /
> Silver cups and flasks
> bursting with choice honey
> and on golden sofas,
> conversations and libations!
>
> Beautiful and splendid youth,
> pure and virginal maidens,
> together all night
> will dance and listen to the lutes.[41]

[39] Seydou, *La poésie mystique peule du Mali*, p. 260, vv. 50–1.
[40] Seydou, *La poésie mystique peule du Mali*, p. 198, v. 19, p. 200, v. 23.
[41] Seydou, *La poésie mystique peule du Mali*, pp. 238–40, vv. 29–32.

Depreciating the lowly world especially inspires the poet's verbosity; hence, in his poem IV, Mouhammadou Abdoullâye Sou'âdou[42] urges his brothers to 'dread God's punishments in order to follow the path of Truth'.[43] His admonishments and advice frame thirteen verses. After a verse in which he proclaims, 'renounce love for this world' (v. 9), 'this world' becomes the 'protagonist' with each remaining verse beginning with 'He . . . He who . . .', in opposition to the end word-rhyme, 'Truth'. This personification bears all the scorn owed to this world; indeed, the term designating it, borrowed from Arabic *dunyā* can be found in v. 9 as *dunyaa*. In the ten following verses, the pronouns, articles, and all participles and adjectives designating it have negative connotations and include, among others, the body and its less-noble parts, and animals, including the dog or the hyena. In addition, all the misdeeds of the world occur in a series of realistic images, which, borrowed from the everyday environment, are meant to be striking and demonstrative:

> [He] Who is nothing but poisoned darts
> cannot be one with the Truth!
> He who in vermin finds his end
> he who leads astray the jackals
> he who makes birds cry
> blinds the Truth!
> He who sets traps
> on sandy dunes and arid lands
> / . . . / obscures the Truth! . . .
> He who renders perfume into stench
> / . . . / becomes deaf to the Truth![44]

Later in the poem, the descriptions extolling the Prophet are built in a series of animated scenes. One of the favourite themes involves a long march of a group of the faithful walking in the footsteps of the Messenger. Thus, seventeen of the

[42] Mouhammadou Abdoullâye Sou'âdou (1820–57) is said to have been in contact with Al-Bakkâye Kounta, adept of the Qādiriyya, which seems to be confirmed in a passage of his second poem where he lauds Sheikh Jaylaanu (al-Jīlānī).

[43] Seydou, *La poésie mystique peule du Mali*, pp. 294–305.

[44] Seydou, *La poésie mystique peule du Mali*, pp. 296–9, vv. 10–13.

twenty-eight verses of the poem by Âmadoun Fôdiya Moussa, titled 'Horsemen', portray the men and their steeds in exalted but realistic terms, depicting the action in quasi-cinematographic style:

> What could be more beautiful for the Chosen-one than his early-morning horse ride!
> At brisk pace, they head steadfastly for the ponds where they will spend the day,
> we hear the clicking of the stirrups like the clicking of bracelets
> and we witness the muffled sweat beneath the saddles, sliding along the straps!
> At sunset, at your command, they dismount, Muḥammad!
> / . . . /
> When the front-runners receive the order, only then do they bolt
> and, after their departure, as they move away, a cloud of dust arises,
> the steeds move deeper in the infinity of the desert as if into a refuge
> and we see among them the shining light of He-who-is-worthy-of-praises
> and just as the sun has set, there still remains the brightness of the face of Aḥmad![45]

The verses that follow list the different coats of the steeds ('immaculate white, bay, brown with black knees') and the equipment of the valiant knights ('spears at an angle, swords hung on the saddles, quivers worn over the shoulder'). They draw a series of life-like paintings of the journey of Aḥmad's army. The poem ends on a description of Paradise, 'the reward bestowed to Aḥmad's companions! Hark, the description of the Eternal Resting Place!'

In the effusive allegory of a valiant journey in the footsteps of the 'Messenger', the poem, 'A Long Voyage'[46] by Alfâ Bôkari Mahmoudou, is equally descriptive but much more mystically inspired. It includes all the common themes: prayer and grace rendered unto God; recalling the life and destiny of the Prophet, the Last Judgement, Paradise, and so on. It also revives the personal quality of the mystical experience:

[45] Seydou, *La poésie mystique peule du Mali*, p. 192, v. 1, p. 194, v. 6.

[46] This poem is composed in *takhmīs*, namely, stanzas (in the case of our poem 125 stanzas) of five lines each, the fifth line ending with a single rhyme through the whole poem, and the first four lines rhyming with each other, but changing from one stanza to the next.

/ . . . /
Emulating the Messenger's braves, bursting with the same passion,
I left in the evening, following in the tracks of those who went before me.
/ . . . /
I will enter the wild without fear, even in the dead of night
I will march headstrong, I will not rest, even if exhausted
by no means resolved to lie down, even should I fall overcome by sleep!
My Messenger set me ablaze, reaching him is my only goal,
however slow it might be, I will not lose patience on the journey leading to Aḥmad![47]

Here, it is not the victorious train of the Companions that haunts the poet's imagination, but rather his own progress in the hope of joining 'Aḥmad's people'. As precise as the description of each action may be, each image summoned and each term used is charged with symbolic meaning and is part of an allegorical discourse – the only verbal resource available to communicate in this realm of spirituality. Indeed, in this context, ordinary discourse proves to be inadequate and everyday vocabulary does not befit the theme of spiritual love, which permeates Sufi thought and practices.

Love and Truth

This notion of 'love' has in fact been discussed by theologians and, in some contexts, it has even been the subject of controversy amongst scholars. The best examples are the debates around the two terms *maḥabba* and *ʿishq*. In the case of Fulani poetry, love's only object is Muḥammad. The mediation of divine love through the love of the Prophet allows the poet to evoke this emotional and personal dimension of one's relationship to the divine. Yet, at the same time, the metaphors used find their origins in the Qurʾān and are well established in Sufi poetry as well.

In his poems devoted to the Prophet, Mouhammadou Abdoullâye Sou'âdou sometimes uses a realistic lexicon to express his love for the Prophet, while at others, his images and metaphors are more subtle. For example, in his poem VIII, he uses both nuanced terms to express feelings

[47] Seydou, *La poésie mystique peule du Mali*, p. 74, vv. 7–8, p. 76, vv. 12–13.

of love, and resorts to more abrupt terms to describe the effects of this love on his body:

> Aḥmad so haunts my thoughts that I am beside myself
> Aḥmad so haunts my thoughts that I moan and wither away
> Under the weight of the love gripped in my heart
> and if I do not moan, so strong is the embrace, that I weep.
> Aḥmad is the obsession of all my nights and all my days,
> so deep is my devotion for Aḥmad that I dream of it and become delirious!
> Each night I weep, in my thirst for Aḥmad
> and, filled with love, I burst into tears and complaints.
> My lungs and liver are torn asunder because of Aḥmad
> to the point where they only hang by a thread, lest I die![48]

In these few verses, three Fulani terms are used for expressing feelings of love, and they characterise its various facets or phases. The first and most common, *gilli* (2nd and 4th verse), is associated with an emotion that affects the heart. The second, *beegeede* (3rd verse), corresponds to subtle and pure feelings of love experienced both by the poet and by God towards the Prophet. The third, *sawqu* (borrowed from the Arabic *shawq*, 'ardent desire') refers to the passionate desire to reach one's beloved.

In his poem X, M. A. Sou'âdou describes the least pure stage of love, the *sawqu*, but, this time, the risk of triviality provoked by this term – evoking the 'ardent desire' that dries up the heart – is quickly negated by metaphor, spun from end to end, playing on flora and on aquatic imagery:

> I wanted to create a poem of manly ardour
> and out of the sweetness of the love for the Prophet it was created.
> His love ran through my veins until it made me suffer
> until I perished like a wilted tree, dry and the first to be cut down.
> Like a breeze of the dry season has dried up a tree in a luscious wood,
> likewise we all fade under the torrid spell of our love for the Chosen-one.
> May this poem purify all the vices present in the heart
> and may it fill it with truths until, fully satisfied, this heart will overflow!

[48] Seydou, *La poésie mystique peule du Mali*, p. 358, vv. 19–22.

And may all persons with a vessel come rinse it properly, use it to draw water,
fill it, and load it on their head in order to drink and thus regain life.
May we let truth sprout from within, becoming beautiful and renewed,
/ . . . /
And once it is well watered, it will develop, spread its branches and its shade
then flower, bud, burgeon and bear fruit . . .
Then the fruit will ripen so that we can cut them and let them fall to enjoy and
may each passerby
select some, eat his fill, and be satisfied.
Sated, he will be filled with the strength to act, filled with endurance and
perseverance,
harnessed with seven shoulder belts, he will combat Satan and thus make
him flee.[49]

Here the poet still wants to be the privileged mediator; but since human language is ineffective in translating mystical experience, he complicates the metaphor: the truths his words wish to convey are holy water and fertile water; yet, in the plant imagery, the tree does not represent the devotee burning with love, but, rather the Truth sown in his heart, which, like the tree regenerated by water, will spread its branches, bear countless fruits, and then serve as spiritual provision for his disciples.

And, as we have seen throughout these passages, the two recurrent themes, Love and Truth, represent the two notions that drive every spiritual impulse. To convey them, several conventional motifs are often used: light (*nūr*) and illumination (Q. 24, 35, 57, 9 and 28, and so on), thirst and quenching.

Water and Light

The main metaphors are those related to water, but more precisely, those combining the elements of water and light.

Thus, in the verses above (pp. 4 and 5), the term 'quenched' and the two key words, 'Truth' and 'Light', mark the shift from a realistic and commonplace description of the impact of this ecstatic love – a truly spiritual intoxication that

[49] Seydou, *La poésie mystique peule du Mali*, pp. 382–4, vv. 5–13. The subsequent verses describe the seven harnesses that serve to preserve the sins caused by: hearing, seeing, and the heart, hands, legs, mouth and *pudenda*.

physically affects the poet – towards an imaginative evocation of his mission as mediator of revealed truths:

stricken by hiccups, I pour out the light of Muḥammad!
Through my wails I warn my parched loved ones: come drink!
He who to the Good was promised will surely be quenched by the light of
Muḥammad.[50]

This motif of quenching combined with light is apparent in all of these poems:

The Messenger drank abundantly from the light of Prophecy!
The Messenger drank abundantly from the light of the Apostolate!
The Messenger drank abundantly from the light of the Science of Truth!
The Messenger drank abundantly from the light of Humanity!
The Chosen-one also benefited from the light of a true soul
he, quenched by the light of felicity, expanded its sphere!
/ . . . /
the lights he diffuses have forever sealed his longevity!
He who, in the Lord, douses himself with truth, in truth, is indeed Aḥmad![51]

In contrast, the motif of thirst combined with darkness is equally as important when calling on others to adhere to the quest for Truth:

I am creating my own sermon for humans
who have succumbed to deceit, attaching themselves indefinitely to it
And abandoning the Truth however radiant in order to engage in the
terrifying wilderness of an ignorance that cannot even spark any light.
There, they suffer from tremendous thirst for having vowed themselves to
this ignorance.
/ . . . /
Deafened by thirst, they cannot be summoned to respond:
in the deep wilderness of ignorance, those to whom we speak will understand
nothing.[52]

50 Seydou, *La poésie mystique peule du Mali*, p. 396, vv. 16–17.
51 Seydou, *La poésie mystique peule du Mali*, p. 90, vv. 43–4.
52 Seydou, *La poésie mystique peule du Mali*, p. 340, vv. 4–7.

Other imaginative interpretations tied to water are found in the stream where one is immersed, as well as the beneficial downpour. Thus, the faithful who 'longs to follow the Messenger':

> will gird himself, putting all his energy into imitating him, his zeal and
>   resolve to search
> for a way to bathe in love, while his gusts of wind blow onto him
> until his heart is carried away by the torrent of the Chosen-one
> in turn, sinking or emerging in the flow of his thoughts for Aḥmad.
> I beg my Master to let me have this privilege and
> if I cannot swim in it, may I at least drink from a generous chalice.[53]

And Alfâ Bôkari Mahmoudou, in his poem directly addressed to God: 'Oh You, whose reign is eternal . . .', evokes his abundant acts of generosity using the following imagery:

> I will render an image of divine generosity
>   and understand this, oh humans!
>   / . . . /
> An immense cloud released its rain
>   a tornado poured down, doling itself out
>   pools and rivers were supplied,
>   and each was provided with what was intended for it.
> An uproar resounded in the wilderness
>   that even the ears of the deaf could hear
>   and the thirsty rejoiced in drinking
>   and were delivered of all thirst.[54]

What dominates is the association of all of these aquatic images with light and, especially, the light emanating from Aḥmad. In his devout exaltation, Alfâ Bôkari Mahmoudou exposes how Muḥammad is a refraction of God's Light:

[53] Seydou, *La poésie mystique peule du Mali*, p. 92, vv. 49–50.

[54] Seydou, *La poésie mystique peule du Mali*, p. 154, vv. 38–40.

Within you, Generous-Reed-Pen has drunk seven strengths
and the celestial canopy has received all its harmony from this double saturation.
With your light, the divine throne was inundated, beneath it, it expanded
And the seventy sails, Privileged-One, you are the one who saturated them, lavishing upon them up to your last drop
so greatly they draw their light, and this evermore, from Aḥmad![55]

You are the one who illuminated the sun . . ., the full moon . . ., the stars,
the Great Tablet . . ., the Horn-of-light . . ., the Kawthar . . .![56]

As for Mouhammadou Abdoullâye Sou'âdou, he describes the Chosen-one's ascension, straddling the Burāq,[57] in the eighth poem in his repertoire dedicated to the Prophet. The Prophets who came to greet him as saying:

from Aḥmad's light all creations owed their existence
such that, Canopy, Throne, Reed-Pen, and Tablets, everything likewise,
from the earth to the highest of heavens, thanks to Aḥmad, was illuminated . . .[58]

What may be seen as a hyperbole for some is the poet's aestheticisation of the theological concept of Muḥammad's Light (*al-anwār Muḥammadiyya*). This image reflects the exaltation abundantly expressed in these 'songs', whose authors' mystical impulses projected them into a world they could only describe using poetic language, appealing to the imagination in order to convey the complexities of these 'spiritual realities'.

[55] Seydou, *La poésie mystique peule du Mali*, p. 108, vv. 85–6.

[56] Thus, the poet attributes the Prophet with: if not all of creation, at least the light that illuminates both the realm of the stars and the divine: the Generous-Reed-Pen designates the supreme Reed Pen with which, according to tradition, God determined everyone's destiny on the Destiny Tablet. But here, it represents the divine Verb that was received and transmitted by the Prophet Muḥammad; the Great Tablet is the celestial tablet where all divine decrees figure or the sacred Tableau on which an angel records the actions of people; the Horn-of-light designates the Trumpet of the Last Judgement, as described by al-Ghazālī (*al-Durra al fākhira*, p. 38).

[57] Burāq, according to tradition, is the creature sent to Muḥammed for his celestial ascent.

[58] Seydou, *La poésie mystique peule du Mali*, p. 356, vv. 13–14.

This mystical poetry, with the spread of Sufi brotherhoods in Sub-Saharan Africa, appeals in all social strata of the population, from the most literate to the most humble. By sharing with their interlocutors the emotions drawn from their intimate and personal experiences, the poets inspired reviving the collective poetic dimension of faith. In order to reach both the mind and heart of human beings, the divine message is interpreted and communicated in poetic discourse. Symbolic, allegorical and metaphorical expression is the best way to convey and transmit a message that borders on the ineffable. The mediation of song adds to poetry's evocative power by bringing into vibration, in unison, the very being of both the one who delivers the message and the one who receives it. Both spiritually merge in this communion of faith, which indeed was the ultimate goal of these poets who are religious, mystical, and engaged.

Bibliography

Abitbol, Michel, *Tombouctou et les Arma. De la conquête marocaine du Soudan nigérien en 1591 à l'hégémonie de l'empire peul du Macina en 1833* (Paris: Maisonneuve et Larose, 1979).

Al-Ghazālī, Abū Ḥāmid Muḥammad. *Al-durra al-fākhira fī kashf ʿulūm al-ākhira* [La Perle précieuse, ou, Le livre des morts], trans. L. Gauthier (Leipzig: Otto Harrassowitz, 1925).

Al-Ḥallāj, Akhbār, *Recueil d'oraisons et d'exhortations du martyr mystique de l'islam Husayn Ibn Mansur Hallaj*, trans et annotation Louis Massignon and Paul Kraus (Paris: Éditions J. Vrin, collection 'Études musulmanes', [1957] 1975).

Anawati, G. C. and Gardet, Louis, *Mystique musulmane* (Paris: Librairie philosophique J. Vrin, 1968).

Bâ, Amadou Hampâté and Cardaire, Marcel, *Tierno Bokar, le sage de Bandiagara* (Paris: Présence africaine, 1957).

Bâ, Amadou Hampâté and Lilyan Kesteloot, *Kaïdara. Récit initiatique peul*, Classiques africains No. 7 (Paris: Julliard, distribué par Karthala, 1969).

Berque, Jacques, *Les dix grandes odes arabes de l'Anté-Islam. Les Muʿallaqât* traduites et présentées par Jacques Berque (Paris: Sindbad, La Bibliothèque arabe, 1979).

Brenner, Louis, *West African Sufi: The Religious Heritage and Spiritual Search of Cerno Bokar Saalif Taal* (London: Hurst, 1984).

Cuoq, Joseph M., *Les musulmans en Afrique* (Paris: Maisonneuve et Larose, 1975).

Cuoq, Joseph M., *Histoire de l'islamisation de l'Afrique de l'Ouest, des origines à la fin du XVIe siècle* (Paris: Geuthner, 1984).

Djian, Jean-Michel, *Les manuscrits de Tombouctou. Secrets, mythes et réalités* (Paris: JC Lattès, 2012).

Eguchi, Paul K. (trans.), *Poem of Repentance*, African Languages and ethnography IV (Tokyo: ILCAA, 1976).

Gaden, Henri, *Tyam Mohammadou Aliou, La Vie d'El Hadj Omar. Qacida en poular*, transcription, traduction, notes et glossaire, Henri Gaden (Paris: Institut d'ethnologie, 1935).

Haafkens, Johannes, *Chants musulmans en peul. Textes de l'héritage religieux de la communauté musulmane de Maroua. Cameroun* (Leiden: Brill, 1983).

Hiskett, Mervyn, *The Sword of Truth: The Life and Times of the Shehu Usuman Dan Fodio* (New York: Oxford University Press, 1973).

Hunwick, John. O., *Arabic Literature of Africa: The Writings of Western Sudanic Africa*, vol. 4 (Leiden: Brill, 2003).

Kane, Ousmane and Triaud, Jean-Louis, *Islam et islamismes au sud du Sahara* (Paris: IREMAN-Karthala-MSH, 1998).

Kermani, Navid, *God is Beautiful: The Aesthetic Experience of Quran*, trans. Tony Crawford (Malden, MA: Polity, 2015).

Laoust, Henri, *Essai sur les doctrines sociales et politiques de Taki-d-Din Ahmad b. Taimiya*: a Canoniste hanbalite né à Harran en 661/1262, mort à Damas en 728/1328 (Le Caire: Recherches d'archéologie, de philologie et d'histoire, t. X, 1939).

Levtzion, Nehemia, *Islam in West Africa: Religion, Society and Politics to 1800* (Aldershot: Variorum, 1994).

Piga, Adriana, *Les voies du soufisme au sud du Sahara*, Parcours historiques et anthropologiques, Préface Louis Triaud (Paris: les Éditions Karthala, 2006).

Robinson, David, *La guerre sainte d'al-Hajj Umar* (Paris: Karthala, 1988).

Robinson, David and Triaud, Jean-Louis (eds), *Le temps des marabouts. Itinéraires et stratégies islamiques en Afrique occidentale française, 1880–1960* (Paris: Karthala, 1997).

Sanankoua, Bintou, *Un empire peul au XIXe siècle. La Diina du Maasina* (Paris: Karthala, 1990).

Schmidt, Jean-Jacques, *Les Mou'allaqât, poésie arabe préislamique* (Paris: Seghers, 1978).

Seydou, Christiane, '*Majjaado Alla gaynaali*, poème en langue peule du Foûta-Djalon', *Cahiers d'Études Africaines* 24(6) (1966): 643–81.

Seydou, Christiane, '"Le Chameau" : poème mystique ou . . . pastoral?' in *Itinérances en pays peul et ailleurs*, Mélanges à la mémoire de Pierre-Francis Lacroix, réunis par l'ERA 246 du CNRS (Paris: Mémoires de la Société des Africanistes, 1981), vol. 2, pp. 25–52.

Seydou, Christiane, *Bergers des mots, poésie peule du Massina*, Classiques africains 24 (Paris: Les Belles Lettres, distribué par Karthala, 1991).

Seydou, Christiane, 'Poésie religieuse et inspiration populaire chez les Peuls du Foûta-Djalon', *Journal of African Cultural Studies* 14(1) (2001): 23–47.

Seydou, Christiane, 'Prône contre le tabac. Un manuscrit peul du fonds Vieillard', in Pascal Boyeldieu and Pierre Nougayrol (eds), *Langues et cultures. Terrains d'Afrique*, hommages à France Cloarec-Heiss, Collection Afrique et Langage No. 7 (Louvain and Paris: Peeters, 2004), pp. 147–53.

Seydou, Christiane, *La poésie mystique peule du Mali*, Introduction Louis Brenner (Paris: Karthala, 2008).

Sow, Alfâ Ibrâhîm, *La Femme, la Vache, la Foi*, Classiques africains 5 (Paris: Julliard, distribué par Karthala, 1966).

Sow, Alfâ Ibrâhîm, *Le Filon du bonheur éternel* par Mouhammadou-Samba Mombéyâ, Classiques africains 10 (Paris: Armand Colin, distribué par Karthala, 1971).

Triaud, Jean-Louis and David Robinson (eds), *La Tijâniyya. Une confrérie musulmane à la conquête de l'Afrique* (Paris: Karthala, 2000).

Trimingham, J. Spencer, *A History of Islam in West Africa* (Oxford: Oxford University Press, 1974).

Willis, John Ralph (ed.), *Studies in West African Islamic History, vol. 1: The Cultivators of Islam; vol. 2: The Evolution of Islamic Institutions; vol. 3: The Growth of Arabic Literature* (London: Frank Cass, 1979).

6

VANISHING ART, GENRE-MAKING: THE UYGHUR STORYTELLING TRADITION AND ITS HERITAGISATION

Musapir[1]

In 2009, tens of thousands of people came from all over the Uyghur homeland to the annual festival at the *mazar* (shrine) of Imam Asim in the Khotan desert to pray, heal, make merit and be a part of the community. During the festival, this holy land was transformed into an animated bazaar where merchants sold their wares to pilgrims, and where musicians, storytellers, and other talented individuals gathered crowds to showcase their skills and crafts. Among the activities such as games, children playing and Sufi rituals, it was hard to miss the crowds that gathered around a handful of storytellers. Hundreds of men, women and children sat on the sand, some eating snacks, focusing on an old man in the centre playing instruments and performing lively stories. I was captivated by his facial expressions and hand gestures, the fast-changing pace of the music, and the audience's dramatic and emotional responses, which included tears. After the performance, I interviewed the storyteller and asked for the name of the story. He said it was a *dastan* about the hero Siyit Nochi. Another storyteller explained that it was the *Qisse of Fatima*. I had learned about the oral literature forms called *dastan* and *qisse* from books and had read written versions when I was growing up. But my visit to the Imam Asim Mazar festival was the first time I had seen a

[1] Musapir is the pen name of the author of this chapter.

live performance and a deeply engaged audience response. I returned there every Thursday in May 2009 and listened to many other storytelling performances. I was struck between the mismatch between what I had read and what storytellers told me, as well as what I saw and heard in their vibrant performances infused with Islam.

Dastan (*dástán*, *dāstān*), *qisse* (*qissah*) and *hikmet* (*hikāyat*) are forms of oral literature combining narrative and music.[2] Wide-ranging in content and style, and performed in many different spaces, from shrines and mosques to marketplaces, construction sites and private homes, they have circulated in various languages and forms, both oral and written, through what are today Iran, Turkey, South Asia and Central Asia.[3] Uyghur ethnographer Qurban Metturdi argues that Central Asian communities, including the Uyghurs, historically accepted and developed the flourishing storytelling tradition along with Islam and Sufism, integrating their existing unique musical styles, stories, and religious beliefs and practices, all of which continued to develop and change.[4] These expressive traditions are therefore what we might consider

[2] I use Romanised spellings without accents in conformity with the system generally used in Uyghur studies (and Central Asian studies more generally).

[3] On the Indo-Persian context, see Pasha M. Khan, *The Broken Spell: Indian Storytelling and the Romance Genre in Persian and Urdu* (Detroit, MI: Wayne State University Press, 2019); Julia Rubanovich, 'Tracking the Shahnama Tradition in Medieval Persian Folk Prose', in Charles Melville, Gabrielle van den Berg and Julia Rubanovich (eds), *Shahnama Studies* (Leiden: Brill, 2011), pp. 11–35; Qurat-ul-Ain Shirazi and Ghulam Sarwar Yousof, 'Historical and Cultural Relevance of the Adventures of Amir Hamza', *International Journal of English and Literature* 4(6) (2013): 259–63; Quratulain Shirazi, 'Reconfiguring Dástán Tradition as a Commemorative Narrative of Power Structures, Charismatic Leadership, and Sainthood in North India', *Journal of Religion and Popular Culture* 28(2/3) (2016): 145–62. On the Turkic/Central Asian context, see Hasan Bülent Paksoy, *Alpamysh: Central Asian Identity Under Russian Rule* (Pittsburgh, PA: Association for the Advancement of Central Asian Research, 1989); Alexandre Papas, *Thus Spake the Dervish: Sufism, Language, and the Religious Margins in Central Asia, 1400–1900* (Leiden: Brill, 2019); Karl Reichl, *Singing the Past: Turkic and Medieval Epic Poetry* (Ithaca, NY: Cornell University Press, 2000); UNESCO, 'Arts of the Meddah, Public Storytellers', 2008, available at: https://ich.unesco.org/en/RL/arts-of-the-meddah-public-storytellers-00037.

[4] Qurban Metturdi, '维吾尔族说唱艺术' (Lexicological Analysis of Uyghur Meddah)', *Journal of the Central Academy of Drama* 2(148) (2013): 26–30.

as part of an evolving 'Muslim-but-not-only'[5] World Literature complex,[6] transcending national borders and taking on localised forms. As performative traditions rooted in both oral and written culture and incorporating a breadth of genres (poetic, narrative, musical) and forms of knowledge (religious, historical, cultural, philosophical, ethical), *dastan*, *qisse* and *hikmet* also transcend 'literature' in the narrow modernist sense.[7]

While much of the scholarship on *dastan* and *qisse* takes a historical perspective, I have been studying them as part of the living culture of the Uyghur homeland, today governed as the Xinjiang Uyghur Autonomous Region (hereafter Xinjiang) under the People's Republic of China. Among Uyghurs, as among other Indigenous communities, oral tradition is a way to convey traditional knowledge and to form and strengthen their communities. To be a storyteller, what we call *meddah*, *qissekhan*, *dastanchi*, *wahiz* and *büwi*, has for centuries been a venerated profession in which Islamic culture and faith is deeply embedded. Yet in English-language scholarship on Indo-Persian *dastan* and *qisse*, these traditions have commonly been defined or referred to as a 'romance' genre, while in work on Turkey and Central Asia, they are largely introduced as romances and epic tales. In his contribution to this volume, Khan discusses the 'epistemologically based devaluation' of *qisse* (or *qissah*) in India under British colonialism. Defined as belonging to the Orientalising world-literary 'romance' genre, *qisse* was 'consigned to little more than antiquarian significance', representing a backward, irrational and superstitious world 'that Europe had left behind for modernity'. This view of *qisse* became dominant among Indian as well as British elites, superseding the understanding and value of *qisse* as articulated by Persian- and Urdu-language storytellers.

In this chapter, I turn to examine *dastan*, *qisse* and *hikmet* as vanishing expressive traditions under contemporary Chinese communist settler colonialism, and the epistemic violence caused by efforts to integrate them into

[5] Pasha M. Khan, 'A Fine Romance', Chapter 11, this volume.

[6] See the introduction to this volume, Chapter 1.

[7] On the more general problem of Islamic literature exceeding restrictive Eurocentric definitions of literature, see Sarah Bin Tyeer and Claire Gallien's introduction, Chapter 1, to this volume.

the 'world' of the multinational Chinese nation and its world heritage – world heritage like world literature being organised on the premise of national traditions. My aim is twofold. First, to introduce *dastan*, *qisse* and *hikmet* and the professional storytellers who are the carriers of these traditions, based on my observations of performances and interviews with contemporary Uyghur storytellers between 2008 and 2016. These storytellers have been practising this profession for life and I have tried to understand how they frame their art and how they explain their stories and their craft. I argue that it should be understood as a holistic expressive heritage and epistemology. Second, to critically examine the documentation, categorisation and heritagisation of Uyghur storytelling by Uyghur folklorists working under the constraints of Chinese Communist Party ideology and policy, and to show what has been rendered invisible in the process. In particular, I highlight how these processes have divorced the Uyghur storytelling tradition from the Islamic culture and practices integral to both its literary content and its meaning and practice in everyday life.

Dastan, Qisse and *Hikmet*

In the years following my visit to the Imam Asim Mazar festival, I visited many other *mazar* festivals, bazaars and Sufi gatherings, listening to many other stories, and interviewing more storytellers to understand the depths of this performative tradition. What captured my attention was how they explained the stories to me. As had been the case at Imam Asim Mazar, storytellers did not provide consistent information about genre; the same story might be called a *qisse* by some, and a *dastan* by others. Similar to Khan in his historical research on the Indo-Persian context, I found that definitions of the terms *dastan*, *qisse* and *hikmet* could 'slide toward each other along a continuum', with a considerable area of overlap.[8] This was not only in terms of their respective length as Khan notes, but also depended on the social context in which they were performed. What was a *qisse* or *dastan* at a *mazar* might be a *hikmet* at a funeral. While I provide a brief introduction to these art forms here, this fluidity is important to bear in mind as these three forms exist and inform each other as part of a greater body of work. Storytellers

[8] Khan, *The Broken Spell*, p. 9.

themselves showed little interest in classifying or defining their verbal art or their profession. What excited them were the content, music and details of the story.

Khan's conceptualisation of *dastan* and *qisse* as an encompassing 'verbal art' to emphasise their performativity,[9] is very much relatable to Uyghur storytelling traditions. While he writes from a historical Persian and Urdu perspective, I noticed remarkable similarities between his account of those expressive cultures and those that I witnessed being performed among contemporary Uyghurs. In the Uyghur context, *dastan* can refer to literary works that narrate certain events in a poetic way,[10] such as the *Qutadgubilik* by the eleventh-century philosopher Yusuf Khas Hajib, and the *dastan* of Parhad-Sherin by the fifteenth-century poet Alisher Navai.[11] *Dastan* is also the largest oral narrative tradition among Uyghurs. *Dastan* can tell an immense range of stories, including tales of lovers, religious figures and warriors among many others. The main events of the complex stories that oral *dastan* dramatically recount are narrated in prose, while the inner lyrical feelings of the characters are expressed in poetic language. These poetic parts are rhythmically accompanied by traditional Uyghur musical instruments. The flexibility of *dastan* storytelling is considerable, making improvisation possible in order to highlight certain episodes. Performances can be prolonged or shortened, although it is not acceptable to change central details such as the name of the hero, his spiritual journey or the main war. Many *dastans* have different variants according to the local oasis region in which they are performed, such as in the accompanying music (*ahang*) and dialect. *Ahang bek muhnim* ('the melody is very important') is a remark I heard often among Uyghur Elders.

Uyghur scholars make a clear distinction between written and oral *dastan*. According to Osman Ismail Tarim, written *dastan* are always created entirely in poetics. In contrast, oral *dastans* – which he refers to as 'folk *dastan*' – are a mixture of prose and rhyme, strong in musical tone, and disseminated orally

9 Khan, *The Broken Spell*, p. 1.

10 Osman Ismail Tarim, personal communication, 2009.

11 See Yusuf Khas Hajib, *Wisdom of Royal Glory (Kutadgu Bilig): A Turko-Islamic Mirror for Princes*, trans. Robert Dankoff (Chicago: University of Chicago Press, 1983), for a translation of *Qutadqubilik* (*Kutadqu Biliq*).

by dedicated professional performers.[12] This makes them much more complex, colourful and well received by ordinary Uyghurs, Tarim claims.[13] Unless otherwise specified, in this chapter I am referring to these oral *dastans*.[14] However, it is important to emphasise that there is a reciprocal relationship between Uyghur written and oral literary culture, which feed and borrow from each other,[15] as was also the case in Persian and Urdu *qisse* traditions.[16] Storytellers would read literary works and improvise from them, while classical writers would hear and write the stories that they performed. I also found that storytellers would write down *dastan*s to circulate among their students and, more recently, to document and preserve stories that they are no longer able to perform (a point to which I will return).

During my fieldwork, I found that religious and historically themed *dastan*s were the most popular among everyday Uyghur audiences. The different *dastan*s that I heard included two of the most popular, *Abdurrahman Pasha* and *Siyit Nochi*, both local heroes who fought against Qing rulers in late nineteenth-century Khotan and Kashgar. I saw these *dastan*s as a precious window onto Uyghur history and epistemology. Similarly, in the Qomol region in northeastern Xinjiang, heroic *dastan*s had continued to be popular, such as those of Yachibeg and Omer Batur,[17] both of whom were rebellious figures and

[12] Osman Ismail Tarim, 'The Types of Uyghur Folk Dastan' *Journal of Xinjiang University* 32(4) (2012): 1–8.

[13] Tarim, 'The Types of Uyghur Folk Dastan'.

[14] For an introduction to Uyghur *dastan* that emphasises the traditions of repertoire, pedagogy and performance practices in terms of content and melody, see Rahile Dawut and Elise Anderson, 'Dastan Performance Among the Uyghurs', in Elmira Köchümkulova, Saida Daukeyeva and Theodore Levin (eds), *The Music of Central Asia* (Bloomington: Indiana University Press, 2015), p. 468. For accompanying video excerpts of several different *dastan* performances filmed between 2009 and 2010, see Rahile Dawut and Elise Anderson, 'Audio & Video Tracks: Dastan Performance among the Uyghurs', *The Music of Central Asia*, 2015, available at: https://www.musicofcentralasia.org/Tracks/Chapter/24.

[15] On the connection between the oral and the written in Uyghur culture more generally, see Rian Thum, *The Sacred Routes of Uyghur History* (Cambridge, MA: Harvard University Press, 2014).

[16] See Khan, *The Broken Spell.*

[17] See at: https://www.uyghur-archive.com/diyarim/bbs/diyarim7250.html.

leaders of the Qomol farmers' revolt who fought against the Zunghar Mongols in the seventeenth century. As one storyteller in Qomol put it, 'heroes die but their stories do not'.

Religiosity is ingrained in Uyghur *dastan* performances, most of which at least start or end with prayers. Although Uyghurs are usually described as Sunni Muslims, Shia Islamic motifs and narratives such as the stories of Ali and Fatima and their sons Hasan and Husayn are very popular in Uyghur *dastan* traditions. These stories were until recently performed not only at large *mazar* pilgrimages but also in smaller gatherings, for example, as an integral part of funeral ceremonies. They are poetically written with a rhythmic nature and are attributed to Ahmat Yesewi (1093–1166), who founded the first Turkic-Sufi order, or to other Sufi literary legends. As one storyteller told me in 2009, 'Yesewi wrote 4,444 *dastan* for us, but only 400 of them came to us.' Yesewi's poetry is widely circulated among Uyghurs and is embedded in many rituals and storytelling traditions.

Dastan and *qisse* are often used as interchangeable terms for stories about prophets and Islamic saints by storytellers. In the Uyghur language, *qisse* has multiple meanings and broad connotations just like *dastan*. Many *dastan* of particular figures are also referred to as *qisse*, for example, *Qisse of Chin Moden*, *Qisse of Tumur Khalipe* or *Qisse of Prophet Muḥammad*. A common recurring expression in many *dastans* is '*el-qisse*', meaning 'this *qisse* continues as such', which is frequently used by storytellers to create a pause before changing the characters, location or the direction of the story. The *Dictionary of the Uyghur Language*, created by Uyghur cultural elites, defines *qisse* as an epic narrative created in the style of legend and myth.[18] When I was growing up, I frequently encountered the word *qisse* in the titles of books, plays, movies and television series that told historical stories. For example, the well-known Chinese novel *Sanguo Yanyi*, or *The Three Kingdoms*,[19] is translated in Uyghur as *Uch Padishahliq Heqqide Qisse*. I also enjoyed reading the *qisses* of the reformist Islamic educator Abdukadir Damolla (1862–1924) and of Nuzugum, a nineteenth-century

[18] *Dictionary of the Uyghur Language*, vol. 3 (Beijing: Minzu chubanshe, 1990), p. 425.

[19] *Sanguo Yanyi* is more commonly known in English as *The Romance of Three Kingdoms*.

female Uyghur hero said to have been martyred by the Qing emperor.[20] As a young Uyghur, I therefore understood *qisse* to be synonymous with historical stories. Later, through first-hand experience and discussions with locals, I learned that *qisse* is more than just a genre of historical storytelling. A *qisse* is a story, a legend and even a way of expressing certain events, which involves grand narratives along with a personal biography.

Despite these broader meanings, among storytellers I found that *qisse* was primarily associated with the stories of the prophets of Islam. Perhaps the biggest *qisse* text, familiar to every Uyghur, is *Qissesul Enbiya*, the *Qisse of Prophets*. I remember this as my grandparents' favourite book to read aloud to us and to ask us to read to them. It was so famous that when I asked Elders what they knew about *qisse*, or what is *qisse*, they often asked if I was referring to the *Qisse of Prophets*. The Uyghur version, published in 1981, is based on the Chagatai (eastern Turkish) manuscript written in 1310 by Nesiridin Rabghuzi.[21] This is just one of many versions of the *Qisse of Prophets*, which has been described as a 'genre' in and of itself.[22] The Rabghuzi text contains forty-four *qisse*s of different prophets and saints in Islamic history. In his review of a 1995 edition with English translation, Dankoff remarks on the popularity of Rabghuzi's text among readers of Chagatai since it was first completed in the fourteenth century, as well as its importance for Turkologists and 'all interested in Islamic cultural history'.[23] Among contemporary Uyghur storytellers, the popularity of this book had made *qisse* almost synonymous with stories of prophets, which were most commonly performed at *mazar*s and Sufi gatherings, and in other religious spaces.

While *dastan* and *qisse* are some of the lengthier forms of Uyghur oral folk literature, *hikmet* is a shorter variation, as is also generally the case in the

[20] See Kate Abramson, 'Gender, Uyghur Identity, and the Story of Nuzugum', *Journal of Asian Studies* 71(4) (2012): 1069–91.

[21] For a critical edition of this text with accompanying English translation and glossary, see Nesiridin Rabghuzi, *The Stories of the Prophets: Qisas al-Anbiya: An Eastern Turkish Version*, trans. and ed. H. E. Boeschoten, M. Vandamme and S. Tezcan (Leiden: Brill, 1995).

[22] See, for example, Micheal Pregill, '*Qiṣaṣ al-Anbiyā*' as Genre and Discourse. From the Qur'ān to Elijah Muhammad', *Mizan* 2(1) (2017).

[23] Robert Dankoff, 'Review: Ragbhuzi's Stories of the Prophets', *Journal of the American Oriental Society* 117(1) (1997): 115.

Indo-Persian context.[24] The literal meaning of *hikmet*, an Arabic loanword, is wisdom, philosophy, rationale and/or underlying reason.[25] The *Dictionary of the Uyghur Language* provides a similar definition: wise, knowledgeable and the understanding of something difficult or hidden.[26] However, as a type of expressive culture or verbal art, *hikmet* are Sufi poems that convey Islamic philosophy and stories of prophets or saints. They are more poetic than *qisse* and much shorter than *dastan*. However, as with *dastan* and *qisse*, there is overlap and fluidity. Text and music understood to be *qisse* in one context is understood and performed as *hikmet* in another. In particular, stories about the day or event of a central character's death are *qisse* or *dastan* when performed at *mazar*s, but *hikmet* at funerals. The most obvious example is the *Qisse of Karbala*, which is performed as part of the *hälqä-sohbät* ritual and identified as *hikmet* in those ritual settings. The *Qisse of Fatima's Death* and the *Qisse of the Death of Prophet Muḥammed* are also widely performed *hikmet* at funerals in southern Xinjiang. Rachel Harris experienced the performance of *hikmet* during her fieldwork in a village in southern Xinjiang in 2009, as well as among Uyghur diasporic communities in Central Asia in 2015/16. She notes that they are put to song and music and play 'a part in rituals of mourning and healing, and as a part of regular spiritual practice in both men's and women's gatherings'.[27] As a child, I always wanted to attend funerals since I found great interest and beauty in the stories and melodies of *hikmet*, which remind us that everyone dies. I clearly remember the strong emotional response they provoked, which Harris identifies as both grief and 'awe of God's power'.[28]

As this brief summary of *dastan*, *qisse* and *hikmet* shows, there exists a fluid nature between all three performative art forms. During my upbringing and fieldwork, I cannot recall any storyteller consciously declaring the genre

[24] Khan, *The Broken Spell*, pp. 9–10.

[25] Hans Wehr, *A Dictionary of Modern Written Arabic, Arabic–English*, ed. J. Milton Cowan (Wiesbaden: Harrassowitz, 1980), p. 197.

[26] *Dictionary of the Uyghur Language*, vol. 2, p. 580.

[27] Rachel Harris, 'Text and Performance in the Hikmät of Khoja Ahmad Yasawi', *Rast Musicology Journal* 7(2) (2019): 2152. See also Rachel Harris, *Soundscapes of Uyghur Islam* (Bloomington: Indiana University Press, 2020), p. 70.

[28] Harris, Soundscapes of Uyghur Islam, p. 33.

of his performance before or after he began. They are consistently borrowing from each other in terms of format and content as part of a holistic expressive verbal art intertwined with Islamic culture and practice.

Genre-making, Heritagisation and Erasure

Although *dastan*, *qisse* and *hikmet* have been integrated into Uyghurs' everyday lives, there have been very few written transcriptions of them, let alone systematic research, and they have generally been excluded from textbooks and collections of Uyghur folk literature. The late Abdukerim Rahman (1941–2020), for example, created a highly influential categorisation of Uyghur folk literature into eleven genres, inspired by the 'father of Chinese folklore studies' Zhong Jingwen.[29] This system became embedded in pre- and post-secondary school Uyghur textbooks and incorporated a wide range of oral literature from legends, myths, epic poems and fables to didactic humorous stories, jokes, boasts, proverbs and riddles. But the kind of story performances I saw at Imam Asim are entirely absent; they are not even included as an example. As far as I have seen, they are also excluded from the anthologies of oral literature compiled by local state cultural bureaus, from the regional down to township level. The reasons for their exclusion are complex and worthy of more detailed discussion elsewhere. Suffice it here to note that it relates in part to their strong connections to Sufism, which is marginalised in the Uyghur context. Sufism has been criticised by Uyghur intellectuals and opposed by Islamic revivalists, as well as targeted by the Chinese state, to the extent that many Uyghurs hide their Sufi identity.[30]

Despite the general marginalisation of Uyghur storytelling traditions, there were efforts among Uyghur folklorists, including Abdukerim Rahman, to collect them, resulting in the publication of collections of 'representative' *dastan* as a genre of Uyghur folk literature. These efforts started in the early 1960s. In an interview, Abdukerim Rahman said that he and other Uyghur folklorists wanted to document and publish these stories before they disappeared, but they were under the intense pressure of the Maoist political campaigns of the day. This led them to exclude what they thought might be too

[29] Abdukerim Rahman, *Uyghur Folklore* (Urumqi: Xinjiang University Press, 2002).

[30] I will examine this triple marginalisation of Uyghur Sufism more fully in a future publication.

'superstitious' and religious, keeping only the main narrative and standardising and modernising the language. During the Cultural Revolution, many of the stories they had collected were lost. Following the reinstitution of folklore studies in China in 1978,[31] the process restarted and several volumes of collected *dastan* were published, most in the 1990s and 2000s. However, these collections do not even come close to illustrating the deep cultural meaning of *dastan* as embedded in our daily lives. The versions documented by Swedish Turkologist Gunnar Jarring (1907–2002) in the late 1920s and 1930s are much closer to the stories I heard performed than those published by Uyghur folklorists.

First, a considerable amount of what defines these verbal arts was left out, including the music, performance practice, variations, and their social contexts and functions. As Michael Long examines in his study of the canonisation of the Mongol Janggar epic, when Chinese government agencies and local cultural elites began collecting and publishing oral folk literature in the late 1970s and early 1980s, they narrowed verbal art down to a written format, treating it 'as an oral *text* rather than as a socially implicated performance'.[32] In the published collections of *dastan* we find no reference to music, performance context, local variation or lineage of transmission – elements deemed by storytellers to be central to *dastan*. Abdukerim Rahman explained that for the purposes of publication they also changed the language to a more standard literary language. This process of textualisation of oral tradition is, of course, not unique to China. In their introduction to the vast and diverse musical and performative history of northern Indian art forms, Francesca Orsini and Katherine Schofield note how texts that had once been 'recited, sung, danced, and enacted have been territory ceded to scholars of literature and religion, who have generally acknowledged their aural and performative dimensions but gone little further'.[33] Texts become fixed and come

[31] See Michael D. R. Long, 'Finding the "Epic of Jangar": The Literary Construction of an Early Oirat Epic in the Xinjiang Uyghur Autonomous Region', *Asian Ethnicity* 22(1) (2021): 90–104.

[32] Long, 'Finding the "Epic of Jangar"', p. 94.

[33] Francesa Orsini and Katherine Butler Schofield, *Tellings and Texts: Music, Literature, and Performance in North India* (Cambridge: OpenBooks, 2015), p. 4.

to 'appear to exist in separate domains sealed by boundaries of script and literacy', rather than as works that circulated 'thanks to oral transmission, translation, exposition, and memorisation'.[34]

Secondly, the folklorists were working under the constraints of national political interests and Chinese Communist Party ideology, which required them to 'separate the "healthy" from the "reactionary", and to criticize "backward and reactionary elements" and "eliminate them" through their revision work.'[35] Religious content, themes and language were a particular target for elimination, as religiosity has long been attributed as backwards, superstitious or feudal in the national narrative of China as a modern atheist nation-state; religion has also been increasingly tightly regulated since the 1980s. Since *qisse* and *hikmet* were implicitly defined as 'religious' they were excluded from official published collections and have been rendered largely invisible. Although religiosity also runs through *dastan*, through a careful process of selection and revision, folklorists were able to construct *dastan* as a genre of folk literature associated with romance, in particular love stories, or as belonging to the world folk epic tradition, akin to the Mongol Janggar, Kyrghz Manas, Greek Iliad or Tibetan Gesar epos.

Any stories that folklorists were worried might be politically sensitive or problematic were excluded – not only the stories of prophets and saints, but also the widely performed *dastan* of heroes who had led local revolts. But the process of erasing 'problematic' content from *dastan* went beyond the careful selection of particular stories, characters and events as representative. It also involved changing the language and way of narrating to erase any explicitly Islamic content, themes or frames. For example, in the original version of the famous love story *Gherip Senem*, prayer often frames the characters' actions and time is marked by the five daily Islamic prayers. But in the revised version, 'At the time of morning prayer . . . [this happened]' was changed to 'After the sunrise . . . [this happened].' In the original version, when Senem is longing for her lover, she prays to Allah. In the printed version, she cries.

With the rise of a global intangible cultural heritage (ICH) industry in the 2000s, the Chinese Communist Party was eager to promote its version

[34] Orsini and Schofield, *Tellings and Texts*, p. 9.

[35] Long, 'Finding the "Epic of Jangar"', p. 98.

of the Chinese nation's multi-ethnic 'Chinese' ICH on the world stage.[36] This created space for Uyghur folklorists to document Uyghur verbal arts as living tradition and performance. In 2004, China became a signatory to UNESCO's 2003 Convention for the Safeguarding of the ICH of humanity. Over the following years, renowned ethnographer Rahile Dawut, who had been visiting *mazars* since 1995, secured funding from the World Oral Literature Project and the Firebird Foundation to document variations of Uyghur *dastan* in their authentic settings, creating a research centre at Xinjiang University. Uyghur cultural elites put great efforts into enlisting various forms of cultural expression as ICH, including *dastan*, since this would place them under legal protection and provide access to state funding. Osman Ismail Tarim attempted to highlight the richness of *dastan* beyond romance by developing a categorisation based on their contents and themes: heroic *dastan*, love *dastan*, historic *dastan* and advisory *dastan* to name a few.[37] Nevertheless, in its successful applications to enlist *dastan* as ICH at the regional level (2007) and then national level (2009), the Xinjiang Folk Literature Association primarily promoted love *dastan*s as '*dastan*'. This inadvertently narrowed the definition of what should and could be 'safeguarded' following the enlistment.

Ultimately Uyghur folklorists were hoping to mirror the success of the Kyrgyz Manas epic, which was inscribed on the UNESCO representative ICH of humanity list under China in 2009,[38] along with the Tibetan Gesar epic tradition.[39] However, the complexity of the language and music of *dastan*s and their sheer variety posed challenges. Moreover, it was in 2009 that the limited space for Uyghur religious and cultural expression started to contract following inter-ethnic violence in Urumqi, the capital of Xinjiang. There was a further push to cleanse *dastan* of all religious and historical elements, placing the emphasis on music and romance in the

[36] Anon., 'You Shall Sing and Dance: Contested "Safeguarding" of Uyghur Intangible Cultural Heritage', *Asian Ethnicity* 22(1) (2020): 121–39.

[37] Tarim, 'The Types of Uyghur Folk Dastan'.

[38] See at: https://ich.unesco.org/en/RL/manas-00209. Kyrgyzstan was subsequently successful in having *Manas* separately listed in 2013 as one of the Kyrgyz epic trilogy. See at: https://ich.unesco.org/en/RL/kyrgyz-epic-trilogy-manas-semetey-seytek-00876.

[39] See at: https://ich.unesco.org/en/RL/gesar-epic-tradition-00204.

belief that it might still be possible to achieve UNESCO status. But the political climate for Uyghurs continued to worsen with China's launch of its so-called People's War on Terror (*renmin fankong zhanzheng*) in 2014 and anti-extremism campaign. In 2017, almost all Uyghur folklorists who had been working on heritagisation and documentation efforts, including Rahile Dawut and Abdukerim Rahman, were arrested or disappeared.

The construction of folk literature genres, especially for the sake of categorising cultural heritage and deciding what is worthy of preservation, is an inherently colonial way of studying Indigenous heritage. It diminishes its power and complexity and role in Uyghur life. By recording, documenting and publishing what they could, Uyghur folklorists have at least salvaged parts of the Uyghur storytelling tradition. But in the process of constructing *dastan* as a folk literature genre and form of 'Chinese' world heritage from sanitised fragments, Uyghur verbal arts have been divorced from the world of Islamic cultures and practices. The risk is that these state-approved fragments come to stand in for the whole, rendering much of the Uyghur storytelling tradition invisible, and superseding its meaning and importance as circulated and practised in the community for generations. For me, this was heart-wrenchingly visible during fieldwork in 2015 and 2016, when I found storytellers attempting to survive (politically and economically) by learning and reciting from published *dastan*, rather than performing what they had learned from their masters. But before going on to discuss this erosion of the Uyghur storytelling profession, we will first turn to examine it in its broader performative and historical context among Uyghurs and in the broader Islamic world.

Performance of Music and Narrative: *meddah, dastanchi, qissekhan, büwi*

Dastan, *qisse*, and *hikmet* as a living tradition are performed and transmitted by artists variously known among Uyghurs as *meddah*, *dastanchi*, *qissekhan*, *waiz*, *ashiq*, *elneghme* and *büwi*. Although Uyghur elites trying to theorise those terms made clear distinctions between them during our interviews, these distinctions always mismatched what I saw and heard from practitioners. In my experience, artists and members of the public usually used terms interchangeably or according to context, with variations common in different regions. For example, in Khotan *dastanchi* and *waiz* were used interchangeably, in Kashgar, *dastanchi* and *elneghme*. In my conversations with storytellers, it became clear that they had multiple identities. Most identified as Sufi or *elneghme* (lit: folk artists), while some also called themselves *meddah*, *waiz* or *dastanchi*. Some identified as healers or *bahshi*. The exception to this fluidity was the term *büwi* as it is reserved exclusively for women, who perform in private spaces; the *meddah*, *dastanchi* and *qissekhan* who perform at *mazar*, *bazaar* and *meshrep* are male. Despite this fluidity in the use of terms, my impression was that the categorisation and heritagisation of *dastan*, combined with the politicisation of religiosity, had led to *dastanchi* becoming the more common and preferred term (a point to which I will return).

Given the fluidity in terms on the ground and the politics of public self-identification, I use the generic English term 'storyteller' to refer to these artists. However, it should be emphasised that, as cultural gatekeepers who express tremendous talent in music, melody and dramatic performance, they are doing much more than telling a story. While performing a *dastan*, for example, a single skilled storyteller is able to convincingly perform the roles of numerous characters. They will often perform a few pieces of music before commencing a *dastan* performance, and a few storytellers will usually come together to support each other's performances.[40] Hearing the music, people nearby realise that a *dastan* is about to be performed and gather in a circle around the storyteller. In the past, *dastans* might be performed over a period of several days; every day the audience returned, hoping to hear the end. For local cultural gatherings, hosts would find the best storyteller in town to act as host and perform until the next morning as most of the guests would stay overnight. Many storytellers would also perform for the village where they were labouring (*hashar*) in the fields or building roads or canals. As well as creating a vibrant and vivid form of performance art, these artists almost always appeared to lead Islamic rituals and act as spiritual healers.

Storytellers in Islamic cultures are often thought of as male, but among Uyghurs female storytellers, or *büwi*, perform *dastan* or *hikmet* in much smaller, closed Sufi gatherings such as *dhikir* or *khetme* ceremonies.[41] They

[40] See also Dawut and Anderson, 'Dastan Performance'.

[41] Harris speaks of *khetme* (*khätmä*) as a recitation from the Qur'ān with emotional and spiritual significance among Uyghur women. Harris, *Soundscapes of Uyghur Islam*, pp. 58–60.

are generally women with deep religious knowledge. My grandmother was a *büwi*. She would lead the act of washing bodies for funerals and performed numerous *hikmet* at *nezir* (Uyghur mourning ceremonies) and other cultural gatherings. She had many students to whom she taught the Qur'ān, *hikmet* and other religious knowledge. As Harris puts it, "[*büwi*] are respected women within the local community who perform rituals of cleansing or expulsion, mourning and commemoration, and prepare the bodies of deceased women for burial."[42] One *büwi* I interviewed in 2011 was extremely charismatic, and her voice could draw considerable emotion from the audience. This naturally made her a leader as everyone would sit and listen to her. She told me that she thanked Allah for her voice; because of it she could sing, preach, give advice to youths, organise community activities and bring people together. Singing the *hikmet*, she said, was a reminder of the brevity of life and that we should not put too much importance on worldly possessions. As she performed it for the community, this *büwi* demonstrated the importance of *hikmet* as a form of Islamic communication.

Before performing independently, it is expected that *dastanchi* or *büwi* apprentices train for years with their masters (*ustaz*) to understand the craft, study recitation and master a musical instrument. As one Elder informed me, without a blessing from a senior *meddah*, *dastanchi* or *büwi* one cannot be an independent performer. The special master and apprentice (*ustaz–shagirt*) relationship that I witnessed during fieldwork deeply impressed on me how traditional epistemology is reproduced. It also speaks to the larger cultural ecology of these craftsmanship forms in Central Asia.

Like the *dastan*, *qisse* and *hikmet* they perform, contemporary Uyghur storytellers share many characteristics with the storytellers who historically carried these verbal arts through Persian, South Asian and Turkic societies. In general, *meddah* (*meddaḥ*, *maddaḥ* and *maddah*) is the most common and widespread term for professional storytellers in the Islamic world. It is commonly interpreted as the Arabic word for 'one who praises',[43] an understanding that is

[42] Rachel Harris, 'Harmonizing Islam in Xinjiang: Sound and Meaning in Rural Uyghur Religious Practice', in Ildiko I. Bellér-Hann and Trine T. Brox (eds), *On the Fringes of the Harmonious Society* (Copenhagen: NIAS Press, 2013), p. 293.

[43] Boratav, Pertev Naili, 'Maddāḥ', in Peri Bearman et al. (eds), *Encyclopaedia of Islam, Second Edition*. Brill online, 2012.

reflected in contemporary Uyghur understandings of *meddah* as an umbrella term for storytellers. When I asked Uyghur Elders 'what is *meddah?*' most replied, 'the one who praises Allah (*allahni medhiyliguchi*) and spreads Allah's words'. Historian Alexandre Papas has written much on the subject of *meddah* in Central Asia, identifying them as travelling artists who performed and entertained in exchange for food and resources.[44] Showing the continuity of *meddah* in Iran and Central Asia since at least the fifteenth century, Papas notes that Sufi scholar, writer and poet Ḥusayn Wā'iẓ Kāshifī (1461–1504), who lived in Nishapur, Masshad and Herat, discussed different types of *meddah* 'distinguishable by their literary attitudes' and aptitudes.[45] Uyghur poet Abdullah Poskami, writing in the early twentieth century, makes reference to both *meddah* and *qissekhan* ('reciter of stories'), professions that he presents as arbiters of 'true knowledge'.[46]

In 2008, Turkey was successful in inscribing 'Arts of the Meddah, Public Storytellers' on the UNESCO Representative List of the Intangible Cultural Heritage of Humanity. Similar to the role and performance spaces of *meddah* in the Uyghur homeland, the UNESCO listing describes them as storytellers who historically performed as both educators and entertainers in 'caravanserais, markets, coffeehouses, mosques and churches', where they 'transmitted values and ideas among a predominantly illiterate population'.[47] However, Papas makes an interesting distinction between the *meddah*s of the Ottoman Empire, whose stories became increasingly secular, and those of Central Asia, who maintained the religious character of their repertoires.[48] Ablet Yasin's ethnography of Sufis in the Khotan region (southwest Xinjiang) shows that in the early twenty-first century *meddah*s not only continued to transmit cultural history and memory among Uyghurs, but also acted as significant carriers of Sufi rituals and healing practices.[49] I found that some Uyghur

[44] Papas, *Thus Spake the Dervish*, p. 183.

[45] Papas, *Thus Spake the Dervish*, p. 183.

[46] Poskami, *Kitabi Ăbdullah*, (Ürümchi: Xinjiang Publishing House, 2004) 260–261; also cited in Thum, *The Sacred Routes of Uyghur History*, p. 119.

[47] UNESCO, 'Arts of the Meddah, Public Storytellers'.

[48] Papas, *Thus Spake the Dervish*, p. 185.

[49] Ablet Yasin, 'Study of Sufism in Khotan Region', manuscript of Master's thesis, Xinjiang University, 2009. Yasin is another Uyghur intellectual who disappeared in 2017.

storytellers felt that the very name *meddah* should be sacred, since it refers to one who praises Allah and delivers Allah's wisdom. This description resonates with the historical significance of *meddah*, highlighted by Papas, who describes them as touching on 'the listeners' religious feelings by recounting the life of the Prophet of Islam, or the tribulations of Sufi saints, with many marvellous details and moral lessons'.[50] However, under the anti-Islamic policies of the Chinese Communist Party, this religiosity has not only been excised from published collections of *dastan*, but also from the practices of storytellers.

Vanishing Space, Vanishing Text, Vanishing People

Little did I realise when I attended the Imam Asim Mazar festival in 2009 that this would be my first and last time to witness it. When I returned in 2012 and 2015, the pilgrimage site was empty. In the extreme silence of this holy land, I could hear those stories repeating in my head. The Chinese Communist Party has committed itself to the desecration and complete removal of Uyghur cultural, social and religious sites, including 8,500 mosques,[51] despite its claims to protect them. Satellite imagery of the destroyed *mazar* of Imam Asim speaks for itself. Beyond the loss of the site's physical landmarks is the even deeper loss of the stories and culture that had been cultivated and performed there for generations. Since 2014, Islamic belief and practice have been targeted under China's so-called People's War on Terror. Even state-recognised imams have been prosecuted, let alone other religious figures in the community.[52] With the appointment of a new Party Secretary to Xinjiang in 2016, everyday life has been brought under heightened and highly policed state surveillance,[53] and

[50] Papas, *Thus Spake the Dervish*, p. 184.

[51] Chris Buckley and Austin Ramzy, 'China is Erasing Mosques and Precious Shrines in Xinjiang', *New York Times*, 25 September 2020; Mao Weihua and Aybek Askhar, 'Xinjiang Rejects US' Report on Mosques', *China Daily*, 18 July 2020.

[52] See at: BBC, https://www.bbc.com/news/world-asia-china-56986057.

[53] Josh Chin and Clément Bürge, 'Twelve Days in Xinjiang: How China's Surveillance State Overwhelms Daily Life', *The Wall Street Journal*, 19 December 2019; *New York Times*, 'Document: What Chinese Officials Told Children Whose Families Were Put in Camps', 16 November 2019; Sarah Parvini, '"They want to erase us". California Uighurs Fear for Family Members in China', *LA Times*, 9 August 2019.

since 2017 more than 1 million Uyghurs are estimated to have been taken into so-called 're-education camps' to correct their thoughts.[54]

These policies have had a profound effect on the ways Uyghurs can express their faith and storytellers can practice their craft,[55] creating large-scale disruption in cultural transmission from one generation to the next. Ethnomusicologist Mu Qian, who studied *dastan* from a master *dastanchi* in Khotan in 2014–15, found that it was increasingly difficult to learn, perform and continue *dastan* practice.[56] Requirements to obtain special permission for gatherings of more than ten people and prohibitions on public preaching of religious content, enforced through frequent police visits to practitioners' homes, greatly affected *dastanchi*s' ability to make any living with their art. As the space to perform such rituals continued to shrink, one *büwi* told me that she wrote down what she sang; since she does not sing often, she is afraid of forgetting. Many other storytellers who I interviewed kept, copied, and hid manuscripts and recordings of different *dastan*s, *qisse*s and *hikmet*s in an attempt to preserve them.

Meanwhile, physical and cultural spaces like sacred landscapes, shrines, Uyghur *muqam*, *meshrep*, rituals and other gatherings have been banned or destroyed, leaving almost no public spaces for *dastanchi*, *meddah* and *qissekhan* to perform. As some pointed out, the Great Famine (1958–62) and Cultural Revolution (1966–76) almost completely eradicated public performances of our oral traditions and culture, but even during these devastating times *dastan* still continued underground and were performed in the community. Now, with the intensity of state surveillance it is almost impossible to carry on even in private. With the criminalisation of consuming texts in the Uyghur language, especially texts that have elements of Islam, *dastanchi*, *meddah* and *büwi* also now have nothing to perform with. Performing, for example, the

[54] Adrian Zenz, 'New Evidence for China's Political Re-Education Campaign in Xinjiang', *Jamestown Foundation* 18(10) (2018): 1–45; S. Nebehay, 'U.N. says it has Credible Reports that China Holds Million Uighurs in Secret Camps', *Thomson Reuters*, 10 August 2018.

[55] Amy Anderson and Darren Byler, '"Eating Hanness": Uyghur Musical Tradition in a Time of Re-education', *China Perspectives* 2019-3 (2019): 17–26.

[56] Mu M. Qian, 'Experiencing God in Sound: Music and Meaning in Uyghur Sufism', PhD thesis, University of London, 2018.

Qisse of Karbala, or the *dastan* of *The Death of Prophet Muḥammad* can be reason alone to be taken to a re-education camp to correct so-called extremist behaviours.[57] One recent Uyghur exile reports that in some villages it is now hard to find *büwi* or other religious specialists to lead funerals according to traditional protocols. The fear of performing religiosity even in private has had a devastating effect on the Uyghur community. People are afraid to even talk about these subjects or to keep their manuscripts at home, let alone to teach them.

At the same time, *dastan* as a national-level ICH and *dastanchi* as the carriers of this heritage are ostensibly safeguarded under Chinese law. It is here that we see how the restrictive construction of *dastan* as a genre – and what has been included and excluded in the process – is directly affecting the survival of these cultural practitioners. My impression from what I saw and heard on the ground is that *dastanchi* has become the more common term, even though Elders commented that it was not a term widely used until a few decades ago. Some said that they would have called themselves a *meddah* or *waiz* before, but now preferred *dastanchi*. I found *qissekhan* to be the least-used term. I assume that this has to do with the strong association between *qisse* and *The Qisse of Prophets*; any mention of the prophets in public is a punishable crime in current-day Xinjiang. In public state media, *dastanchi* are introduced as highly skilled musicians who tell romance stories. *Dastanchi* is therefore a safer term. Moreover, if a storyteller gains official recognition as a *dastanchi*, they will get a government stipend.

It is important to recognise storytelling as a profession and livelihood; people would pray at the end of each performance and offer their appreciation to storytellers in cash at the end of their performances. One storyteller explained that he had been a storyteller and musician for his whole life. With the closing of cultural spaces such as *bazaar*s or *mazar*s, he had lost his livelihood and, along with it, his status as a provider for his family. He had little experience and few skills to do other work. It was in such circumstances that I found some storytellers vying to become state-designated *dastanchi* so that they could still work and receive a modest stipend. In Qomul region, I even found

[57] Austin Ramzy and Chris Buckley, '"Absolutely No Mercy": Leaked Files Expose How China Organized Mass Detentions of Muslims', *New York Times*, 16 November 2019.

two female performers listed as *dastanchi* intangible cultural heritage bearers. It transpired that they used to be called *büwi*. Since *büwi* largely practice in the private space of the home, they have been largely invisible to scholars studying *dastan* traditions. They were also excluded from discussions on the preservation of Uyghur intangible cultural heritage. At the same time, the religious nature of private gatherings of female practitioners has meant that they have come under state scrutiny and become a target of surveillance. Overall, being a *büwi* narrating religious content is extremely precarious. It is therefore not surprising that some *büwi* – like some *meddah* and *qissekhan* – appear to have attempted to reinvent themselves as state-approved *dastanchi*.

The implications of this reinvention go beyond what people call themselves. *Dastanchi* is a term that reflects the combination of narrative and musical talent among storytellers performing *dastan*, who accompany their own performance on traditional Uyghur instruments such as the *rawap*, *dutar* and *tembur*, and in some cases their canes. However, as a profession it has been reshaped to align with national narratives of the Chinese state, which means foregrounding themes of love and morals and reducing – or these days completely eradicating – Islamic content. Many of the practitioners I met (before the commencement of mass detentions) were already in survival mode. They were having to learn the *dastan* that had been revised and published, rather than performing what they had learned from their masters. To avoid persecution, they usually tried to emphasise their musical talents in a bid to be recognised as musicians. I also saw some *dastanchi*s volunteer for local propaganda choirs, especially in the wake of the 2015 campaign to eradicate religious extremists, which rejected any form of Islamic expression.[58] Achieving the status of a 'red singer' was not only politically safer but allowed them to generate some income by performing at weddings.

State efforts to eradicate religious content from everyday life have backed these artists and their art forms into a corner, often forcing them to choose between their heritage or the continued practice of their art, sanitised of their religion and culture. In the words of a common Uyghur expression, Islam and Uyghur culture are mixed together like milk with

[58] On this campaign, see Maya Wang and Sophie Richardson, '"Eradicating Ideological Viruses": China's Campaign of Repression Against Xinjiang's Muslims', *Human Rights Watch*, n.d.

water. The attempt to separate them imposes tremendous physical, mental and spiritual harm.

Conclusion

The fluidity of Uyghur storytelling and the complex influence and interaction between *dastan*, *qisse* and *hikmet*, between orality and text, between literary and epistemic genres, and between local, Islamic, national and other worlds has yet to be properly recognised within Islamic studies. The relationship between *dastan*, *qisse* and *hikmet* is best understood in the frame of a holistic expressive heritage and epistemology embodied in a way of life, which does not lend itself easily to being categorised. During my field work, I initially tried to define performances according to genre and to figure out which kind of storyteller was called what name. But talking with Elders made me realise what was most important for them: the rights to continue their practice, the interconnected relationships between the stories, the music, the performances, Islam and their spirituality, and the importance of their practice in our community life.

As this chapter has shown, efforts to collect and standardise Uyghur *dastan* as a genre and to transform it into representative 'world' heritage have ironically severed the links between Uyghur oral literature and the worlds (local, Islamic, Turkic) in which it was formed, circulated, transformed and transmitted. *Dastan* and *qisse*, as stories and verbal art that have circulated through Islamic cultures from Turkey through Persia to South and Central Asia, have already been devalued through the European Orientalist gaze and their reductive classification as a romance genre. As living verbal art forms embedded in everyday Uyghur life, they are now under renewed threat from the stringent restrictions that the Chinese state has imposed on them in an effort to control Uyghur communities physically, spiritually, culturally and emotionally. Under the colonial and Islamophobic gaze of the Chinese state, *qisse* and *hikmet* have been rendered invisible, while *dastan* has been purged of the religiosity that was integral to both its literary content and performance.

The Uyghur storytelling tradition should be seen as having its own knowledge systems, protocols, musical elements and performance, which are essential for the spiritual life of Uyghurs. I emphasise that this is a heritage embodied in our life, rituals and ancestral land. Reducing it to a particular genre or musical style diminishes its value and only furthers the deconstruction of living culture under the colonial gaze. Uyghur folklorists have attempted to salvage what they can, but the process of selection and revision involved in preservation and categorisation efforts has inadvertently played into the hands of an atheist state that attempts to secularise, if not eliminate, all art and literature with religious content. Giving detailed ethnographic accounts of what I saw, listened to and learnt from Elders can act as a counterpoint. However, this is a heritage that needs to be spoken, performed and received. Simply transcribing and textualising performances or recording them on film will not preserve or continue *qisse*, *hikmet* and *dastan*. For this, we need to reclaim the physical and cultural spaces in which they have thrived, such as *mazar* shrines, Uyghur *muqam*, *meshrep*, Sufi rituals and other gatherings, as well as the knowledge and authority of Elders. We also need to support traditional learning systems such as that of master and apprentice (*ustaz–shagirt*) and the continuity of storytelling as a cultural ecology.

At the present moment, such aspirations remain out of reach. Compared with the ongoing human rights atrocities in Xinjiang, the destruction of cultural spaces, and the criminalisation of Uyghur culture, a discussion on the epistemic violence effected through genre-making and heritagisation might not feel so urgent. Yet I argue that it is important precisely in showing how colonial powers dismantle and appropriate living heritage, and in highlighting what has been written, documented and officially preserved, and what has not. We should keep in mind how future generations will learn and reclaim what is vanishing today. When this next generation comes together to study and revitalise Uyghur storytelling traditions, I hope that my observations and analyses will give them a direction and framework for their endeavours.

Bibliography

Abramson, Kate, 'Gender, Uyghur Identity, and the Story of Nuzugum', *Journal of Asian Studies* 71(4) (2012): 1069–91.

Anderson, Amy and Darren Byler, '"Eating Hanness": Uyghur Musical Tradition in a Time of Re-education', *China Perspectives* 2019-3 (2019): 17–26.

Anonymous, 'You Shall Sing and Dance: Contested "Safeguarding" of Uyghur Intangible Cultural Heritage', *Asian Ethnicity* 22(1) (2020): 121–39.

Boratav, Pertev Naili, 'Maddāḥ', in Peri Bearman et al. (eds), *Encyclopaedia of Islam, Second Edition* Brill online, 2012.

Buckley, Chris and Austin Ramzy, 'China is Erasing Mosques and Precious Shrines in Xinjiang', *New York Times*, 25 September 2020, available at: https://www.nytimes.com/interactive/2020/09/25/world/asia/xinjiang-china-religious-site.html.

Chin, Josh and Clément Bürge, 'Twelve Days in Xinjiang: How China's Surveillance State Overwhelms Daily Life', *The Wall Street Journal*, 19 December 2019, available at: https://www.wsj.com/articles/twelve-days-in-xinjiang-how-chinas-surveillance-state-overwhelms-daily-life-1513700355.

Dankoff, Robert, 'Review: Ragbhuzi's Stories of the Prophets', *Journal of the American Oriental Society* 117(1) (1997): 115–26.

Dawut, Rahile and Elise Anderson, 'Dastan Performance Among the Uyghurs', in Elmira Köchümkulova, Saida Daukeyeva and Theodore Levin (eds), *The Music of Central Asia*. Bloomington: Indiana University Press, 2015), pp. 406–21.

Dawut, Rahile and Elise Anderson, 'Audio & Video Tracks: Dastan Performance among the Uyghurs', *The Music of Central Asia*, 2015, available at: https://www.musicofcentralasia.org/Tracks/Chapter/24.

Dictionary of the Uyghur Language, 6 vol., (Beijing: Minzu Chubanshe, 1990).

Hajib, Yusuf Khas, *Wisdom of Royal Glory (Kutadgu Bilig): A Turko-Islamic Mirror for Princes*, trans. Robert Dankoff (Chicago: University of Chicago Press, 1983).

Harris, Rachel, 'Harmonizing Islam in Xinjiang: Sound and Meaning in Rural Uyghur Religious Practice', in Ildiko Bellér-Hann and Trine T. Brox (eds), *On the Fringes of the Harmonious Society* (Copenhagen: NIAS Press, 2013), pp. 293–317.

Harris, Rachel, 'Text and Performance in the Hikmät of Khoja Ahmad Yasawi', *Rast Musicology Journal* 7(2) (2019): 2152–68.

Harris, Rachel, *Soundscapes of Uyghur Islam* (Bloomington: Indiana University Press, 2020).

Khan, Pasha M., *The Broken Spell: Indian Storytelling and the Romance Genre in Persian and Urdu*, ed. Donald Haase (Detroit, MI: Wayne State University Press, 2019).

Long, Michael D. R., 'Finding the "Epic of Jangar": The Literary Construction of an Early Oirat Epic in the Xinjiang Uyghur Autonomous Region', *Asian Ethnicity* 22(1) (2021): 90–104.

Mao Weihua and Aybek Ashkar, 'Xinjiang Rejects US' Report on Mosques', *China Daily*, 18 July 2020, available at: https://global.chinadaily.com.cn/a/202007/18/WS5f12dc94a31083481725a75e.html.

Metturdi, Qurban, '*维吾尔族说唱艺术"麦达赫"的词源学考析* (Lexicological Analysis of Uyghur Meddah)', *Journal of the Central Academy of Drama* 2(148) (2013): 26–30.

Mu Qian, 'Experiencing God in Sound: Music and Meaning in Uyghur Sufism', PhD thesis, University of London, 2018.

Nebehay, Stephanie, 'U.N. Says it has Credible Reports that China Holds Million Uighurs in Secret Camps', *Thomson Reuters*, 10 August 2018.

New York Times, 'Document: What Chinese Officials Told Children Whose Families Were Put in Camps', 16 November 2019, available at: https://www.nytimes.com/interactive/2019/11/16/world/asia/china-detention-directive.html?mtrref=www.google.com&assetType=REGIWALL.

Orsini, Francesa and Katherine Butler Schofield, *Tellings and Texts: Music, Literature and Performance in North India* (Cambridge: OpenBook, 2015).

Paksoy, Hasan Bülent, *Alpamysh: Central Asian Identity Under Russian Rule* (Pittsburgh, PA: Association for the Advancement of Central Asian Research, 1989).

Papas, Alexandre, *Thus Spake the Dervish: Sufism, Language, and the Religious Margins in Central Asia, 1400–1900* (Leiden: Brill, 2019).

Parvini, Sarah, '"They Want to Erase Us". California Uighurs Fear for Family Members in China', *LA Times*, 9 August 2019, available at: https://www.latimes.com/local/lanow/la-me-california-uighur-muslims-china-20190610-story.html.

Poskami, Ăbdullah, *Kitabi Ăbdullah* (Ürümchi: Xinjiang Publishing House, 2004).

Pregill, Michael, with Marianna Klar and Roberto Tottoli, 'Qiṣaṣ al-Anbiyāʾ as Genre and Discourse. From the Qurʾān to Elijah Muhammad', *Mizan* 2(1) (2017), available at: https://mizanproject.org/journal-post/qisas-al-anbiya-as-genre-and-discourse.

Rabghuzi Al-, *The Stories of Prophets: Qisas al-Anbiya an Eastern Turkish Version*, trans. and ed. H. E. Boeschoten, M. Vandamme and S. Tezcan (Leiden: Brill, 1995).

Rahman, Abdukerim, *Uyghur Folklore [Uyghur Folklori]* (Urumqi: Xinjiang University Press, 2002).

Ramzy, Austin and Chris Buckley, '"Absolutely No Mercy": Leaked Files Expose How China Organized Mass Detentions of Muslims', *New York Times*, 16 November 2019, available at: https://www.nytimes.com/interactive/2019/11/16/world/asia/china-xinjiang-documents.html.

Reichl, Karl, *Singing the Past: Turkic and Medieval Epic Poetry* (Ithaca, NY: Cornell University Press, 2000).

Rubanovich, Julia 'Tracking the Shahnama Tradition in Medieval Persian Folk Prose', in Charles Melville, Gabrielle van den Berg and Julia Rubanovich (eds), *Shahnama Studies* (Leiden: Brill, 2011), pp. 11–35.

Shirazi, Qurat-ul-Ain and Ghulam Sarwar Yousof, 'Historical and Cultural Relevance of the Adventures of Amir Hamza', *International Journal of English and Literature* 4(6) (2013): 259–63.

Shirazi, Quratulain, 'Reconfiguring Dástán Tradition as a Commemorative Narrative of Power Structures, Charismatic Leadership, and Sainthood in North India', *Journal of Religion and Popular Culture* 28(2/3) (2016): 145–62.

Tarim, Osman Ismail, 'The Types of Uyghur Folk Dastan', *Journal of Xinjiang University* 32(4) (2012): 1–8.

Thum, Rian, *The Sacred Routes of Uyghur History* (Cambridge, MA: Harvard University Press, 2014).

UNESCO, 'Arts of the Meddah, Public Storytellers', 2008, available at: https://ich.unesco.org/en/RL/arts-of-the-meddah-public-storytellers-00037.

Wang, Maya and Sophie Richardson, '"Eradicating Ideological Viruses": China's Campaign of Repression Against Xinjiang's Muslims', *Human Rights Watch*, n.d., available at: https://www.hrw.org/report/2018/09/09/eradicating-ideological-viruses/chinas-campaign-repression-against-xinjiangs.

Wehr, Hans, *A Dictionary of Modern Written Arabic, Arabic–English*, ed. J. Milton Cowan (MacDonald & Evans, 1961; Wiesbaden: Harrassowitz, 1980).

Yasin, Ablet, 'Study of Sufism in Khotan Region', manuscript of Master's thesis, Xinjiang University, 2009.

Zenz, Adrian, 'New Evidence for China's Political Re-Education Campaign in Xinjiang', *Jamestown Foundation* 18(10) (2018): 1–45.

CIRCULATION, TRANSLATION, REREADING

7

FRIEDRICH RÜCKERT (1788–1866) AND HIS POETIC TRANSLATION OF THE QUR'ĀN[1]

Georges Tamer and Cüneyd Yıldırım

For a long time, it was only scholars of German language and literature who saw themselves as responsible for the study of the distinguished German poet Friedrich Rückert (1788–1866). Primarily for technical reasons they eschewed the translations of Eastern classics made by that poet. Too great was the oeuvre, which included patriotic hymns, romantic poetry and classical philology, and too little their expertise in Islamic culture and history. Thus, Rückert's 'oriental' side received little attention, until more recent German scholars of Islamic studies, such as Annemarie Schimmel (1922–2003),[2] Wolfdietrich Fischer (1928–2013)[3] and Hartmut Bobzin,[4] drew attention to

[1] The chapter follows the guidelines of the *Encyclopaedia of Islam*, 2nd edition, when transcribing Arabic and Persian names and terms. Like everything in it, the authors are also responsible for the translations from German.

[2] See Annemarie Schimmel, *Friedrich Rückert: Lebensbild und Einführung in sein Werk* (Freiburg: Herder, 1987); Annemarie Schimmel, *Rückert zu Ehren: Zwischen Orient und Okzident* (Schweinfurt: Rückert-Gesellschaft, 1985); Annemarie Schimmel, *Weltpoesie ist Weltversöhnung* (Würzburg: Ergon, 1996).

[3] See Wolfdietrich Fischer and Rainer Gömmel (eds), *Friedrich Rückert. Dichter und Sprachgelehrter in Erlangen* (Neustadt an der Aisch: Degener, 1990).

[4] Bobzin is the editor of Rückert's Qur'ān translation. See Friedrich Rückert (trans.) and Hartmut Bobzin (ed.), *Der Koran in der Übersetzung von Friedrich Rückert* (Baden-Baden: Ergon, 2018).

it. Thanks to them, this important dimension of Rückert's oeuvre has become increasingly important in research as well as in the poet's public perception. Contributions from Islamic Studies have now become an integral part of the yearbooks of the German Rückert Society. In the context of post-colonial literary criticism, initial signs of research on Rückert in English-speaking academia are also observable.[5]

Friedrich Rückert was born on 16 May 1788 in Schweinfurt into a bourgeois, Franconian-Protestant milieu. As the son of a lawyer, he began studying law in the winter of 1805/6 in accordance with his father's wishes, but changed to philology following his own inclination. In this, he earned his doctorate in 1811 at the University of Jena, which at that time was renowned for its lectures in philosophy and philology. He gained his initial fame as a poet with his *Geharnischten Sonetten* (*Armoured Sonnets*, 1814), which he dedicated to the German campaign of liberation against Napoleonic rule. A few years later, he wrote *Liebesfrühling* (*Lovespring*, 1821), one of the most popular collections of German love poems of the nineteenth century. In 1826, the University of Erlangen appointed Rückert to the Chair of Oriental Philology, for which he had qualified with his translation of the *Maqāmāt* by the Arab author al-Ḥarīrī (1054–1122). During his time in Erlangen, he published further translations of important poetic works from Arabic, Persian and Sanskrit, before leaving for Berlin, where he became professor from 1841 to 1848. After his return from the Prussian capital to his Franconian homeland, he remained there until his death on 31 January 1866.[6]

Rückert is the foremost representative of a tendency within German Romanticism to which German Literary Criticism has given the term *orientalising poetry* ('Orientalisierende Dichtung').[7] In this context, he is mentioned alongside Johann Wolfgang von Goethe (1749–1832), August Graf von Platen (1796–1835), Georg Friedrich Daumer (1800–75), Ferdinand

[5] See Tuska Benes, 'Transcending Babel in the Cultural Translation of Friedrich Rückert (1788–1866)', *Modern Intellectual History* 8(1) (2011): 61–90.

[6] Hartmut Bobzin, 'Friedrich Rückert – Der "orientalische Dichter und Philologe"', in Mark-Georg Dehrmann and Alexander Nebrig (eds), *Poeta Philologus: Eine Schwellenfigur im 19. Jahrhundert* (Bern: Peter Lang, 2011), pp. 69–70.

[7] Günther Schweikle and Irmgard Schweikle (eds.), *Metzler Literatur Lexikon. Begriffe und Definitionen* (Stuttgart: Johann Benedict Metzlersche Verlagsbuchhandlung, 2007), 556.

Freiligrath (1810–76) and Friedrich Bodenstedt (1819–92).[8] The focus of these authors was on elements that were foreign to them, exotic and magical in terms of content and form. Their main inspiration was the exoticism of the *Arabian Nights*, which were first made accessible through Antoine Galland's French translation in 1704.[9]

In distinction to Edward Said's term orientalism, scholars like Claire Gallien propose the term pseudo-orientalism for fanciful literature, which makes use of the cultural data collected by Orientalist scholars only to create fiction. According to this model, orientalism forms the basis of pseudo-orientalism. What is further crucial for that distinction is the production of power-knowledge in which pseudo-orientalism is not directly involved.[10] Following this terminology, Rückert's engagement with Islam was both orientalist as well as pseudo-orientalist, even if the latter seems to have outweighed the former.[11] In combining both types, he marks a special status in the history of European literature.

The emergence of German orientalising poetry stems from the desire of some German poets to establish a universal poetry by adopting themes and styles of foreign cultures.[12] This cultural project of national significance responded to Goethe's call to create *Weltliteratur* (World Literature) out of German literature. This led to a focus on the so-called Orient, which went

[8] Hans-Günther Schwarz, *Orient – Okzident: der orientalische Teppich in der westlichen Literatur, Ästhetik und Kunst* (München: Iudicium, 1990), p. 40; Wolfdietrich Fischer, 'Die Wahrnehmung des Orients in der deutschen Literatur der ersten Hälfte des 19. Jahrhunderts', in Hartmut Bobzin et al. (eds), *Jahrbuch der Rückertgesellschaft* (Würzburg: Ergon, 2008), vol. 17, p. 63.

[9] Fischer, 'Die Wahrnehmung', p. 60.

[10] Claire Gallien, *L'Orient anglais. Connaissance et fictions au XVIIIe siècle* (Oxford: Voltaire Foundation, 2011), pp. 30–1, 75, 174. It is open for discussion how the work of German (pseudo-)Orientalists had an influence on the image of Islam that was prevailing during the short Orient interaction of Kaiser Wilhelm's Deutsche Reich (1888–1918). For its Intelligence Bureau for the East (*Nachrichtenstelle für den Orient*) was involved in spreading pan-Islamism in the Islamicate world.

[11] This statement requires a comprehensive analysis, which the scope of this chapter does not offer.

[12] Ahmed Hammo, 'Die Bedeutung des Orients bei Rückert und Platen', unpublished PhD dissertation, Albert-Ludwigs-Universität Freiburg, 1971, p. 165.

back to the assumption that this was home to a primeval mythology from which all other mythologies arose and that Oriental poetry reflected most clearly.[13] Thus, the focusing on foreign poetry was regarded as preparatory for any search for truth. Rückert was convinced that by exploring foreign languages one could feel the essence of the originally unified worldview.[14] In line with Goethe, he also expressed his conviction of the necessity for universal poetry with his often-quoted formula 'world poetry is world reconciliation' ('*Weltpoesie allein ist Weltversöhnung*').[15]

With his *West-Eastern Divan*, the masterpiece of the German pseudo-orientalist literary genre that was first published in 1819, Goethe had a considerable influence on Rückert. This influence is most evident in his earliest works, for example, in the drama *Der Scheintod* (*The False Death*) and *Die Türkin* (*The Turkish Woman*), both written in 1812. In *Der Scheintod*, a comedy in three acts, he introduces the reader into a fantastic image of the world of the Abbasid caliph Hārūn al-Rashīd (766–809).[16] *Die Türkin* deals with the fate of the fictive princess Archilde, set into an imaginative oriental scenario including Christian crusades. Both dramas, which represent Rückert's first conception of the Orient, are clearly inspired by fabrications from the *Arabian Nights* and therefore contain pseudo-orientalism that is imaginative Oriental projections. In the course of expanding his language skills in the following years, he added translating to his initial imitating and adapting method. To make this development clear, this chapter continues with an overview of Rückert's creative as well as academic treatment of both Islamic and Islamicate literature,[17] what became his full-time profession when

[13] Hammo, 'Die Bedeutung'.

[14] Friedrich Rückert, *Friedrich Rückert's gesammelte poetische Werke*, vol. 8 (Frankfurt am Main: Sauerländer, 1868), p. 22.

[15] Qiu Kong, *Schi-King. Chinesisches Liederbuch*, trans. Friedrich Rückert (Altona: Hammerich, 1833), p. 6.

[16] See Friedrich Rückert, *Der Scheintod. Lustspiel in drei Aufzügen* (Schweinfurt: Förderkreis der Rückert-Forschung, 1970).

[17] The terminological distinction between the religion of Islam (or Islamdom) and the Islamicate (culture) goes back to the American historian Marshall Hodgson. In his *The Venture of Islam*, he argues that the cultural manifestations in the lands inhabited by Muslims do not always

he accepted the chair for Oriental philology in Erlangen. It concludes with a brief analysis of the main peculiarities of the poet's Qurʾān translation. Pointing at the context of this literary as well as scholarly work will reveal that the (pseudo-)orientalist oeuvre of Rückert was embedded in the German cultural project of creating World Literature.

From Free Imitation to Imitative Translation

Differing from other orientalising German poets, Rückert felt the necessity to study the relevant languages before he started developing his world poetry. He was aware of the fact that a better adaptation of foreign poetry required an exact knowledge of the relevant cultural and religious circumstances. Thus, a study of sources, even beyond poetry, was indispensable.[18] Rückert's translations of Arabic, Persian and Sanskrit literary classics formed a significant part of his oeuvre. The image of the Orient in his works changed with the increasing acquisition of specialist knowledge both in the languages and in cultural history. In 1818, Rückert intensified his Arabic and Persian studies after his encounter with one of the great Orientalists of his time, Josef von Hammer-Purgstall (1774–1856).[19] He later acquired many other languages and dialects of the Near East, including Coptic and Hebrew, through self-study, and continued to deepen this linguistic knowledge throughout his life. Thanks to these extensive language skills, Rückert was appointed full professor in Erlangen in 1826. From then on, he was able to earn his living through philological studies.[20] This also confirms his preference for philology over the production of pleasing poetry as he had expressed two years earlier:

> Two things are now much closer to my heart than all poetic fame: firstly, to educate my boys . . . secondly to bring the Oriental studies, into which I . . .

directly refer to religion. For them, he thus proposed the term 'Islamicate'. See Marshall G. S. Hodgson, *The Venture of Islam: Conscience and History in a World Civilization* (Chicago: University of Chicago Press, 1974), vol. 1, p. 58.

[18] Wolfdietrich Fischer, 'Das Islamverständnis Friedrich Rückerts', in Wolfdietrich Fischer and Rainer Gömmel (eds), *Friedrich Rückert. Dichter und Sprachgelehrter in Erlangen* (Neustadt an der Aisch: Degener, 1990), p. 118.

[19] Bobzin, 'Friedrich Rückert', pp. 71–3.

[20] Hammo, 'Die Bedeutung', pp. 65.

threw myself completely, so far that they finally give the world a yield and me a livelihood.[21]

Rückert understood the turn to Oriental philology as an emancipation from Greek for the benefit of German culture.[22] This idea clearly shows the influence of the German philosopher and theorist of Romanticism Friedrich Schlegel (1772–1829), who preceded Rückert by combining his enthusiasm for the Orient with serious philological study. However, Schlegel devoted himself to Sanskrit and not to Arabic. This was due to his conviction that India was the origin of the European–Christian civilisation and that there are ties between German and Sanskrit in terms of linguistic history.[23] Corresponding to the emphasis on Sanskrit by Schlegel at that time, Rückert recommended his students in Erlangen to learn Arabic first, then Sanskrit and, finally, Persian and Turkish as the third and fourth language.[24]

Rückert's perception of the Orient changed over time with his philological studies. When he started with writing a series of ghazals in the style of Jalāl al-Dīn al-Rūmī (1207–73) in 1819, his wish was to convey the ideas of the Persian Muslim poet.[25] He did this not by translating, but by more freely imitating, a practice comparable to what Goethe had done in his *West-Eastern Divan*. It was Rückert's mentor, the Austrian Hammer-Purgstall, whose translations of some of Rumi's ghazals served him as an inspiration. Two years later, Rückert continued by imitating another Persian classic: again, it was Hammer-Purgstall's *Geschichte der schönen Redekünste Persiens* (*A History of Fine Persian Rhetoric*, 1818) that inspired him to his Ḥāfiẓ (1315–90) imitations under the title *Östliche Rosen* (*Eastern Roses*, 1821). This interest in Ḥāfiẓ

21 Rückert, *Friedrich Rückert's gesammelte poetische Werke*, vol. 12, p. 423.

22 Benes, 'Transcending Babel', pp. 68, 71.

23 See Chen Tzoref-Ashkenazi, 'India and the Identity of Europe: The Case of Friedrich Schlegel', *Journal of the History of Ideas* 67(4) (2006): 713–34.

24 Sabine Mangold, *Eine 'weltbürgerliche Wissenschaft'. Die deutsche Orientalistik im 19. Jahrhundert* (Stuttgart: Franz Steiner Verlag, 2004), p. 56.

25 Friedrich Rückert, *Orientalische Dichtung in der Übersetzung Friedrich Rückerts* Annemarie Schimmel (ed.) (Bremen: Carl Schünemann Verlag, 1963), p. 51.

was in line with the trend initiated by Hammer-Purgstall that other German-speaking poets apart from Goethe and Rückert followed.[26] In the context of his *Östliche Rosen*, he wrote to his Viennese teacher that this time he was more concerned with the form than with the spirit of the Persian poems.[27] This statement can be interpreted as a development of his method from free imitation to a greater focus on the original form.

While interest in Rumi waned, Rückert returned to Ḥāfiẓ in later years. His favourite pupil, Paul de Lagarde, published Rückert's translations of forty-two ghazals and twenty-eight quatrains (*rubāʿiyyāt*) from the Divan of Ḥāfiẓ in 1877, the work having been originally finished 1847. According to Annemarie Schimmel, these translations are philologically accurate and very close to the Persian original. Thus, they differ significantly from the products of the Ḥāfiẓ culture within German nineteenth-century poetry.[28]

In his later years, Rückert also turned his focus to two other classics of Persian poetry: Saʿdī (between 1213/1219–92) and Jāmī (1414–92). The first of the two was already a familiar name to German experts and lovers of foreign literature. In 1653, the scholarly diplomat Adam Olearius translated the *Gūlistān* (*The Rose Garden*) of Saʿdī into German, twenty years after the first French translation. Still in the seventeenth century, *Bustān* (*The Garden*), another of Saʿdīs famous didactic poems, was also translated into German. In this way, this text came to the attention of Goethe and Herder, who received it with enthusiasm. In Rückert's lifetime, several editions of both texts as well as translations were available on the German book market. Under these circumstances, Rückert's works on Saʿdī failed to attract attention and were only published posthumously. However, some information is available about his sources and working method: for the *Bustān* he used the London edition

26 Among these poets are G. F. Daumer (1800–75), Fr. Bodenstedt (1819–92) and H. Bethge (1876–1946).

27 Rückert, *Orientalische Dichtung*, p. 73.

28 The Persian edition on which Rückert based his translations from the Divan is unknown. The later standardised, successful edition by Rosenzweig-Schwannau, which Rückert was to acquire, was not published until 1858. Rückert, *Orientalische Dichtung*, pp. 76–7; Herman Kreyenborg, 'Friedrich Rückert als Interpret orientalischer Dichtung', in Wolfdietrich Fischer (ed.), *Friedrich Rückert im Spiegel seiner Zeitgenossen und der Nachwelt* (Wiesbaden: Harrassowitz, [1927] 1988), pp. 275–6.

of Forbes Falconer from 1838, while for other poems, he referred to the collection that was published in Calcutta in the years 1791–5 by H. J. Harington. Usually, he borrowed the text from a library and copied it by hand. In doing so, he made notes and compiled a glossary. He also studied the context of his subject: on Saʿdī he read John Malcom's *History of Persia*, d'Herbelot's *Bibliothèque orientale* and *L'Histoire des Mongols de Perse*, edited by Etienne Marc Quatremère.[29]

Like Saʿdī, Jāmī was not Rückert's discovery. Jāmī's epic *Yūsuf wa-Zuleikhā*, a poetic adaptation of the Qurʾānic story of Joseph and Potiphar's wife in couplet form (*mathnawī*), was available as a complete translation by Rosenzweig-Schwannau from 1824. A few years later, in 1831, Rückert translated large parts of Jāmī's Divan. His source was a manuscript held in the library of the city Gotha. He published parts of that translation between 1844 and 1852 in the German academic journal *Zeitschrift der Deutschen Morgenländischen Gesellschaft*.[30]

Rückert, who never published an edition of an original Arabic or Persian text, relied on the basic research of other orientalists. In 1822, Silvestre de Sacy (1758–1838) had published the *Maqāmāt* (*The Assemblies*) of al-Ḥarīrī (1054–1122), a collection of some fifty coherent, entertaining stories in rhyming prose. After the private purchase of this edition 'for a small fortune',[31] Rückert immediately set about producing a suitable translation into German. This proved to be a particular challenge, prompting him to opt for an imitation rather than an adequate translation in order to meet his aesthetic ambitions. This imitation was partly published in 1826. In 1837, already standing with both feet on the ground of philology, Rückert's Ḥarīrī appeared more or less complete, with the exception of a few *maqamas*.[32] With the self-criticism of a serious philologist, he claimed at this point that the text was untranslatable:

[29] Rückert, *Orientalische Dichtung*, pp. 129–32.

[30] Ibid. pp. 158–9; Kreyenborg, 'Friedrich Rückert als Interpret', p. 276.

[31] Annemarie Schimmel, *Friedrich Rückert. Lebensbild und Einführung in sein Werk* (Göttingen: Wallstein Verlag, 2016), p. 94.

[32] Kreyenborg, 'Friedrich Rückert als Interpret', p. 268; Karl Macke, 'Friedrich Rückert als Übersetzer', in Wolfdietrich Fischer (ed.), *Friedrich Rückert im Spiegel seiner Zeitgenossen und der Nachwelt* (Wiesbaden: Harrassowitz, [1896] 1988), p. 258.

> I think it will always remain, as it is now, untranslatable, not because of the difficulty of the form, which has begun to be overcome here, nor because of certain details of the content that are suppressed or changed by the current editor . . . but because the core itself, the centre of many of his *maqamas* is something that sticks to the original language and disappears with it.[33]

The poetic translations of the following years increased in philological accuracy. *Rostem und Suhrab*,[34] published in 1838, is a story from the monumental Persian epic *Shahnameh* written by Firdawsī (940–1019/25?). It deals with the encounter of the hero Rostem with his son, unknown to him, in a battle that culminates in the death of the latter. Half a century later, the literary remains reveal that Rückert had transferred the complete *Shāhnāme* into German without publishing it.[35] The eminent historian of the Qur'ān, Theodor Nöldeke (1836–1930), later praised that translation as Rückert's best work because of its philological value.[36]

Even in his years as a scholar, Rückert never gave up free, creative imitation. A testimony of his innovative approach to the history and culture of the Islamicate world is his original, pseudo-orientalist *Sieben Bücher morgenländischer Sagen und Geschichten* (*Seven Books of Eastern Legends and Stories*, 1837). The structure of this collection of narrative poems imitates that of classical Islamic historiography. As far as the literary style is concerned, the work is reminiscent of the great Persian moralising poets such as Rūmī, Sa'dī and Jāmī. It begins with the prophets from Ādam to Yaḥyā (John the Baptist). Surprisingly, Jesus is missing, which may be because Rückert did not want to provoke his German Christian readers with the Islamic view of Jesus. The second chapter deals with the history of early Islam, the third with the pre-Islamic history of Arabs and Persians. The following three chapters present more or less chronologically famous Muslim rulers, beginning with the four caliphs and ending with the Safavid Shāh Ismā'īl and one of the few

33 Kreyenborg, 'Friedrich Rückert als Interpret', p. 268.

34 See Friedrich Rückert, *Rostem und Suhrab. Eine Heldengeschichte in zwölf Büchern* (Erlangen: Bläsing, 1838).

35 See Firdawsī, *Firdosis Königsbuch*, trans. Friedrich Rückert, 3 vols (Berlin: Georg Reimer, 1890–4).

36 Schimmel, *Friedrich Rückert: Lebensbild*, pp. 86–7.

female rulers, Raziya Sultana of Delhi. While in the first six chapters, Rückert transforms mythical and historical material into partly instructive and partly informative poems, entertaining stories predominate in the seventh chapter. *Der Kater* ('The Cat'), for example, beautifully illustrates a popular variant of *jinn* belief and the everyday use of pious practices. It is about a jinn that has taken the form of a cat and lives in the house of a pious sheikh. This sheikh secretly hears his cat talking to another jinn that is outside the window and wants to enter. This is not possible, the cat tells his fellow, because the sheikh had spoken the name of God about the door lock. The sheikh has done the same with the food and drink in his house, which is why the cat is not able to hand over anything. The cat-jinn then advises the other jinn to go to the neighbour, who is not that pious and therefore more exposed to jinn maltreatment.[37]

In works like *Sieben Bücher morgenländischer Sagen und Geschichten*, Rückert articulated a conception of Oriental wisdom that serves as a universal intellectual resource. This is only partly referring to Islam, and largely refers to what he thought of as Indian religion. In *Die Weisheit des Brahmanen* (*Wisdom of the Brahmin*, 1836–9), a monumental collection of didactic poems, Rückert communicates his own worldview as an Indian sage. This original work ingeniously combines all the knowledge that he acquired in the course of his philological and cultural studies.[38] In it, he processes and interweaves the material of his Sanskrit studies, as in the *Nal und Damajanti*[39] and *Gita Govinda*,[40] with the content and couplet form of the Persian Muslim poets to create a universalistic and pantheistic teaching poem. At the same time, it contains signs suggesting a restrained position towards Islam and the Prophet Muḥammad. In one poem, for example,

[37] Rückert, *Friedrich Rückert's gesammelte poetische Werke*, vol. 4, pp. 259–60.

[38] See Christine Maillard, 'Friedrich Rückerts westeuropäischer Brahmane', in York-Gothart Mix (ed.), *Das Völkereintrachtshaus. Friedrich Rückert und der literarische Europadiskurs im 19. Jahrhundert* (Würzburg: Ergon 2012), pp. 221–45.

[39] See Friedrich Rückert, *Nal und Damajanti. Eine indische Geschichte* (Frankfurt am Main: Sauerländer, 1828).

[40] See Jayadeva, *Gitagovinda. Das Indische Hohelied des bengalischen Dichters Jayadeva* trans. Friedrich Rückert, ed. Herman Kreyenborg (Leipzig: Insel, 1919).

it is stated that truth differs concerning time and place ('Ein jeder Glaube . . .').[41] It goes on to say that Muḥammad was perfect for his age and region but would not fit in another time and place. In the following lines, Rückert advises his reader to thank God for giving him a better holy book at a better place. This can be understood either as the Bible or, due to his character as a Brahmin, Indian holy scriptures.[42]

The figure of the Indian sage in *Die Weisheit des Brahmanen* represents Rückert's Oriental universalism at its best. When it comes to Arabic Islam, represented in the image of Muḥammad, his idea of a universalistic Oriental cultural heritage gives way to cultural relativism. His sympathies for the religion of the Brahmins, or rather for its representation, was clearly an expression of the enthusiasm of German romanticists for India that grew with the publication of Friedrich Schlegel's *Über die Sprache und Weisheit der Inder* (*On the Language and Wisdom of the Indians*, 1808).

Rückert's categorisation of non-European languages and cultures, in which his Orientalism is apparent, pales in comparison with his enormous willingness to study Arabic. An outstanding example of his mastery of that language, as well as his sensitivity to Islam, is the partial translation of the Qur'ān he worked on between 1820 and 1846. Having never received attention during his lifetime, and only published posthumously, it is celebrated today as a German translation that imitates the original style of the Arabic holy book successfully.[43]

The Poetic Translation of the Qur'ān

Rückert is one of the leading figures at the beginning of the emancipation of Oriental philology from Christian theology within early nineteenth-century German academia. Many of the important pioneers of that new Oriental philology in German-speaking countries were not theologians and academics, but members of the upper class. As diplomats and ambassadors, they were in close contact with Islamic cultures, learned their languages, and collected

[41] Friedrich Rückert, *Die Weisheit des Brahmanen* (Göttingen: Wallstein, 1998), vol. 2, p. 356.

[42] Ibid. p. 458.

[43] Ibid. *Der Koran*, p. xxxv.

antiques and manuscripts.[44] Among them was Hammer-Purgstall, who, after his training as a translator at the court of the Habsburgs, lived in Constantinople and Cairo from 1799 to 1807. After his return, his encounter with Friedrich Schlegel must have convinced him that the study of Oriental languages should have the same significance as Greek and Latin philology.

Hammer-Purgstall passed on to his pupil Rückert his broad interest in different aspects of Islamic cultures with a special focus on poetry and history.[45] He had an idea of what a Qur'ān translation should look like, having translated a selection of *suras* himself, paying close attention to the rhymes. Rückert was a reader of Hammer-Purgstall's *Fundgruben des Orients* (*Treasure Trove of the Orient*, 1808–18), a journal in which the Viennese presented pieces of his translations. Its second issue contains the poetic translation of the last forty *suras*, preceded by a programmatic preface. In this, Hammer-Purgstall declares the Qur'ān as a masterpiece of Arabic poetry and explains that:

> In order, then, to exploit the poetic content of the Qur'ān as faithfully as possible, the translation must not only keep pace with the original, but also keep the same tone. The final rhymes of the verses must be translated into rhymes, which so far has not been done in any of the translations known to us, and which could not be done more faithfully in any European language than in the German one . . . which is not alien to any stroke of the heavens, which elicits the germs of its peculiar culture from every soil, and which carefully preserves them.[46]

The examples of Rückert's translations given below illustrate the extent to which the poet-scholar followed Hammer-Purgstall's method of translation, which focused on two principles: the imitation of the structure of every verse and the translation of rhymes into rhymes.

Rückert's interest in the Qur'ān did not remain constant in his life. Rather, there were two phases in which he devoted himself to the holy book of Islam:

[44] Mangold, *Eine 'weltbürgerliche Wissenschaft'*, p. 44.

[45] Ibid. p. 47.

[46] Joseph Hammer-Purgstall, *Fundgruben des Orients. Mines de l'Orient 2*, 1811, pp. 25–6.

one was during his time as a private scholar in Coburg between 1820 and 1826; and the other between 1836 and 1846 as a professor in Erlangen.[47] Rückert's translation did not appear during his lifetime, for the main reason that he lacked a financial sponsor for the completion of that project. Hartmut Bobzin, editor of Rückert's translation of the Qurʾān, noticed from Rückert's correspondences that the publishers' interest in such a translation changed from time to time. In 1823, Rückert tried to attract F. A. Brockhaus (1772–1823), editor of the famous encyclopaedia of the same name, for the publication of his translation of some *suras*, but without success. The publisher did not respond to Rückert's request to increase his fee.[48] This was four years before Goethe made his views on World Literature public. It can only be speculated that Brockhaus considered a large-scale project of a German Qurʾān translation to be unpromising. It is possible that it seemed to him to be unprofitable scholarship. It then took Rückert ten years to revive his motivation and to resume his plan. The reason for his renewed interest in such a project was the publication of a low-priced Arabic edition of the Qurʾān by the Arabist Gustav Flügel (1802–70) in 1834, which Rückert purchased himself. From then on, he was no longer dependent on libraries for this.[49]

In addition to purely Arabic editions of the Qurʾān, Rückert, like his predecessors, also relied on Maracci's edition including its traditional Muslim commentary.[50] Bobzin also reports that Rückert used for his work an edition of the commentary by al-Bayḍāwī, the Arabic–Latin dictionary of Jacob Golius and George Sale's notes to his Qurʾān English translation titled *Preliminary Discourse*.[51] However, Rückert did not attach too much importance to the Muslim commentaries. For the most part, he did not find them helpful. Instead, he considered the Qurʾān itself to be sufficient.[52] For his own commentary, he started in *al-Baqarah*, the second and longest *sura*, referring to the Qurʾān's biblical context by quoting relevant passages from the Old

[47] Rückert, *Der Koran*, pp. iv, xxv–xxviii.

[48] Ibid. pp. xxi, xxiii, xxvi.

[49] Ibid. p. xxiii.

[50] Ibid. p. x.

[51] Ibid. p. xxv.

[52] Ibid. pp. 8–9.

Testament.[53] However, Rückert then abandoned this intertextual analysis, which apart from *al-Baqarah* does not appear, in favour of a self-referential analysis that compares Qur'ānic statements from different passages with each other.

According to Bobzin, Rückert never planned a complete translation. The *suras* that are missing completely are 69 (*al-Ḥāqqah*), 71 (*Nūḥ*), 78 (*al-Naba'*), 85 (*al-Burūj*), 86 (*al-Ṭāriq*), 87 (*al-A'lā*), 88 (*al-Ghāshiyah*), 89 (*al-Fajr*), 90 (*al-Balad*), 98 (*al-Bayyinah*), 99 (*al-Zalzalah*) and 104 (*al-Humaza*). More noteworthy is the deliberate omission of verses in *suras* he translated. His own notes and commentaries show that he avoided translating content that he found uninteresting. This included legal topics such as matrimonial and inheritance law as well as moral themes. In contrast, he was particularly interested in everything he called mythical and historical. Among them were stories about prophets, their opponents, ancient peoples, angels and jinns.[54] Nevertheless, as is clear from the list above, he did not translate some of the early Meccan *suras* known for their expressive imagery of the Last Judgement and Hell. According to Bobzin, Rückert's omission of Qur'ānic material was always intentional. Regarding those Meccan *suras*, it is probable that Rückert skipped those passages due to the repetitive quality of its contents. The Last Judgement and Hell are, after all, often-repeated Qur'ānic themes.

Rückert also took the liberty of changing the order of verses to suit his idea of how it should have been. In this, he already anticipated the approach of later scholars, who would completely question the structure of the Qur'ān, as Muslims knew it.[55] Right at the beginning of his commentary on the second *sura* (*al-Baqarah*), Rückert notes that this *sura* lacks any order. He interprets this circumstance as an attempt by either the Prophet or the collectors of the revelation to summarise various things. Accordingly, unlike Muslim commentators, he claims that this must be the last Medinan *sura*, not the first.[56]

Two illustrative examples of Rückert's highly individual and creative rearrangement of the Qur'ān are *sura* 24 *al-Nūr* ('das Licht') and 37 *al-Ṣāffāt*

[53] Rückert, *Der Koran*, p. 7.

[54] Ibid. p. xxxi.

[55] Ibid. pp. xxxi–xxxii.

[56] Ibid. p. 4.

('Die Reihenführerinnen'). He comments on the former as follows: 'Cut into pieces, with omission of single verses and parts.'[57] With this in mind, he places verses 23–26 starting with *inna lladhīna yarmūna* ('Fürwahr, die da beschmitzen') between the ninth (*wa-l-khāmisa* . . .: 'Das fünfte . . .') and eleventh verse (*inna lladhīna jāʾū* . . .: 'Die da mit Lügen kommen'), while dropping the tenth completely. After verse 34 (*wa-la-qad anzalnā* . . .: 'So haben wir herabgesendet . . .'), it goes on with verses 47–57 (*wa-yaqūlūna* . . .: 'Sie sagen . . .'), then continuing with verses 62–64 (*innamā l-muʾminūna* . . .: 'Allein die Gläubigen'), leaving out 58–61. Verses 35–45, which begin with the famous Light Verse (*Allāhu nūru l-samāwāt* . . .: 'Gott ist das Licht des Himmels . . .'), Rückert places at the end as if they were the finale of the *sura*.[58] Verses 57–61, which Rückert ignored, deal with rules of moral conduct in the family, especially with regard to the protection of privacy. According to these, a child who has reached puberty should ask for permission at certain times of the day before entering the parents' room. Furthermore, they announce that women in advanced age are allowed to remove the veil under certain circumstances. Rückert may have considered this too trivial, or he may not have found a solution to include these verses into the scheme of his translation, as some of them obviously differ in length.

Rückert's method of rearrangement was twofold. On the one hand, he followed the advice of Hammer-Purgstall by focusing on the end rhymes in the Arabic original. Convinced of his poetic ability, he thought he could better relate the verses to each other than the editors of the Qurʾān. On the other hand, he gave extra attention to the content. He attempted to distinguish more clearly between different topics, whose transitions in the Qurʾān are not always easy to follow. This is clearly visible in *sura* 37, which Rückert divided into three parts regarding the topics in it. After identifying related topics, he put the verses together accordingly. One topic Rückert recognised in *sura* 37 is Abraham's sacrifice (vv. 99–113); another is the story of Jonas (vv. 139–148). He then linked together the remaining verses, which traditionally form the beginning and the end of the *sura* and which, in Rückert's view,

[57] 'Zerlegt in einzelne Stücke, mit Auslassung einzelner Verse und Partien', in Rückert, *Der Koran*, p. 264.

[58] Ibid. pp. 264–73.

have no connection to the two topics mentioned. He guessed to have discovered in verse 165 a response to the oath with which the *sura* begins. Accordingly, the two verses that belong together are 'By those lined up in ranks' (*wa-l-ṣāffāti ṣaffa*) and 'We are indeed the ones lined up in ranks' (*wa-innā la-naḥnu l-ṣāffūn*). In his own harmonious way, Rückert composes a semantic unit from these remaining verses. After verses 165 and 166, he thus continues with verses 180, 181 and 182, while ignoring 167–179. Corresponding to this rearrangement, the following order of verses would result in Arabic:

> 165 wa-innā la-naḥnu l-ṣāffūn[a]
> 166 wa-innā la-naḥnu l-musabbiḥūn[a]
> 180 subḥāna rabbika rabbi l-ʿizzati ʿammā yaṣifūn[a]
> 181 wa-salāmun ʿalā l-mursalīn[a]
> 182 wa-l-ḥamdu li-llāhi rabbi l-ʿālamīn[a]

Here it becomes clear that Rückert put the respective verses in a new relation to each other in accordance with their end rhymes, as can be seen at the transition from verse 166 to 180. In addition, a look into Marmaduke Pickthall's English translation of the Qurʾān reveals the effect that rearrangement has on the content. For this purpose, the corresponding verses in English are set in the order suggested by Rückert, as follows:

> 165 Lo! We, even We are they who set the ranks.
> 166 Lo! We, even We are they who hymn His praise.
> 180 Glorified be thy Lord, the Lord of Majesty, from that which they attribute (unto Him)
> 181 And peace be unto those sent (to warn).
> 182 And praise be to Allah, Lord of the Worlds![59]

Rückert thus understood the part of the *sura* that remains when the two stories of Abraham's sacrifice and the prophet Jonas are separated as a speech by the angels culminating in a praise of God.

[59] Marmaduke Pickthall, *The Meaning of the Glorious Koran* (New York: Alfred A. Knopf, 1930), pp. 463–4.

As three illustrative examples of the poetic value of Rückert's translation, the *suras* 112 (*al-Ikhlāṣ*), 95 (*al-Tīn*) and 97 (*al-Qadr*) are presented here. In *al-Ikhlāṣ*, Rückert succeeds in remaining highly faithful to the Arabic original.

Original:
1 Qul huwa llāhu aḥad^{un}
2 Allāhu ṣ-ṣamad^{u}
3 Lam yalid wa-lam yūlad
4 Wa-lam yakun lahū kufuwan aḥad^{un}

Rückert:
1 Sprich: Gott ist Einer,
2 Ein ewig reiner,
3 Hat nicht gezeugt und ihn gezeugt hat keiner,
4 Und nicht ihm gleich ist einer.[60]

In this very short *sura*, which is so crucial for the conception of Islamic monotheism, the characteristics of Rückert's poetic Qurʾān translation are evident. On the one hand, he keeps the syntax of the Arabic original as far as possible; on the other, he imitates its rhyme. The former characteristic is clearly visible in the first verse: it corresponds absolutely to the original. The latter characteristic, the rhyme of the original, is also visible here in the German version. In the original, the word *aḥad* gives the rhyme that is 'Einer' (the One) in German. *Aḥad* is followed by *ṣamad*, a much speculated name of God, which Rückert translates as 'ewig reiner' (eternally pure) to keep the rhyme, although the meaning he gives to *ṣamad* is highly questionable.[61] The third verse corresponds to the syntax of the Arabic original; but in order to keep the rhyme as in the original, Rückert lets the verse end with another word in German: 'keiner' (none), which corresponds to the negation in the sentence, but not to *yūlad*. The translation of the last verse again equals the Arabic.

[60] Rückert, *Der Koran*, p. 490.

[61] Pickthall, for example, translates *ṣamad* with 'the eternally Besought of all'. See Pickthall, *The Meaning*, p. 676.

Similarly successful as *al-Ikhlāṣ* is the translation of *al-Qadr*, another early Meccan *sura*.

Original:

1 innā anzalnāhu fī laylati l-qadrⁱ
2 wa-mā adrāka mā laylatu l-qadrⁱ
3 laylatu l-qadri khayrun min alfi shahrⁱⁿ
4 tanazzalu l-malāʾikatu wa-l-rūḥu fīhā bi-idhni rabbihim min kulli amrⁱⁿ
5 salāmun hiya ḥattā maṭlaʿi l-fajrⁱ

Rückert:

1 Wir sandten ihn hernieder in der Nacht der Macht.
2 Weißt du, was ist die Nacht der Macht?
3 Die Nacht der Macht ist mehr als was
In tausend Monden wird vollbracht.
4 Die Engel steigen nieder und der Geist in ihr,
Auf ihres Herrn Geheiß, daß alles sei bedacht.
5 Heil ist sie ganz und Friede, bis der Tag erwacht.[62]

In the original, the last word of the first verse, *qadr*, marks the rhyme of the whole *sura*. Rückert's translation fits with this arrangement by ending with 'Macht' as the translation of *qadr* and thus giving the rhyme for the other verses. However, those German words that rhyme do not correspond to those in the Arabic original. In this case, Rückert preferred rhyme to the reproduction of Qurʾānic syntax. This is appropriate in view of the expressiveness of the short Meccan *suras*. Furthermore, 'Macht' for *qadr* reflects only one aspect of the complex meaning of the word given by the majority of Muslim scholars. Again, however, the power of expression outweighs philological rigour by combining 'Nacht' and 'Macht'.

It requires a lot of ingenuity to meet all the linguistic specifications of the Qurʾān poetically in another language. In particular, it seemed a major challenge to keep the rhyme by using an equivalent word in German. Therefore, Rückert made ample use of assonances. For this, the translation of the *sura al-Tīn* is a fine example.

[62] Rückert, *Der Koran*, p. 478.

Original:

1 wa-l-tīni wa-l-zaytūn[i]
2 wa-ṭūri sīnīn[a]
3 wa-hādhā l-baladi l-amīn[i]
4 la-qad khalaqnā l-insāna fī aḥsani taqwīm[in]
5 thumma radadnāhu asfala sāfilīn[a]
6 illā lladhīna āmanū wa-ʿamilū l-ṣāliḥāti fa-lahum ajrun ghayru mamnūn[in]
7 fa-mā yukadhdhibuka baʿdu bi-l-dīn[i]
8 a-laysa llāhu bi-aḥkami l-ḥākimīn[a]

Rückert:

1 Bei Feige und Olive,
2 Und bei des Berges Giebeln,
3 Und diesem Friedensgebiete!
4 Wir schufen erst den Menschen nach dem schönsten Bilde,
5 Dann ließen wir ihn sinken in die tiefste Tiefe,
6 Die ausgenommen, die glauben und das Gute thun,
Lohn ungemessner ist für diese.
7 Was zweifelst du noch am Gericht?
8 Ist Gott der gerechteste Richter nicht?[63]

The first three verses consist of oaths typical of the style of many Meccan *suras*. Here God swears by the fig, the olive, Mount Sinai and the 'secure settlement' (*al-balad al-amīn*). Rückert begins the first verse with a literal translation. For the following verse, he obviously found no rhyming solution for *sīnīn*, which would be 'Sinai' in German. In favour of a relatively acceptable assonance in the form of an old-fashioned word for summit ('Giebel'), Rückert renounces the mention of Mount Sinai and thus the biblical reference of the *sura*. Verses 1–6 follow the same assonance, with which the last two verses break. This is because the poet preferred here the imitation of the syntax of the Arabic original to the rhyme. This also includes letting the verses end with the German equivalents of the words with which the verses conclude. Thus, *dīn* corresponds to the German word for court ('Gericht'), which Rückert obviously did not want to renounce, unlike Mount Sinai. The

[63] Rückert, *Der Koran*, p. 476.

'nicht' in the last verse rhymes with 'Gericht', which, however, does not mark the final word in the Arabic, but rather a shift of the interrogative particle at the beginning of the verse ('a-').

To sum up, Rückert succeeded in keeping a good balance between the two principles of Hammer-Purgstall's method, although he did not always cope with implementing them as well as in *sura al-Ikhlāṣ*, 112, which was probably due to the brevity of the *sura*. The longer a *sura* was, the more complicated the poetic translation became. Apart from those two principles, the imitation of sentence structure and the translation of rhymes into rhymes, the recurring iambic rhythm of Rückert's translations is striking. This is something that the Viennese Orientalist had also implied, but which only a master poet like Rückert was capable of creating. The rhythm is completely lacking in Hammer-Purgstall's attempts at poetic translations.[64] It is precisely this lyrical quality, paired with a philological and cultural–historical sensitivity, that distinguishes Rückert's translations so much from other attempts.

During his lifetime and in the decades that followed, only his closest associates knew his work on the Qurʾān. From one of the pioneers of modern critical Qurʾān research and late contemporary of the master poet, Theodor Nöldeke, there is no statement concerning that translation, although he was among the admirers of Rückert's *Shāhnāme*. After Rückert's death, three manuscripts from his literary remains appeared that contained translations from the Qurʾān. Their first edition was published in 1888, on the hundredth anniversary of his birth, on behalf of his family, but almost another 100 years passed before an intellectual audience started to appreciate that work. To mention only a few judgements, Annemarie Schimmel can certainly be considered the greatest admirer of Rückert's poetic Qurʾān translations within academia. Already in 1963, thus three decades before the new edition of Rückert's Qurʾān, she stated that the poet-scholar had succeeded in reproducing the solemn diction of the Arabic original in the German language as far as possible.[65] Navid Kermani, a prominent German Muslim intellectual, who is the author

[64] Bobzin compares the two on the basis of their translation of *sura* 88 (al-Ghashiyyah). Rückert's translation there goes back to a manuscript consisting of attempts, which, for some reason, was not intended for publication. Rückert, *Der Koran*, pp. xix–xxii.

[65] Rückert, *Orientalische Dichtung*, p. 203.

of academic studies on Islam as well as fictional and non-fictional best sellers, celebrates Rückert's translation for wonderfully demonstrating that poetry is the transition from language to music.[66] Murad W. Hofmann (1931–2020), a German convert to Islam and former ambassador to Algeria and Morocco, differed quite strongly in his judgement. He considered that Rückert's German adaptation of the original Qurʾānic style 'sounds childish'.[67]

Conclusion

The idea of creating German world poetry was a self-confident expression of bourgeois cosmopolitanism. Thus, Rückert's studies on Islam formed part of a larger national project whose significance depended on political realities. Rückert never started a trend, but rather followed broader tendencies that began with Herder, Goethe and Schlegel, and which were pushed forward by the Viennese Hammer-Purgstall. German translations of mainly Persian poets, above all Ḥāfiẓ, were so numerous in his time that it happened that Rückert's contributions to that field came too late to be noticed. Further discouraged by the failure of the liberal German March Revolution in 1848, he abandoned his project of world poetry and returned to literary classicism. This is perhaps the main reason why his translation of the Qurʾān did not appear during his lifetime. From 1848 until the 1880s, there was simply no demand for it.[68] Tastes in poetry had changed in the meantime. Younger generations of poets in particular perceived Rückert's language as overly artificial, peculiar and even unpleasant.[69]

The Rückert expert and internationally renowned Islamic scholar Annemarie Schimmel summarises Rückert's career by saying that he was too philological for some and too poetic for others.[70] As far as the latter is concerned, his partial translation of the Qurʾān has indeed not aroused the interest of German scholars on Islam even after it was published. In questioning the composition of the holy

[66] Navid Kermani, *Gott ist schön. Das ästhetische Erleben des Koran* (Munich: C. H. Beck, 1999), 183.

[67] Murad W. Hofmann, 'Germany and the Qur'an', *Journal of Qur'anic Studies* 2(1) (2000): 144.

[68] Benes, 'Transcending Babel', pp. 88–90.

[69] 'Friedrich Rückert and his Works', review of the *North American Review*, 1 October 1869, p. 584.

[70] Schimmel, *Weltpoesie*, pp. 7–8.

book, he preceded later academic research, even though his effort was not to be recognised. His emphasis on the lyrical form has hardly encouraged anyone in Islamic (former Oriental) Studies to do further research in this respect.[71] Accordingly, Rückert's project of a poetic Qur'ān translation stands alone; nevertheless, experts now consider it to be successful in combining both philological reliability and aesthetic value.

Bibliography

Benes, Tuska, 'Transcending Babel in the Cultural Translation of Friedrich Rückert (1788–1866)', *Modern Intellectual History* 8(1) (2011): 61–90.

Bobzin, Hartmut, 'Friedrich Rückert – Der "orientalische Dichter und Philologe"', in Mark-Georg Dehrmann and Alexander Nebrig (eds), *Poeta Philologus: Eine Schwellenfigur im 19. Jahrhundert* (Bern: Peter Lang, 2011), pp. 67–82.

Firdawsī, *Firdosis Königsbuch*, trans. Friedrich Rückert, 3 vols (Berlin: Georg Reimer, 1890–4).

Fischer, Wolfdietrich, 'Das Islamverständnis Friedrich Rückerts', in Wolfdietrich Fischer and Rainer Gömmel (eds), *Friedrich Rückert. Dichter und Sprachgelehrter in Erlangen* (Neustadt an der Aisch: Degener, 1990), pp. 117–30.

Fischer, Wolfdietrich, 'Die Wahrnehmung des Orients in der deutschen Literatur der ersten Hälfte des 19. Jahrhunderts', in Hartmut Bobzin et al. (eds), *Jahrbuch der Rückertgesellschaft* (Würzburg: Ergon, 2008), vol. 17, pp. 59–72.

Fischer, Wolfdietrich and Rainer Gömmel (eds), *Friedrich Rückert. Dichter und Sprachgelehrter in Erlangen* (Neustadt an der Aisch: Degener, 1990).

Gallien, Claire, *L'Orient anglais. Connaissance et fictions au XVIIIe siècle* (Oxford: Voltaire Foundation, 2011).

Hammer-Purgstall, Joseph, *Fundgruben des Orients. Mines de l'Orient 2*, 1811.

Hammo, Ahmed, 'Die Bedeutung des Orients bei Rückert und Platen', unpublished PhD dissertation, Albert-Ludwigs-Universität Freiburg, 1971.

Hodgson, Marshall G. S., *The Venture of Islam: Conscience and History in a World Civilization*, 3 vols (Chicago: University of Chicago Press, 1974).

Hofmann, Murad W., 'Germany and the Qur'an', *Journal of Qur'anic Studies* 2(1) (2000): 143–7.

Jayadeva, *Gitagovinda. Das Indische Hohelied des bengalischen Dichters Jayadeva*, trans. Friedrich Rückert, ed. Herman Kreyenborg (Leipzig: Insel, 1919).

[71] One exception is Kermani, *Gott ist schön*; English: Kermani, *God is Beautiful: The Aesthetic Experience of the Quran* (Cambridge: Polity, 2014).

Kermani, Navid, *Gott ist schön. Das ästhetische Erleben des Koran* (Munich: C. H. Beck, 1999).

Kermani, Navid, *God is Beautiful: The Aesthetic Experience of the Quran* (Cambridge: Polity, 2014).

Kong, Qiu, *Schi-King. Chinesisches Liederbuch*, trans. Friedrich Rückert (Altona: Hammerich, 1833).

Kreyenborg, Herman, 'Friedrich Rückert als Interpret orientalischer Dichtung', in Wolfdietrich Fischer (ed.), *Friedrich Rückert im Spiegel seiner Zeitgenossen und der Nachwelt* (Wiesbaden: Harrassowitz, [1927]1988), pp. 261–88.

Macke, Karl, 'Friedrich Rückert als Übersetzer', in Wolfdietrich Fischer *Friedrich Rückert im Spiegel seiner Zeitgenossen und der Nachwelt* (Wiesbaden: Harrassowitz, 1988 [1896]), pp. 232–60.

Maillard, Christine, 'Friedrich Rückerts westeuropäischer Brahmane', in York-Gothart Mix (ed.), *Das Völkereintrachtshaus. Friedrich Rückert und der literarische Europadiskurs im 19. Jahrhundert* (Würzburg: Ergon 2012), pp. 221–45.

Mangold, Sabine, *Eine 'weltbürgerliche Wissenschaft'. Die deutsche Orientalistik im 19. Jahrhundert* (Stuttgart: Franz Steiner, 2004).

North American Review, The, 'Friedrich Rückert and his Works', Review, 1 October 1869, pp. 584–94.

Pickthall, Marmaduke, *The Meaning of the Glorious Koran* (New York: Alfred A. Knopf, 1930).

Rückert, Friedrich, *Nal und Damajanti. Eine indische Geschichte* (Frankfurt am Main: Sauerländer, 1828).

Rückert, Friedrich, *Rostem und Suhrab. Eine Heldengeschichte in zwölf Büchern* (Erlangen: Bläsing, 1838).

Rückert, Friedrich, *Friedrich Rückert's gesammelte poetische Werke*, 12 vols (Frankfurt am Main: Johann David Sauerländer, 1868/9).

Rückert, Friedrich, *Orientalische Dichtung in der Übersetzung Friedrich Rückerts*, ed. Annemarie Schimmel (Bremen: Carl Schünemann Verlag, 1963).

Rückert, Friedrich, *Der Scheintod. Lustspiel in drei Aufzügen* (Schweinfurt: Förderkreis der Rückert-Forschung, 1970).

Rückert, Friedrich, *Die Weisheit des Brahmanen*, 2 vols (Göttingen: Wallstein, 1998).

Rückert, Friedrich, *Der Koran in der Übersetzung von Friedrich Rückert*, ed. Hartmut Bobzin (Baden-Baden: Ergon, 2018).

Schimmel, Annemarie, *Rückert zu Ehren: zwischen Orient und Okzident* (Schweinfurt: Rückert-Gesellschaft, 1985).

Schimmel, Annemarie, *Friedrich Rückert: Lebensbild und Einführung in sein Werk* (Freiburg: Herder, 1987).

Schimmel, Annemarie, *Weltpoesie ist Weltversöhnung* (Würzburg: Ergon, 1996).

Schimmel, Annemarie, *Friedrich Rückert: Lebensbild und Einführung in sein Werk* (Göttingen: Wallstein Verlag, 2016).

Schwarz, Hans-Günther, *Orient – Okzident: der orientalische Teppich in der westlichen Literatur, Ästhetik und Kunst* (München: Iudicium, 1990).

Schweikle, Günther and Irmgard Schweikle (eds), *Metzler Literatur Lexikon. Begriffe und Definitionen* (Stuttgart: Johann Benedict Metzlersche Verlagsbuchhandlung, 2007).

Tzoref-Ashkenazi, Chen, 'India and the Identity of Europe: The Case of Friedrich Schlegel', *Journal of the History of Ideas* 67(4) (2006): 713–34.

8

THE 'ISLAMIC' *ARABIAN NIGHTS* IN WORLD IMAGINARIES

Muhsin J. al-Musawi

This chapter argues that the conflation between Islam and the *Arabian Nights* is not a straightforward trajectory. If this conflation was less noticeable in the first half of the eighteenth century, interested scholars, Orientalists like Sir William Jones, physicians, antiquarians and philologists began late in the century to trace Islamic echoes, and manners and customs that they associated with Islamic societies. In other words, the issue of attachment to and detachment from the tales is also intertwined with and entangled in the rising aspirations of the empire. Involvement in the colonial conquest often led pillars of this conquest, its savants, and entrepreneurs of the East India Company and the Royal Society of Bengal to treat the *Nights* as documents. The first Governor of the Presidency of Fort William in Bengal and the head of the Supreme Council of Bengal, Warren Hastings (1732–1818), was among early enthusiasts of Galland's *Nights* as a document. The first de facto Governor-General of Bengal (1772–85) was often cited in support of Antoine Galland's translation of *Mille et une nuits. Contes arabes* (1704–12/17) as representative of Islamic societies.[1] The celebration that Galland's edition enjoyed could not last forever. With the increasing philological interest in the *Nights* as a significant document for royal societies and others concerned with 'useful knowledge', the search for

[1] See Muhsin J. al-Musawi, *Scheherazade in England* (Washington, DC: Three Continents, 1981), p. 28.

complete manuscripts turned into a relentless mania that drove many in Egypt and South Asia to stitch together tales from different sources to claim complete manuscripts.[2]

Such is the clamour around the Macan manuscript (Calcutta II) that it was claimed as the most complete against the incomplete Galland's manuscript and its siblings. William Hay Macnaghten, later the Secretary to the Secret and Political Department in Calcutta, and Henry Torrens of the College of Fort William and the Royal Society of Bengal were among the new breed of Orientalists who took the *Nights* as their property to be made available to speakers of Arabic and English. As argued and documented by scholars, such appointees to India's General Committee of Public Instruction like Charles E. Trevelyan (1833) would argue strongly for providing the English-speaking world with a complete manuscript.[3] That was Sir William Hay Macnaghten's opinion. As a distinguished Arabist, he argued for the need to have this early nineteenth-century manuscript published and translated because of 'the credit which must accrue to our nation, from presenting to the Musulman population of India, in a complete and correct form and in their own classical language, these enchanting tales'.[4]

The phenomenal popularity of the *Thousand and One Nights* (*Arabian Nights*) upon its advent in France (1704–12), England and the rest of Europe, incited and consolidated old and new impressions of Islam and the Arabs.[5]

[2] D. B. MacDonald, 'A Preliminary Classification of some MSS of the Arabian Nights', in Thomas Walker Arnold and Reynold Alleyne Nicholson (eds), *A Volume of Oriental Studies Presented to Edward G. Browne* (Cambridge: Cambridge University Press, 1922), pp. 304–21; and D. B. MacDonald, 'The Earlier History of the Arabian Nights', *JRAS* 3 (1924): 353–97.

[3] For more, see Paulo Lemos Horta, *Marvellous Thieves: Secret Authors of the Arabian Nights* (Cambridge, MA: Harvard University Press, 2017), pp. 107–13

[4] Cited by Robert Irwin, *The Arabian Nights: Tales of 1001 Nights*, trans. Malcolm C. Lyons with Ursula Lyons; Introduced and annotated by Robert Irwin (London: Penguin, 2008), 2: xv.

[5] For more on the advent of the *Thousand and One Nights*, see Duncan Black MacDonald, 'A Bibliographical and Literary Study of the First Appearance of the Arabian Nights in Europe', *Library Quarterly* 2(4) (1932): 387–420; see also Duncan Black MacDonald, 'On Translating the Arabian Nights', *The Nation* 71 (August 30, 1900): 167–8, 185–6; and Charles Knipp, 'The Arabian Nights in England: Galland's Translation and Its Successors', *Journal of Arabic Literature* 5(1) (1974): 44–54. See also Muhsin al-Musawi, 'The Arabian Nights in Eighteenth-Century English Criticism', *Muslim World* 67 (1977): 12–32; and al-Musawi, *Scheherazade in England.*

Although there was an active translation from Arabic in philosophy, science and other fields of 'wisdom'[6] in the seventeenth century, these were not as popular and therefore had less impact in sapping the theological and political foundations of medieval fear and antagonism. The *Nights* was to play multiple roles, depending on readerships. Its appeal to newly emerging readerships could be viewed as an expected response to an entertaining narrative; a response that was not lost on the anonymous Grub Street translator who coined the most popular title, *The Arabian Nights' Entertainments*.

The story is different among the learned: if Alexander Pope and a large number of the litterateurs were enthusiastically drawn to this new and compelling narrative, the case was not so for Addison, Steele, Voltaire and Johnson, for example, who were more given to using the Oriental mode for moralistic, satiric and philosophical purposes.[7] Islam did not figure prominently as religion in these writings. It is rather a blurred and shady background that would gradually unfold as the polarised Other, as in Lord Byron's (1788–1824) eastern poems.[8] Islam and the East are presented as being synonymous with Ottomans, the Turks that Byron identifies with despotism, abduction and violence. Otherwise, the East serves to exoticise a scene, to intensify strangeness and difference as in William Beckford's (1760–1844) *Vathek*. The latter was written in French (1782) and translated into English (1786), to be one of the most inspiring narratives to the Romantic movement.[9] It partly draws on the Abbasid caliph al-Wathiq's (d. 847) biographies to come up with a different image that speaks

[6] G. J. Toomer, *Eastern Wisdom and Learning: The Study of Arabic in Seventeenth-Century England* (Oxford: Oxford University Press, 1996); also Raymond Schwab, *Oriental Renaissance: Europe's Rediscovery of India and the East, 1680–1880* (New York: Columbia University Press, 1984); and especially, Norman Daniel, *Islam, Europe and Empire* (Edinburgh: Edinburgh University Press, 1967).

[7] See Husain Fareed Ali Haddawy, 'English Arabesque: The Oriental Mode in Eighteenth-Century English Literature', unpublished PhD dissertation, Cornell University, 1962; and Martha Pike Conant, *The Oriental Tale in England in the Eighteenth Century* (New York: Columbia University Press, 1908).

[8] There are many studies of Byron's eastern tales, but see Peter J. Kitson, 'Byron and Post-Colonial Criticism: The Eastern Tales', in Jane Stabler (ed.), *Palgrave Advances in Byron Studies* (London: Palgrave Macmillan, 2007), pp. 106–29.

[9] P. F.. More, *The Drift of Romanticism* (New York: Houghton Mifflin, 1913), p. 33.

directly to Beckford's own aspirations and acts of defiance. The Abbasid caliph's quest for knowledge and his relentless aspiration to experiment in chemistry and to further the rationalist school of thought could have been the spark that set Beckford's imagination on fire. In *Vathek*, the Abbasid caliph was collapsed with Satan's defiance and the pre-Romantic search for the vast and the boundless. The image of the 'flaming heart' that Beckford assigns to the protagonist best stands for Beckford's strong Romantic impulse. No other image proved to be as compelling.[10] In other words, appropriation of Islamic history and the *Arabian Nights* narrative was part of a simmering Romantic challenge to the rigid rationality of the Augustans. Islam was only a site for projections. Until the last decades of the eighteenth century, what drew attention was regional rather than theological difference.

Islam and the *Arabian Nights*: A Modern Concoction?

Hence, it may sound surprising to argue that a more systematic conflation of the *Arabian Nights* with Islam is a modern concoction, that is, a late eighteenth-century one that had its paradigmatic materialisation in writing only in early nineteenth-century Europe. To recapitulate, this conflation with Islam did not form a noticeable case upon the first advent of the *Nights* in translation and appropriation in France (1704–12), and simultaneously in England. Indeed, there was a tendency to lay the blame for lack of attention to manners and customs on the English Grub Street translator (1705–6). When the Revd Edward Forster undertook a retranslation in 1802, his justifications, as well as those of his later editor G. Moir Bussey (1839, 1842 editions), rest on the understanding that the first English translator was behind some omissions and inadequacies. Forster and Moir Bussey relied on the authority of Warren Hastings, 'whose long residence in the East, and many acquirements, admirably qualified him to express a correct opinion on the subject, must be admitted to have some weight'.[11] The translator and editor added a quote from Hastings: 'Galland has selected the best of the tales, and

[10] More, *The Drift of Romanticism*.

[11] 'Introductory Preface', *Arabian Nights' Entertainments*, trans. Revd Edward Forster. Carefully revised with an explanatory and historical introduction with twenty-four engravings from designs by Robert Smirke (London: J. Thomas, 1842), p. 70.

rendered those which he has given us, if not quite faithfully, yet with the costume and manners perfectly correct, and the language both elegant and Oriental. Our English translations of his work are mean and coarse beyond criticism.'[12] This conflation began to take shape in the first half of the nineteenth century when a branch in philological inquiry in France and Germany in particular argued a racial classification of language into families, Aryan and Semite.[13] Thus, while a visible line of writing on the *Nights* is more concerned with its 'beauties',[14] or morals in Richard Johnson's (i.e., Revd J. Cooper) usage in 1790, or of its aesthetic qualities that highlight the narrative power of the tales, there are other lines that are no less influential insofar as the makeup of a pseudo-Oriental/Islamic imaginary is concerned. To elaborate further on the Lacanian use of imaginary, it is worthwhile to reference Jacques Lacan's question in a comment on Melanie Klein who 'tells us that objects are constituted by the interplay of projections, introjections, expulsions, reintrojections of bad objects . . . don't you have the feeling that we are in the domain of the imaginary?'[15] A set of values and linguistic and symbolist practices inclusive of projections, illusions and seductions function among readers and communities whereby the *Nights* turns into a nexus that feeds imaginaries of Islam, its rituals and caliphs, especially Harun al-Rashid, as will be shown in due course. As a frequent reference, Lady Mary Wortley Montagu's (1689–1762) letters from Turkey are worth citing. She began writing in 1717. These letters present a different image of an Ottoman

[12] Forster, Introductory Preface', *Arabian Nights' Entertainments.*

[13] See Muhsin al-Musawi, *The Arabian Nights in Contemporary World Cultures* (Cambridge: Cambridge University Press, 2021), pp. 20–2, 46,154–5, 255–6, 263, 286; see also Edward Said, *Orientalism* (New York: Random House-Vintage, 1978), pp. 136–47.

[14] J. Cooper, *The Oriental Moralist; or the Beauties of the Arabian Nights Entertainments* (London: Newbery, 1790); Cooper, *Beauties of the Arabian Nights Entertainments, Consisting of the Most Entertaining Stories* 2nd edn (London: Newbery, 1792); see also Hari Mohan (ed.), *Beauties of the Arabian Nights* (Calcutta, 1839).

[15] The notion is explained in Jacques Lacan, 'The Function of Language in Psychoanalysis', in *Speech and Language in Psychoanalysis*, trans. Anthony Wilden (Baltimore, MD: Johns Hopkins University Press, 1973), p. 74; cited in Gregor Campbell, 'Imaginary/symbolic/real', in ed. Irena R. Makaryk (ed.), *Encyclopedia of Contemporary Literary Theory: Approaches, Scholars, Terms* (Toronto: Toronto University Press,1995), pp. 560–1.

seraglio that titillated a class fed on strict rules of composition and meagre awareness of life elsewhere.[16] Circulated privately in 1724, Lady Mary wrote her letters to prove that, 'excepting the enchantments', the tales depict 'a real representation of the manners' in Turkey.[17] Like some travellers, she read scenes of difference there through silhouettes and images that were made available in Antoine Galland's version of *Les mille et une nuits: contes arabes* (*The Thousand and One Nights, Arabian Tales*, 1704–12). In other words, the *Nights* participated in the appearance of multiple readings of the Middle East region, the Orient of early England before the shift of the term to reference Southeast Asia. This takes place not because the *Nights* offers an exact picture of the region. Its storytelling power, imaginative fecundity and strangeness to relatively insular societies evoke projections and dreams. A vast imaginary has been growing since then where desires are played out as evidenced in an enormous body of writings, illustrations, pantomimes, harlequins, plays, poems and subsequently films.

Not to confuse these diverse lines in approaching the *Nights*, we can probably think of the aristocrat, novelist and racist theorist Arthur de Gobineau (1816–82) in his *Essai sur l'inégalité des races humaines* (*Essay on the Inequality of Human Races*; 1853–5) and Jean-Baptiste Fourier's 'Preface' to the *Description of Egypt*, as another line that either defines language as a racial category in the case of Gobineau or looks demeaningly upon Islam and the Arabs as a damaging presence to ancient civilisations as argued in Jean-Baptiste Fourier's preface (1768–1830).[18] Fourier's essentialist view of Arabs as of 'fixed opinions and customs' and of the 'unintelligibility' of the Qur'ān as deterrence to progress are partly conversant with Gobineau's later assumptions and set a dominating defining category that finds in Ernest Renan a formidable exponent. The *Nights* is not absent from this discussion, it is

[16] Lady Mary Wortley Montagu, *The Complete Letters*, ed. Robert Halsband, 3 vols (Oxford: Clarendon, 1965–6), vol. 1, p. 15.

[17] Cited in all-Musawi, *Scheherazade in England*, pp. 14–15.

[18] *Description de l'Égypte* (*Description of Egypt*), French Government, 1809–22. For an intelligent reading, see Anne Godlewska, 'Map, Text and Image: The Mentality of Enlightened Conquerors: A New Look at the Description de l'Égypte', *Transactions of the Institute of British Geographers* 20(1) (1995): 5–28 at 7–8.

often called upon to ascribe disorganisation, lack of symmetry and restraint to Islam. In matters of origin of the *Nights*, the blame is levelled at the Arabic process of accretion that befell an otherwise different *Hazar Afsaneh*. The divide among scholars on the basis of the early history and origination of the *Nights* should not be shrugged off as mere quibbling. *New* philology built among other things on this divide to argue a Sanskrit or Persian origin. One can cite cases in the Arabian composite collection that demonstrate lack of the Enlightenment-cherished tenets of good composition as espoused by notables like Bishop Atterbury who rebuffed Alexander Pope's celebration of Galland's translation.[19] Impatient with different compositions, and unfamiliar with classical Arabic tradition, some eighteenth- and nineteenth-century writers expressed views that ended up in an imaginary of racial divides.

From Gobineau to Renan

The case of Gobineau is more complicated than that of the English essayist and Romantic Thomas De Quincey (1785–1859), or at a later stage that of the English banker, economist, literary critic and journalist Walter Bagehot (1826–77), the editor and co-founder of the *National Review* (1855) and the editor for seventeen years of *The Economist* (since 1861). In the words of Professor Pierre-Louis Rey, Joseph Arthur de Gobineau considers the *Nights* a Persian text: 'During his adolescence in Brittany, he had become enamoured of the *Thousand and One Nights*. "All he dreamed of were mosques and minarets, he said he was a Muslim, ready to make his pilgrimage to Mecca", recounted one of his childhood friends.' Furthermore, 'as soon as he arrived in Paris in 1835, he started taking Persian lessons with Quatremère at Le Collège de France, before giving into the Orientalist fashion of the time in a long poem titled *Dilfiza* (1837).'[20] His appointment in 1855 as secretary to the diplomatic mission in Tehran for three years and his second visit there in January 1862, as plenipotentiary minister, brought him closer to rituals and practices of dervishes, Shia Islam, Sufism, Bábism and traditional theatre as shown in his essays on Shīʿī *taʿziyeh* or what the influential essayist and poet

[19] Al-Musawi, *Scheherazade in England*, pp. 16–17.

[20] See at: https://heritage.bnf.fr/bibliothequesorient/en/joseph-gobineau-art, last accessed 28 August 2020.

Matthew Arnold calls 'Persian Passion Play',[21] which responds with admiration to Gobineau's writings in this direction. The trio, Gobineau, Renan and Arnold, read there an agnostic scientism that better met their rejection of the divine. While enchanted by life there, Gobineau wrote in imitation of the *Thousand and One Nights*. His mixed views, pseudo-Oriental mode and disenchantment with revolutionary France, well fitted him in that equipoise between the drift of Romanticism and the reality of colonial expansion. His life story and record, as well as his writings, demonstrate that effort to find an anchor outside the immediate French context while also applying a discriminating racial reading of the Other. The *Nights* serves a number of imaginaries verbally constructed by people like him. Thus, one part in the *Nights* is 'Oriental', while the other manifests fortitude and exposition of ancient habits of valour and manliness. Islam is reduced to rituals as perceived in *taʿziyah* (Shīʿī mourning) processions in Iran commemorating the challenge posed by the Prophet's grandson (d. 680) against Umayyad usurpers, and the ultimate massacre of him, his family and companions. Pierre-Louis Rey writes of his tales as follows: 'As an allusion to the *Thousand and One Nights*, he nicknamed the three heroes of his *Pléiades* "Calenders, sons of kings". Above all, his *Nouvelles asiatiques* (1876) illustrated this nostalgia.' Tinged with racial discrimination, and a number of essentialisms, Gobineau departs from the mainstream of the Oriental mode. Upon reflecting on his Oriental stories, Rey writes,

> Three of the six tales ('L'Illustre Magicien', 'Histoire de Gambèr-Aly', 'La Guerre des Turcomans') depict with both humour and tenderness the failings of modern Persians (dissimulators, versatile, taken in by anything shiny); two others ('La Danseuse de Shamakha' and 'Les Amants de Kandahar') exalt individuals who, amid the mountains of the Caucasus or Afghanistan, have managed to keep the strength of character and nobility of their original culture.[22]

[21] R. H. Super (ed.), *Prose Works of Matthew Arnold* (Ann Arbor: University of Michigan Press, 1960–74), VII (1970): 22. For more, see Geoffrey Nash, 'Aryan and Semite in Ernest Renan's and Matthew Arnold's Quest for the Religion of Modernity', *Religion & Literature* 46(1) (2014): 25–50.

[22] See at: https://heritage.bnf.fr/bibliothequesorient/en/joseph-gobineau-art, last accessed 28 August 2020.

He adds, 'When he uses an emphatic, florid style, we can wonder if he is mocking or entering into a complicity with Orientals, but this ambiguity adds to the charm of his stories.'[23] Situating the last two tales in the mountains of the Caucasus, the presumed birthplace of the Aryan race, Gobineau draws a radical difference between characters in his five tales. The Aryan shows strength and nobility in comparison with the rest! In the end, this last space, the borders of the Caucasus and its people, suits his racist theory, his exaltation of the birth of an Aryan race! Nevertheless, he comes up in *Trois ans en Asie* with such a sweeping conclusion that sums up the pitfalls of his essentialisms: 'Asia is an extremely seductive dish, but it poisons those who eat it.'[24]

Although this waywardness and difficult navigation between a racist reading of human communities and his essentialist view of Asia while meaning only Iran and Caucasus heights sound nonsensical nowadays, their correspondence to and concomitance with similar views passed by architects of empire and their resurgence in times of trouble and war indicate that they are central to the rhetoric of empire. This is why views passed by the Schlegel brothers and accepted by Oetrup with respect to the origins of the *Nights* cannot be bypassed as sporadic or uneventful.[25] With their specialisation in Sanskrit, the Schlegel brothers August Wilhelm Schlegel (1767–1845) and Friedrich von Schlegel (1772–1829) often depreciate the possibility of an Arab-Islamic *Arabian Nights* when it comes to the study of origins. If they ever grant a romanticised nod to the Arab, it is reserved to the Bedouin whom von Hammer-Purgstall views as a model for a defiant and independent romantic spirit that urban life domesticates and flattens.[26] A philological–historical line is well

[23] See at: https://heritage.bnf.fr/bibliothequesorient/en/joseph-gobineau-art.

[24] See at: https://heritage.bnf.fr/bibliothequesorient/en/joseph-gobineau-art.

[25] See Muhsin Mahdi, *The Thousand and One Nights* (Leiden: Brill, 1995), pp. 1–2. More on this point in al-Musawi, *The Arabian Nights in Contemporary World Cultures.*

[26] Joseph von Hammer-Purgstall, 'On Arabic Poetry, Especially the Romance of Antar', *New Monthly Magazine* 13 (1820): 12–18, 151–61; Friedrich von Schlegel, *Lectures on the History of Literature, Ancient and Modern, from the German*, 2 vols (Edinburgh: Blackwood, 1818); Henry Torrens, 'Remarks on M. Schlegel's Objections to the Restored Editions of the Alif Leilah, or Arabian Nights' Entertainments', *Journal of the Asiatic Society*, n.s. 25 (1838): 72–7; W. C. Taylor, 'Professor Schlegel and the Oriental Translation Fund', *Foreign Quarterly Review* 11 (1833): 315–33.

exemplified in Sylvestre de Sacy's contributions, not only to the study of the *Arabian Nights*,[27] but also to the translation and study of Arabic literature and *grammatica* as in his *Principles of General Grammar*.[28] His reflections on those views of Joseph von Hammer-Purgstall (1774–1856) as well as Edward William Lane's (1801–76) contributions in this respect are important in setting the stage for further philological research that has substantiated a constellation of studies and grids that impact the formation of ideas about the *Nights* and its presumed religio-social and historical dimensions.[29]

While not necessarily accurate, these discussions happened to work within a certain constellation, and they were bound to leave indelible marks on an imaginary that collapsed Islam, Arabs and 'Orientals'. In other words, a certain Europeanised 'Islamic' imaginary has been gathering force since these nineteenth-century debates. Muhsin Mahdi makes significant contributions to disentangle this mass of documents and conjectures. He raises questions with respect to this body of fervent writings and presumptions that evolved into a fight over origins: 'How did they come to think that a collection of stories presumably originating in ancient India could survive transmission from one culture to another, from one language to another, and from one storyteller to another and yet remain identifiable in eighteenth-century Paris or Cairo as belonging to a particular nation?'[30] Nevertheless, and notwithstanding this

[27] Baron de Sacy, 'On the Origin of the "Arabian Nights"', XXVIII (July 1829), 560–6 (repr. in *Selections from the Asiatic Journal*, covering January 1816 to December 1829 (Madras, 1875), 996–1001); Silvestre de Sacy and Antoine Isaac (1758–1838), supplemental essay to Galland's *Les mille et une nuits* (Paris: Bourdin, 1860); and *Les mille et une nuitscontes arabes, traduits par Galland*, Illustrés par M. M. Francais, H. Baron, ed. Wattier, Laville, etc. Revus et corrigés sur l'édition princeps de 1704, augmentés d'une dissertation sur les Mille et une nuits, par Sylvestre de Sacy. More in al-Musawi, *Scheherazade in England*, p. 166.

[28] See at: http://onlinebooks.library.upenn.edu/webbin/book/lookupname?key=Silvestre%20de%20Sacy%2C%20A.%20I.%20(Antoine%20Isaac)%2C%201758-1838, last accessed 2 September 2020.

[29] Joseph von Hammer-Purgstall, 'Sur l'Origine des Mille et une Nuits', *Journal Asiatique* 10 (1827): 253–56; Joseph von Hammer-Purgstall, 'Note: Sur l'origine persane des Mille et une Nuits', *Journal Asiatique* 3(8) (1839): 171–6; Edward William Lane, *The Thousand and One Nights, Commonly Called, in England, the Arabian Nights' Entertainments*, 3 vols (London: Charles Knight, 1839–41) (with a foreword and substantial review).

[30] Mahdi, *The Thousand and One Nights*, pp. 1–2.

significant effort to disentangle a history of fictional literature, the latter – known worldwide under the title *Arabian Nights* or *Thousand and One Nights* – has been a compelling factor in the creation of an imaginary that has collapsed Islam, the Arabs and sometimes 'Orientals' or 'Asiatics'. Different tributaries happened to generate images of the Muslim and the Arab or the Turk, but the collection, with its composite content,[31] is not divested of Islamic markers.[32] Narrative attributes, presumptuous insertions, and Islamic or non-Islamic themes and images gather force to provide Western audiences over time with a captivating imaginary that occasionally, if not often, displaces factual detail.

Axial Patterns in a Dominating Imaginary

This imaginary has these axial patterns:

1. *A Rationale for Popularity and Fashion*: As popularity among rising reading publics cannot be dismissed out of hand, this wide approval was deliberately rationalised to fit into a scale of cultural prioritisation. If the urban Arab, the city dweller, is no longer the carrier of the admirable qualities of valour and nobility, as the German school of the Schlegels argues, their choice falls on an old Sanskrit or Persian dynasty that fits well the ascending Aryan presumption that learned Orientalists like Henry Torrens refuted. Indeed, we can cite Schlegel's argument for a Sanskrit origin, and the counter-narrative and detailed refutation by Henry Torrens as examples of the raging controversy on origins.[33] His brother Friedrich was no less reluctant to make concessions on matters of descent or origin. Like his brother, and notwithstanding fluctuations in his early and later career, he is more given to racial classifications and prioritisations. Thus, after reading Goethe's *Divan*,

[31] See Nabia Abbott, 'A Ninth-Century Fragment of the "Thousand Nights" New Light on the Early History of the Arabian Nights', *Journal of Near Eastern Studies* 8(3) (1949): 161.

[32] For a detailed study of the Islamic elements in the tales, ironic or otherwise, see Muhsin al-Musawi, *The Islamic Context of the Thousand and One Nights* (New York: Columbia University Press, 2009).

[33] For more, see al-Musawi, *Scheherazade in England*, p. 43; Torrens, 'Remarks on M. Schlegel's Objections to the Restored Editions of the Alif Leilah or Arabian Nights' Entertainments', pp. 161–8.

for example, he wrote, 'It is strange to see how in his old age he has suddenly started behaving in such a Turkish manner.'[34]

2. *Racial and Spatial Imaginaries*: The other side in the discussion of 'origins' relates to place: was it Egypt as Edward William Lane forcefully argues and substantiates with heavy annotations on manners and customs; or could it be Baghdad and Syria? At the outset, this discussion is not tightly tied to the issue of an 'Islamic' imaginary. But it is. If Lane's substantiation of an Egyptian orientation is substantiated by experiential detail and readings, other Orientalists like de Sacy, the *Athenaeum* reviewer between 1820 and 1860, Francis Palgrave (Deputy Keeper of the Public Record Office, 1838–61), and many others argue for the *Arabian Nights* as a consortium, a collection that had a multiple genealogy as shown in von Hammer-Purgstall's unearthing of tenth-century Baghdadi documents proving the existence in Arabic of a claimed translation of an Indo-Persian *Hazar Afsana* (*Thousand Fables*) that was to undergo redactions, revisions, additions and appropriation, as demonstrated in 1949 by Nabia Abbott's 'A Ninth-Century Fragment'.[35] The European discovery of such historical evidence gave way to further conjectures that confused the Indo-Persian source with the ultimate evolution or outgrowth of a *Thousand and One Nights*. It helped advocates of racial conceptualisations to speak of a Sanskrit or Persian *Nights*.

3. *The 'Orient of Poets'*: This phrase was coined by the English poet and essayist Leigh Hunt in his *London Journal* of October 1834. There he wrote, 'Hail, Araby and Persia! – not the Araby and Persia of the geographer, dull to the dull, and governed by the foolish – but the Araby and Persia of books, of the other and more real East . . . the Orient of Poets, the magic lands of the child, the ineffaceable recollection of the man.'[36] Literary readings offer probably the most sustainable imaginary insofar as the common reader is concerned. The Romantics, the aesthetes and late Romantics are unconcerned with the issue of place or race. The tales for them are Arabian tales as the

[34] Schlegel to Dorothea, 13 October 1819. Cited in Ian Almond, *History of Islam in German Thought from Leibniz to Nietzsche* (New York: Routledge, 2010), p. 89.

[35] Abbott, 'A Ninth-Century Fragment', pp. 129–64.

[36] Leigh Hunt, 'On Genii and Fairies of the East, the Arabian Nights', *Leigh Hunt's London Journal* 1(30) (22 October 1834): 233–7.

endearing Grub Street title tells them. George Meredith advises his readers to think like an Arab to enjoy reading or to write in this vein. In other words, early Romantics like the poet and essayist Leigh Hunt and or Victorians like Alfred Lord Tennyson (1809–92) and William Ernest Henley (1849–1903) were in tune with a literary imaginary offered by the *Nights* and reconstrued in poems like Lord Tennyson's famous 'Recollections of the Arabian Nights'. The captivating power of the tales is given a direction that is in tune with a literary imaginary whereby invocations of an aesthetic experience take place. The conflation between Harun al-Rashid Abbasid Baghdad and a palace of art for a consummate poetic reverie is at the base of what is meant by the 'orient of poets', an imaginary that takes leave of history and geography to create a realm of art:

> Thence thro' the garden I was drawn –
> A realm of pleasance, many a mound,
> And many a shadow-chequer'd lawn
> Full of the city's stilly sound,
> And deep myrrh-thickets blowing round
> The stately cedar, tamarisks,
> Thick rosaries of scented thorn,
> Tall orient shrubs, and obelisks
> Graven with emblems of the time,
> In honour of the golden prime
> Of good Haroun Alraschid.
>
> With dazed vision unawares
> From the long alley's latticed shade
> Emerged, I came upon the great
> Pavilion of the Caliphat.
> Right to the carven cedarn doors,
> Flung inward over spangled floors,
> Broad-based flights of marble stairs
> Ran up with golden balustrade,
> After the fashion of the time,
> And humour of the golden prime
> Of good Haroun Alraschid.

Henley's 'Arabian Nights' Entertainments', which he dedicates to the American writer and art critic Elizabeth Robins Pennell (1855–1936), is no less powerful. Its galaxy of names and stories may not sound of relevance to Islam. But, in the end, every name and story as recollected beckons to cities, territories and people who involve all, caliphs and wazirs, calendars and rovers, seamen and women of every sort, along with practices and rituals that appeal to readers more than historical narratives or political accounts:

I was – how many a time! –
That Second Calendar, Son of a King,
On whom 'twas vehemently enjoined,
Pausing at one mysterious door,
To pry no closer, but content his soul
With his kind Forty. Yet I could not rest
For idleness and ungovernable Fate.
And the Black Horse, which fed on sesame
(That wonder-working word!),
Vouchsafed his back to me, and spread his vans,
And soaring, soaring on
From air to air, came charging to the ground
Sheer, like a lark from the midsummer clouds,
And, shaking me out of the saddle, where I sprawled
Flicked at me with his tail,
And left me blinded, miserable, distraught
(Even as I was in deed,
When doctors came, and odious things were done
On my poor tortured eyes
With lancets; or some evil acid stung
And wrung them like hot sand,
And desperately from room to room
Fumble I must my dark, disconsolate way),
To get to Bagdad how I might. But there
I met with Merry Ladies. O you three – Safie, Amine, Zobeide – when my heart
Forgets you all shall be forgot!

The poem reconstructs in verse a number of tales that happen to occupy the poet's memory and force themselves on an imagination that has to share its enchantment with the people he loves. The process of reading as reflection and imagining is best captured in the following verses in this long poem:

> Then, as the Book was glassed
> In Life as in some olden mirror's quaint,
> Bewildering angles, so would Life
> Flash light on light back on the Book; and both
> Were changed. Once in a house decayed
> From better days, harbouring an errant show
> (For all its stories of dry-rot
> Were filled with gruesome visitants in wax,
> Inhuman, hushed, ghastly with Painted Eyes),
> I wandered; and no living soul
> Was nearer than the pay-box; and I stared
> Upon them staring-staring.

4. *A Disenchanting Real*: It is not enough to reference the novelist, poet and critic George Meredith (1829–1909) to comprehend a sober-minded reading of the *Nights* in relation to conflictual imaginaries that happened to sweep France, Germany and England in particular, where projections of personal desires overrode realities and also blurred a possibility of navigation between imaginaries and 'realties'. Meredith takes Lane's translation and annotation as a significant moment in disenchantment. It saps the Romantic foundations of an imaginary, its vastness, strangeness, and boundless opportunities and replaces all with a 'reality' that Lane's translation exemplified and presented in annotations and review. As argued in *Scheherazade in England*, George Meredith's own criticism of Oehlenschlager's *Aladdin* in the *Westminster* of 1858,[37] emphasises that Lane presents a complex East that is disenchanting and also compelling for being different from the European Romantic projections. Hence, comes Meredith's warning not to adopt the Oriental mode as a showcase for reveries and obsessions: he argues 'against the adoption of an Oriental model, or an Eastern theme, when they [writers]

[37] Cited and argued in al-Musawi, *Scheherazade in England*, pp. 98–9. Meredith's appeared as 'A Review of Ochlenschläger's *Aladdin*', in *Westminster Review* LXIX, n.s., XIII (1858), 291–93 at 292.

are peculiarly labouring under personal emotion'.[38] To dismantle the imaginary that Meredith was bent on doing could not a be an easy job, not only because it was already a dominating tide in Romantic projections of an East, but also because the reality that Edward William Lane strives to present cannot be attainable unless writers are ready to outstep their own subjectivity and read Arabs, culture and locale as they are. Meredith knows that this is not an easy task: 'because few have sufficient strength of sympathy and imagination combined to cast themselves loose from the West, and start freely; and moreover it requires a subtle dramatic and a mimetic power not common'. Even if capable of representations of an East that generate an imaginary, pseudo-Orientalism fails in the end because such striving to reach and present life in the East requires a sincere and adequate acquaintance with the Orient as one's own. Otherwise, writers 'may amass heaps of imagery, and paint the desert in vivid colours, but they will never themselves be taken for Arabs. The East teems with passion, sentiment, poetry, and humour, but these qualities are all entirely of a different texture from ours.'[39] The only way to write in the Oriental mode is to bypass Otherness and let oneself get submerged in another culture. The writer 'must not only look on, his imagination must live in, the desert and the Arabian mind'.[40]

5. *Dispensers of an Imaginary*: As usual in literature, every age has its own preferences; and cynics and rebels are prone to dismantle the grand reverie evoked and sustained by a pleasant reading. The early European manipulation of the Oriental mode for satiric, moralistic and philosophical purposes gave way to the cynicism of many, including Edgar Allan Poe in his 'The Thousand-and-Second Tale of Scheherazade' (1845),[41] and not ending with James Alroy Flecker's (1884–1941) drama *Hassan: The Story of Hassan of Baghdad* (1922) that angered William Butler Yeats for its disenchanting misanthropic mode. Yeats' 'The Gift of Harun al-Rashid' (1924) runs counter to Flecker's and

[38] Meridith, 'Review of Ochlenschläger's *Aladdin*'.

[39] Meridith, 'Review of Ochlenschläger's *Aladdin*'.

[40] Meridith, 'Review of Ochlenschläger's *Aladdin*'. See al-Musawi, *Scheherazade in England*, pp. 98–9.

[41] Edgar Allan Poe, 'The Thousand-and-Second Tale of Scheherazade', *Godey's Lady's Book* (February 1845).

similar accounts or representations.[42] As a recapitulation on Tennyson's 'Recollections . . .', Yeats' poem celebrates the caliph as a lover of art whose gifts are no less than poetic inspiration, fecund imagination and impetus to write. The dispensers of an imaginary happened to be too cynical or humorous to stay in the web of an imaginary sustained by poets, artists and essayists. The latter group might have been waning under the encroachment of virtual venues, but not for the novelist A. S. Byatt who even produced a new edition of selected tales from Sir Richard Francis Burton's *Thousand and One Nights* (2001).[43]

6. *Dissociating Genre from Race*: Another line of analysis that debunks certain imaginaries may well relate to burgeoning theorisations of novelistic writing. Thomas Warton's (1728–90) well-known ventures in this respect suggest idleness and credulity of Eastern monarchs and the nature of climate were behind the origin of fiction among the Arabs and Easterners. For Warton, Arabia became the locale where fiction took root.[44] This led to John Dunlop's *History of Fiction* (1814), where he argues that idleness, fecundity of imagination and climate gather forces in the character of the Arab. In an informed rebuff, Sir Francis Palgrave wrote back: 'we have very little confidence in the influence supposed to be exercised by climate over the moral character of mankind: we doubt whether genius of any kind rises or falls with the mercury in the thermometer'. Concluding that John Dunlop 'Wartonizes in his turn,' Palgrave chastises upholders of attitudes that convey 'the conceited airs of superiority with which our writers usually regard the Asiatics.'[45] With his acquaintance with archival material and mastery of analysis, Francis

[42] William Butler Yeats, 'The Gift of Harun Al-Raschid', *The Dial* (1924).

[43] A. S. Byatt, *The Arabian Nights: Tales from a Thousand and One Nights* (Modern Library Classics) 1st Modern (New York: Modern Library Edition, 2001).

[44] This conceptualisation started early on with P.-D. Huet's *A Treatise of Romances and Their Original* (London, 1672) (S. Lewis's trans., 1715); and Thomas Warton, 'On the Origin of Romantic Fiction in Europe', prefixed to vol. I of his *History of English Poetry* (London, 1774–81).

[45] Francis Palgrave, 'Dunlop's History of Fiction', *Quarterly Review* XIII (1815): 384–408 at 388. See also al-Musawi, *Scheherazade in England*, p. 73. On circumstantial theory in the second half of the eighteenth century, see al-Musawi, ibid., p. 34, fn. 33.

Palgrave dismantles this tendency to Wartonise, that is, writing in the manner of Thomas Warton and his association of the rise of fiction with climate. The implications of Warton's line of conjecture are many, as circumstantial theory gave birth to a poetics of atomisation,[46] its focus on the desert and sand as analogous to a presumed lack of organic unity in Arabic poetry. This same line of thought appears in the platitudes of Sir Alfred Lyall whom Lord Cromer profusely quoted,[47] and who was the brother of Sir Charles James Lyall, the illustrious translator of the *Muʿallaqāt*.[48] That same streak of thinking, but using psychological and sociological analysis, appears in Raphael Patai's *The Arab Mind* (1973).[49]

These are only some variations on the power of a collection to incite discourse and invoke multiple readings, and thence imaginaries. This field of knowledge, which has continued to invite further discursive input by a large body of scholars, continues to inspire imaginaries that engage with the *Nights* as either a pure compelling narrative as argued, for example, by the English poet and critic Leigh Hunt (1784–1854), Jorge Luis Borges (1899–1986) and Georges May among writers,[50] or a picture of non-literary contexts, as discussed by the English economist and neo-classicist writer Walter Bagehot, and many others. The dialogue among these perspectives indicates the problematic involved in the desiring subject, and its predication onto a colonial desire. Schools of thought that took the *Nights* as a field of ethno-theological study happened to operate within a colonial script where colonial desire proliferates in expansion, exploitation, manipulation of power, and also the reproduction of a self-image outside the metropolitan centre. Thus, in terms of image-making and creation of an imperial imaginary of an Orient, even a

[46] Palgrave, 'Dunlop's History of Fiction'.

[47] On Sir Alfred Lyall, see Said, *Orientalism*, pp. 38–9.

[48] Sir James Lyall, *Translations of Ancient Arabic Poetry, Chiefly Pre-Islamic, with Introduction and Notes* (London: William & Norgate, 1885); *The Mufaddaliyat: An Anthology of Ancient Arabian Odes*, compiled by al-Mufaddal son of Muhammad, according to the recension and with the commentary of Abu Muhammad al-Qasim ibn Muhammad al-Anbari, edited for the first time by Charles James Lyall (Oxford: Clarendon, 1918–24).

[49] Raphael Patai, *The Arab Mind* (New York: Charles Scribner's, 1973).

[50] Georges May, *Les mille et une nuits d'Antoine Galland, ou, Le chef-d'oeuvre invisible* (Paris: PUF, 1986).

devotee to the *Book of the Thousand and One Nights* like Sir Richard Francis Burton is no more than an actor in the dynamics of culture and empire. Edward Said argues in view of Burton's statements like 'Egypt is a treasure to be won': 'we must recognize how the voice of the highly idiosyncratic master of Oriental knowledge informs, feeds into the voice of European ambition for rule over the orient'.[51]

To perceive and conceptualise scholars' attention to the *Nights* as an Arabo-Islamic document,[52] and its popular proliferation in almost every venue, the role of nineteenth-century writing in envisioning a worldwide imaginary invites further exploration. Alongside the venues already discussed, it is worthwhile to mention prominent scholars' focus on the *Nights* throughout the nineteenth and early twentieth century, the period that, for Renan, signifies European modernity that coincides with an increasing interest in the region and its geographies, manners, customs, natural resources and people.

In his articulation and use of Orientalism as a field of knowledge that is rooted in philology, Renan argues: 'Philology is the *exact science* of mental objects. It is to the sciences of humanity what physics and chemistry are to the philosophic sciences of bodies.'[53] Every subsequent image-making of Islam and the Orient that makes use of the foundational scholarship of de Sacy, von Hammer-Purgstall, George Lamb, Edward Forster, Richard Gough, Jonathan Scott and John Richardson has to pass through a number of lenses,[54]

[51] Said, *Orientalism*, p. 196.

[52] As early as 1811, we have G. S. Beaumont, *Arabian Nights' Entertainments: Or, the Thousand and One Nights, Accurately Describing the Manners, Customs, Laws, and Religion of the Eastern Nations*, 4 vols (London: Mathews & Leigh, 1811).

[53] Translated and quoted by Said, *Orientalism*, pp. 132–3.

[54] George Lamb, Edward Forster and John Richardson wrote prefaces to their adaptations or translations of the *Nights*: George Lamb, *New Arabian Nights' Entertainments*, selected from the original MS. By Joseph von Hammer; now first translated into English, 3 vols (London: Henry Colburn, 1826), with a preface; Edward Forster, *The Arabian Nights*, 5 vols (London: Miller, 1802), with a preface; Richard Gough (trans. and ed.), *Arabian Nights Entertainments*, 4 vols (London: Longman, 1798), with a preface; and Jonathan Scott, *The Arabian Nights Entertainments*, with etchings by A. Lalauze, 4 vols (London: Nimmo, [1811] 1883). John Richardson issued two relevant books, *Dissertation on the Language, Literature, and Manners of the Eastern Nations* (Oxford: Clarendon, 1778); and *A Grammar of the Arabic Language* (London: Murray, 1776).

and one of them like that of Gobineau, Ernest Renan and Fourier leaves an indelible mark on a supremacist rhetoric that ends up with the debasement of Others. Like any great book of a composite nature and enchanting narrative, the *Nights* offers itself easily to different readings and dispositions; it also charms and changes readers' dark sides.[55] Writings that happen to accumulate and gather around the Orient are not homogeneous, but the rhetoric of empire also gathers its material from these that feed into and better suit its message. But this venue is not as simple as it sounds.

Prominent translations or editions also impact responses among proponents of colonialism, racism and discrimination against women. Gobineau's mixed response to the *Thousand and One Nights* was probably inspired by Galland's version; but he was definitely conversant with the ongoing discussion of origins as proposed in a number of introductions or epilogues to other versions, especially Galland's version with de Sacy's appended study.[56] But he could have read von Hammer's edition of extra tales that were translated into French by G. S. Trébutien (1826).[57] What counts is his view that the *Arabian Nights* is Persian; and it is also Asiatique. As I argued in *The Arabian Nights in Contemporary World Cultures*, the sparingly edited Galland's translation was all the rage in Paris and London, and nobody remained untouched by the tales for better or worse.

Galland and Lane: Emergence of Incompatible Imaginaries

Along with multiple factors that relate to the rise of middle-class reading publics and the undeveloped art of narrative, the relative absence of substantial translations from the enormous classical and medieval Arabic cultural production allowed the *Thousand and One Nights* to be at the centre of attention. Its

[55] See Robert Irwin, 'The Dark Side of the Arabian Nights', n.d., available at: https://www.criticalmuslim.io/the-dark-side-of-the-arabian-nights, last accessed 28 August 2020.

[56] More popular in France were these contributions by Baron de Sacy: Silvestre de Sacy, 'Mémoire sur l'origine du recueil de conts intitulé Les Mille et une Nuits', *Mémoires de l'Académie des inscriptiones et belle lettres* 10 (1829): 30–64; and Baron de Sacy, 'Recherches sur l'oringine du recueilde contes intitulé les Mille et une Nuits', *Revue de Paris* 5 (1829): 65–76.

[57] In English, see Lamb, *New Arabian Nights' Entertainments*. French and English editions relied on August E. Zinserling's German translation, 1823.

first translator and editor, Antoine Galland (1646–1715), writes of Eastern manners and diverse representations of faiths and regions, but not of a specifically Islamic text. He writes of the tales in his preface as follows:

> They must also be pleasing, because of the account they give of the customs and manners of the eastern nations, and of the ceremonies of their religion, as well Pagan as Mahometan, which are better described here than in any author that has wrote of them, or in the relations of travellers. All the eastern nations, Persians, Tartars, and Indians, are here distinguished, and appear such as they are, from the foreign to the meanest subject; so that without the fatigue of going to see those people in their respective countries, the reader has here the pleasure to see them act, and hear from them speak.

But the power of this translation derives from Galland's knack for storytelling. In D. B. MacDonald's words, 'He was a born story-teller; he had a flair for a good story and a knack to re-tell it well.'[58] He made a few changes to the formulaic frame and the division into Nights,[59] and effected stylistic changes to accommodate the text to French decorum and minimised the invocations of God. The success, as evidenced in reprints, continuations, imitations, retranslations and serialisations was incomparable to any other reception. It took France, then England, and Europe by surprise and changed for good the dry rules set by Boileau. Martha Pike Conant wrote in her dissertation that came out in book form in 1908: 'In France, the popularity of these fantastic and marvellous stories, restless in plot and exuberant in colour, had testified to a truant desire to escape from the strict artistic rules and classical ideals of masters like Boileau. Conditions were similar in England.'[60] Jorge Luis Borges adds more to this conclusion in his 'The Thousand and One Nights': 'It might be said that the Romantic movement begins at the moment when someone, in Normandy or in Paris, reads The Thousand and One Nights. He leaves the world legislated by Boileau (d. 1711) and enters the world of

[58] D. B. MacDonald, 'Alf Laila wa-laila', *The Encyclopaedia of Islam, Supplement* (Leiden: Brill, 1938), pp. 17–21 at 17.

[59] See Mahdi, *The Thousand and One Nights*, pp. 39–49.

[60] Conant, *The Oriental Tale in England*, p. 247.

Romantic freedom.'[61] Galland established the canon for the *Arabian Nights*, as argued by Borges in his 'The Translators of the Thousand and One Nights', but he also offers a translation that is largely responsible for an active image-making of the East, and the Arabs. It was disturbing to eighteenth-century rules of composition, the emphasis on restraint and the fear of extravagant imagination. Indeed, Samuel Johnson has as title for a chapter in his pseudo-Oriental tale *Rasselas* (1759) 'The dangerous prevalence of imagination'.[62] Less given to divine referentiality, eighteenth-century writings focus more on the general than the particular, and more on the human than the sacred. Even pseudo-Oriental tales like the ones written by Voltaire (1694–1778) and Samuel Johnson attempt either to flaunt and mock a trendy infatuation with the 'Orient' as in (*Zadig*, 1747) or, in the case of Johnson's (1709–84) *Rasselas* (1759), to represent Abyssinia (Ethiopia) as lacking knowledge in comparison with England and France. And as 'knowledge will always predominate over ignorance, as man governs the other animals',[63] colonisation is advocated as a blessing![64]

Each translation opens up different horizons and expectations, but one can agree with Borges that Galland and later Mardrus allow enough space for imagination to construct an Orient.[65] As noticed earlier, Leigh Hunt calls this the 'Orient of poets'. It is nowhere, but it remains vast and free enough to let imagination roam. Hunt draws a picture that readers of Galland and later Mardrus cherish and recall with love. In his *London Journal* of October 1834, Leigh Hunt hailed this vision of the Orient as follows: 'Hail gorgeous East! . . . the Orient of Poets, the magic lands of the child, the ineffaceable recollection of the man.' Writing about new translations of the *Arabian Nights* for the *London and Westminster Review* (October 1839), Hunt argues as to why he was

[61] Jorge Luis Borges, 'The Thousand and One Nights', trans. Eliot Weinberger, *The Georgia Review* 38(3) (1984): 564–74 at 572.

[62] Samuel Johnson, *The History of Rasselas, Prince of Abissinia* (London: Penguin, [1759] 1976), pp. 133–4.

[63] Johnson, *The History of Rasselas*, p. 63.

[64] See Muhsin al-Musawi, 'Rasselas as a Colonial Discourse', *CIEFL Bulletin* n.s. 8(1) (1996): 47–60.

[65] J. C. Mardrus (ed.), *Le livre des mille nuits et une nuit* (Paris: Éditions de la Revue blanche, 1899–1929, 1900–4).

more attuned to Galland's version against the heavily annotated one by Edward William Lane: 'What is more valuable in the "Arabian Nights" is not what concerns the Arabs as Arabs, but what concerns all the world as men, women, and children – as lovers of surprising adventures, of visions, of luxuries, of beauty, of pomp and power, of endless variety and vicissitude.'[66] In 1834, and under the unchallenged lure of Galland's version, Leigh Hunt sums up the components of a Romantic imaginary that cares less for Islamic practices and manners and customs:

> To us, the Arabian Nights are one of the most beautiful books in the world: not because there is nothing but pleasure in it, but because the pain has infinite chances of vicissitude, and because the pleasure is within the reach of all who have body and soul, and imagination. The poor man there sleeps in a door-way with his love, and is richer than a king. The Sultan is dethroned tomorrow, and has a finer throne the next day. The pauper touches a ring, and spirits wait upon him. You ride in the air; you are rich in solitude; you long for somebody to return your love, and an Eden encloses you in its arms. You have this world, and you have another. Fairies are in your moon-light. Hope and imagination have their fair play, as well as the rest of us. There is action heroical, and passion too: people can suffer, as well as enjoy, for love; you have bravery, luxury, fortitude, self-devotion, comedy as good as Moliere's, tragedy, Eastern manners, the wonderful that is in a common place, and the verisimilitude that is in the wonderful calendars, cadis, robbers, enchanted palaces, paintings full of colour and drapery, warmth for the senses, desert in arms and exercises to keep it manly, cautions to the rich, humanity for the more happy, and hope for the miserable.[67]

In other words, the *Arabian Nights* as offered in Galland's version evokes an imaginary Orient, whereas annotated translations call on verifiable or credible associations that could meet the interests of the bourgeoisie and also the interests of the empire overseas. Both directions provide their imaginaries, but the replication of a presumed Islam appears more in response to Edward

[66] Leigh Hunt, 'New Translations of the Arabian Nights', *London and Westminster Review* (October 1839), p. 111.

[67] Hunt, 'Genii and Fairies of the East, the Arabian Nights', pp. 233–7.

William Lane's translation that appeared first in thirty-two serialised parts in 1838.[68] Supplemented with enormous body of notes to discuss manners and customs and reference everything as presumably practised in Egypt, certified by the learned, or mentioned in classical tradition, Lane's *Nights* leaves little space for imaginative flights, but it revives an interest in comparisons with England at the height of its imperial glory.[69]

Edward William Lane and the Authentication Mania

No wonder that Edward William Lane's copious notes to his translation of the book of the *Thousand and One Nights* from the Bulaq edition and double-checked against available editions[70] invited his nephew Stanley-Lane Poole to prepare them in book form under the title *The Arabian Society in the Middle Ages*, which complements Lane's book *Manners and Customs of the Modern Egyptians* (1836).[71] These were backed at a later stage by his *Lexicon* (in eight parts, 1863–91). Islam looms large in these two books, and the *Nights* appears as an Islamic document. It is not surprising that Lane exercised an unusual impact on the field. It is mainly due to this impact that the *Nights* was systematically conflated with Islam and the Arabs. Even its supernatural element, its marvels and magic, is rationalised as common faith among Muslims, medieval and modern. When illustrators for more than three centuries have tried to capture Scheherazade's flowing narrative, they often end up with a mixed plateau where projections or denials maintain a tenuous relationship to an encompassing cultural script. The symbolic, the real and the imaginary become blurred as they are played out in a domain that lures,

[68] Edward William Lane (trans. and ed.), *A New Translation of the Tales of a Thousand and One Nights; Known in England as the Arabian Nights' Entertainments* (London: Charles Knight, 1838–40) (in 32 pts.).

[69] For more on this point, see al-Musawi, *Scheherazade in England*, pp. 91–114.

[70] Lane, *A New Translation of the tales of a Thousand and One Nights*, with copies notes by Edward William Lane, illustrated with many hundred wood-cuts. This is followed by his *The Thousand and One Nights, commonly called, in England, the Arabian Nights' Entertainments.* A new translation from the Arabic, with copious notes, illustrated by William Harvey, 3 vols (London: Charles Knight, 1839–41). With a foreword and substantial review essay.

[71] Stanley Lane-Poole (1854–1931), *Arabian Society in the Middle Ages: Studies from The Thousand and One Nights* (London: Chatto & Windus, 1883).

disenchants and erases its signifieds. Some prominent contemporary scholars get trapped in Lane's version of the *Thousand and One Nights*, its enormous annotation that drove the Arabian Knight and unique rebel Richard F. Burton to provide his documentary surplus of notes, 'Terminal Essay' and 'A Biography of the Book and Its Reviewers Reviewed'.[72] Indeed, to write a 'biography' of the *Thousand and One Nights* is an instance of genuine encapsulation of the power of the *Nights* in impacting worldwide imaginaries. Illustrious scholars like Mia Gerhardt, Fedwa Malti-Douglas and Andre Miquel find it difficult to speak of a composite work in terms of totality and wholeness. Thus, Malti-Douglas addresses only the frame to conclude that 'the frame of the *Nights* is certainly in the Islamic mainstream'.[73] If she means the Scheherazade/Shahryar story, it is not Islamic; but if she means other embedded and frame tales like 'The Merchant and the Demon', then narrative functions within an Islamic understanding of a universe of jinn and humans. Andre Miquel sums the real, the symbolic and the imaginary in historical terms. 'Islamic civilization expressed in Arabic encompasses a very long history. The *Arabian Nights* follows it over nearly ten centuries.'[74] Gerhardt relies more on F. Gabrieli's discussion of the amalgamated composition that has the veneer of Arabic, but not the robust material of the classical tradition. 'This is the inevitable result of the long historical process which has led to the actual form of the "1001 Nights", in which several cultural periods are superposed and amalgamated, that of classical Arabic civilization being not the most conspicuous, not the best preserved.'[75]

Lane's edition was to generate such conversations, but not Galland's. Even when Jonathan Scott reproduced and edited Galland (1811), translating

[72] See al-Musawi, *Scheherazade in England*, pp. 115–43; al-Musawi, *The Arabian Nights in Contemporary World Cultures*, pp. 136–7.

[73] Fedwa Malti-Douglas, *Woman's Body, Woman's Word: Gender and Discourse in Arabo-Islamic Writing* (Princeton, NJ: Princeton University Press, 1991), p. 24.

[74] Andre Miquel, 'The Thousand and One Nights in Arabic Literature and Society', in Richard G. Hovannisian and Georges Sabag (eds), *The Thousand and One Nights in Arabic Literature and Society* (Cambridge: Cambridge University Press, 1997), pp. 6–13 at 7.

[75] Translated and cited in Mia Gerhardt, *The Art of Storytelling: A Literary Study of the Thousand and One Nights* (Leiden: Brill, 1963), p. 4.

additional new tales with a lengthy introduction on manners and customs,[76] he could not go beyond a contemporaneous conversation. But Lane's came at an opportune time, the heyday of the realistic novel, and the preparation of the Crystal Palace exhibition to celebrate the expansive empire. In a note on his significant poem, 'Recollections of the Arabian Nights', Alfred Lord Tennyson wrote: 'I had only the translation from the French of Galland – of the Arabian Nights – when this was written, so I talked of sofas, etc. Lane was yet unborn.'[77] The phrasing is important, for Galland offers a compelling narrative to conjure up images and details, but Lane's edition with its notes and illustrations freezes any conjecture, it confines imagination. Hattersley wrote a long article for *The Dublin Review* (February 1940) in which he celebrates the edition because it places 'the reality bodily before us'.[78] This 'reality', and no matter how representationally confining, is to inform a worldwide imaginary about Islam that cannot be easily dislodged. It allows such essentialist readings as the Israeli Orientalist Raphael Patai's *The Arab Mind* (1973). In other words, and regardless of Lane's good intentions, representational knowledge functions as a one-track informant that allows little space for contending views. William Harvey's illustrations, 'under the eye of Mr. Lane', cannot be overestimated.[79] They freeze scenes and offer all illustrators and painters some material to build genealogies of an Orient and Islam that take the lead from a narrative that in its late fourteenth-century manuscript claims no more than itself. B. E. Pote wrote to the *Foreign Quarterly Review* on the power of Harvey's illustrations as 'the very dreams of the reader's own imagination spontaneously wrought into shape, and phantastically weaving them adown the margin as he reads the tale . . . constantly giving to unformed

[76] Scott, *The Thousand and One Nights; or the Arabian Nights' Entertainments*; W. E. Griffis (ed.), *Alif Laila wa Leila: The Arabian Nights Entertainments*; adapted for American readers from the text of Jonathan Scott, with an introduction, 4 vols (Boston, MA: Lothrop, 1891).

[77] Cited by Leila Ahmed, *Edward W. Lane: A Study of His Life and Works and of the British Ideas of the Middle East in the Nineteenth Century* (London: Longman, 1978), p. 143, from Alfred Lord Tennyson, *Works*, with notes by the author. Edited with a memoir by Hallam Lord Tennyson (London, 1913), 897.

[78] M. Hattersley, 'The Arabian Nights' Entertainments', *Dublin Review* VIII (February 1840): 105–33 at 127.

[79] Austin Dobson, *Thomas Bewick and His Pupils* (London, 1884), p. 213.

and embryo conception, the force and finish of reality'.[80] Lane's contemporaries, as reviewed in *Scheherazade in England*, consider his version to be the real *Arabian Nights*, conflated for good with Islam, a point that the *Eclectic Review*, the *Athenaeum*, the *Foreign Quarterly Review* and many others celebrated.[81]

Incitement to Comparisons: Rites of Passage

It was not coincidence that John Payne allowed his nine-volume translation in 1882–4,[82] with three more volumes later, to be used in full by Richard Francis Burton. The aesthete, poet and Arabist saw in hindsight the drift towards ethnology and anthropology. Henceforth, a large industry grew around the *Nights* that in turn informed and fed imaginaries. If Galland inspires 'Recollections of the Arabian Nights' as the most powerful poem that testifies to a realm of art, presided over by the benevolent caliph Harun al-Rashid, later editions force different images and recollections. Walter Bagehot's significant essay 'The People of the Arabian Nights' is a counterpoint to Tennyson's 'Recollections' and Leigh Hunt's criticism.[83] Bagehot thinks of the transition from Galland to Lane as a rite of passage: 'As it is impossible to revive the old feelings in their old force, it is pleasant, if we wish to re-peruse the Eastern stories, to have them in a form like that given to them by Mr. Lane; sufficiently different to leave our minds free from old distractions, and faithful enough to give play to a new set of interests.'[84] This rite of passage applies to many careers and individuals; it signifies a departure from the Romantic craze of projections to

[80] B. E. Pote, 'Arabian Nights', *Foreign Quarterly Review* XXIV (1839): 139–68 at 157.

[81] See Muhsin al-Musawi, 'Lane and The Victorian Literary Scene', in *Scheherazade in England*, pp. 91–114.

[82] John Payne (trans.), *The Book of the Thousand Nights and One Night*: now first completely done into English prose and verse, from the original Arabic, 9 vols (London: Printed by Villon Society for private subscription and private circulation, 1882–4) (with well-informed book-length essay appended to vol. 9); and John Payne, *Tales from the Arabic of the Breslau and Calcutta* (1814–18) editions of the *Book of the Thousand Nights and One Night*, not occurring in the other printed texts of the work, now first done into English, 3 vols (London: Villon Society, private subscription and circulation, 1884).

[83] Walter Bagehot, 'The People of the Arabian Nights', *National Review* IX (July 1859): 44–71.

[84] Bagehot, 'The People of the Arabian Nights', p. 47.

an analytic mode that argues the relative absence of deep interiorisation of character and the emphasis on action as a condition of possibility whereby medieval Islam had its impositions of conformity: 'as beliefs never questioned and responsibilities never lifted'.[85] He ends up with a conclusion that converses with some basic Orientalist tenets. He argues that Islam as a political system 'opens a minimum of play for the faculties, [and] in which genius and industry are no stepping-stones to advancement, and incapacity and negligence no bar to favour'.[86] The *Nights* becomes Bagehot's bedrock to analyse Islam. Bagehot's wording, his emphasis on 'people', and his navigation between the *Nights* and Lane's notes, and probably Harvey's illustrations, signal the height of conflation that began ramblingly in Jonathan Scott's introduction (1811) on manners and customs, along with the emphasis on the need to authenticate the *Nights* against multiple manuscripts. Although not an Orientalist, his roles as businessman, journalist, founder of a powerful journal and man of letters situate Bagehot at the heart of empire, its reading of other cultures and representations of Islam, and along with it the whole region. His appreciation of the role of the caliph Harun al-Rashid recapitulates Tennyson's 'Recollections'; but his reading differs from Tennyson who had Galland's version for envisioning a realm of art. Bagehot writes: 'The presence of this defined and imposing character, wielding irresponsible power and commanding unlimited resources . . . this stately, magnificent centrepiece gives a certain unity and substance to this collection of tales, which even with its aid they too much want: for the book is, in many respects, a jumbled gathering.'[87] Years later, John Payne argues against al-Rashid as caliph; his role as just and fair is disputed.[88] He presents the caliph as given to 'furious outbursts of passionate frenzy'. As for the presentation of the monarch as benevolent, Payne suggests: 'a great portion of the collection was taken bodily from notes or compilations prepared at his especial instance by the celebrated poets and musicians . . . that illustrated his court'.[89] These

[85] Bagehot, 'The People of the Arabian Nights', p. 56.

[86] Bagehot, 'The People of the Arabian Nights', p. 55.

[87] Bagehot, 'The People of the Arabian Nights', p. 63.

[88] John Payne, 'The Thousand and One Nights', *New Quarterly Magazine* 2 pts (January/April 1879): 1:150–74, 2:377–401.

[89] Payne, 'The Thousand and One Nights', 1:161.

opposite representations are to inform the makeup of an imaginary: Tennyson–Bagehot's representation based on the *Nights* leads us to William Butler Yeats' famous poem 'The Gift of Haroun al-Rashid';[90] whereas John Payne's informs J. E. Flecker's popular play *Hassan* (in five acts) that was rebuffed for its negative representation of the caliph.[91] No matter how we read representations as central to Western imaginaries of Islam, trendy 'realism' that gave way to naturalist explorations and Burton's superfluity proves no less forceful than the supernatural in either enhancing an illustration industry or shedding into cinematic production. When editing a popular abridged version of Galland's, Lawrence Housman wrote in celebration of Arthur Boyd Houghton's illustrations because they 'supply humour or pathos or character-drawing, which the story itself quite failed to convey. In his hands, Aladdin's mother becomes a character of delicious comedy.'[92] A genealogical illustration production that struck roots in late eighteenth-century Europe, in France, England and Germany, proved to be both a blessing and a curse. As a blessing, it gives form to storytelling and brings it closer to audiences worldwide. Nineteenth-century drawings continue to provide material for the reproduction of the *Thousand and One Nights*, feeding multiple voicings across borders. As a curse it invites ditties such as the one that prologues Disney's production of Aladdin that manifests how stereotyping operates as serious racial injustice.[93] It reads as follows: 'Oh I come from a land / From a faraway place / Where the caravan

[90] William Butler Yeats, 'The Gift of Haroun al-Rashid', was written in 1923, appeared in the American journal *The Dial* (1924) and first appeared in *English Life and the Illustrated Review* (January 1924).

[91] James Elroy Flecker, *Hassan: The Story of Hassan of Baghdad and How he Came to Make the Golden Journey to Samarkand* (London: Heinemann, 1922).

[92] Lawrence Housman, 'Introductory Essay', *Arthur Boyd Houghton: A Selection of His Work* (London: Kegan Paul, 1896), p. 24. See also al-Musawi, *Scheherazade in England*, p. 100.

[93] Christopher Wise, 'Notes from the Aladdin Industry: Or, Middle Eastern Folklore in the Era of Multinational Capitalism', in Brenda Ayers (ed.), *The Emperor's Old Groove: Decolonizing Disney's Magic Kingdom* (New York: Peter Lang, 2003), pp. 105–14; Dianne Sachko Macleod, 'The Politics of Vision: Disney, Aladdin, and the Gulf War', in Brenda Ayers (ed.), *The Emperor's Old Groove: Decolonizing Disney's Magic Kingdom* (New York: Peter Lang, 2003), pp. 179–92; and Timothy R. White and James Emmet Winn, 'Islam, Animation and Money: The Reception of Disney's Aladdin in Southeast Asia', *Kinema* (1995), available at: http://www.kinema.uwaterloo.ca/white951.html, last accessed 23 December 2020.

camels roam. / Where they cut off your ear / If they don't like your face. / It's barbaric, but hey, it's home.' This popular production, directed by Guy Ritchie, with a budget of US$183 million, incites critics to admire its art and cinematography, but bemoan its departure from the original.[94] There is always 'collateral' damage, as Jack Shaheen's comprehensive survey of cinematography shows. The post-industrial era witnesses raids on the *Arabian Nights* and its orphan tales that are no less violent than wars of intervention.[95] Muhsin Mahdi is right in concluding that: 'For the eighteenth-century, the *Nights* was the "Orient", and the orient was the world of Muslims and Ottomans.'[96] The neat conclusion could have been qualified a bit to suggest the limits of that imaginary before the advent of Lane. Although the age of empire and then the post-industrial society differ from the eighteenth century in focus, the *Nights* remains a point of reference to the Orient. The major translations, along with that of Enno Littmann continue to feed image-making not because the tales allow such excursions, but primarily because the surplus of notes redirect attention from the art of storytelling to the ethnographic and racial side.

Bibliography

Abbott, Nabia, 'A Ninth-Century Fragment of the "Thousand Nights" New Light on the Early History of the Arabian Nights', *Journal of Near Eastern Studies* 8 (1949): 129–64.

Ahmed, Leila, *Edward W. Lane: A Study of His Life and Works and of the British Ideas of the Middle East in the Nineteenth Century* (London: Longman, 1978).

[94] 'Though the story of Aladdin begins and ends familiar, there is a different tale told and we see the rise of a different Sultan which is neatly written and brought out', available at: https://www.behindwoods.com/english-movies/aladdin/aladdin-review.html, last accessed 23 December 2020.

[95] See at: https://www.latimes.com/local/obituaries/la-me-jack-shaheen-20170713-story.html, last accessed 23 December 2020. Shaheen convinced Disney to change a few things that had already appeared in early Disney versions. Jack Shaheen, *Reel Bad Arabs: How Hollywood Vilifies a People*, 3rd edn (Northhampton, MA: Olive Branch Press, 2014). See also Wise, 'Notes from the Aladdin Industry', pp. 105–14; and White and Winn, 'Islam, Animation and Money'.

[96] Mahdi, *The Thousand and One Nights*, p. 4. See also al-Musawi, 'The Arabian Nights in Eighteenth-Century English Criticism', pp. 12–32.

Almond, Ian, *History of Islam in German Thought from Leibniz to Nietzsche* (New York: Routledge, 2010).

Al-Musawi, Muhsin Jasim, 'The Arabian Nights in Eighteenth-Century English Criticism', *Muslim World* 67 (1977): 12–32.

Al-Musawi, Muhsin Jasim, *Scheherazade in England: A Study of Nineteenth-Century English Criticism of the Arabian Nights* (Washington, DC: Three Continents Press, 1981).

Al-Musawi, Muhsin Jasim, 'Rasselas as a Colonial Discourse', *CIEFL Bulletin* 8(1) (1996): 47–60.

Al-Musawi, Muhsin Jasim, *The Islamic Context of the Thousand and One Nights* (New York: Columbia University Press, 2009).

Al-Musawi, Muhsin Jasim, *The Arabian Nights in Contemporary World Cultures* (Cambridge: Cambridge University Press, 2021).

Arberry, Arthur J., 'Oriental Pearls Strung', *BSOAS* 11(4) (1946): 699–712.

Bagehot, Walter, 'The People of the Arabian Nights', *The National Review* IX (July 1859): 44–71.

Beaumont, G. S., *Arabian Nights' Entertainments: Or, the Thousand and One Nights, Accurately Describing the Manners, Customs, Laws, and Religion of the Eastern Nations*, 4 vols (London: Mathews & Leigh, 1811).

Behindwoods Review Board, 'Aladdin Movie Review', Behind Woods, n.d., available at: https://www.behindwoods.com/english-movies/aladdin/aladdin-review.html, last accessed 23 December 2020.

Borges, Jorge Luis, 'The Thousand and One Nights', trans. Eliot Weinberger, *The Georgia Review* 38(3) (1984): 564–74.

Byatt, A. S., *The Arabian Nights: Tales from a Thousand and One Nights* (New York: Modern Library Classics, 2001).

Campbell, Gregor, 'Imaginary/Symbolic/Real', in Irena R. Makaryk (ed.), *Encyclopedia of Contemporary Literary Theory: Approaches, Scholars, Terms* (Toronto: Toronto University Press, 1995), pp. 560–1.

Conant, Martha Pike, *The Oriental Tale in England in the Eighteenth Century* (New York: Columbia University Press, 1908).

Cooper, J., *The Oriental Moralist; or the Beauties of the Arabian Nights Entertainments* (London: Newbery, 1790).

Cooper, J., *Beauties of the Arabian Nights Entertainments, Consisting of the Most Entertaining Stories*, 2nd edn (London: Newbery, 1792).

Daniel, Norman, *Islam, Europe and Empire* (Edinburgh: University Press, 1967).

de Sacy, Silvestre, 'Mémoire Sur l'origine Du Recueil de Conts Intitulé Les Mille et Une Nuits', *Mémoires de l'Académie des Inscriptiones et Belle Lettres* 10 (1829): 30–64.

de Sacy, Silvestre, 'On the Origin of the "Arabian Nights"', XXVIII (July 1829), pp. 560–66 (repr. in *Selections from the Asiatic Journal*, covering January 1816 to December 1829 (Madras, 1875), 996–1001).

de Sacy, Silvestre, 'Recherches Sur l'origine Du Recueilde Contes Intitulé Les Mille et Une Nuits', *Revue de Paris* 5 (1829): 65–76.

Description de l'Égypte, French Government, 1809.

Dobson, Austin, *Thomas Bewick and His Pupils* (London, 1884).

Flecker, James Elroy, *Hassan: The Story of Hassan of Baghdad and How He Came to Make the Golden Journey to Samarkand* (London: Heinemann, 1922).

Forster, Edward (trans.), *The Arabian Nights*, 5 vols (London: Miller, 1802).

Forster, Edward (trans.), *Arabian Nights' Entertainments* (London: J. Thomas, 1842).

Galland, Antoine (trans.), *Les Mille et Une Nuits* (Paris: Bourdin, 1860).

Gerhardt, Mia, *The Art of Storytelling: A Literary Study of the Thousand and One Nights* (Leiden: Brill, 1963).

Godlewska, Anne, 'Map, Text and Image: The Mentality of Enlightened Conquerors: A New Look at the Description de l'Égypte', *Transactions of the Institute of British Geographers* 20(1) (1995): 5–28.

Gough, Richard (trans.), *Arabian Nights Entertainments*, 4 vols (London: Longman, 1798).

Griffis, W. E. (trans.), *Alif Laila Wa Leila: The Arabian Nights Entertainments*, 4 vols (Boston, MA: Lothrop, 1891).

Haddawy, Husain Fareed Ali, 'English Arabesque: The Oriental Mode in Eighteenth-Century English Literature', unpublished PhD dissertation, Cornell University, 1962.

Hammer-Purgstall, Joseph von, 'On Arabic Poetry, Especially the Romance of Antar', *New Monthly Magazine* 13 (1820): 12–18, 151–61.

Hammer-Purgstall, Joseph von, 'Sur l'Origine Des Mille et Une Nuits', *Journal Asiatique* 10 (1827): 253–6.

Hammer-Purgstall, Joseph von, 'Note: Sur l'origine Persane Des Mille et Une Nuits', *Journal Asiatique* 3(8) (1839): 171–6.

Hattersley, M., 'The Arabian Nights' Entertainments', *Dublin Review* VIII (February 1840): 105–33.

Horta, Paulo Lemos, *Marvellous Thieves: Secret Authors of the Arabian Nights* (Cambridge, MA: Harvard University Press, 2017).

Housman, Lawrence, 'Introductory Essay', in *Arthur Boyd Houghton: A Selection of His Work* (London: Kegan Paul, 1896), pp. 11–29.

Huet, Pierre-Daniel, *A Treatise of Romances and Their Original*, trans. S. Lewis (London: Flower-de-Luce & Sun, 1715).

Hunt, Leigh, 'On Genii and Fairies of the East, the Arabian Nights', *Leigh Hunt's London Journal* 1(30) (1834): 233–7.

Hunt, Leigh, 'New Translations of the Arabian Nights', *London and Westminster Review* XXXIII (1839): 101–37.

Irwin, Robert (ed.), *The Arabian Nights: Tales of 1001 Nights, vol. 1: Nights 1 to 294*, trans. Malcolm C. Lyons and Ursula Lyons (London: Penguin, 2008).

Irwin, Robert, 'The Dark Side of "The Arabian Nights"', *Critical Muslim*, n.d., available at: https://www.criticalmuslim.io/the-dark-side-of-the-arabian-nights, last accessed 28 August 2020.

Johnson, Samuel, *The History of Rasselas, Prince of Abissinia* (London: Penguin, 1976).

Kitson, Peter J., 'Byron and Post-Colonial Criticism: The Eastern Tales', in Jane Stabler (ed.), *Palgrave Advances in Byron Studies* (London: Palgrave Macmillan, 2007), pp. 106–29.

Knipp, Charles, 'The Arabian Nights in England: Galland's Translation and Its Successors', *Journal of Arabic Literature* 5(1) (1974): 44-54.

Lacan, Jacques, *Speech and Language in Psychoanalysis*, trans. Anthony Wilden (Baltimore, MD: Johns Hopkins University Press, 1973).

Lamb, George (trans.), *New Arabian Nights' Entertainments*, 3 vols (London: Henry Colburn, 1926).

Lane, Edward William (trans.), *The Thousand and One Nights, Commonly Called, in England, the Arabian Nights' Entertainments*, 3 vols (London: Charles Knight, 1839).

Lane-Poole, Stanley, *Arabian Society in the Middle Ages: Studies from The Thousand and One Nights* (London: Chatto & Windus, 1883).

Les mille et une nuits, contes arabes, traduit par Galland, Illustrés par M. M. Français, H. Baron, ed. Wattier, Laville, etc. Revus et corrigés sur l'édition princeps de 1704, augmentés d'une dissertation sur les Mille et une nuits, par Sylvestre de Sacy.

Lyall, Sir James (trans.), *Translations of Ancient Arabic Poetry, Chiefly Pre-Islamic, with Introduction and Notes* (London: William & Norgate, 1885).

MacDonald, Duncan Black, 'On Translating the Arabian Nights', *The Nation* 71 (1900): 167-8, 185-6.

MacDonald, Duncan Black, 'A Preliminary Classification of Some MSS of the Arabian Nights', in Thomas Walker Arnold and Reynold Alleyne Nicholson (eds), *A Volume of Oriental Studies Presented to Edward G. Browne* (Cambridge: Cambridge University Press, 1922), pp. 304–21.

MacDonald, Duncan Black, 'The Earlier History of the Arabian Nights', *Journal of the Royal Asiatic Society of Great Britain and Ireland* 3 (1924): 353–97.

MacDonald, Duncan Black, 'A Bibliographical and Literary Study of the First Appearance of the Arabian Nights in Europe', *Library Quarterly* 2(1) (1932): 387–420.

MacDonald, Duncan Black, 'Alf Laila Wa-Laila', in M. Th. Houtsma, A. J. Wensinck, Willi Heffening, Evariste Lévi-Provençal, and H. A. R. Gibb (eds), *The Encyclopaedia of Islam, Supplement* (Leiden: Brill, 1938), pp. 17–21.

Macleod, Dianne Sachko, 'The Politics of Vision: Disney, Aladdin, and the Gulf War', in Brend Ayers (ed.), *The Emperor's Old Groove: Decolonizing Disney's Magic Kingdom* (New York: Peter Lang, 2003), pp. 179–92.

Mahdi, Muhsin, *The Thousand and One Nights* (Leiden: Brill, 1995).

Malti-Douglas, Fedwa, *Woman's Body, Woman's Word: Gender and Discourse in Arabo-Islamic Writing* (Princeton, NJ: Princeton University Press, 1991).

Marble, Steve, 'Jack Shaheen Dies; Scholar Persuaded Disney to Alter "Aladdin" as He Fought Hollywood's Racial Stereotypes', *Los Angeles Times*, 13 July 2017.

Mardrus, J. C. (ed.), *Le livre des mille nuits et une nuit* (Paris: Éditions de la Revue blanche, 1899).

May, Georges, *Les Mille et Une Nuits d'Antoine Galland, Ou, Le Chef-d'oeuvre Invisible* (Paris: PUF, 1986).

Meredith, George, 'Review of Ochlenschläger's *Aladdin*', Westminster Review LXIX, n.s., XIII (1858): 291–3.

Miquel, André, 'The Thousand and One Nights in Arabic Literature and Society', in Richard G. Hovannisian and Georges Sabag (eds), *The Thousand and One Nights in Arabic Literature and Society* (Cambridge: Cambridge University Press, 1997), pp. 6–13.

Mohan, Hari (ed.), *Beauties of the Arabian Nights* (Calcutta, 1839).

Montagu, Lady Mary Wortley, *The Complete Letters*, ed. Robert Halsband, 3 vols (Oxford: Clarendon, 1965).

More, P. E., *The Drift of Romanticism* (New York: Houghton Mifflin, 1913).

Muhammad, al-Mufaddal ibn and Charles James Lyall (eds), *The Mufaddaliyat: An Anthology of Ancient Arabian Odes* (Oxford: Clarendon, 1918).

Nash, Geoffrey, 'Aryan and Semite in Ernest Renan's and Matthew Arnold's Quest for the Religion of Modernity', *Religion & Literature* 46(1) (2014): 25–50.

Palgrave, Francis, 'Dunlop's History of Fiction', *Quarterly Review* XIII (1815): 384–408.

Patai, Raphael, *The Arab Mind* (New York: Charles Scribner's, 1973).

Payne, John, 'The Thousand and One Nights', *New Quarterly Magazine* (January/April 1879): 150–74, 377–401.

Payne, John (trans.), *The Book of the Thousand Nights and One Night*, 9 vols (London: Villon Society, 1882).

Payne, John, *Tales from the Arabic of the Breslau and Calcutta*, 3 vols (London: Villon Society, 1884).

Poe, Edgar Allan, 'The Thousand-and-Second Tale of Scheherazade', *Godey's Magazine and Lady's Book (1844–1848)*, pp. 2, 61, 1845.

Pote, B. E., 'Arabian Nights', *Foreign Quarterly Review* XXIV (1839): 139–68.

Rey, Pierre-Louis, 'Joseph-Arthur de Gobineau (1816–1882)', n.d., BnF Shared Heritage, available at: https://heritage.bnf.fr/bibliothequesorient/en/joseph-gobineau-art, last accessed 28 August 2020.

Richardson, John, *A Grammar of the Arabic Language* (London: Murray, 1776).

Richardson, John, *Dissertation on the Language, Literature, and Manners of the Eastern Nations* (Oxford: Clarendon, 1778).

Said, Edward, *Orientalism* (New York: Random House-Vintage, 1978).

Schlegel, Friedrich von, *Lectures on the History of Literature, Ancient and Modern, from the German*, 2 vols (Edinburgh: Blackwood, 1818).

Schwab, Raymond, *The Oriental Renaissance: Europe's Rediscovery of India and the East: 1680–1880*, trans. Gene Patterson-Black and Victor Reinking (New York: Columbia University Press, 1984).

Scott, Jonathan, *The Arabian Nights Entertainments*, 4 vols (London: Nimmo, 1811).

Shaheen, Jack, *Reel Bad Arabs: How Hollywood Vilifies a People*, 3rd edn (Northhampton, MA: Olive Branch Press, 2014).

Stetkevych, Jaroslav, 'Arabic Poetry and Assorted Poetics', in M. H. Kerr (ed.), *Islamic Studies: A Tradition and Its Problems* (Malibu: Undena Publications, 1980), pp. 102–23.

Super, R. H. (ed.), *Prose Works of Matthew Arnold*, vol. VII (Ann Arbor: University of Michigan Press, 1960).

Talib, Adam, *How Do You Say 'Epigram' in Arabic? Literary History and the Limits of Comparison* (Leiden: Brill, 2018).

Taylor, W. C., 'Professor Schlegel and the Oriental Translation Fund', *Foreign Quarterly Review* 11 (1833): 72–7.

Tennyson, Alfred Lord, *Works*, ed. Hallam Lord Tennyson (London, 1913).

Toomer, G. J., *Eastern Wisedome and Learning* (Oxford: Oxford University Press, 1996).

Torrens, Henry, 'Remarks on M. Schlegel's Objections to the Restored Editions of the Alif Leilah, or Arabian Nights' Entertainments', *Journal of the Asiatic Society* 63 (1837): 161–8.

Warton, Thomas, 'On the Origin of Romantic Fiction in Europe', in *History of English Poetry*, vol. 1 (London, 1774).

White, Timothy R. and James Emmet Winn, 'Islam, Animation and Money: The Reception of Disney's Aladdin in Southeast Asia', *Kinema*.

Wise, Christopher, 'Notes from the Aladdin Industry: Or, Middle Eastern Folklore in the Era of Multinational Capitalism', in Brenda Ayers (ed.), *The Emperor's Old Groove: Decolonizing Disney's Magic Kingdom* (New York: Peter Lang, 2003), pp. 105–14.

Yeats, William Butler, 'The Gift of Harun Al-Raschid', *The Dial*, 1924.

9

WHERE IS WORLD LITERATURE?

Hamid Dabashi

You know this journey is not toward the heavens –
Towards Mars,
This eternal bloodsucker —
Or towards Venus
This horrid widow-whore wolf
Who knows no sorrow
Who used to toast her ominous drink with Hafez and Khayyam,
And dance wildly like a gypsy girl?
And now drinks with MacNeice or Nima –
And tomorrow will drink to whoever comes after us –
It is not towards them.

Mehdi Akhavan-e Sales, 'Chavoshi'

I would like to begin this chapter by sharing a memory. A few years after I finished my doctoral degree at the University of Pennsylvania in 1984, I went down to Philadelphia to have lunch with the late George Makdisi (1920–2002), the eminent scholar of the social and intellectual history of Islam and Christianity with whom I had the rare privilege of working as a graduate student. There were two towering minds on our campus in the late 1970s and early 1980 (I am sure there were more but I was particularly interested in these two) with whom I was closely affiliated: Philip Rieff and George Makdisi, a Freudian cultural sociologist and an intellectual historian, respectively, who very much shaped the contours of my own critical thinking.

While Rieff put a Freudian twist to my sociological imagination, Makdisi taught me how to tease out literary humanism from the domineering Islamic scholasticism.

George and I sat at a table in our Faculty Club at the corner of Locust Walk and 36th Street, picked up our food, ordered our drinks and began to catch up. I had finished my postdoctoral at Harvard and had started teaching at Columbia. My youthful essay, 'Symbiosis of Religious and Political Authorities in Islam' (1987) was still very much on George's mind and he was eager to talk about my arguments. We talked and reminisced from here and there until we came to talk about his most recent book, *The Rise of Humanism in Classical Islam and the Christian West: With Special Reference to Scholasticism* (1990),[1] a book I deeply admired and closely read after its sister volume, *The Rise of Colleges: Institutions of Learning in Islam and the West* (1981),[2] on which he was working while I was his student and published it when I had graduated. I began politely and gently sharing with him that I did not think the rise of Adab was entirely because of Qur'ānic eloquence and had to do with the cosmopolitan context of Baghdad. As an intellectual historian George was suspicious of all such sociological observations, but with impeccable grace, patience and gentility that was definitive toto to his character he engaged me in conversion. We finished our lunch, said farewell and parted ways.

I saw George on another occasion before his passing, when while vacationing with my family in Booth Bay Harbor, Maine, I accidentally ran into him in the parking lot of a motel where we were staying and he joyously showed me his back trunk full of books he was carrying while taking a break from his office on Penn campus. Years went by, George passed away in 2002, and I finally published my own book on Adab, *The World of Persian Literary humanism* (2012), dwelling mostly on the Persian Adab to the East of Muslim world, and in which I extended Makdisi's exquisite study to the Persian world, parting ways with him in my main arguments, while admiring, to this day, his comparative attractions to the Mediterranean basin. As a

[1] See George Makdisi, *The Rise of Humanism in Classical Islam and the Christian West: With Special Reference to Scholasticism* (Edinburgh: Edinburgh University Press, 1990).

[2] See George Makdisi, *The Rise of Colleges: Institutions of Learning in Islam and the West* (Edinburgh: Edinburgh University Press 1981).

Christian Arab, Makdisi's preoccupation was very much on the borderlines of scholasticism and humanism in the eastern Mediterranean world. Mine went eastward towards the Persianate world, where I had discovered a different set of theoretical considerations that had surfaced there and required attention.

The rich and expanding scholarship on Adab preceded that conversation between me and my mentor, and has now expanded far and wide into literary traditions in Indo-Persian, Central Asian, and Ottoman territories. The classic works collected in the edited volume of Barbara Daly Metcalf, *Moral Conduct and Authority: The Place of Adab in South Asian Islam* (1984) has now led to more recent works on multiple cites of literary humanism. While the pioneering work of George Makdisi was instrumental in my own work, the equally important work of South Asian scholars like Irfan Habib and Mozaffar Alam resulted in the excellent works of Sunil Sharma and others. The links among these areas have remained mostly unexamined. But the more crucial issue is the fact that these multiple sites, as exemplified in Makdisi, Metcalf and my own work is the fact that these simultaneous and concurrent worlds were at once concomitant and yet insular, and precisely in their varied polyfocality they point to the interpolated worlds of literacy humanism in Muslim worlds.

'Islam' as a Floating Signifier

The idea of Islam as a floating signifier to be considered as the framework of a different conception of world literature brings to the forefront of our critical thinking not only the variety of languages in which Muslims have realised their poetic and literary works, but also when similar literary works are translated into a language like Arabic, Persian, Turkish or Urdu that have historically been called 'Islamic languages'. We do not ordinarily think of English, French, Spanish or Portuguese as Islamic languages, and yet from Aristotle to Derrida and from Homer to Neruda they have been translated into these 'Islamic languages' and thus entered the domain of the worldly disposition of being a literate Muslim. Such a perspective will have overcome the self-centring Euro-universalism of 'World Literature' as North American and western European literary critiques have articulated it. But, at the same time, this very conception of Islam, open-ended as it is, cannot be fetishised unto itself and must be remembered as a quintessentially dialogical proposition in which all its moral and intellectual movements from the very beginning have been rooted in non-Islamic contexts. Masterpieces of Arabic and Persian literary traditions, from *Arabian Nights* to *The Shahnameh* have been actively incorporated into European bourgeois public spheres, and in turn they have reverberated back on the layered disposition of the Muslim world. Add to that the fact that there are increasing numbers of Muslims who live in Europe and North America and who produce their literary work in their new languages, a fact that is compromised by creating the alienating pigeon hole of 'diasporic literature'. The fact is that English, French, German, Italian, Spanish, etc have now also become 'Muslim languages'.

While writing my book on *The Shahnameh: The Persian Epic as World Literature* (2019),[3] I had an occasion to reflect on an incident in one of my classrooms while teaching the Persian epic when in the course of a class presentation on the *Shahnameh* illustrations a student was deeply impressed by the sudden realisation that in every frame of a painting she was observing how the whole epic dwelled. On this occasion, I had reasons to share with my students the sense of tragic totality when listening to the recitations of the iconic Palestinian poet Mahmoud Darwish (1941–2008) of his own poetry, declaring the triumphant tragedy of his own people. For all I know, I then speculated, Darwish had no knowledge of Ferdowsi, perhaps had never even read the *Shahnameh*, even in its Arabic translation that goes back to Fath ibn Ali Bundari Isfahani's (1190–1245) translation. But the sense of the fragility of fate evident in Darwish's poetry is and remains, in and of itself, decidedly epic.

Of this I was confident, and so I shared with my readers, for I know from our own examples in Iran when we read poets like Anna Akhmatova, Mahmoud Darwish, Faiz Ahmad Faiz, Nazem Hekmat, Aimé Césaire, Pablo Neruda, Nazik Al-Malaika, Langston Hughes or Vladimir Mayakovski in the same breath. We read them, I said in my book, with a sense of enabling tragic fragility of time and space, both ours and yet paradoxically not ours. I had then added to their company our own towering national poets Ahmad Shamlou and Forough Farrokhzad and said how our active memories of the

[3] See Hamid Dabashi, *The Shahnameh: The Persian Epic as World Literature* (New York: Columbia University Press, 2019).

Shahnameh were the foregrounding of our reading of all these poets, and their (always) tenuous nostalgia for our future. I then wondered if we were to put all those poets together – Darwish from Palestine, Faiz from Pakistan, Hekmat from Turkey, Neruda from Chile, Mayakovski from Russia, Shamlou from Iran, and Césaire from the West Indies to Africa and the whole Negritude Movement – if any assumption of 'World Literature' were to account for *the world* of this particular constellation of poets – not their names and perhaps even a few of their poems, but the world they had come together to form and in which their particular poetry meant and signified something beyond their individual importance.

What and where was *the world* these poets had inhabited and into which we were welcomed? They came from different homelands: Palestine, Iran, Russia, Turkey, Chile, the Afro-Caribbean basin, the United States and Pakistan. On the surface of the map these countries and climes have scarce anything to do with each other – and for sure make a mockery of the whole notion of 'the West'. They do not belong to 'the West' and they do not belong to 'the East' of that 'West'. One of them is still under European colonial occupation, and the rest are all over the map – some decolonised, some colonising, others neo-colonised. So how could they form any 'world' and where would that world be actually located? There is only one abiding sense in which these seven or even more poets had come together: the fact that my entire generation was reading them in Persian, in my mother tongue. Darwish wrote in Arabic, Hekmat in Turkish, Neruda in Spanish, Mayakovsky in Russian, Langston Hughes in English, Faiz in Urdu, Césaire in French and only Shamlou in Persian. Were they not to be translated into Persian how in the world could we possibly read them, let alone read them together, let alone see them come together to facilitate a meaningful and enabling world for us, a world in which we lived and breathed and thought and believed and loved and acted – the world from which I now write?

If Persian as a language that is deeply accentuated in its Islamic and pre-Islamic heritage is the home of a worldly poetic imagination not just its own but also those it has happily welcomed home to itself, then the question is no longer 'what is world literature' but far more importantly 'where is world literature?' By posing the question 'what is world literature', the leading theorists of the idea have in fact consolidated the Eurocentric assumption that its home is English, or French, or German or any other of the so-called 'European languages' in which they write and ask this question and then theorise, and which we post-colonials have happily confiscated for our own counter-theoretical purposes. But even in this very confiscated language we can also ask if world literature can be done, performed, staged and theorised in decidedly non-European languages – such as Arabic, or Persian, or Urdu or Turkish, all of them the languages of the Muslim world that have now in fact also become 'European languages', but even more widely in Chinese, Swahili or Malayalam. More pointedly we might even add: what happens to the so-called 'European languages' like French, Spanish or English when they are appropriated by a Césaire or Neruda, or this very prose I write in English, and brought home to their colonised people? If so, then the task ahead of us is to discover those worlds (always in plural) outside the imperial geography of 'World Literature' as it has been hitherto understood and one-sidedly theorised. We the inhabitants of the real world do not belong to that World in 'World Literature' except as subordinate non-subjects. That 'World' in that 'World Literature', I have proposed, is a decidedly European world, the result of an imperial designation, no matter how critically theorists from inside the frame seek 'to problematise it', for in it lurks the ideology of a global domination we have sought to overcome and dismantle to liberate the real world. In fact, without dismantling that world, as Fanon correctly diagnosed in his *Wretched of the Earth* (1961), it is impossible even to be born into the real world. Our kind of cogito, to paraphrase Enrique Dussel in his *Philosophy of Liberation* (1977), is contingent on dismantling the conquiro of the world that has found itself on our collective de-subjection, subjugation, robbing us of our very humanity.

Just like Arabic or Turkish or Urdu right next to it, Persian is no ordinary language. It is the language of Ferdowsi, Rumi, Nezami, Attar, Amir Khosrow, Jami and Sa'di, among scores of other towering poets, philosophers, mystics and metaphysicians. Performing a poetic impulse in this language resonates and echoes with the two conflating classical and contemporary worlds together. We are, in short, reading Darwish, Hekmat, Neruda, Mayakovski, Hughes and Faiz in the language of Rudaki, Ferdowsi, Rumi, Sa'di and Hafez, Ghalib, Iqbal and now, of course, Nima and Shamlou. These two conflating worlds expound and expand their horizons to create and craft their own contemporary world – a world beyond the reach of those who have just read any classical Persian poet without these contemporary poets singing in their ears, or those who have read these contemporary poets in their Arabic, Turkish, Urdu, Spanish, English or Russian originals in the context of different worldly framings. These poets have brought their worlds home to reside in Persian, as Persian has offered its historical hospitality to welcome them home to its variegated worlds.

Reworlding Literature

One of my contentions in my book on *The Shahnameh: The Persian Epic as World Literature* has been the ideological hegemony of 'World Literature' as it has been articulated by a handful of western European and North American literary theorists from Goethe to Damrosch. In this book I opted to map out the three conflating worlds in which (1) the Persian epic was created, (2) the world it creates, and (3) the world in which it has been read. I did so in order to expose and disrupt the ideological provenance of 'World Literature' as we have received it today. That work was preliminary to a more seminal argument. In this chapter I wish to make that argument in a more purposeful way: that if we put these poets together, living as they did at the time when I was reading them in Persian in Iran before having set foot outside Iran, a particularly poignant world arises, deeply rooted in an Islamic language for which 'World Literature' has afforded no theoretical imagination, no spatial domain, or even any mere clue, and in fact even today it cannot accommodate without immediately dismantling itself. The task ahead of us is no longer to beat the dead horse of 'World Literature' – as Euro-Americans have theorised it. The task ahead is the mapping out of different worlds it has systematically and epistemically violated, distorted as it has colonially dominated.

Reading these poets working as they do with multiple languages and yet coming to us as they did in Persian frames pushes the question of world literature (again I must emphasise the real world not the Eurocentric 'World' of their 'World Literature') into decidedly 'non-European languages' and imaginaries – in a way that the very ideological apparatus of 'Western languages' starts to crumble. It brings the landscapes of places like Chile, Russia, Palestine, Africa, the Caribbean, Latin America, the United States, and the Arab and Muslim world into a new conception of worldliness. This wider horizon of 'Islamic languages', namely, when Arabic, Persian, Turkish or Urdu hosts the world, is entirely invisible to the naked eyes of Orientalists and 'World Literature' aficionados alike. We need to rediscover and theorise that world. We are the products of that world, before the Euro-Universalism of 'World Literature' was allowed to cast its gaze upon the world their imperial and colonial benefactors had silenced and facilitated for them.

Decolonising literary thinking will have to begin with liberating the theoretical language from its stagnant suffocation inside the imperial attitude of the so-called 'European languages'. The presence of poets like Aimé Césaire, Pablo Neruda or Vladimir Mayakovski in the same community while they wrote in French, Spanish and Russian – all ordinarily assimilated into 'European languages', liberates the colonial claims of Europe over these languages. Europe cannot cross borders into other continents and cultures where the brutally colonised have learned their French and English and when they talk back still call those languages 'European'. These languages, as I always say, have been confiscated by the world at large the same way that Native Americans confiscated the Winchester guns of their tormentors and conquerors and started shooting back at them. We own these languages. We have given them new zest, power and meaning. There are more of us speaking English, French and Spanish in Asia, Africa and Latin America than they do in Europe. These are no longer 'European languages'. I thus go much further than Arundhati Roy, who in a brilliant recent essay wrote (in English): 'Writing or speaking in English is not a tribute to the British Empire . . . it is a practical solution to the circumstances created by it.'[4] It is much more than 'a practical solution'. It is a revolutionary confiscation of what rightfully belongs to us by virtue of an entire history of our anti-colonial and anti-imperial battles. My right to the English language was sealed in 1953 when the British MI6 and the US CIA came to my homeland and staged a military coup against our democratically elected prime minister and turned my homeland effectively into their colony and military base. Each of us on the colonial map of the world have a similar history with English, French, Italian, Spanish, etc. Today, from Mexico to

[4] See Arundhati Roy, 'What is the Morally Appropriate Language in Which to Think and Write?' Literary Hub, 25 July 2018, available at: https://lithub.com/what-is-the-morally-appropriate-language-in-which-to-think-and-write.

Argentina, there is no question that Spanish is their language which they confiscated from Spain. There should never be a question that English is also an Indian, an Arab, an Iranian and an African language.

The question is not just the historical provenance of a literary language. The question is also the literary imageries that go into the making of a language. When Darwish or Hekmat or Faiz or Shamlou perform their poetries in Arabic, Turkish, Persian or Urdu their words and imageries resonate with the classical poetry they have both inherited and overcome. As they introduce new imageries from their daily lives, they encounter the innate echoes of those imageries with the classical heritage they are regaining and overcoming. The verticality of that imaginative encounter with the past then interfaces with the horizontality of their own contemporary poets from around the globe that once translated into Persian had to wrestle with the classical antiquities of these words. Categorically denied any access to the multi-lingualism of this dialectic, the Eurocentricity of the European and American theorists completely compromise what they call 'World Literature'. The world that these poets create is a real world, not a theoretical world, a fictive, imperial world.

Let me be more specific: the historic succession of Persian poets from Rudaki to Ferdowsi, Rumi, Sa'di, Amir Khosrow, Bedil and Hafez, all the way to the threshold of colonial modernity had created the world of Persian literary humanism in the larger context of Muslim worldly consciousness – a subject I have explored in detail in my *Persian literary Humanism* (2012). The moment when these contemporary poets from Darwish to Neruda were translated into Persian, entirely unbeknownst to themselves they had entered the variegated domains of that worldly literature. This appropriated and incorporated them into a world their poetry in of itself had not anticipated. When these poets were translated into English, French or German, they were branded as having entered into 'World literature'. But when they were translated into Persian (or Arabic, Turkish or Urdu) they were lost to a *terra incognito*. The task facing us is to see what happens when these *horizontal* translations take place. Poets like Darwish, Hekmat, etc. have scarce become part of a world literature in the shadow of the hegemony of what Euro-American literary scholars call 'World Literature' – and in the dark shadow of that oblivion they are not even seen let alone recognised or theorised. The

Eurocentric project of cannibalising them into the minced meat of 'World Literature' will have to be replaced by placing them in the worldly habitat of alternative worlds that hosted and empowered them long before 'the West' had named itself the epicentre of universe. Allamah Mohammad Iqbal brought Dante, Goethe, Rumi and Hafez together into the bosom of his Persian poetry, and created a world in his two (among other) masterpieces, *Asrar-e-Khodi* (*Secrets of Selfhood*) and *Romuz-e-Bekhodi* (*Mysteries of Selflessness*). That world is real, and that is real world literature, and that real world and that world literature are beyond the reach of what in Europe and the United States passes as their 'World Literature'.

I happen to have read these poets in Persian, in my homeland, never having yet set foot outside Iran. An Egyptian might have read them in Arabic, a Pakistani in Urdu, a Turk in Turkish, to which we might also add a Russian, a Hispanic or an Afro-Caribbean who may have also read them in Russian, Spanish or French. The point is the theoretical prospect of seeing how a worldly literature is possible outside the Euro-American axis of 'World Literature'. The task here is not just decolonising but in fact decentring literary theory. I have done my modest share of it in my work. Here I continue picking up from where I had left off by thinking through the hospitalities of a language like Persian or Arabic or Turkish or Urdu when hosting these poets. The task at hand is no longer just naming and shaming the Eurocentricism of the literary theory. We need to begin mapping out the future of post-'Western' literary theory. That theory can be done and is done as much in Arabic and Turkish and Persian as it can be done in liberated English, French or German. The entire history of this 'World Literature' as it is defined on North American campuses covers less than two hundred years, ever since Goethe (1749–1832) saw the sparkles of a few ghazals of Hafez in German translation and thought he had seen the light. To think that the literary heritage of Sanskrit, or Persian, or Chinese or Arabic has to come and ask permission to sit at the feet of this 'World Literature' is the epitome of an imperial arrogance that has long since lost its legitimacy and yet it still feigns authority.

Where in the World?

Far more important than the self-centring question '*what* is world literature', which posits subjective authority for the questioner and denies it to world literature, we need to wonder 'where' is world literature, where is it located, on the premise of what conception of territoriality, and what sort of a knowing or unknowing subject does it implicate? All the varied and conflating worlds we inhabit point to multiple imaginative geographies that mark the location of cultures and with it the liberation geography that reimagines and reasserts the idea of 'the world' in a way that, for example, the prominent Spanish historian and linguist Américo Castro did in his monumental book *The Spaniards: An Introduction to their History* (1948),[5] or Fernand Braudel in his *The Mediterranean and the Mediterranean World in the Age of Philip II* (1949),[6] or José Martí in 'Our America' (1891),[7] or Immanuel Wallerstein's world-systems theory (1974–89),[8] or Gayatri Spivak in her *Other Asias* (2007).[9] Equally crucial is to map out the succession of colonial, anti-colonial, decolonial, neo-colonial and post-colonial revolts against this world system – against globalisation as the systematic abuse of labour by capital. Upon such worlds these poets begin to find kindred souls that override their geographies and create their own emerging worlds, in which we then dwell. Much is indeed lost in translation, but much more is gained in the shadows of those originals – those paratextual foregrounding of what they actually and potentially mean. These worlds are not all presentist for the Mediterranean world of Ibn Khaldun (d. 1406) in his *Muqaddimah* or the comparatist imagination of Alberuni (d. *c.* 1050) in his *India* all come together to map out the imaginative geography of a succession of worlds that have defined the contours of our trans-historicity.

In reconfiguring such a world, we need to come to terms with the spatial politics of being in the world – and the unfolding territorialities of such worlds. The French Marxist sociologist Henri Lefebvre has proposed the idea of 'the third space': first, is the physical space, second, is the mental space and,

[5] See Américo Castro, *The Spaniards: An Introduction to their History* (Los Angeles: University of California Press, [1948] 1971).

[6] Fernand Braudel, *The Mediterranean and the Mediterranean World in the Age of Philip II* (Berkeley: University of California Press, [1949] 1995).

[7] For an electronic edition of Jose Marti's 'Our America' see at: https://writing.upenn.edu/library/Marti_Jose_Our-America.html.

[8] Immanuel Wallerstein, *The Modern World-System*, 3 vols (Berkeley: University of California Press, 1974–89).

[9] See Gayatri Chakravorty Spivak, *Other Asias* (Oxford: Wiley-Blackwell, 2007).

third, is the social space.[10] Where exactly is this social space? Here another theorist of space become crucial: Edward Soja's notion of 'Third Space' works through what he calls spatial trialectics. Soja's Third Space is both real and imagined.[11] The idea of Third Space is open-ended, miasmatic, cumulative or an evolving trialectics. While Soja points to hybridity and the duality becoming trialectical and thus the third space opening up onto new horizons, I have proposed an interstitial space, which is hidden to both First and Second spaces to sustain the subversive power of art on that interstitial space that the post-colonial state loses all its relevance.[12] Such theorisations of interstitial spaces – neither here nor there but always already somewhere else – have crucial consequences for the changing idea of 'world literature', for it shifts the territorial location of the literary act entirely outside the colonial fiction of 'the West' and re-places it on the factual site of where this very dangerous delusion of 'the West' has left of our humanity lives.

As another cogent example of the interstitial space, I might suggest the idea of the 'Persianate World', which was first introduced by the American Orientalist Marshall Hodgson in the 1970s and has more recently found popularity among a number of North American scholars.[13] Contrary to any attempt to fix and locate this Persianate world, it is indeed an interstitial space, for the term Persianate tries to designate the Persian or Iranian which are always already floating signifiers. From India to Transoxiana, Central Asia, the Caucasus, through the current border of Iran and deep into the Ottoman Empire from Europe to North Africa the Persianate world has had textual evidences of mobile significations. The ancient roots of this fact have to do with the imperial origins of the terms all the way back to the Achaemenid Empire, and some of it with the multicultural disposition of the Islamic empires that have followed it. As a result, the Persian in the Persianate has intertextual presence in Arabic, Turkish, Urdu

[10] See Henri Lefebvre, *The Production of Space*, trans. Donald Nicholson-Smith (Oxford: Blackwell, 1991).

[11] See in particular, Edward W. Soja, *Seeking Spatial Justice* (Minneapolis: University of Minnesota Press, 2010).

[12] See the chapter on 'Interstitial Space of the Art of Protest' in my recent book, *The Emperor is Naked: On the Inevitable Demise of the Nation-State* (London: Zed Books, 2020), pp. 118–51.

[13] See, for example, Nile Green, *The Persianate World: The Frontiers of a Eurasian Lingua Franca* (Oakland: University of California Press, 2019).

and Bengali, which in turn implies a far more interpolated presence of proto-Iranian leitmotifs from pre-Islamic deep into the Islamic periods. In my *Persophilia: The Persian Culture on the Global Scene* (2015), I have also explored the effervescence of the Persianate themes in the European context from Aeschylus' *Persians* to Xenophon's *Cyropaedia* and far beyond from Classical Antiquity and the Hebrew Bible into the active formation and transformation of the European bourgeois public sphere. The interstitial spatiality of the Persianate therefore remains potent precisely because it is indeterminate and coterminous with its own deterritorialisations.[14] It is precisely that Persianate world that is enriched, conflated and further interpolated by translations reaching from the sixth-century Pahlavi rendition of *Panchatantra* into the Arabic of Ibn al-Muqaffa's *Kelilah and Dimnah* to the twentieth-century translations of Darwish, Neruda, or Mayakovsky into Persian.

That brings us back to a reconsideration of the very idea of 'the world' and worldliness in an Islamic (or Chinese, or Indian, or African, etc) context. In the Islamic context, the word *Dunya* in Arabic, Persian, etc. is usually paired with the word *Din* (tentatively translated as Religion), or *Uqba*ʾ (the Other World), or *Akhira* (Day of Judgement, aka Yaum al-Din, Day of Resurrection). The idea of the world in Islamic culture is therefore inflected with a transcendent world, for there is no Donya without Din, and there is no Din without Donya. This is a fundamentally different conception of the world than, say, Heideggerian Worldliness, or Being-in-the-World – for being in Donya here also means being in the Din. In the Qurʾān we read: 'Thereupon Allah Granted the reward of the world as well as a better reward of the World to Come. Allah loves those who do good' (Q. 3:148). A prophetic *ḥādith* says 'al-Donya Mazriʾat al-Akhira/the World is the field of the Next World.' So this world is pivoted towards the world to come – this world has the inflection of the other world. Dunya is not a philosophical speculation. It is a theological immanence – it is integral to a sustained binary. It is therefore not 'secular' for it is sacred – it is the farm where we cultivate to reap in the world to come. This contingency of the world makes it transitory, immanent

[14] I have developed this idea further in my 'Nations without Borders', in Asef Bayat and Linda Herrera (eds), *Global Middle East: Into the Twenty-First Century* (Oakland: University of California Press, 2021), pp. 60–76.

and through the idea of '*Vahdat al Wujud/Unity of Being*' it is co-immanent with the divinity that dwells in it. This space is neither local nor global, neither solitary nor comparative, for it is always already contingent, interstitial, amorphous, permeable, immanent – somewhere between Din and Donya, between transcendence and immanence.

That both real and liberating conception of the world enables us to free our thinking of not just 'the West' but of 'the East' too as they both have been colonially co-created to impose their fake veracity. So where is world literature today? It is in Manus Island refugee camp in Australia where Behrooz Boochani, a Kurdish Iranian refugee, tapped his bestselling memoir on his cellphone in Persian, had it translated into English and published to a global reception. Rosi Braidotti's *Nomadic Subjects* had been mapping out the contours of such nomadic subjectivity in purely abstract philosophical terms.[15] As a Kurdish Iranian in search of his own homeland, Boochani had lived that nomadic life which eventually landed him in a refugee camp in a remote island as a persona non grata.[16]

Boochani's *No Friend but the Mountains: Writing from Manus Prison*, is an account of homelessness, of his meanderings from his homeland to Indonesia to Christmas Island and ultimately landing on Manus island, where he writes about his and his fellow inmates' conditions. Like Boochani's memoire, the real and factual world literature is homeless for the subject it informs and that informs it is nomadic. The monadic world of world literature as it is performed by Euro-universalists corresponds to an imperial episode of their 'West' that has long since imploded. The dyadic world they manufactured between 'World Literature' and 'Third World Literature' has fallen flat on its face. The example of Arabic and Persian literary humanism (Adab) – or those written in Chinese, Turkish, Malayalam or Swahili – points to half-a-dozen such worlds from India to Iran, to Central Asia, the Ottoman and the Arab and African worlds. The introduction of non-Muslim into Muslim languages

[15] See Rosi Braidotti, *Nomadic Subjects: Embodiment and Sexual Difference in Contemporary Feminist Theory* (New York: Columbia University Press, 2011).

[16] For a review of Boochani's *No Friend but the Mountains: Writing from Manus Prison.* see J. M. Coetzee, 'Australia's Shame', New York Review of Books, 26 September 2019, available at: https://www.nybooks.com/articles/2019/09/26/australias-shame.

has today expanded these horizons beyond any colonial demarcations or post-colonial protest. From my fateful proximity to my late mentor George Makdisi in the 1980s to the writing of this meditation on the whereabouts of world literature, the factual evidence of the world of our experiences has taught us much more humility in deciphering our worldly habitat.

Bibliography

Braidotti, Rosi, *Nomadic Subjects: Embodiment and Sexual Difference in Contemporary Feminist Theory* (New York: Columbia University Press, 2011).

Braudel, Fernand, *The Mediterranean and the Mediterranean World in the Age of Philip II* (Berkeley: University of California Press, [1949] 1995).

Castro, Américo, *The Spaniards: An Introduction to their History*, trans. Willard F. King and Selma Margaretten (Los Angeles: University of California Press, 1971).

Coetzee, J. M., 'Australia's Shame', New York Review of Books, 26 September 2019, available at: https://www.nybooks.com/articles/2019/09/26/australias-shame.

Dabashi, Hamid, *Persophilia: The Persian Culture on the Global Scene* (Cambridge, MA: Harvard University Press, 2015).

Dabashi, Hamid, *The Shahnameh: The Persian Epic as World Literature* (New York: Columbia University Press, 2019).

Dabashi, Hamid, 'Interstitial Space of the Art of Protest', in *The Emperor is Naked: On the Inevitable Demise of the Nation-State* (London: Zed Books, 2020), pp. 118–51.

Dabashi, Hamid, 'Nations without Borders', in Asef Bayat and Linda Herrera (eds), *Global Middle East: Into the Twenty-First Century* (Oakland: University of California Press, 2021), pp. 60–76.

Green, Nile, *The Persianate World: The Frontiers of a Eurasian Lingua Franca* (Oakland: University of California Press, 2019).

Lefebvre, Henri, *The Production of Space*, trans. Donald Nicholson-Smith (Oxford: Blackwell, 1991).

Makdisi, George, *The Rise of Colleges: Institutions of Learning in Islam and the West* (Edinburgh: Edinburgh University Press, 1981).

Makdisi, George, *The Rise of Humanism in Classical Islam and the Christian West: With Special Reference to Scholasticism* (Edinburgh: Edinburgh University Press, 1990).

Marti, Jose, 'Our America', available at: https://writing.upenn.edu/library/Marti_Jose_Our-America.html.

Roy, Arundhati, 'What is the Morally Appropriate Language in Which to Think and Write?' Literary Hub, 25 July 2018, available at: https://lithub.com/what-is-the-morally-appropriate-language-in-which-to-think-and-write.

Soja, Edward W., *Seeking Spatial Justice* (Minneapolis: University of Minnesota Press, 2010).

Spivak, Gayatri Chakravorty, *Other Asias* (Oxford: Wiley-Blackwell, 2007).

Wallerstein, Immanuel, *The Modern World-System*, 3 vols (Berkeley: University of California Press, 1974–89).

SECULAR–NON-SECULAR

10

PRAISING THE PROPHET MUḤAMMAD IN CHINESE: A NEW TRANSLATION AND ANALYSIS OF EMPEROR ZHU YUANZHANG'S *ODE TO THE PROPHET*

Haiyun Ma and Brendan Newlon[1]

There is a poem composed in classical Chinese titled *baizizan*, or 'One Hundred Words of Praise', which is an ode to the Prophet Muḥammad. Chinese Muslim intellectuals since the Ming–Qing period have attributed the poem to the founding emperor of the Ming dynasty, Zhu Yuanzhang (r. 1368–98). Some go as far as to think of the Ming royal family as patrons of Islam, and even claim that the poem reveals Zhu Yuanzhang to have been a Muslim.[2] The attribution to Zhu has been a matter of scholarly debate. However, in the light of the pervasive influence of Muslims in early Ming China, diplomatic interaction and letter exchange between the Ming and the Muslim rulers in Central Asia such as Tamerlane and his successors,[3] and

1 Brendan Newlon authored the initial chapter draft, translation and analysis. Haiyun Ma contributed additional historical and scholarly content and assisted in revisions for the final publication.

2 For a study of intimacy between the Ming royal family and Islam, see Yusuf Chang, 'The Ming Empire: Patron of Islam in China and Southeast–West Asia', *Journal of the Malaysian Branch of the Royal Asiatic Society* 61(2) (255) (1988): 1–44.

3 For a study of Ming–Tamerlane relation, see E. Bretschneider, *Medieval Researches from Eastern Asiatic Sources*, vol. 2 (New York: Barnes & Noble, 1967); Sir Henry Yule (ed.), *Cathay and the Way Thither* (London: Printed for the Hakluyt Society, 1913–16).

sweeping Islamisation in fifteenth-century Central Asia after Mongol rule make it likely that Zhu, like any worldly person of his time, would at least have been familiar with Muslims and Islam, including poems praising the Prophet Muḥammad that were in circulation in Eurasia at the time. It is certainly possible that Zhu or one of his contemporaries or successors possessed the requisite knowledge of Islamic texts and traditions to compose *baizizan*. Furthermore, a close textual analysis of the poem itself reveals a great deal about its author.

The history of the Ming dynasty (1368–1644) is a testament to the unprecedented impact of Muslims in diplomacy, as demonstrated by the great maritime expeditions led by Muslim admiral Zheng He and his Ḥanafī Muslim associates[4] that traversed the Indian Ocean and generated more knowledge about overseas practices of Islam from Southeast Asia to East Africa.[5] At the same time, the Ming government introduced nativist cultural assimilation policies to Sinicise – or more accurately, *Han*-ify – subject populations that were not ethnically or culturally Han, such as Mongols and various Muslim groups. As a result of these policies some Muslim communities adopted Confucian literary styles and the Chinese language – again, more accurately the dialects favoured by the Han. Some communities were said to have become Confucian Muslims or Muslim Confucians.[6] The relative success of Muslim

[4] A recent discovery of a Chinese–Malay text reveals a hidden Muslim network that supported Zheng He's voyages in the Indian Ocean. For a translation and discussion of this text, see 'Chinese Muslims in Java in the 15th and 16th Centuries: The Malay Annals of Sémarang and Cérbon', trans. and with comments by Hermanus Johannes de Graaf, Theodore G. Th. Pigeaud and M. C. Ricklefs (Monash Papers on Southeast Asia No 12, 1984)

[5] For a study of Zheng He, see Edward L. Dreyer, *Zheng He: China and the Oceans in the Early Ming Dynasty, 1405–1433* (Pearson College Div, 2006). For a documentation of various Muslim countries, peoples and products, see Ma Huan, *Ying-Yai Sheng-Lang: Overall Survey of the Ocean's Shores* (1433), trans. Feng Cheng-Chün and J. V. G. Mills, 2nd edn (Thailand: White Lotus, 1996).

[6] For a study of Confucian Muslims and their Han Kitab literature, see Donald Leslie, *Islam in Traditional China: A Short History to 1800* (Canberra: Canberra College of Advanced Education, 1986). And more recently, James D. Frankel, *Rectifying God's Name* (Honolulu: University of Hawai'i Press, 2011) and Kristian Petersen, *Interpreting Islam in China: Pilgrimage, Scripture, and Language in the Han Kitab* (Oxford: Oxford University Press, 2018).

communities through that enculturation into Han Chinese societies is a primary factor explaining why Chinese Muslims tend to remember or document the Ming dynasty nostalgically as a golden age of Islam in China. During this period, Hui (Sinicised) Muslims prospered, not only because existing families and communities thrived, but also because they were deeply involved in majoritarian Han Confucian societies and attracted a greater number of Han Chinese converts to the religion. These political, cultural and social changes gradually and jointly produced a class of Hui Muslim literati and a new literary genre of translated Islamic texts in the Chinese language or the Han kitab, a bilingual portmanteau joining 'Han' from Chinese and 'kitab' from Arabic to mean 'Chinese books'. Ming period Hui cultural expression was not limited to literature; in the early twentieth century, Chinese Muslims rediscovered rich Islamic archaeological sites and historical sources in coastal Chinese cities such as Quanzhou.

In retrospect, Hui Muslims attribute the growth and well-being of their community during the Ming period in part to Muslim-friendly actions and Islam-protective policies initiated by the dynasty's founder, the Hongwu Emperor Zhu Yuanzhang. Zhu is remembered as a supporter of Muslims and an admirer of Islamic traditions. Throughout his life, he reportedly surrounded himself with Muslims, both in his personal affairs and in connection with official matters of state:

> His original war band, made up of men like Hu Dahai and Chang Yuchu, is described as heavily Muslim. Remarkably, so too is his very family; according to Chinese Muslim tradition Zhu Yuanzhang's first wife, Empress Ma (Ma Hou), was a Muslim; he also had an adoptive Muslim son, Mu Ying; brother; and father-in-law, Guo Zixing.[7]

[7] Zvi Ben-Dor Benite, 'The Marrano Emperor: The Mysterious Bond between Zhu Yuanzhang and the Chinese Muslims', in Sarah Schneewind (ed.), *Long Live the Emperor!: Uses of the Ming Founder across Six Centuries of East Asian History* (Minneapolis, MN: Society for Ming Studies, 2008). In a footnote, Benite adds: 'On Mu Ying see "Mu Ying," DMB, 1079–83, in which Frederick Mote specifically rejects the claim that Mu was a Muslim; On Empress Ma see "Empress Ma," DMB, 1023–26, in which Chou Tao-chi does not refer to the Empress as Muslim.'

Several historians, including Jin Jitang and Fu Tongxian, went so far as to claim that Zhu Yuanzhang himself was a Muslim. Fu explains that 'the attitude of the Ming emperors was partial toward Islam and they held it in the highest esteem. It is probable that Taizu Zhu Yuanzhang was a follower of the Islamic Teaching.'[8] For those who subscribe to the narrative of a Muslim Ming emperor, the smoking gun is the emperor's positive public engagement with the religion of Islam:

> For instance, in the early years of Emperor Hongwu's reign in the Ming Dynasty His Majesty ordered mosques to be built in Xijing and Nanjing [Xi'an and Nanjing, the historical capital cities], and in southern Yunnan, Fujian and Guangdong. His Majesty also personally wrote *baizizan* [a eulogy] in praise of the Prophet's virtues.[9]

The text of *baizizan*, a poetic ode presented below as the *One Hundred Words of Praise*, lauds Islam and praises the Prophet Muḥammad. Determining Zhu's personal and inner religious leaning may ultimately prove impossible from the available Chinese official historical data written by non-Muslims, but this poem has indisputably been written in the authorial tone of a believer.

The outstanding question is whether the ode was truly composed by Zhu, or whether it was merely attributed to him posthumously by later sources. Zvi Ben-Dor Benite has raised several questions about the sources which attribute authorship of the ode to Zhu and hint at his openly or secretly possessing a Muslim identity. For example, he notes that although Zhu lived in the late fourteenth century, the earliest known extant record of the

[8] Fu Tongxian (傅统先) (1934), *Zhongguo hui jiao shi* (中国回教史). 中国: 商务印书馆. http://goo.gl/Lkcv9a, 60; Jin Jitang (金吉堂) (1935), *Zhongguo hui jiao shi yan jiu* (中国回教史研究) (*A Historical Study of Islam in China*). 北平: 成达师范出版部, 154. Both were cited in, Benite, 'The Marrano Emperor: The Mysterious Bond between Zhu Yuanzhang and the Chinese Muslims', pp. 276–7.

[9] Maria Jaschok and Jingjun Shui, *The History of Women's Mosques in Chinese Islam: A Mosque of Their Own* (London: Curzon Press, 2000), 77.

ode is a prefatory document published in the *Real Commentary on the True Teaching* (*Zhengjiao zhenquan*), the famous book by Wang Daiyu (1580–1660) that initiated the so-called 'Han Kitab' genre of Islamic literature in the Chinese language. Moreover, he argues that the authenticity and dating of that document is dubious.[10] Benite emphasises that within 'conventional histories such as the *Official History of the Ming Dynasty (Mingshi)* or the *Veritable Records of the Ming Dynasty (Ming shilu)* . . . there is no evidence that [Zhu Yuanzhang] favored Islam, let alone surrounded himself with Muslims'.[11] He also highlights differences between how Zhu's edicts appear in official Ming dynasty records and how they have been remembered in early Qing dynasty Muslim sources. Benite notes that although these edicts appear unremarkable in official records, Chinese Muslim accounts sometimes record them with slightly different wording that makes them seem partial towards Muslims, and theorises that Chinese Muslims promoted a narrative emphasising their positive relationship with the previous dynasty's rulers out of concern for how the newly ascendant Qing rulers might treat them.[12] This is a reasonable thesis, and it would have been just as natural for Chinese Muslims to be nervous about the rise of a new ruling dynasty as it would have been for any other vulnerable minority group within Chinese society. Yet this does not preclude the possibility that court historians might have avoided declaring the emperor's affinity for Islam or revealing a pro-Muslim bias in his policies. For contemporary scholars, the caveat in dealing with conflicting narratives like these is distinguishing between a 'loud silence' and an *argumentum ex silentio*. In other words, a shortage of documentation supporting a thesis is not the same as discovering evidence against it.

At the very least, it is not difficult to imagine that an emperor of the Ming dynasty would have been familiar with Islamic teachings and philosophy. Muslims had long since made up a significant portion of the population in Central Asia and in several regions of China. Any well-travelled person

[10] Benite, 'The Marrano Emperor', pp. 278–9.

[11] Benite, 'The Marrano Emperor', p. 277.

[12] Benite, 'The Marrano Emperor', p. 291.

of that period probably interacted with Muslims quite regularly, and savvy politicians of every era study the demographics of their region, as observed and documented by Ming envoys to western regions such as Chen Cheng.[13] A century earlier, Kublai Khan (1215–94), the founder of the Yuan dynasty (1206–1368), similarly recognised the importance of learning about the religions of his empire and its neighbours. He reportedly confided in Marco Polo (1254–1324) that:

> There are four prophets who are worshiped and to whom everybody does reverence. The Christians say that their God was Jesus Christ; the Saracens Mahomet; the Jews Moses; and the idolaters Sagamoni Burcan [the Shakyamuni Buddha], who was the first god to the idols; and I do honour and reverence to all four, that is to him who is the greatest in heaven and more true, and him I pray to help me.[14]

Emperors Zhu and Kublai were both conquerors governing a vast territory of diverse populations, so a cosmopolitan and tolerant attitude towards religious diversity was pragmatic. For Zhu in particular, knowledge of Muslim customs would have been practical for diplomatic, economic, political and even personal reasons. Under the preceding Mongol Yuan dynasty, Eurasian trade routes were re-established and maintained, and many of the merchants who travelled or who worked with the Mongol rulers as Ortoq were Muslims. By the late fourteenth century when Zhu established the Ming dynasty, various Muslim powers controlled most of the territories in Eurasia. In other words, Zhu established the Ming dynasty in the midst of what must have seemed to him an overwhelmingly Muslim world.[15]

[13] For a study of Ming–Tamerlane relations, see Bretschneider, *Medieval Researches from Eastern Asiatic Sources*.

[14] Morris Rossabi, *Khubilai Khan: His Life and Times* (Berkeley: University of California Press, 1988).

[15] Brendan Newlon, 'Muslim Community Maps of 14th Century Asia', available at: https://goo.gl/uxKPbg, last accessed 14 April 2018. Satellite imagery © 2018 Landsat/Copernicus, Data SIO, NOAA, US Navy, NGA, GEBCO, IBCAO. Map Data © 2018 Google, ORION-ME, Zenrin.

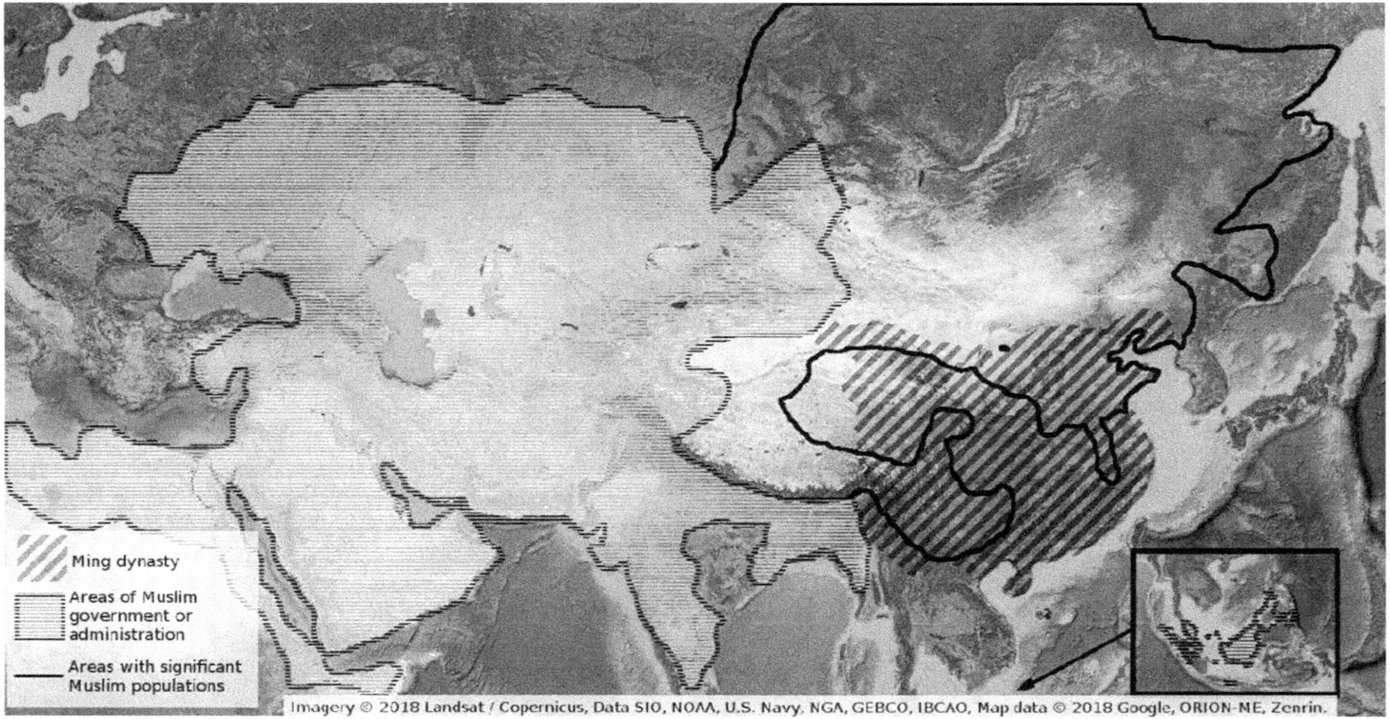

Map showing the estimated regions governed by Muslim administrations by the early fourteenth century, areas in Asia with significant Muslim populations, and the territory of the Ming dynasty. © 2018 Brendan Newlon.

The territory the Ming state inherited from the Yuan dynasty was not an enclave without Muslims either. As a consequence of the Yuan dynasty's practice of preferentially assigning official positions to the *semu* (various non-Han, non-Mongol) people of Central Asia, Muslims and their families became established in numerous provinces to occupy imperial military or bureaucratic positions, especially in southwest coastal provinces such as Fujian where Muslims had dominated maritime trade for several centuries, most notably by the Pu family during the Song–Yuan period.[16] According to the historical encyclopaedia compiled by the Persian vazīr Rashīd al-Dīn Ṭabīb (1247–1318) around 1300, four of the twelve administrative districts of the early Yuan empire were governed by Muslims, and at the time of his writing, 'all the inhabitants [of Yunnan] are Mahomedans'.[17] The influence of these population demographics persisted through the Ming period, making basic familiarity with Islamic teachings and Muslim social customs politically indispensable. Zhu Yuanzhang's son, Zhudi 朱棣, even issued an edict protecting a model Muslim leader, Mir Hajj 米里哈只.[18] In his account of a journey to the Ming capital of Beijing, Persian ambassador Ghiyāth al-Dīn Naqqāsh mentioned a powerful Hajj official at the Ming court who was in charge of Persian ambassadors.[19] Interestingly, some of the iconic blue and white porcelain of the imperial house of the Ming bear Islamic calligraphy,[20] an uncommon and unusual practice throughout Chinese history. Muslim individuals, communities and religious or cultural expressions were prevalent and highly visible at the time.

[16] For a study of Muslim merchants in coastal regions, especially in Fujian and Guangdong, see John W. Chaffee, *The Muslim Merchants of Premodern China: The History of a Maritime Asian Trade Diaspora, 750–1400* (Cambridge: Cambridge University Press, 2018).

[17] Yule, *Cathay and the Way Thither*, vol. 3, p. 126.

[18] The copy of this edict can be accessed at China's Cultural Palace of Nationalities 民族文化, available at: http://www.cpon.cn/special/details/42.html.

[19] For an account of Ghiyāth al-Dīn Naqqāsh's journey to Beijing, see Hafiz-i Abru, *A Persian Embassy to China Being An Extract from Zubdatu't tawarikh of Hatīz Abru*, trans. K. M. Maitra (New York, 1970).

[20] For a study of Ming-era blue-and-white porcelain with Islamic calligraphy, see James Frankel, 'Muslim Blue, Chinese White: Islamic Calligraphy on Ming Blue-and-white Porcelain', *Orientations* 49(2) (2018): 2–7.

Another important dimension to the discourse of a Muslim Ming emperor is the role of oral history. It is overwhelmingly the narratives passed down within Chinese Muslim families and communities that recall the emperor either as a Muslim or as someone who was sympathetic towards Islam. Although some contemporary historians consider oral history to be less reliable than written records, others regard oral transmission to be reliable, particularly within societies that value oral culture highly, as is common among Muslim communities.[21] Benite acknowledges that 'it is impossible to know exactly when and how specific oral traditions were born', but he recognises that there is something remarkable about the prevalence and distribution of these traditions, and wonders how it 'became a perception *collectively* shared by Chinese Muslims living in separate communities all over China'.[22]

Future research might examine the merits of specific oral histories and family memories regarding Islam shared among Chinese Muslims. It may be helpful to interrogate what can be understood from the lack of corroborating evidence in court records and official histories often written by a later dynasty that replaced the former and, as part of the conquest project, wrote the history of the former. In some cases, imperial historians are known to have distorted the record, as was the case of Ming Confucian officials who intentionally destroyed records in the imperial archives that focused on Muslims, including records of Zhenghe's Indian Ocean voyages.[23] Contemporary scholarship must therefore engage extensively in critical historiography and ethnography, and any scholar undertaking such a study should be aware of an uncommon quality that may be assumed about the narrators of these particular oral traditions: their heritage exists at the intersection of several classes of people who take great pride in memorisation and high-fidelity narrative transmission.

Among Muslims, memorisation and oral transmission have always been central to the preservation and propagation of the religion. Most Muslims – and all

[21] Jaclyn Jeffrey (ed.), *Memory and History: Essays on Recalling and Interpreting Experience* (Lanham, MD: University Press of America, 1994); Vansina, Jan. 2017. *Oral Tradition: A Study in Historical Methodology* (London: Routledge, Taylor & Francis Group).

[22] Benite, 'The Marrano Emperor', p. 278.

[23] For a discussion of Ming official's destruction of archival sources on Zhenghe, see Hui Chun Hing, 'Huangming zuxun and Zheng He's Voyages to the Western Oceans', *Journal of Chinese Studies* 51 (2010): 67–85.

Muslim scholars – devote themselves to memorising passages of the Qur'ān. It is not uncommon for scholars or even lay Muslims to memorise the entire Qur'ān, and any practising Muslim must necessarily memorise at least a few chapters to recite while performing daily religious prayers. Moreover, few communities in the world have ever been as intensely focused on the preservation, transmission and authentication of oral traditions as the Muslim scholars of Central Asia whom many Chinese Muslims regard as either biological or intellectual ancestors. That was the cultural and educational environment which produced the legendary memories of Muslim scholars like al-Dārimī (797–869), al-Bukhārī (810–70), Muslim ibn al-Ḥajjāj (815–75), al-Tirmidhī (824–92), Abū Manṣūr al-Māturīdī (853–944) and Fāṭima bint Muḥammad al-Samarqandī (d. 1185), all of whom were experts in a range of Islamic sciences.[24] These and other Muslim scholars of Central Asia were particularly influential in developing the methodology of *ḥadīth* narrative analysis (*ʿilm al-ḥadīth*), which is the science of rigorously and systematically evaluating the authenticity of statements concerning the life and sayings of the Prophet Muḥammad as conveyed through written or oral transmission. A significant aspect of the identities of Chinese Muslims who narrated stories about the emperor is that they valued and felt connected to that Islamic scholarly heritage through family lineage or through the educational lineages of their religious teachers. It is reasonable to expect that they would value and be capable of narrative fidelity when transmitting information that is important to their religious history.

Also among these narrators were Muslim scholars who simultaneously belonged to the Chinese Confucian literati class. Like Wang Daiyu, they claimed descent from earlier scholars who had earned government positions after demonstrating scholarly excellence through the imperial examinations. Notably, the imperial examination system rewarded the ability of candidates to memorise and recall great volumes of literary knowledge.[25] In the political

[24] Al-Dārimī, al-Bukhārī, Muslim ibn al-Ḥajjāj and al-Tirmidhī contributed significant collections of *ḥadīth*. Abū Manṣūr al-Māturīdī was one of two systematic theologians who defined Sunni orthodoxy. Fāṭima bint Muḥammad al-Samarqandī was an expert Ḥanafī jurist.

[25] Wang Daiyu, for example, was a Chinese Muslim Scholar and recounted that one of his ancestors was a scholar personally recognised and appreciated by Emperor Zhu Yuanzhang. Benite, 'The Marrano Emperor', p. 281.

and social context of the Ming and Qing dynasties in which the relevant narratives of Zhu were first recorded, a strong and reliable memory was considered the hallmark of intelligence and a fundamental aspect of education.[26] In summary, because of the significant esteem with which memory and oral traditions were regarded by their communities, the oral histories and family narratives passed down among Chinese Muslim communities deserve due consideration as potential sources of reliable historical data. Without evidence of forgery, Muslim oral histories about Zhu should not be discounted.

Determining whether Zhu was Muslim or even whether he was the true author of the *baizizan* is not essential to an analysis of the ode itself. However, if the traditional attribution of the *baizizan* to Zhu is accurate, his ode praising the Prophet Muḥammad would have been among the earliest known royal texts to express Islamic themes in Chinese. Significantly, considering its composition in Chinese language and in the classical *shī* poetic style of matching four-character couplets that originated in the Tang dynasty, *baizizan* must be understood as a native Chinese literary expression of Islamic values.[27] For both reasons, *baizizan* represents a tipping point after which Islam can be discussed as a religion of China rather than merely as a religion practised in China. The ode's publication is therefore one of the most important milestones in the history of Islam in China and East Asia. The complete poem is presented below with an original English translation and is followed by a detailed analysis.[28]

[26] A. K. C. Leung, 'Elementary Education in the Lower Yangtze Region in the Seventeenth and Eighteenth Centuries', in Benjamin A. Elman and Alexander Woodside (eds), *Education and Society in Late Imperial China, 1600–1900* (Berkeley: University of California Press, 1994), p. 394; Zvi Ben-Dor Benite. *The Dao of Muhammad: A Cultural History of Muslims in Late Imperial China* (Cambridge, MA: Harvard University Asia Center, 2010), pp. 91–2.

[27] For more information about the styles and history of Chinese poetry, see Zong-qi Cai, *How to Read Chinese Poetry: A Guided Anthology* (New York: Columbia University Press, 2008), p. 14.

[28] Mandarin pronunciation guide: qián kūn chū shǐ / tiān jí zhù míng / chuán jiào dà shèng / jiàng shēng xī yù / shòu shòu tiān jīng / sān shí bù cè / pǔ huà zhòng shēng / yì zhào jūn shī / wàn shèng lǐng xiù / xié zhù tiān yùn / bǎo bì guó mín / wǔ shí qí yòu / mò zhù tài píng / cún xīn zhēn zhǔ / jiā zhì qióng mín / zhěng jiù huàn nàn / dòng chè yōu míng / chāo bá líng hún / tuō lí zuì yè / rén fù tiān xià / dào guàn gǔ jīn / xiáng xié guī yī / jiào míng qīng zhēn / mù hǎn mò dé / zhì guì shèng rén

	One Hundred Words of Praise	**百字讚**
1 2	*The universe began with the heavenly tablet recording his name. The religion-delivering great sage, born in the western realm.*	乾坤初始，天籍注名。 傳教大聖，降生西域。
3 4	*Conferring and receiving heavenly scripture in thirty parts, universally transforming all created beings. Master of the trillion rulers, leader of the ten thousand sages.*	授受天經，三十部冊， 普化眾生。億兆君師， 萬聖領袖。
5 6 7 8	*Assisted by destiny, protector of the humanity. In each of the five prayers, he silently supplicates for their total well-being. His intention is that Allah should remember the needy. Deliver them from tribulations to safety. Knower of the unseen.*	協助天運，保庇國民。 五時祈祐，默祝太平。 存心真主，加志窮民。 拯救患難，洞徹幽冥。
9 10	*Exalted above every soul and spirit, free from any blameworthy deeds. A mercy to all of the worlds, whose path is preeminent for all time.*	超拔靈魂，脱離罪業。 仁覆天下，道冠古今。
11	*Renounce false religions; return to The One – that is the religion called the Pure and True.*	降邪歸一，教名清真。
12	*Muḥammad is the most noble sage.*	穆罕默德，至貴聖人。

Rhetorically, the ode can be divided into three sections forming a persuasive argument with two premises and a conclusion. The first section (lines 1–4) introduces the Prophet in a universal context, identifying him as the most important feature in the universe's creation. Since his message provides the only means of universal salvation, his rank is praised above all rulers and sages. The second section (lines 5–8) offers a candid glimpse into basic tenets of Islam and the heart and private thoughts of the Prophet, whose sincerity, humility and selfless concern for others are revealed as he supplicates in prayer. In the final section of the poem (lines 9–12), the tone shifts again. Unlike the sense of cosmic significance in the first section or the intimate compassion reflected in the second section, the third section confronts the reader directly with an appeal to embrace the path of Islam. The argument can be paraphrased as follows:

Premise 1: The entire universe is centred upon this supreme sage who brought a comprehensive scripture from heaven.

Premise 2: He epitomises the sage ruler whose sole concern is humanity's well-being.

Conclusion: Therefore, his teaching is the only path worthy to be followed, so embrace the Pure and True teaching of Islam!

This argument is tailored to address the concerns of a neo-Confucian worldview: the Great Dao is universal, so it can originate from the East or the West. Islam originated in a distant land, but, as with Buddhism, its universal scope makes it a valid foundation for Chinese society and moral values. The noble qualities embodied in the Prophet Muḥammad epitomise the Confucian ideal of a sage ruler whose virtues can propagate through every level of society to bring about universal harmony. His comprehensive teaching completes and supersedes all others, therefore adopting it must be understood as no less than an ethical imperative from a neo-Confucian perspective.

Several things make the language and style of this poem fascinating. Classical Chinese poetry uses an abbreviated form of language which often affords a degree of interpretive ambiguity. This poem uses ambiguous grammar structures, homophones and familiar phrases to convey multiple layers of meaning when read in the context of the religious and philosophical discourse of the period. In places, it is clearly evocative of set phrases from Islamic traditions that would have been immediately recognisable to Muslim readers, even in translation.

For example, the poem opens with a comment about the first moments of creation: 'the universe began with the heavenly tablet recording his name' (line 1). Prophetic narrations (*ḥadīth*) seem to differ about what Allah created first. According to one narration, the first thing to be created was the heavenly pen, whereupon Allah commands it to write on a heavenly tablet the destinies of all that will exist from that moment until the Day of Judgement.[29] According to other narrations, the first thing Allah created was the light of

[29] The word I have translated above as 'heavenly tablet' (line 1) is more properly a register, which combines the function of pen and tablet within one word. This narration is well known and can be found in the *Sunan* of Tirmidhī and *Sunan* of Abī Dawūd, and in the *Musnad* of Imām Aḥmad.

the Prophet Muḥammad (*nūr Muḥammad*) meaning, perhaps, his soul, or the blessed essence of truth and goodness that the Prophet would embody in the world.[30] In this line, the character used for 'his name' (名 *míng*) is homophonic with the character for a shining light (as in 光明 *guāngmíng*) and nearly homophonic to the word for an individual's nature and life (as in 性命 *xìngmìng*) or life and destiny (as in 命运 *mìngyùn*). In eight Chinese characters, the author manages to reconcile the ideas expressed in both narrations and hint at their commentary by explaining that the pen and tablet came into existence through the action of declaring the name of the Prophet. The Prophet existed, at least in a nominal sense, and recording that sacred truth was the first action by which the universe was inaugurated. Furthermore, it is possible that homophones were intended to evoke a sense of the Prophet as a shining light and hint at the centrality of his life to God's predestined plan for creation. This nuanced handling indicates the author's skill in engaging metaphysical questions that Muslim philosophers have struggled with and which are still debated among Muslims today.

Several lines in the ode are reminiscent of passages from other famous Islamic texts. For example, the phrase 'exalted above every soul and spirit' (line 9) was probably intended as a translation of 'Muḥammad is the noble leader over both worlds and both creations'. The reference to 'both worlds and both creations' is to humans and jinn; souls and spirits, and this is one of the most memorable lines in al-Būsīrī's (d. 1294) poem al-*Kawākib al-duriyya fī madḥ khayr al-bariyya* ('celestial lights in praise of the best of all creation'), more commonly known as the *burda*.[31] The *burda* is a poem that, like the *baizizan*, eloquently praises the Prophet Muḥammad. The *burda* was highly acclaimed and gained widespread popularity immediately after it was composed, and the practice of reciting it is a central element of *mawlid* celebrations commemorating the Prophet's birth.[32] It is not uncommon to find Sufis

[30] See Sayyid Rami al-Rifai, *The Light of Allah in the Heavens and the Earth: The Creation of the Atom (24:35) and the Physics of Spirituality*, https://ghayb.com/wp-content/uploads/2015/09/The-Light-Of-Allah-In-The-Heavens-and-The-Earth-The-Creation-Of-The-Atom-24-35-and-The-Physics-Of-Spirituality.pdf Sunnah Mu'akada, 2016, p. 122

[31] Al-Buṣīrī, *The Mantle Adorned: Translated, with Further Poetic Ornaments* (London: Quilliam Press, 2005). Numerous recordings of the poem being recited exist, for example, 'The Mantle of Praise by the Adel Brothers', Apple Music, n.d., available at: https://music.apple.com/au/album/the-mantle-of-praise/1171287717, last accessed 26 July 2020.

[32] For more on the *burda* and the *mawlid* celebrations see Chapter 4 by Walid Ghali in this volume.

or 'Darwish' (*dieliweishi*), mentioned in Yuan historical accounts, and the *burda* probably first reached China through the Sufi orders of Central Asia in the context of celebrating the *mawlid*.[33] If so, it would have been familiar to Chinese Sufi and Muslim communities in the early fourteenth century before *baizizan* was composed. Muslims reading the *baizizan* who knew the *burda* would have recognised similarities between the two poems immediately.

Several other lines in the *baizizan* have close parallels in the *burda*. For example, 'the universe began with the heavenly tablet recording his name' (line 1), resembles 'without him this world would never have come into being!'[34] Where the *baizizan* exalts the Prophet as the 'master of the trillion rulers, leader of the ten thousand sages' (line 4), the *burda* confirms that 'his form and character surpassed even the previous prophets, and none have approached him in knowledge or nobility'.[35] The *baizizan* nostalgically recalls the Prophet as the 'protector of humanity' because 'his intention is that Allah should remember the needy. Deliver them from tribulations to safety, knower of the unseen' (line 5). Similarly, the *burda* recalls that he was 'concerned for our welfare, he did not confuse us with matters we could not fathom', and adds 'nor should we doubt a prophet when he speaks of the unseen'.[36] The Qur'ān indicates that the Prophet is the final messenger whose teaching is the culmination and pinnacle of religion by giving him the titles, 'Messenger of Allah, and the Seal of the Prophets' (Q. 33:40). The *baizizan* affirms the same, saying, '. . . whose path is preeminent for all time' (line 10). The *burda*

[33] Since texts such as the *burda* are most often transmitted orally, it is impossible to determine when it first became popular among Muslims in China, however, we do know that a complete Chinese translation of the *burda* was recorded by Yusuf Ma Dexin (d. 1874) under the title *tianfang shijing* (*The Classic of Arabian Poetry*). Ma Dexin mentions it because it was already a longstanding classic. Devin DeWeese writes about a fifteenth-century Central Asian commentary on the *burda*. See Devin A. DeWeese, *The Kashf Al-Hudā of Kamāl Ad-Dīn Ḥusayn Khorezmī: A Fifteenth-Century Sufi Commentary on the Qaṣīdat Al-Burdah in Khorezmian Turkic* (Bloomington: Indiana University Press, 1985).

[34] Imām Buṣīrī, 'The Fez Singers', and Bennis Abdelfettah, *The Burda of Al-Busiri: The Poem of the Cloak*, trans. Hamza Yusuf, audio CD edn (Thaxted: Sandala, 2002), p. 10

[35] *The Burda of Al-Busiri: The Poem of the Cloak*, p. 10

[36] *The Burda of Al-Buṣīrī: The Poem of the Cloak*, pp. 12, 22.

makes the same point: 'all the previous prophets and messengers gave precedence to you . . . What preeminence you have been entrusted with!'[37]

The poem makes other references to the Qur'ān and famous sayings of the Prophet. For example, 'in each of the five prayers, he silently supplicates for their total well-being' (line 6) recalls what the Prophet told his wife 'Aishah about his constant concern for his community:

> Aishah narrated: 'Once, when I saw the Prophet in a good mood, I said to him: "O Messenger of Allah! Supplicate to Allah for me!" So, he said: "O Allah! Forgive Aishah her past and future sins, what she has hidden, as well as what she has made apparent." So, I began smiling, to the point that my head fell into my lap out of joy. The Messenger of Allah said to me: "Does my supplication make you happy?" I replied: "And how can your supplication not make me happy?" He then said: "By Allah, it is the supplication that I make for my Ummah in every prayer."'[38]

The fact that the Prophet supplicates for his community (*umma*) in each prayer is related explicitly in this narration, while the fact that he does so silently is indicated by the fact that 'Aishah, who regularly observed him in prayer, had never heard the supplication before. *Baizizan* here expands the concept of community (*umma*) to mean humanity, which obviously includes the Chinese.

The description of the Prophet in *baizizan* as 'A mercy to all of the worlds' (line 10) is taken directly from the Qur'ān: 'And We have not sent you except as a mercy to all of the worlds' (Q. 21:107).[39] The description, 'leader to the ten thousand sages' (line 4) can be read as a translation of the Prophet's honorific titles *sayyid al-anbiyā'* and *imām al-mursalīn*, 'chief of all prophets' and 'leader of all Messengers'.

The final lines of the *baizizan* are references to the Qur'ān and could be read in a number of ways. They could be read as a political rectification of Islam as orthodoxy, as a declaration of the author's conversion to Islam, or as a call by the author for the listener to convert to Islam. 'Renounce false

[37] *The Burda of Al-Buṣīrī: The Poem of the Cloak*, p. 30.

[38] Ṣaḥīḥ Ibn Ḥibbān 7266

[39] A more literal translation of this line would be 'Mercy to all under Heaven'.

religions; return to The One' (line 11) is a compound statement that first negates false faith and then affirms true faith, perfectly mirroring the compounding of negation and affirmation within the core teaching of Islam: 'so know that there is no deity except Allah' (Q. 47:19), and it reflects the concept of *tawḥīd*, or the Islamic affirmation of God's oneness. The *baizizan* continues, 'that is the religion called Islam' (line 11), which echoes the Qur'ān in saying, 'Indeed, the religion with Allah is Islam' (3:19) and 'Today, I have perfected your religion for you, and have completed My blessing upon you, and chosen Islam as your religion' (Q. 5:3). Of course, the final line, 'Muḥammad is the most noble sage' (line 12) is a stand-in for the Qur'ānic statement, 'Muḥammad is the Messenger of God' (48:29) as it would be translated through a Chinese neo-Confucian cultural filter.[40]

There are also aspects of *baizizan* that reflect knowledge of Islamic traditions beyond direct textual references or translations. The phrase 'conferring and receiving heavenly scripture in thirty parts' (line 3) points to the custom of dividing the text of the Qur'ān into thirty sections (*juz'*, pl. *ajzā'*) to facilitate reciting it from beginning to end over the course of a month, as Muslims worldwide often do during Ramaḍan. In contrast to the more outwardly apparent division of the Qur'ān into 114 chapters, these 'thirty parts' are primarily experienced in the domain of a believer's practice because they allow Muslims who recite the Qur'ān with regularity to pace their reading. Thirty parts is also the division used when memorising the Qur'ān. After the first chapter, one proceeds to memorise the rest of the Qur'ān one *juz'* at a time. Describing the Qur'ān as divided into thirty parts rather than 114 chapters indicates that the author is relating to the Qur'ān in the context of its memorisation or recitation as a religious and devotional practice. In other words, the author was probably a practising Muslim or was thoroughly familiar with Islamic practices, and not someone who had merely seen a written copy of the Qur'ān.

The placement of the word 'intention' in the line 'his intention is that Allah should remember the needy' (line 7) can only be understood in terms

[40] Stewart called this phenomenon in the translation of religious concepts an attempt to locate cultural 'equivalence' between technical terms that serve analogous purposes in two cultural contexts. See Tony K. Stewart, 'In Search of Equivalence: Conceiving Muslim–Hindu Encounter through Translation Theory', *History of Religions* 40(3) (2001): 260–87.

of Islamic ethical philosophy, which locates intention as the determining factor in an action's moral value. This principle was elaborated from the famous prophetic narration, 'actions are but by intention . . .'[41] The author comments on the sincere intention of the Prophet to emphasise his virtue and selfless concern for others. The pride of place given to intention indicates that the author knew that prophetic narration and understood how its commentary is understood within the Muslim philosophy of ethics.

The phrase 'free from any blameworthy deeds' (line 9), summarises the orthodox Sunni doctrine of immaculacy (*ʿiṣma*), which maintains that all prophets were divinely protected from ever committing sinful or blameworthy actions. The Persian theologian Fakhr al-Dīn al-Rāzī (d. 1210) dedicated a treatise entirely to explaining this point and providing the scriptural proofs which established it as a cornerstone of orthodox creed. The fact that he wrote this treatise, titled 'The Immaculacy of the Prophets' (*ʿiṣmat al-anbiyāʾ*) implies that in the late twelfth or early thirteenth century, theologians were debating this doctrine, which prompted Rāzī's comprehensive response. However, by the time *baizizan* was written, the author asserts the point with simple confidence. This statement would not have been made so clearly by someone who relied either upon a limited selection of basic Islamic texts or upon knowledge passed down within local Muslim communities. The author of *baizizan* was someone who kept up to date with the latest religious discourse emerging from Central Asian centres of Islamic scholarship.

The ode also incorporates expressions commonly found in Chinese Buddhist and Confucian literary traditions. For example, 'universally transforming all created beings' (line 3) is a set phrase used in Buddhist texts. The phrase appears in the Chinese translation of the Avatamsaka sutra (*c.* 699): 'the Buddha's disciple dwelling here acts as a wheel-turning king, universally teaching living beings to practice the ten goods'.[42] Transferring this particular phrase from the context of Buddhism to the context of Islam in China is significant, because after

[41] Yaḥyā b. Ṣharaf al-Nawawī, Ezzedin Ibrahim and Denys Johnson-Davies (trans.), *An-Nawawi's Forty Hadith* (Salimiah, Kuwait: International Islamic Federation of Student Organizations, 1982), p. 26.

[42] In Chinese: '佛子住此作輪王 普化眾生行十善.' Buddhist Text Translation Society, *Introducing the Avatamsaka Sutra* (Talmage, CA: Buddhist Text Translation Society, 1980).

Buddhism, Islam was the first foreign religious tradition to gain a significant following in China and represent itself as a universal teaching. By appropriating this phrase, the author is declaring Islam's naturalisation; despite its foreign origins, the universal scope of Islam makes it a Chinese religion through the same universalising expression that naturalised Buddhism in China. Using the Confucian term 'sage' (*shèng*) to translate 'prophet' and describing Islam as a way or path (*dào)* (line 10) or a teaching (*jiào*) (line 11) further naturalises it as a principled model of social propriety and ethical ideal within the same tradition as the teachings of Confucius and Mencius.

The phrase 'renounce false religions; return to The One' (降邪歸一 *xiángxié guīyī*) (line 11) is a strategic modification of the phrase 'the unification of the three teachings' (三教歸一 *sānjiāo guīyī*). The latter summarises the neo-Confucian doctrine of religious syncretism formulated during the Song dynasty which became increasingly popular in the Ming and Qing dynasties. In that discourse, 'unification of the three teachings' meant combining elements of Confucian, Buddhist and Taoist teachings into a unified religious system in which each of the three traditions could address a different area of human concern: Confucianism governed social ethics; Taoist rituals mediated ongoing relationships between humans and spiritual beings; and Buddhist rituals pacified deceased spirits and provided a road map for the affairs of the hereafter.[43] The way the phrase is modified in *baizizan* lampoons that doctrine by implying that any religion which is incapable of satisfying all aspects of human existence comprehensively is no more than a false or heretical teaching and deserves to be abandoned. Linguistically, this lampoon alters the grammar of the phrase from a four-character noun–noun construct, roughly meaning 'three teachings unification', into a pair of two-character verb–object phrases meaning 'renounce false religions; return to The One'. Changing the grammar isolates the character *guī* as a separate verb meaning 'return' and homophonically 'conversion' (*guī*) instead of the compound word 'unification'. While 'return' might seem like a strange verb to use when exhorting someone to convert to Islam, the explanation lies in a prophetic

[43] Clifford Plopper traces the idiom to a sixteenth-century novel, *Investiture of the Gods* (封神演义 Fēngshén Yǎnyì). See Clifford H. Plopper, *Chinese Religion Seen through the Proverb*, 2nd edn (Shanghai: Shanghai Modern Publishing House, 1935), p. 16.

narration that describes Islam as the natural religion followed by all humans at birth – it is only later that the pure religious inclinations (*fiṭra*) of a child are altered by the efforts of parents and other socialising forces.[44] The concept of return is also notably reflected in the fact that Chinese Muslims are called the Hui people, using the Chinese character that means 'to return'.

At the same time, the call to renounce false or heterodox religions evokes the Islamic narrative of abrogating or correcting earlier religious teachings. According to this narrative, the original revelations of Judaism, Christianity and Sabean gnosticism had become corrupted over time, and Islam was a call to return to their common origin: affirming the truth of God's oneness. As Islam reached more distant regions, Muslims viewed other religions analogously in terms of the same narrative. In China, it can be assumed that Muslims viewed Confucianism, Buddhism and Taoism through the same narrative lens. This is implied by the preceding line '. . . path pre-eminent for all time' (line 10). The poem's conclusion (lines 10–11) could just as easily be read in a more confrontational tone: 'this path (*dào*) supersedes (*guàn*) all prior (*gǔ*) and contemporary (*jīn*). Subdue (*Jiàng*) those heresies (*xié*) and return to oneness (*guīyī*) [in] the religion (*jiào*) named (*míng*) pure and true (*qīngzhēn*) [Islam]'.

Another strong possibility is that the poem's final lines represent the Islamic testification of faith (*al-shahāda*), that 'there is no deity worthy of worship except Allah, and Muḥammad is the Messenger of Allah'. Traditionally, uttering this phrase constitutes a formal conversion to Islam. The *shahāda* consists of two parts: a negation of false deities and an affirmation of the one supreme deity. The Arabic phrase, *lā ʾilāha ʾillā-llāh*, might literally be rendered 'no [false] gods – only the one God'. If we read the emperor's phrase (降邪歸 – *Jiàng*xié guīyī) (line 11) as a parallel of this construction, it can be read as a declaration mirroring the *shahāda*: '[I] reject false faiths, returning to The One'. The possibility of this interpretation is strengthened by the fact that the phrase 'return to The One' (歸 – *guīyī*) is homophonic with the verb 'to convert' (皈依 – guīyī) from one religion to another. In an oral recitation, the lines would sound identical to 'renounce false religions; convert to

[44] *Ṣaḥīḥ Muslim*, Q. 46:36.

the religion called Islam', or, as a more personal statement, 'I renounce false religions and convert to the religion called Islam'.

A contextualised reading of the poem may suggest the way Islam was Sinicised during the Ming dynasty. The Ming defeat of the preceding non-Han Mongol Yuan dynasty and the restoration of Han cultures through forced assimilation or Sinicisation posed a challenge for Chinese Muslims. By presenting the authenticity and orthodoxy of Islam as a consistent continuation of the same *dao* of Daoism, Confucianism and Buddhism already familiar and accepted within Chinese society, the poem serves to justify the orthodoxy of Islam not only philosophically, but also, more importantly, politically through a top-down approach in the new culturally nativist Ming dynasty. In other words, the poem can be seen as a political rectification and justification of Islam presented in a way that could be acceptable in the Sinicising Ming context.

Multiple readings are also possible for the phrase 'the most noble sage' (*zhìguì shèngrén*) (line 12). In the above translation, the first two characters are interpreted as a superlative title describing the Prophet as 'the most noble'. However, 'the most noble' could refer to a noun standing for one of the ninety-nine names of God.[45] In that case, it would be read as the second half of the *shahāda*: 'Muḥammad, sage of the Most Noble', or 'Muḥammad is the messenger of God'. In fact, it would be difficult to express the same meaning more eloquently within the poem's strictly metered format. Considering the ease with which the line could be read in this way and the expectation that a work in this genre would include the *shahāda*, the parallel was probably intentional.

In conclusion, whether Emperor Zhu Yuanzhang authored this poem or implicitly intended to declare himself Muslim by glossing the Islamic testification of faith in the final lines may be impossible to determine with absolute certainty from a historical and official perspective. Traditional narratives

[45] It is not clear which of the ninety-nine names might have been intended. The names that strike me as the most likely possibilities are 'The Self-Sufficient' (*al-ghanī*), 'The Possessor of Ultimate Majesty and Generosity' (*dhū'l jalāl wa'l-ikrām*), 'The Benefactor' (*al-nafi'*), 'The Enricher/Emancipator' (*al-mughnī*), 'The Most High' (*al-'alī*), 'The Most Generous' (*al-karīm*), 'The Ultimate Ruler of all Creation' (*al-malik*), or 'The Exalted above all Creation' (*al-mutakabbir*).

conveyed within Muslim communities affirm it, but even those present contradictions. For example, the author obviously possessed a broad understanding and awareness of current Islamic scholarly discourse, but this contrasts significantly from the impression of Zhu Yuanzhang that is conveyed in an anecdote recounted by Chinese Muslims. In the anecdote, Zhu neglects to remove his shoes before stepping into a mosque. An associate quickly informs him of his gaffe, whereupon Zhu replies, 'I did not know the custom'.[46] Mosque attendance and communal worship are core aspects of how Islam has been practised by Muslims in all eras and in all regions. In stark contrast to the level of knowledge demonstrated by the author of *baizizan*, this account depicts Zhu as someone who is ignorant of basic Islamic customs. The only way to reconcile this story with the claim that Zhu authored *baizizan* would be to suggest that this incident must have occurred before he embarked upon a path of religious scholarship. Or perhaps accidentally committing this blunder was the impetus that impelled the emperor to learn more about Islam. Or perhaps the anecdote that ridiculed Zhu was a later composition for the purpose of neutralising and nullifying Zhu's praise on the Prophet.

Bibliography

Abdelfettah, Bennis, *The Burda of Al-Busiri: The Poem of the Cloak*, trans. Hamza Yusuf, audio CD edn (Thaxted: Sandala, 2002).

Abru, Hafiz-i, *A Persian Embassy to China Being An Extract from Zubdatu't tawarikh of Hatīz Abru*, trans. K. M. Maitra (New York, 1970).

Al-Buṣīrī, *The Mantle Adorned: Translated, with Further Poetic Ornaments* (London: Quilliam Press, 2009).

Al-Nawawī, Yaḥyā b. Sharaf, *An-Nawawi's Forty Hadith*, trans. Ezzedin Ibrahim and Denys Johnson-Davies (Salimiah, Kuwait: International Islamic Federation of Student Organizations, 1982).

Al-Rifai, Sayyid Rami, *The Light of Allah in the Heavens and the Earth: The Creation of the Atom (24:35) and the Physics of Spirituality*, https://ghayb.com/wp-content/uploads/2015/09/The-Light-Of-Allah-In-The-Heavens-and-The-Earth-The-

[46] Shujiang Li and Karl W. Luckert, *Mythology and Folklore of the Hui: A Muslim Chinese People* (New York: SUNY Press, 1994), p. 235; Benite relates this story in his analysis of Chinese Muslim narratives about Zhu Yuanzhang as a Muslim. See Benite, 'The Marrano Emperor', p. 275.

Creation-Of-The-Atom-24-35-and-The-Physics-Of-Spirituality.pdf (Sunnah Mu'akada, 2016).

Benite, Zvi Ben-Dor, 'The Marrano Emperor: The Mysterious Bond between Zhu Yuanzhang and the Chinese Muslims', in Sarah Schneewind (ed.), *Long Live the Emperor!: Uses of the Ming Founder across Six Centuries of East Asian History* (Minneapolis, MN: Society for Ming Studies, 2008).

Benite, Zvi Ben-Dor, *The Dao of Muhammad: A Cultural History of Muslims in Late Imperial China* (Cambridge, MA: Harvard University Press, 2010).

Bretschneider, E., *Medieval Researches from Eastern Asiatic Sources*, vol 2 (New York: Barnes & Noble, 1967).

Chaffee, John W., *The Muslim Merchants of Premodern China: The History of a Maritime Asian Trade Diaspora, 750–1400* (Cambridge: Cambridge University Press, 2018).

Cai, Zong-qi, *How to Read Chinese Poetry: A Guided Anthology* (New York: Columbia University Press, 2008).

Chang, Yusuf, 'The Ming Empire: Patron of Islam in China and Southeast–West Asia', *Journal of the Malaysian Branch of the Royal Asiatic Society* 61(2) (255) (1988): 1–44.

DeWeese, Devin A., *The Kashf Al-Hudā of Kamāl Ad-Dīn Ḥusayn Khorezmī: A Fifteenth-Century Sufi Commentary on the Qaṣīdat Al-Burdah in Khorezmian*, Turkic Text edition, translation and historical introduction (Bloomington: Indiana University Press, 1985).

Dreyer, Edward L., *Zheng He: China and the Oceans in the Early Ming Dynasty, 1405–1433*, Pearson College Div, 2006.

Frankel, James D., *Rectifying God's Name* (Honolulu: University of Hawai'i Press, 2011).

Frankel, James D., 'Muslim Blue, Chinese White: Islamic Calligraphy on Ming Blue-and-white Porcelain', *Orientations* 49(2) (2018): 2–7.

Fu, Tongxian (傅統先), *Zhongguo hui jiao shi* (中國回教史) [*History of Islam in China*] (China: Shangwu yinshuguan, 1934).

Hing, Hui Chun, 'Huangming zuxun and Zheng He's Voyages to the Western Oceans', *Journal of Chinese Studies* 51 (2010): 67–85.

Jaschok, Maria and Jingjun Shui, *The History of Women's Mosques in Chinese Islam: A Mosque of Their Own* (London: Curzon Press, 2000).

Jeffrey, Jaclyn (ed.) *Memory and History: Essays on Recalling and Interpreting Experience* (Lanham, MD: University Press of America, 1994).

Jin, Jitang (金吉堂). *Zhongguo hui jiao shi yan jiu* (中國回教史研究) [*A Historical Study of Islam in China*] (Peking: Chengda shifan chubanshe, 1935).

Leslie, Donald, *Islam in Traditional China: A Short History to 1800* (Canberra: Canberra College of Advanced Education, 1986).

Leung, A. K. C., 'Elementary Education in the Lower Yangtze Region in the Seventeenth and Eighteenth Centuries', in Benjamin A. Elman and Alexander Woodside (eds), *Education and Society in Late Imperial China, 1600–1900* (Berkeley: University of California Press, 1994), p. 394.

Li, Shujiang and Karl W. Luckert, *Mythology and Folklore of the Hui: A Muslim Chinese People* (New York: SUNY, 1994).

Ma, Huan, *Ying-Yai Sheng-Lang: Overall Survey of the Ocean's Shores* (1433), trans. Feng Cheng-Chün and J. V. G. Mills, 2nd edn (Thailand: White Lotus, 1996).

Petersen, Kristian, *Interpreting Islam in China: Pilgrimage, Scripture, and Language in the Han Kitab* (Oxford: Oxford University Press, 2018).

Plopper, Clifford H., *Chinese Religion Seen through the Proverb* (Shanghai: Shanghai Modern Publishing House, 1935).

Ricklefs, M.C. (ed.), 'Chinese Muslims in Java in the 15th and 16th Centuries: The Malay Annals of Sémarang and Cérbon', Monash University, Monash Papers on Southeast Asia No. 12. 1984.

Rossabi, Morris, *Khubilai Khan: His Life and Times* (Berkeley: University of California Press, 1988.

Scheewind, Sarah (ed.), *Long Live the Emperor!: Uses of the Ming Founder across Six Centuries of East Asian History* (Minneapolis, MN: Society for Ming Studies, 2008).

Stewart, Tony K., 'In Search of Equivalence: Conceiving Muslim–Hindu Encounter through Translation Theory', *History of Religions* 40(3) (2001): 260–87.

Yule, Henry (ed.), *Cathay and the Way Thither: Being a Collection of Medieval Notices of China*, vol. 3 (London: Printed for the Hakluyt Society, 1913).

11

A FINE ROMANCE: TRANSLATING THE *QISSAH* AS WORLD ROMANCE[1]

Pasha M. Khan

World literature is produced when a set of texts is read in a certain way. It is 'a mode of reading' that arises out of the historical and intellectual circumstances of its readers.[2] Therefore, Aamir Mufti has been able to identify a foundational role for Orientalism in the rise of world literature described by David Damrosch, through careful historicisation. Already in Goethe's own time, the 'Orientalist knowledge revolution' that accompanied and enabled the era of Western settler colonialism was the motor for the induction of Orientalised expressive traditions into the world literary system that was taking shape in western Europe and North America.[3] What was the 'world' assumed and conjured by the idea of the 'romance' as a world literary genre, and how did Orientalism produce the space and time of that world? In the present study, I shall argue that the worldwide romance genre, supposed to comprehend the genres of narrative properly referred to as *qissah*,

[1] I am grateful to Aqsa Ijaz for her comments on a draft of this chapter, and to the editors for the many points that they raised to help clarify my arguments. For my title, I am indebted to Ginger Rogers and Fred Astaire. All translations are my own unless otherwise specified.

[2] David Damrosch, *What is World Literature?* (Princeton, NJ: Princeton University Press, 2003), p. 281.

[3] Aamir Mufti, *Forget English! Orientalisms and World Literatures* (Cambridge MA: Harvard University Press, 2016), p. 90.

hikāyat, *dāstān*, *kathā*, etc.,[4] was fashioned in an Orientalising manner that mapped onto the 'Oriental romance' the inert antiquity of the Occidental romance genre, normatively locating the Orient as the ancient origin of the world romance. The smooth consistency of the world romance genre therefore concealed a chrono-Orientalism that made it possible, and that consigned the *qissah* to little more than an antiquarian significance. The world of world romance was one of delightful, obsolete irrelevance, and insofar as Orientals continued to inhabit the world that Europe had left behind for modernity, the schizochronic condition of the world provided a justification for the *mission civilisatrice*. My argument owes a great deal to Sara Grewal's interrogation of the ghazal as lyric, in which she points out how the discourse of the ghazal as world literature conceals the colonial dismissal of the ghazal as 'backward'.[5]

Against the Romance-*Qissah* Translation

The genre of verbal art called the *qissah* or *dāstān* has been referred to in English by a variety of names. At times, these English genre names have been determined in part by the commentator's view of a specific text, as when the story of Amir Hamzah was in 1892 referred to as a 'novel', or when the *Shahnameh* is referred to as an 'epic'.[6] Apart from the protean and therefore rather suitable term 'tale', the genre itself has most often been referred

[4] The terms *qissah*, *hikāyat*, *dāstān* and *kathā* all refer to a narrative genre or genres, most often oral-performative, told by *qissah-khwān*s (*qissah*-reciters), *dāstān-go*s (*dāstān*-tellers), *kathā-kār*s (*kathā*-makers), etc. Distinctions between these genre designations have been made in various places and points in history, but it is difficult to generalise. As an example of such difficulty, in India from the late nineteenth century onward, there was a tendency to imagine that *hikāyat*s are brief narrations, *qissah*s of medium size, and *dāstān*s are lengthy 'epics'. While the above characterisation of the brevity of the *hikāyat* is usually correct, the distinction between *qissah* and *dāstān* is not, historically. One regularly finds long *qissah*s that are divided into shorter *dāstān*s, completely reversing the assumed norms of length.

[5] Sara Grewal, 'Ghazal as "World Poetry": Between Worlding and Vernacularization', *Comparative Literature* 74(1) (2022): 25–51.

[6] ʿAbdullāh Husain Bilgrāmī, *Dastan-e Amir Hamza: An Oriental Novel*, ed. Sajjad Husain (Patna: Khuda Bakhsh Oriental Public Library, 1992); Mahmoud Omidsalar, *Poetics and Politics of Iran's National Epic, the Shahnameh* (New York: Palgrave Macmillan, 2011).

to as 'romance', and not only by nineteenth-century Orientalists. More recent scholars of the *qissah* who work in English have also designated it as 'romance', including William Hanaway, Frances Pritchett, Aditya Behl and myself. In my 2019 study, *The Broken Spell*, I frequently referred to the Urdu and Persian 'romance'. I did so even as I argued that the imposition of this term upon the *qissah* was a distortive one, having faith that an exposition of the distortion would change the signification of the English word in readers' minds and allow the translation to stand.

I no longer believe that such a translation is useful, even if the translator stealthily intends resignification. In *The Broken Spell*, I failed to examine some of my unstated motives, including the assumption that to translate using established categories in the target language is to enact generosity to readers, giving them a starting-point in a system that they already understand.[7] If ever such a generosity were possible, ethically speaking, it would have to involve a target language that lacked the hegemonic power of English. The various genre codes of the *qissah* – and it is important to recollect that there was never any *single* code that could have led us back to a single, essential Islamicate or Indic-Islamicate mindset – should rather have been allowed to stand on their own and related to one another.[8] The sole purpose of comparison with the British romance ought to have been the demonstration of how this translation of a genre term misshaped nineteenth- and twentieth-century readings of *qissah*s among both British Orientalists and Urdu-speaking scholars. Instead, retaining the English translation 'romance' runs the risk of giving license to the sedimented meaning of the term, for resignification is easily elided or forgotten. It is better to let the Urdu genre terms stay in their separate strangeness.

To summarise the production of the assimilative genre equation between romance and *qissah*, we must first consider once more the emergence of the genre code of the novel in eighteenth- and nineteenth-century Britain and France.[9] For the codes of the novel and the romance were formed in relation

[7] Pasha M. Khan, *The Broken Spell: Indian Storytelling and the Romance Genre in Persian and Urdu* (Detroit, MI: Wayne State University Press, 2019), p. 194.

[8] Tzvetan Todorov, *Genres in Discourse* (Cambridge: Cambridge University Press, 1990), p. 198.

[9] For another description of the interdependent emergence of the novel and romance genre codes in western Europe, see Khan, *The Broken Spell*, ch. 6.

and in opposition to one another in a hierarchy wherein the romance was devalued, and the novel exalted as long as it adhered to the ideal code. Understood as romance, the *qissah* was devalued on similar if not identical bases, and in opposition to the novel with its Occidental origin.

In eighteenth-century Britain the superiority of the novel was by no means a given. Though an epistemological hierarchy was emerging wherein the romance would eventually be defined and denigrated with respect to its non-conformance to the dictates of reason and sense, the conformity of the proper novel to rational and empirical reality could be a liability.[10] For the defence of realism was often put forward by novelists who incorporated into their writings subjects that were considered lascivious by their critics. However, alongside the force of market appeal and the waning of the power of the aristocracy with which the romance was associated, the epistemological argument had by the nineteenth century given the triumph to the novel. This was the case even though features associated with the romance continued to appear in novels whose subgenre designations – 'Gothic novels', 'sensation fiction', etc. – signalled their deviation from the normative genre code of the novel.

In my previous work, I have emphasised that the *qissah* was normatively coded as a genre of narratives that, even when they were written, retained in their structure the traces of the oral-performative process whereby they were often produced. One of the results of that very process is that the multigeneric fabric of *qissah*s becomes evident when we look carefully.[11] Thus, any answer to the question 'what was the *qissah*?' is complicated in the first place by the multiplicity of genres running through any given *qissah*, and, indeed, through all texts no matter what their dominant genre. In the second place, disparate codifications of the *qissah* genre existed not only diachronically but also synchronically. Such disagreements about what *qissah*s were reflected contestations about the place of the *qissah* or *dāstān* in Islamic genre hierarchies or systems. Like the romance, the *qissah* genre's value was sometimes challenged

[10] Claire Gallien points out some of the advantages 'Oriental tale' initially enjoyed over the novel, for example, in Claire Gallien, *L'Orient anglais. Connaissances et fictions au XVIIIe siècle* (Oxford: Voltaire Foundation, 2011), p. 34.

[11] Khan, *The Broken Spell*, esp. ch. 3.

because *qissah*s were mendacious or incorporated exaggeration (*mubālaghah*), straying from the standards of intellect (*ʿaql*) and custom (*ʿādat*). Yet I have argued for the unlikelihood that an exclusively rationalist epistemology would have been widespread, notwithstanding how privileged it was among some groups such as the Muʿtazilīs and certain Shiʿīs.[12]

Even if we were to imagine the force and spread of rationalism to be comparable with its force and spread in the post-Enlightenment West, not all *qissah*s exhibited reason-confounding or custom-breaking (*khāriq al-ʿādat*) characteristics. Two points ought to be borne in mind in this regard. First, it may be possible to read non-custom-breaking *qissah*s in terms of the desires of social classes, as Francesca Orsini has suggested. She has stressed the mundaneness of certain *qissah*s such as the *Tale of the Soldier's Son* (*Qissah-i Sipāhī-zādah*), and pointed out that such *qissah*s were popular for reasons linked to the middle-class' appetite for narratives that represented them. She has concluded that, in spite of the reputation of the *qissah* genre for being unchanging, the *Tale of the Soldier's Son* was a new sort of *qissah*, and its newness appears to have been due to the increasing consumption of print by the middle class in the nineteenth century.[13] Such *qissah*s existed long before this period, however, and further research is needed to determine their connection to the socio-economic developments that predated colonialism in India. Secondly, while *qissah*s centred around magic and *tilism*s,[14] like the *Tale of Amīr Hamzah*, appear most egregiously contrary to reason and sense, this impression is based on the assumption that magic was understood to be irrational and invalid. The work of scholars like Matthew Melvin-Koushki is

[12] Khan, *The Broken Spell*, pp. 181–6.

[13] Francesca Orsini, *Print and Pleasure: Popular Literature and Entertaining Fictions in Colonial North India* (Ranikhet: Permanent Black, 2009), p. 116 and ch. 4 more broadly. Cf. Christina Oesterheld, 'Entertainment and Reform: Urdu Narrative Genres in the Nineteenth Century', in Vasudha Dalmia and Stuart H. Blackburn (eds), *India's Literary History* (Dehli: Permanent Black, 2004), pp. 167–212.

[14] In the context of the *dāstān* tradition and especially the tales of Amīr Hamzah, a *tilism* is a world created by means of a magical enchantment consisting of an earthly device constructed in such a way as to harness the astral powers. See Shamsur Rahman Faruqi, *Sāhirī, Shāhī, Sāhib-Qirānī: Dāstān-i Amīr Hamzah kā mutālaʿah*, vol. 3 (New Delhi: Qaumī Council barā'e furogh-i Urdū zabān, 2006), pp. 284–8.

challenging that assumption.[15] If we accept that the occult sciences (*'ulūm-i gharībah*) did not necessarily run counter to the intellect, then Arthur Dudney and Orsini's point that the post-Raj Hindi *dāstān Chandrakāntā* justified its marvels rationally is true of the earlier *tilismī dāstāns*, including the Persian and Urdu tales of Hamzah themselves.[16]

Following the increasing establishment and influence of British education in India, the *qissah* became subject to a different and much more pervasive sort of epistemologically based devaluation, especially after 1857 and the institution of the British Raj. This devaluation was effected in part via the British identification of the *qissah* as 'romance', the appearance of the novel in Indian languages, and the consequent imposition of the same kind of standards to the *qissah* that had been applied to the romance genre in the eighteenth century. Orientalists and colonised Indian intellectuals made certain that genre history repeated itself, and that the novel triumphed over the *qissah* as it had done over the romance. That the *qissah* and romance genres were subject to the same process of devaluation is thus undeniable. But it was the unnecessary equation between the two that served as an instrument of this process.

In resisting translation, I would like to detach the *qissah* as much as possible from the kind of totalising world literary genre systems of the sort that emerged in Goethe's nineteenth-century Europe and developed over the long course of globalisation. The assumption that the romance genre is world-encompassing, and constitutes a 'world genre', must be challenged and rethought, perhaps along with the idea of a world itself. Until we are able to think carefully about each individual world formed by the various world literary systems that exist and have existed, the idea of a (Goethean) 'world

[15] For example, Matthew Melvin-Koushki, 'Powers of One: The Mathematicalization of the Occult Sciences in the High Persianate Tradition', *Intellectual History of the Islamicate World* 5(1/2) (2017): 127–99.

[16] Arthur Dudney, 'Keeping the Magic Alive: How Devakīnandan Khatrī's Chandrakāntā, the First Hindi Best-Seller, Navigates Western Modernity and the Fantastical', unpublished manuscript, 2012, pp. 18–22, available at: http://www.columbia.edu/itc/mealac/pritchett/00urduhindilinks/txt_dudney_chandrakanta.pdf. (Dudney wrote the original version of this paper in 2008.) Orsini, *Print and Pleasure*, pp. 210–11.

literature' is best analysed as a historical object, as Mufti has taken it, rather than as a canon-building project, even if canons are multiple.

Chrono-Orientalism and the Medieval

In the wake of universalising formalist studies like that of Vladimir Propp, Northrop Frye was able to think of the romance as a world genre, with little reflection upon the geographical, temporal or cultural specificity of romances or the local genre designations that were elided by this translation.[17] The assumed sameness of so-called romances across the world may have been even easier to swallow in the mid-twentieth century than it had been in the nineteenth. The ability to believe in sameness would have been due especially to the tendency of formalism and New Criticism to bracket histories outside the history of forms, including eliding the various epistemic histories undergirding the formation of genres assimilated into the category of 'romance'. It would also have been due to the perceived successes of colonialism in spreading Western civilisation and bringing colonised peoples into a relative state of modernity in harmony with the West.

Otherwise, the *qissah* as Oriental romance fit into the world literary system in an asynchronous or 'schizochronic' manner. Mohamad Tavakoli-Targhi has referred to this schizochronia as 'a fractured conception of historical time' that took 'a dehistorized and decontextualized "European rationality" as its scale and referent' and 'denied coevalness' between Western societies and their others.[18] This fractured temporality has enabled a schizochronic Orientalism, or what I am calling 'chrono-Orientalism'. The Orient serves as both contrast and mirror for the Occident, not least in terms of the latter's history. Chrono-Orientalism projects Western pasts onto the East, so that the East becomes comprehensible as a frozen image of a pre-modern era in the history of the West; the Middle Ages, for example. Medievalising, classicising or barbarising, all forms of chrono-Orientalism are useful

[17] Northrop Frye, *Anatomy of Criticism* (Princeton, NJ: Princeton University Press, 1973), p. 307. Vladimir Propp, *The Russian Folktale*, trans. Sibelan Forrester (Detroit, MI: Wayne State University Press, 2012).

[18] Mohamad Tavakoli-Targhi, 'The Homeless Texts of Persianate Modernity', *Cultural Dynamics* 13(3) (2001): 4.

to the West both as justifications for Western power over the East, and as mechanisms whereby the West is able to understand itself. In her analysis of ABC news reporter Diane Sawyer's medievalisation of Afghan women under the backward Taliban, Kathleen Davis suggested that Orientalisms of this sort spatialise time, alongside evolutionist forms of anthropology, placing all societies upon a temporal continuum in which the height of progress is represented by the present.[19]

In nineteenth-century Britain, medievalisation was a particularly common form of Orientalism involved in the translation of genre terms such as *qissah* and *dāstān* by the word 'romance'. The values that people in modern Europe assigned to the Middle Ages were reflected in Orientalist devaluations of the epistemic conditions behind East and Eastern artworks. Like medieval Europe, the East may have been backward, irrational, feudal, cruel, superstitious, libidinous and unfree. These devaluations of the medievalised Orient were nothing less than reflections of the low value that was mis-assigned to the history of Christian-ruled Europe after the fall of Rome; the period vanishingly referred to as the 'Dark Ages'. It was the West's devaluation of a past understood to belong to the West that was transferred onto the East.

This devaluation, which Medievalist scholars are only beginning to correct, appears not to have been fully accomplished in eighteenth-century Britain. In his *Remarks on the Arabian Nights' Entertainments* (1797), Richard Hole claimed to be able to 'trace beneath the disguise of exaggeration, or the shadowy veil of allegory, events and circumstances which confirm the accounts of our early voyagers, or correspond with the observations of philosophic enquiries, belonging to other climes, and born in distant ages'.[20] Hole's project

[19] Kathleen Davis, 'Time Behind the Veil: The Media, the Middle Ages, and Orientalism Now', in Jeffrey Jerome Cohen (ed.), *The Postcolonial Middle Ages* (New York: Palgrave Macmillan, 2000), p. 108.

[20] Richard Hole, *Remarks on The Arabian Nights' Entertainments* (London: Cadell, 1797), pp. 249–50. Quoted in Richard Van Leeuwen, 'The Canonization of the Thousand and One Nights in World Literature', in Dominique Jullien (ed.), *Foundational Texts of World Literature* (New York: Peter Lang, 2011), p. 104. Van Leeuwen suggests that Hole was not denigrating the worldview of the *1001 Nights*, as some have assumed, but that he restated the critique of the 'childishness' of the *Nights* in order to refute it. Ibid., Van Leeuwen, p. 103.

implied a continuity of the present with the past, including the medieval past, that was not particularly in evidence in schizochronic nineteenth-century Orientalist studies. Richard Van Leeuwen argues that this continuity is evinced in Hole's method and the categories he uses, as well as in his representation of the *1001 Nights*. The link that he makes between Oriental and Classical accounts, moreover, implies a more valorised relation, insofar as the Classical period still held value for eighteenth-century Britons, as Claire Gallien has emphasised.[21] As post-industrial modernity and colonialism chugged forward, however, the schizochronia that Tavakoli-Targhi has described became a basic principle of Orientalism.

I certainly do not mean to suggest that the *qissah* as 'Oriental romance' did not have its apologists, both mealy-mouthed and full-throated. Apparently positive remarks were often impossible without chrono-Orientalist bases. It is only that they reflected redemptive orientations towards the West's own past. Nostalgia for pre-industrial-age values and simplicity produced forms of medievalism underpinning species of approbative chrono-Orientalism that were political, though not neatly classifiable by party affiliation. Alice Chandler has documented Tory nostalgia for Britain's bygone chivalry over liberalism, class conflict and rationalism.[22] On the Whiggish side, Thomas Babington Macaulay's infamous *Minute on Indian Education* conveyed a belief in the superiority of British literature, while Macaulay also ridiculed the poet Robert Southey's idealisation of medieval prosperity, and his alleged ignorance of all rational principles.[23] Yet medievalist nostalgia, a largely conservative affect, was not necessarily a Tory feeling. One has only to remember Edmund Burke's lament for the age

[21] Claire Gallien 'From One Empire to the Next: The Reconfigurations of "Indian" Literatures from Persian to English Translations', *Translation Studies* (2019): 7–8.

[22] Alice Chandler, *A Dream of Order: The Medieval Ideal in Nineteenth-Century English Literature* (Lincoln: University of Nebraska Press, 1970), pp. 153ff.

[23] Thomas Babington Macaulay, *Speeches: With His Minute on Indian Education*, ed. G. M. Young, The World's Classics (New York: AMS Press, 1979), pp. 345–61; Thomas Babington Macaulay, *The Complete Writings of Lord Macaulay*, vol. 12 (Boston, MA: Houghton Mifflin, 1900), pp. 153–6. Cf. Chandler, *A Dream of Order*, p. 113.

of chivalry, or witness the liberal John Stuart Mill's enchantment by 'the chivalrous spirit'.[24]

As participants in Romanticism, Whigs and Radicals also made use of a more temporally complicated Middle Ages that was quite different from Macaulay's conception. Although Elizabeth Fay's analysis of Whiggish and Radical medievalism points out its focus on the discontinuity of the medieval past and the nineteenth-century present, it also shows that Whigs and Radicals extracted from the Middle Ages an orientation towards the future located in the past. They did so by focusing on the figure of the hierarchy-disturbing troubadour rather than the knight, and stressing the world-making power of medieval poetry rather than the grim realities of medieval life. In doing so, they turned past possibilities into future hope.[25]

As a mirror for the medieval, the Oriental could be useful as a past phase whose overcoming was a triumph, or as a heterotopia to be desired, at least in certain respects. The Orientalist scholar Duncan Forbes wrote in 1830 a translation of the Persian *Qissah-i Hātim Tā'ī* (*The Adventures of Hatim Taï, A Romance*). In setting out the importance of the translation, Forbes admitted that the tales 'may not perhaps merit from the English reader that interest which the original holds among the natives of the East'. But he argued that it was unfair to condemn the romance of Hātim on account of its 'supernatural' elements, since it was a reflection of a society quite different from that of Victorian England. He explained:

> In Europe the last three centuries have wrought mighty changes in the state of society, while Asia remains, comparatively speaking, unaltered. Among the natives of Persia and Hindustan, the belief in demons, fairies, magicians with their enchanted palaces, and talismans and charms, is as prevalent as it was in Europe in the chivalrous ages that succeeded the crusades. Hence the most celebrated works of fiction in the East abound with the incredible, the

[24] Edmund Burke, *Reflections on the Revolution in France*, ed. Frank M. Turner (New Haven, CT: Yale University Press, 2003), p. 65; John Stuart Mill, *Dissertations and Discussions, Political, Philosophical, and Historical*, 2nd edn, vol. 1 (London: Longmans, Green, Reader & Dyer, 1867), p. 285.

[25] Elizabeth Fay, 'Romantic Medievalism: The Ideal of History', in *Romantic Medievalism: History and the Romantic Literary Ideal* (London: Palgrave Macmillan, 2002), p. 1ff.

> wild, and the marvellous, like the productions of the bards and story-tellers of Provence and their imitators, which enchanted Europe from the twelfth to the sixteenth centuries.[26]

Forbes contends, in other words, that the English ought to give Orientals a break. They are what they are, and they are not us. And, besides, we in the West were also enchanted once, and we got over it. Forbes' argument posits both the dissimilarity of Orient and Occident, on the basis of the discontinuity between the medieval past and the present; and the similarity of Orient and Occident in the past, present-ing the West's own past in another place. The world romance genre is signalled by the reference to Provence, insofar as Provence was understood as the wick that took the spark of the romance from Spain to Europe. It was in the world romance that the past-medieval of the West was brought across time into present-medieval of the East, for the use of the present West.

The notion that the 'Western romance' and the 'Eastern romance' (e.g., the *qissah*) were temporal siblings also enabled Orientalists to pin upon the Orient the schizochronia that haunted the Occidental present. W. J. Clouston's introduction to his *A Group of Eastern Romances and Stories* (1889) revealed two sites of this schizochronia, the working class and the child:

> It has been justly remarked that 'the literature of a nation furnishes the best guide to researches into its character, manners, and opinions, and no department of literature contains a more ample store of data in this respect than the light and popular part consisting of tales, romances, and dramatic pieces'. The lighter literature of medieval Europe affords us an insight into customs, manners, and superstitions which have long passed away; but in 'the unchanging East' the literature of the Asiatic races, produced at the same period, continues to reflect the sentiments and habits of the Hindus, Buddhists, and Muslims at the present day. For among Asiatics belief in astrology, magic, divination, good and bad omens, and evil spirits (rakshasas, divs, jinn, etc.) who are ever eager to injure human beings is still as prevalent as when the oldest of their popular tales and romances were first written. The child-like,

[26] Duncan Forbes, *The Adventures of Hatim Taï: A Romance* (London: Oriental Translation Fund, 1830), p. v.

> wonder-loving Oriental mind delights in stories of the supernatural, and the more such narratives exceed the bounds of human possibility the greater is the pleasure derived from them; – like our own peasantry, who believed (and not so long since) in 'ghosts, fairies, goblins, and witches', as well as in the frequent apparition of Satan in various forms to delude the benighted traveller, and were fond of listening to "tales of the wild and wonderful" during the long winter evenings.[27]

The Orientals, whose taste for Oriental romances reveals their minds, are likened to 'our own peasantry', on the one hand. This comparison demonstrates the correctness of Saree Makdisi's thesis regarding the need for the 'backward' British working class to be westernised.[28] On the other hand, the Oriental, governed by the imagination, is childlike; and, moreover, children are Oriental-like in their wonder. The infantilisation of Orientals, 'half-devil and half-child', by exposing the epistemological deficiency of the Oriental romance, is a way to justify colonialism.

However, the comparison between the Oriental and the child goes both ways, as the following review of Forbes' *Adventures of Hatim Taï* shows:

> There is no use whatever in our sitting down to read the adventures of Hatim Tai, unless we first revive in our souls the rainbow hues of early youth, and recall that inexperienced ardour which prompted us easily to believe in the mystic potency of talismans, and in the obedience rendered to them by genii of earth and air and ocean. We must again believe, as we then believed, that the imagination has a real living world of its own, far apart from this land of spinning-jennies and rail-roads . . . A grave and argumentative treatise might be written on the question, whether the more civilized of mankind have in fact gained any accession to their happiness, by permitting the increase of exact knowledge to limit the free range of the imagination.[29]

[27] W. A. Clouston, *A Group of Eastern Romances and Stories from the Persian, Tamil, and Urdu* (Glasgow: Privately printed, 1889), p. vi.

[28] Saree Makdisi, *Making England Western: Occidentalism, Race, and Imperial Culture* (Chicago: University of Chicago Press, 2014).

[29] Rudyard Kipling, 'The White Man's Burden', in *Complete Verse* (New York: Anchor Press, 1940), pp. 321–3.

Here children are chrono-Orientalised, for, like Orientals, they are imperfectly civilised, playing happily under the spell of the imaginative Oriental romance with its *jinns* and *tilisms*. A history whose telos is Western civilisation, so-called, is crammed into the span of a human life, in such a way that the child imbibing Oriental imagination embodies the presence of the pre-industrial-age past in the nineteenth-century present. Reduced to its pleasure-giving function, the romance crosses time and meridians to appeal against industrial-age reason through the attractive force of the childish reader. The genre of 'children's literature', of which the romance had become a part by the end of the nineteenth century, is steeped in this value.

As Forbes' comments on the *qissah* show most clearly, the usefulness of 'Oriental romances' is, by the nineteenth century, always based on the schizochronic logic of a chrono-Orientalism that usually medievalised the genre and subsumed it into the genre of romance. Appreciation of so-called Oriental romances was most often rooted in an assumption that they mirrored the West's past for it, making it available for the modern West as a heterotopia.

The Oriental Origins of the Romance

Many of the intellectuals who forged the notion of a worldwide romance genre understood the kinship between Western and Eastern romances, so-called, in terms of descent. They considered Eastern romances to be ancestral to the romances of the West, or at least among their forebears. Much like the genealogies of Western science and philosophy that trace their provenance to Muslim thinkers active during the 'Dark Ages' of Europe, the idea of the Eastern romance inspiriting the Western might be understood as a riposte to those who would maintain the purity of the Western tradition. But, in actuality, this idea was more often used in a chrono-Orientalist fashion, to give to the *qissah* and other 'Eastern' genres subsumed under the code of 'romance' an antiquarian relevance only, leaving the Western literary tradition to succeed and outstrip its venerable but somewhat senile progenitor. While Whiggish and child-centred approaches to the 'Oriental romance' might have implied its heterotopic usefulness for the future, this relation to futurity did not mean that its survival was desirable. Rather, it was valuable as a preserver and carrier of the West's own lost excellence. Forever trapped in the past, the *qissah* exhausted its usefulness once it provided the West with the virtues the West had left behind.

The history of the idea of the world literary romance is intertwined with that of the world literary lyric. The latter is the subject of an excellent study by Grewal, and I will not pause to consider it in detail, referring the reader instead to Grewal's work.[30] It is sufficient to say that one of the points of overlap was that the romance was understood to be either a prose or a verse work, and the rhyming verse form was common to both the lyric and the romance. In the quest for the origins of rhyming verse in particular, there arose what Boase called the Hispano-Arab thesis.[31] It has been argued that the 'intercultural origins' of the lyric genre have been erased even as the standard of the lyric was imposed upon 'Oriental' verse forms.[32] Yet the reality is that European scholars from the sixteenth century onward postulated an Oriental origin (which was not necessarily unilineal) for the lyric and the romance genres.

The Hispano-Arab thesis appears early on in Giammaria Barberi's (1519–75) Italian work on the origin of rhymed poetry, which speculated that troubadour lyric poetry originated in the twelfth century with contact between Christians and Muslims in Andalus. His book was not printed until 1790, but his ideas were spread by colleagues in the intervening period.[33] With this idea available, the French scholar Claude Saumaise (1588–1653), 'believed that Spain, after having learned the art of romancing from the Arabs, taught it by its example to all the rest of Europe'.[34] Saumaise's friend Pierre-Daniel Huet, whose 1671 *On the Origin of Romances* (*De l'origine des romans*) was prefaced to a French romance about a Moorish princess, demurred slightly at Saumaise's thesis, but

[30] Grewal, 'Ghazal as "World Poetry"', pp. 25–51.

[31] Roger Boase, *The Origin and Meaning of Courtly Love: A Critical Study of European Scholarship* (Manchester: Manchester University Press, 1977), pp. 62–75.

[32] Mufti, *Forget English!*, p. 72.

[33] Boase, *The Origin and Meaning of Courtly Love*, p. 11. Huet similarly endorsed, in passing, the idea that rhyme originated with the Arabs. See Pierre-Daniel Huet, *Lettre de Monsieur Huet à Monsieur de Segrais de l'origine des romans* (S. Mabre-Cramoisy, 1678), p. 19. The Hispano-Arab thesis appeared almost new in many of its iterations, such as in the enthusiastic researches of Maria Rosa Menocal in the twentieth century, especially Maria Rosa Menocal, *The Arabic Role in Medieval Literary History: A Forgotten Heritage* (Philadelphia: University of Pennsylvania Press, 2004).

[34] Huet, *De l'origine des romans*, p. 131.

not *tout court*. Huet argued at length that the romance's 'invention [was] due to the Orientals, by whom [he meant] the Egyptians, Arabs, Persians, and Syrians'; as well as the Indians and Jews.[35] He only disagreed in part with the Hispano-Arab thesis, objecting that the tales of romancers such as Taliesin predated Tariq b. Ziyād's incursion into the Iberian Peninsula.[36] Huet bent his efforts to showing that the Oriental origins of the romance went much further back to ancient Egypt, and that classical Greek and Latin romancers were Orientals.[37]

Huet's influential thesis emphasised the primordial nature of the Oriental romance as well as Orientals' mendacious tendencies in contrast to the Greeks and Romans. He referred to Strabo (d. *c.* 24 CE) to pronounce that 'the stories of the peoples of the Orient lie aplenty; that they are inexact and little faithful'.[38] He remarked in addition that:

> The Persians were no lesser than the Arabs in the art of lying agreeably . . . There are no poets who equal the Persians of the last few centuries in the license that they take in lying in their histories, and principally those regarding the origin of their religion, and the lives of their saints. They have so disfigured these, whose reality we know owing to the relations of the Greeks and Romans, that we cannot even recognize them.[39]

The invocation of a classical author's judgement upon Oriental mendacity is one of the many ways in which Huet underlined the antiquity of the romance and romancing tendencies in the Orient. The English translation by Stephen Lewis in 1715 carried this emphasis further at times. Huet's essay suggested that, while the Persians had always revelled in lying tales, in 'the last few centuries' their mendacity had increased. That is to say, that Persians were now more than ever identical to what they had always been. At least, however, there is some hint of change over time, even if this hint remains essentialist. Lewis, on the other hand, omitted the temporal qualification, writing that

[35] Huet, *De l'origine des romans*, pp. 10ff. Cf. Boase, *The Origin and Meaning of Courtly Love*, p. 13.

[36] Huet, *De l'origine des romans*, pp. 131–2.

[37] Huet, *De l'origine des romans*, pp. 10–39.

[38] Huet, *De l'origine des romans*, pp. 22–3.

[39] Huet, *De l'origine des romans*, pp. 20, 24–5.

'there are no poets that equal the Persians in license; they give themselves to falsify'.[40] With the slight abbreviation, Lewis left undisturbed the unchanging nature of the mendacious Oriental.

In the aftermath of Lewis' translation into French, the Hispano-Arab thesis regarding romances became relatively common in Britain, and was elaborated with great antiquarian erudition by Thomas Warton in his *History of English Poetry* (1774). Warton argued that, while Gothic forms of chivalry had underlain earlier forms of European romance, they were decisively superseded later on by influences set in motion by the Christian–Muslim encounters in the Crusades and in the Iberian Peninsula.[41] In his essay on 'The Origin of Romantic Fiction in Europe', Warton noted that already the romance 'is generally supposed to have been borrowed from the Arabians'. He clearly assented to this idea and attempted to prove it in detail.[42] He went to great lengths to show that even the Welsh tradition and the Arthurian romances had come about as a result of contact with the Orient through Spain and Brittany.[43] In his concatenation of proofs, Warton made some remarkable generalisations. 'Dragons,' he submitted, 'are a sure mark of orientalism.'[44]

Because Warton's argument hewed closely to the Hispano-Arab thesis as Huet presented it, it assumed that the medieval period was the origin-point of the romance. The romance was a genre of fiction 'entirely unknown to the writers of Greece and Rome', he insisted. By accepting a medieval origin for the romance genre, Warton could portray the romance as an unnatural accretion upon European culture, 'imported into Europe by a people, whose modes of thinking, and habits of invention, are not natural to that country'.[45]

As she admitted in her 1785 essay *The Progress of Romance*, Clara Reeve was only able to read Warton's work after she had completed the majority of her own. Reeve's essay distinguished less starkly than others between

[40] Pierre Daniel Huet, *The History of Romances*, trans. Stephen Lewis (London: Flower-de-Luce and Sun, 1715), p. 26.

[41] Thomas Warton, *The History of English Poetry*, vol. 1 (London: Thomas Tegg, 1840), pp. 112–15.

[42] Warton, *History of English Poetry*, vol. 1, p. i.

[43] Warton, *History of English Poetry*, vol. 1, pp. iv–xv.

[44] Warton, *History of English Poetry*, vol. 1, p. xv.

[45] Warton, *History of English Poetry*, vol. 1, p. i.

Occidental and Oriental romances. Without directly remonstrating with Warton, Reeve objected that 'few have taken proper notice of the Greek Romances, which may justly be deemed the parents of all the rest', and settled upon Homer as the earliest known progenitor of the romance genre, as Claire Gallien has noted.[46] Comparing the *Odyssey* to the *Sindbad* narrative made popular by eighteenth-century translations of the *1001 Nights*, Reeve derived the *Sindbād-nāmah* from the *Odyssey*, reversing the normative chrono-Orientalist sequence.[47] Coeval with Ancient Greece and Rome, Reeve pointed out, were Oriental romances such as *The History of Charoba Queen of Aegypt*, which Reeve herself translated and included with *The Progress of Romance* expressly to prove to a sceptical friend the existence of such works and the fitness of tales by the 'Arabians and Aegyptians' to be termed romances, along with the romances of the Romans and Greeks.[48] The image that Reeve gives of the classical period is one of fluid encounter between West and East. As Huet's essay shows, an emphasis upon the classical period could just as easily have demonstrated the antiquity of East–West distinctions. Reeve's work, along with Hole's, appears remarkable in this regard.

Her work stands out as well as exemplifying the diminishing epistemological assumptions that still led some critics to value the romance, even in the teeth of the novel's success. In her 1790 'Gothic novel' *A Sicilian Romance*, Ann Radcliffe commented upon spiritish agents in her story: 'I will not attempt to persuade you that the existence of such spirits is impossible. Who shall say that anything is impossible to God?'[49] Reeve had similarly prioritised faith in God's power over rational and empirical assumptions, comparing the 'Arabians' favourably to Homer in this regard.

It was also because Reeve was still judging the romance according to a waning eighteenth-century epistemology according to which reason, while important, is not as important as divine power, among other things. Her essay looks askance at Homer for sending the gods on trifling errands, and for

[46] Clara Reeve, *The Progress of Romance*, vols 1 and 2 (New York: Facsimile Text Society, 1930), p. xi; Gallien, *L'Orient anglais*, pp. 136–7.

[47] Reeve, *The Progress of Romance*, vol. 1, p. 23.

[48] Reeve, *Progress of Romance*, vol. 1, p. xii.

[49] Ann Ward Radcliffe, *A Sicilian Romance* (London: T. Hookham, 1792), pp. 82–3.

his far-fetched plots. Homer's 'machinery' is much more exorbitant than the magic of the 'Arabians', which is at least subordinate to and dependent upon the power of a single God.[50] In this reversal of the normative assignment of epistemological value to East versus West, Reeve's work is again a remarkable holdout.

Clara Reeve's work has been unduly neglected by scholars;[51] in many ways it presents a contrast to other eighteenth-century literary-critical opinions, and the views it proffers are certainly set apart from the dominant views of the nineteenth century regarding the romance, Western or Eastern. Reeve's stalwart recognition that certain novels of her own period were also romances is likewise a noteworthy resistance to the absolute death of the romance.[52] Yet her own understanding of epistemological hierarchy and the dominance of the novel is very much visible throughout her essay, particularly when she characterises the novel as having sprung from the romance's 'ruins'.[53] There remains something spectral about her understanding of the romance, in sympathy with Horace Walpole and Radcliffe's covert and haunted romancing, so that the romance genre is still consigned to the past. To be sure, Reeve's delight in re-animating the romance's ghost is quite different from Burke or John Stuart Mill's despondent lamentation for the age of chivalry. But nowhere in her remarks upon Oriental romance specifically is there any acknowledgement of its presence or future. She translated *The History of Charoba* for the same antiquarian purposes that would gain in importance as the British combed Indian *qissah*s in their search for the ancient origins of the world's tales.

The Romance Caught in the Past

Throughout the nineteenth century Orientalists studied and described Indian *qissah*s that had been recently written in Urdu; sometimes, as in the case of the Fort William *qissah*s, under British patronage. Rarely did they acknowledge

[50] Reeve, *The Progress of Romance*, vol. 1, p. 23.

[51] But see, for example, Gallien, *L'Orient anglais*, pp. 136–7, as well as Rosalind Ballaster, *Fabulous Orients: Fictions of the East in England, 1662–1785* (Oxford: Oxford University Press, 2005) for recuperative treatments of Reeve's work.

[52] Reeve, *The Progress of Romance*, vol. 1, p. 119; vol. 2, p. 32.

[53] Reeve, *The Progress of Romance*, vol. 2, p. 8.

the newness of these *qissah*s, keen to portray them instead as windows into an ossified past. In the wake of William Jones' discoveries, Orientalist translators and scholars of *qissah*s like W. J. Clouston traced the worldwide wanderings of tales said to originate in Sanskrit. In his preface to William Ouseley's *Bakhtiyār-nāmah* (1883), Clouston noted that the Persian work under discussion, a version of the *Sindibād-nāmah*, was said by Arab historian al-Masʿūdī (d. 896 CE) to have come from India:

> While India seems to have been the cradle-land of those folktales, yet they came to us chiefly through an Arabian medium: brought to Europe, among other ways by the Saracens who settled in Spain in the eighth century, by crusaders and pilgrims returning from the Holy Land, and also, perhaps, by Venetian merchants trading in the Levant and the Muslim provinces of Northern Africa.[54]

With their discovery of the Indian origins of such tales, Orientalists like Clouston took their chrono-Orientalism beyond the medievalism of the Hispano-Arab hypothesis in the case of the romance genre.

For Clouston it was a fallacy to imagine that Oriental tales could be characterised by newness. The translation of the *qissah* as romance ensured that originality and future importance were denied to the *qissah* in a way that would not have been the case had *qissah*s regularly been understood as novels instead. Clouston dismissed the originality of *qissah*s at length:

> Whatever our modern European authors may do in the production of their novels (the novel has no existence in the East), it is certain that Asiatic writers do not attempt the invention of new 'situations' and incidents. They have all along been content to use such materials as came ready to hand . . . Indeed they usually mention quite frankly in the prefaces to their books from whence they derived their materials.[55]

There are no novels in the East. There are no new ('novel') narratives in the East. There is nothing at all that is novel in the East. The triple meaning of

[54] W. A. Clouston (ed.), *The Bakhtyar Nama: A Persian Romance*, trans. Sir William Ouseley (Larkhall: William Burns, 1883), p. xiv.

[55] Clouston, *A Group of Eastern Romances*, p. xx.

Clouston's parenthetical remark cuts the *qissah* off forcefully from anything but a past and antiquarian relevance, as Clouston emphasised elsewhere:

> So we need not expect to find much originality in later Eastern collections, though they are of special interest to students of the genealogy of popular tales insofar as they contain incidents, and even entire stories and fables, out of ancient books now lost, which have their parallels and analogues in European folklore.[56]

Much like the science and medicine of the Muslims in the Middle Ages, Oriental romances are valuable insofar as they have preserved the past, and especially the past of Europe. They do Europe a favour, at least, in bringing its forgotten past back to it.

By the nineteenth century, understanding the romance as a worldwide genre was a way of revealing past classical and medieval worlds of encounter and circulation between East and West, when the 'natural' European worldview was pliable or weak enough to accept the imprint of the 'Oriental romance' with its wild excess of imagination. The genre wars of the eighteenth century had already ended in the romance's defeat by the novel, and the former's consignment to the museum. Assimilating 'Eastern tales' to a frozen Western genre of narrative was a way of freezing the East as well. The numerous researches that found the Oriental romance to be originary to the Occidental did not, therefore, give it more than an antiquarian importance in the present. Rather, they emphasised its pastness further, rendering it inert along with the civilisation for which it supposedly stood, as it was made to lie fallow and ready for conquest and salvation at the coloniser's hands.

Following the post-Raj inculcation of British ideas into the minds of Urdu-speaking elites and the rise of the novel in Urdu, the most assiduous twentieth-century scholars of the Urdu *qissah* assigned the same antiquarian value to the genre, which they too identified with the romance. Though Shamsur Rahman Faruqi spared it in his riposte to such scholars, it must be said that even the redoubtable research of Gyan Chand Jain was deeply

[56] Clouston, *The Bakhtyar Nama: A Persian Romance*, p. viii.

complicit in the chrono-Orientalist deep-freeze of the *qissah*.[57] A full century passed before Urdu-language scholarship bestowed upon *qissahs* a new regard, independent of the prejudices of the *qissah*-romance translation.

Conclusion: World, Literature and World Romance

Around the same time that the likes of Gyan Chand Jain and Farman Fatehpuri were compiling their great studies of prose and verse *qissahs*, Frye was asserting that the romance, unlike the novel, was not merely Western, but 'worldwide'.[58] Clara Reeve had made a similar remark in 1785: 'Romances are of universal growth, and not confined to any particular period or countries.'[59] The worldwide compass of the romance genre would appear to be a mark of its value over the novel. Yet we must conclude that the translation of the *qissah* genre as a form of world romance was a way of producing an unequal world in which the romance, including the Oriental romance, was caught in a time-freeze from which the West had emerged insofar as it had largely disavowed the romance, notwithstanding certain nostalgic or melancholic gestures. The schizochronic condition of this world, divided between a modern Occident and a still-medieval Orient, meant that in fact the provincialism of the novel signalled the preeminence of the part of the world in which it had arisen. The world spanned by the romance genre was contiguous only geographically, and not temporally. This world's geographical contiguity, and the conviction that the romance stretched across the world, was possible only by means of a chrono-Orientalist, often medievalising equation between the romance, on the one hand, and the *qissah* and other non-Western genres of narrative, on the other.

To what world or worlds did world literature refer, beyond the globalising post-Goethean world at the centre of which Europe stands? Damrosch is careful to include ancient texts such as *Gilgamesh* and the *Cantares Mexicanos*

57 Gyān Cand Jain, *Urdū kī nasrī dāstānen* (Karachi: Anjuman-i Taraqqī-i Urdū, 1969); Shamsur Rahman Faruqi, *Sāhirī, Shāhī, Sāhib-Qirānī: Dāstān-i Amīr Hamzah kā mutālaʿah*, vol. 1 (New Delhi: Qaumī Council barā'e furogh-i Urdū zabān, 1999); Khan, *The Broken Spell*, pp. 205–8.

58 Frye, *Anatomy of Criticism*, p. 307; Dildār ʿAlī Farmān Fathpūrī, *Urdū kī manzūm dāstāneṅ* (Karachi: Anjuman-i taraqqī-i Urdū Pākistān, 1971).

59 Reeve, *The Progress of Romance*, vol. 1, pp. xv–xvi.

in his examination of world literature.[60] However, at least in *What is World Literature?*, we do not find an examination of how 'literature' or 'world literature' was imagined, and world literary systems configured, in pre-Goethean times. We ought to be aware of the trouble with the idea of a unified and timeless 'literature' along with the notion of a unified world.

In my previous work, I eschewed the category of literature in favour of 'verbal art', as a provisional translation of the Arabic and Persian terms *kalām* and *sukhan* (speech), which were the primary focus of post-Sakkākīan and post-Nizāmīan poetics and linguistic study in Arabic, Persian, Urdu, Punjabi and other languages.[61] I used 'verbal art' to translate *sukhan/kalām* rather than 'literature' in part to emphasise the oral-performativity of genres such as the *qissah*, but implicit in this choice was an unease with the category of literature.[62] Mufti has hinted that '*adab*' maps imperfectly onto 'literature'.[63] The

[60] Damrosch, *What is World Literature?*, chs 1–2.

[61] In his *magnum opus* on language, the *Miftāh al-'ulūm* (*Key to the Sciences*), Al-Sakkākī (*c.* 1160–1229) certainly presented his project as a study of the *anwā' al-adab* (types of [linguistic] discipline), but for him and many later commentators, what was under discipline was *kalām* (speech), organised into collocations (*tarākīb*) usually to produce *shi'r* (poetry), but also other forms. See Sakkākī, *Kitāb Miftāḥ al-'ulūm* (Misr: Al-Matba'ah al-Maimanīyah, 1900), p. 2. For an example of a Sakkākīan use of '*tarākīb-i kalām*' in Persian from eighteenth-century India, see Sadr al-Dīn Muhammad b. Zabardast Khan Fā'iz Dihlawī, 'Khutbah', in *Fā'iz Dihlawī aur Dīwān-i Fā'iz*, ed. Sayyid Mas'ūd Hasan Rizwī, 2nd edn (Aligarh: Anjuman Taraqqī-i Urdū Hind, 1964), pp. 150–1. A précis of the importance and influence of Sakkākī's work may be found in Lara Harb, *Arabic Poetics: Aesthetic Experience in Classical Arabic Literature* (Cambridge: Cambridge University Press, 2020), pp. 20–1. For a more comprehensive treatment of Sakkākī's legacy, see William Smyth, 'Controversy in a Tradition of Commentary: The Academic Legacy of Al-Sakkākī's Miftāḥ al-'ulūm', *Journal of the American Oriental Society* 112(4) (1992): 589–97. I should note that by '*kalām*' I do not mean the discipline of 'theology'. The Persian term *sukhan*, also meaning 'speech', was a very common word for forms of verbal art throughout the Persian cosmopolis. It referred especially, but not exclusively, to poetry (*shi'r*, *nazm*). Nizāmī Ganjawī's twelfth-century poem *Haft paikar* (*Seven Beauties*), and especially its preface, provided a model of poetic reflection upon *sukhan* that would be emulated by many thinkers in languages affected by Persian. For a late (1863) but still typical example in Punjabi, see Miyān Muḥammad Bakhsh, *Safar al-'ishq: Saif al-Mulūk*, ed. Muḥammad Sharīf Sābir (Lahore: Sayyid Ajmal Ḥusain Memorial Society, 2002).

[62] Khan, *The Broken Spell*, p. 1.

[63] Mufti, *Forget English!*, pp. 79–80.

term *adab* as it is used today in Urdu is indeed a modern calque, and not a particularly successful calque, either, if we judge it in terms of the quantity of milliseconds many Urdu-knowers require to comprehend this word as meaning 'literature' rather than 'proper conduct'. For 'literature', they are used to simply hearing the loan-word *litrechar*.

Scholars of Arabic have remarked upon the recentness of the literature = *adab* equation, noting that *adab* was a central concept in many Islamic societies, irreducible to the realm of literature or even language.[64] While the meaning of *adab* underwent shifts over the course of its history, by the ninth century it comprised proper conduct, ethics and the knowledge requisite for a person to be recognised as refined.[65] As Sarah Bin Tyeer's work shows convincingly, to study texts from a perspective that assimilates *adab* to 'literature' is to dehistoricise them and subject them to a literary criticism that lies outside the tradition within which such texts arose.[66]

If we wish to look at the *adab* of what we would otherwise call literature – that is, *sukhan*, speech or texts – '*adab*' in South Asia has meant: (1) a particular *limitational discipline* of verbal artistic production, often formalised in the sciences of language (*ʿilm-i maʿānī*, *ʿilm-i bayān*, *ʿilm-i badīʿ*, etc.);[67] (2) it has also meant a certain genre or purpose of texts that strive to be exemplary and inculcate proper conduct and virtues (*akhlāq*) in the hearer.[68] As Prashant Keshavmurthy has noted on lexicographical bases, both of these meanings of

[64] F. Gabrieli, 'Adab', in P. Bearman et al. (eds), *Encyclopaedia of Islam*, 2nd edn, Brill online, 2012, available at: https://referenceworks.brillonline.com/entries/encyclopaedia-of-islam-2/adab-SIM_0293, last accessed 12 April 2022; Kees Versteegh, *Landmarks in Linguistic Thought III: The Arabic Linguistic Tradition* (London: Routledge, 2013); Michael Allan, 'How Adab Became Literary: Formalism, Orientalism and the Institutions of World Literature', *Journal of Arabic Literature* 43(2/3) (2012): 172–96; Sarah R. Bin Tyeer, *The Qurʾan and the Aesthetics of Premodern Arabic Prose* (London: Palgrave Macmillan, 2016). A thought-provoking look at the centrality of *adab* to Islamic sociality is available in Mana Kia, *Persianate Selves: Memories of Place and Origin Before Nationalism* (Stanford, CA: Stanford University Press, 2020).

[65] Gabrieli, 'Adab'.

[66] Bin Tyeer, *The Qurʾan and the Aesthetics of Premodern Arabic Prose*, pp. 8, 10.

[67] Sakkākī, *Kitāb Miftāh al-ʿulūm*, pp. 2–3.

[68] Abū al-Lais Siddīqī and Nasīm Amrohwī, 'Adab', in *Urdū lughat: Tārīkhī usūl par*, available at: http://udb.gov.pk/result_details.php?word=9714, last accessed 19 October 2020.

adab might be generalised as the observance of the limits (*hadd*) of things.[69] Abu al-Lais Siddiqi's Urdu dictionary on historical principles gives Mīr Hasan's influential 1784 *qissah*, *Sihr al-bayān* (*The Sorcery of Expression*), as an early instance of the use of the term '*adab*' to mean poetry and prose, that is, literature. Upon inspecting Mīr Hasan's verses, we nonetheless see that even his use of '*adab*' can be read as corresponding to *adab* as a limitational or exemplificatory discipline of the production of *sukhan*.[70]

In the post-Raj period, it was the second meaning of *adab* as exemplary 'literature' that became dominant in British India, especially but not exclusively in the case of prose. This dominance was due to the influence of colonial ideas regarding the correct purpose of literature, and British enforcement of these ideas both negatively through the (imperfect) surveillance of Indian presses, and positively through the colonial solicitation and celebration of 'prize-winning *adab*', as C. M. Naim explained.[71] That is, prior to the modernist rule of art for art's sake, the British were able to work *through* the exemplificatory logic of *adab* to impose their own worldview upon Indians. Before this worldview took hold, and long before colonialism, Persian- and Urdu-language storytellers (*qissah-khwāns*) had argued for the value of their *qissahs* in an *adabī* mode, on the basis of the linguistic, epistemic and political exemplarity of the tales that they told.[72] Clearly, storytellers and story-writers

[69] Prashant Keshavmurthy, 'The Limits of Islamic Civility in India', in Milad Milani and Vassilios Adrahtas (eds), *Islam, Civility and Political Culture* (Cham: Palgrave Macmillan, 2021), pp. 106–7.

[70] Siddīqī and Amrohwī, 'Adab'.

[71] C. M. Naim, 'Prize-Winning Adab: Five Urdu Books Written in Response to the Gazette Notification No. 791A (1868)', in *Urdu Texts and Contexts* (Delhi: Permanent Black, 2004), pp. 120–50. See also Frances W. Pritchett, *Nets of Awareness: Urdu Poetry and Its Critics* (Berkeley: University of California Press, 1994), chs 11, 12.

[72] Pasha M. Khan, 'What Storytellers Were Worth in Mughal India', *Comparative Studies of South Asia, Africa and the Middle East* 37(3) (2017): 570–87. See especially ʿAbd al-Nabī Fakhr al-Zamānī, 'The Preface and Introduction to the Tirāz Al-Akhbār', in *The Broken Spell: Indian Storytelling and the Romance Genre in Persian and Urdu*, trans. Pasha M. Khan (Detroit, MI: Wayne State University Press, 2019), p. 256; ʿAbd al-Nabī Faḳhr al-Zamānī Qazwīnī, *Tirāz al-akhbār* (Patna, 1633), fol. 19a, 358 (Tehran: Mūzah-i Markaz-i asnād-i Majlis-i shūrā-i Islāmī); Mirzā Amān ʿAlī Ḳhān Ghālib Lakhnawī, *Tarjamah-i Dāstān-i Sāhib-qirān* (Calcutta: Matbaʿ-i Imdādiyyah, 1855), p. 3.

were responding to a pre-colonial idea that exemplarity was valuable, an idea that was part and parcel of the question-horizon of *adab*.[73] But, especially with the rise of the novel, the identification of the *qissah* as romance, and a succession of changing standards for the valuation of literature, the British and elite Indians side-lined such justifications of *qissahs*' worth.

What the British example demonstrates is that it was very much possible for *adab* to be co-opted for colonial purposes, and yet to remain *adab*. Contests surrounding what kind of verbal art was beautiful, ethical or exemplary were nevertheless governed by the horizon of questions of *adab*, within whose framework *adabī* works ought to be read. Reading in this historicised manner necessitates only that we understand *adab*, not that we must agree with all of the formulations, evaluations and exclusions made within its framework.[74] Bin Tyeer avers that '*literary criticism* . . . rests on literary tools and terminologies that are not only alien to the Arab-Islamic literary history and tradition, but also are not part of its cultural experience or literary history'.[75] To cease subjecting a certain body of texts to literary criticism in favour of *adabī* standards is to risk a fissure within world literature, particularly if *adab* is, at least temporarily, unable to make itself accessible or useful to Eurocentric critics and audiences.[76] I believe that such a temporary separation would be beneficial for *adab*.

To return to 'world', insofar as this word denotes the planet that we inhabit, the impulse of twenty-first-century world literary studies has been to chase literary texts across the globe. The synecdochal meaning of 'world' is also important, however, as in the Muslim world, the Indian Ocean world, the Malay world, etc. Here are worlds, within the planet, across which texts may circulate, rather than on a planetary scale. What would it mean for texts to circulate planetarily anyway, unless they were to cover every inch of the planet? Perhaps the 'world' in pre-Goethean world literature can only ever be a synecdoche.

[73] Bin Tyeer, *The Qur'an and the Aesthetics of Premodern Arabic Prose*, p. 8.

[74] Bin Tyeer, *The Qur'an and the Aesthetics of Premodern Arabic Prose*.

[75] Bin Tyeer, *The Qur'an and the Aesthetics of Premodern Arabic Prose*, p. 10.

[76] Alexander Key, 'Arabic: Acceptance and Anxiety', *ACLA State of the Discipline Report: The 2014–2015 Report on the State of the Discipline of Comparative Literature* (blog), 4 March 2015, available at: https://stateofthediscipline.acla.org/entry/arabic-acceptance-and-anxiety.

Keeping in mind that comparison presupposes circulation, the circulatory paths of texts do not remain within world boundaries as we might imagine them. We might say that these paths create worlds, melancholically.[77] Ayuba Sulaiman Diallo held on to West Africa with the Qurʾāns he copied out from memory, after his enslavement and forced journey across the Atlantic to Virginia.[78] Omar ibn Said, similarly enslaved in Charleston, and jailed after running away, inscribed Arabic words in charcoal onto his prison walls, and in ink in his surviving writings.[79] What kind of worlds can we say that such circulations produced?

Among the many worlds that might have been circulation sites for the *qissah* is the so-called Islamic world or Muslim world. Fortunately or unfortunately, Cemil Aydin has shown quite well why the idea of a Muslim world does not hold water very capably.[80] Not long ago, the done thing seemed to be to refer instead, with Marshall Hodgson, to 'Islamdom' or the 'Islamicate' world, as a way of keeping Islam in the picture while dealing with practices, productions, etc., that might not conform to dominant Islamic norms; and with people who might not self-identify as Muslim.[81] Shahab Ahmed has dealt

[77] Regarding the idea of migrant melancholia, see Sara Ahmed, *The Promise of Happiness* (Durham, NC: Duke University Press, 2010), ch. 4.

[78] Sylviane A. Diouf, *Servants of Allah: African Muslims Enslaved in the Americas* (New York: New York University Press, 2013), p. 193.

[79] Ala Alryyes (ed.), *A Muslim American Slave: The Life of Omar Ibn Said* (Madison: University of Wisconsin Press, 2011), p. 86; Diouf, *Servants of Allah*, p. 191.

[80] Cemil Aydin, *The Idea of the Muslim World: A Global Intellectual History* (Cambridge, MA: Harvard University Press, 2017). However, Aydin's narrative regarding the racialisation of Muslims, for which in his view Muslims are partly responsible, needs to be supplemented with Junaid Rana's excellent evisceration of Islamophobia as performed by White supremacists in the United States: the racialisation of many kinds of brown-skinned people (brown Muslims, Sikhs, Arab Christians, Hindus, etc.). Junaid Akram Rana, *Terrifying Muslims: Race and Labor in the South Asian Diaspora* (Durham, NC: Duke University Press, 2011), p. 8. Cemil Aydin, 'After the "Muslim World": Beyond Strategic Essentialism', *The Immanent Frame*, 17 October 2017, available at: https://tif.ssrc.org/2017/10/17/after-the-muslim-world-beyond-strategic-essentialism.

[81] Marshall G. S. Hodgson, *The Venture of Islam: Conscience and History in a World Civilization* (Chicago: University of Chicago Press, 1977), vol. 1, pp. 57–60.

a decisive blow, however, to Hodgson's idea of the Islamicate by questioning the religion-versus-culture dichotomy that enabled Islamic to be distinguished from Islamicate.[82] *What is Islam?* insists instead upon the 'Islamic', including for the meaning-making acts of certain non-Muslims.

The world that Shahab Ahmed refers to as the Balkans to Bengal complex appears, however, to be an Islamic world with more or less the same shape as Hodgson's Islamdom. Despite *What is Islam?*'s critique of Hodgson, its world is carved using the same marginalisations of sub-Saharan Africa and Southeast Asia as *The Venture of Islam*, never mind other places in the world in which Muslims have left traces.[83] The idea of the Balkans to Bengal complex was an effort to combat a focus upon an Islamic 'Old World' of the Arabic-speaking Middle East.[84] But the focus on the Balkans to Bengal complex makes peripheral 'shadows' of other areas like the Malay archipelago and China, said to be 'pregnant' with seed from the centre.[85] If we nevertheless affirm the value of Shahab Ahmed's idea of the Islamic, how could we better imagine the Islamic worlds that may have existed?

A further difficulty is that it is not always useful to reduce such worlds to the Islamic. Peter Gottschalk's review of Shahab Ahmed's book shows the lingering difficulties with the latter's insistence that non-Muslims participating in the Islamic Con-Text are always 'Islamic'. Gottschalk points out that this insistence, illustrated in *What is Islam?* by the example of a Sikh wrestler proclaiming '*Yā ʿAlī!*' upon entering the fray, raises the question of whether the Islamic-ness of this utterance is in terms of intention or only reception

[82] Shahab Ahmed, *What is Islam? The Importance of Being Islamic* (Princeton, NJ: Princeton University Press, 2016), pp. 156–75.

[83] Ahmed, *What is Islam?*, pp. 73–85. Hodgson's student Marilyn Waldman certainly corrected this deficiency in the world put forward by her teacher, however, as Bruce Lawrence has pointed out. See Marilyn Waldman and Malika Zeghal, 'Islamic World', in *Encyclopedia Britannica*, 21 August 2019, available at: https://www.britannica.com/topic/Islamic-world. Bruce B. Lawrence, 'Genius Denied and Reclaimed: A 40-Year Retrospect on Marshall G. S. Hodgson's The Venture of Islam', *Marginalia: Los Angeles Review of Books* (blog), 11 November 2014, available at: https://marginalia.lareviewofbooks.org/retrospect-hodgson-venture-islam.

[84] Ahmed, *What is Islam?*, p. 82.

[85] Ahmed, *What is Islam?*, pp. 80, 82. See Thum's critique in Rian Thum, 'What is Islamic History?' *History and Theory* 58(4) (2019): 17.

within a broader social discourse.[86] Sikh cases are often instructive. The Sikh poet Saundhā's *Hātam-nāmā* (1807/8), a Braj Bhasha and Punjabi translation of the eighteenth-century Persian *Qissah-i Hātim Tā'ī*, presents the ethics of generosity entirely in terms of the value of *dāna* (giving) and *paraupkār* (deeds for the sake of others) as articulated by the Sikh gurus. In the Persian *qissah*, on the other hand, these values had been fixed in an Islamic framework of noble character traits (*makārim al-akhlāq*). This discrepancy does not mean that we must approve of the modern editor's nationalist claim that Saundhā was 'Indianising' the Persian work,[87] but it does indicate that we need a way to speak about texts like the *Hātam-nāmā* that are indeed Islamic in Shahab Ahmed's terms, but not only Islamic.

The *qissah* moved through Islamic-plus worlds along paths leading far from Islamdom or the Balkans to Bengal into White-majority nations. In part, its circulation had the effect that we have seen, of chrono-Orientalist domination and control. However, other aspects of this circulation were more complicated. In Paris, the Arab Christians Diyūnīsūs Shāwīsh (Dom Denis Chavis) and Mīkhā'īl (Michel) Sabbāgh filled their stomachs by bestowing authenticity upon, and even supplying missing tales for, French continuations of the *1001 Nights* (*Mille et une nuits*).[88] The guileful participation of 'Orientals' in Orientalism raises the by now familiar question of how to distinguish between complicity, and 'playing' the coloniser, in the transitive, Black American sense of the term. The journey of Bengali-language *qissahs* of the prophets (*Kasasol ambiā*/*Qisas al-anbiyā'*) from Bengal to Broken Hill, Australia, has been narrated by Samia Khatun in her *Australianama*, a masterfully decolonial work of scholarship that is itself a concatenation of *qissahs*.[89] Khatun's work opens up this question in particular: in what future terms shall

[86] Ahmed, *What is Islam?*, pp. 445–6. Peter Gottschalk, 'The Interpretative Pivot: Hermeneutics and the Contemporary Decline of Islamic Pluralism', *Marginalia: Los Angeles Review of Books* (blog), 26 August 2016, available at: https://marginalia.lareviewofbooks.org/interpretative-pivot-hermeneutics-contemporary-decline-islamic-pluralism-peter-gottschalk.

[87] Dharam Singh, 'Saṅpādakī', in *Hātamnāmā*, by Saundhā (Amritsar: Gurū Nānak Dev University, 1982), pp. 3, 23, 29.

[88] Muhsin Mahdi, *The Thousand and One Nights* (Leiden: Brill, 1995), ch. 2.

[89] Samia Khatun, *Australianama: The South Asian Odyssey in Australia* (London: Hurst, 2018).

we speak of the Muslim-but-not-only worlds of the White settler colonies to which the traces of Islam and Muslims have come?

Bibliography

Ahmed, Sara, *The Promise of Happiness* (Durham, NC: Duke University Press, 2010).

Ahmed, Shahab, *What is Islam? The Importance of Being Islamic* (Princeton, NJ: Princeton University Press, 2016).

Allan, Michael, 'How Adab Became Literary: Formalism, Orientalism and the Institutions of World Literature', *Journal of Arabic Literature* 43(2/3) (2012): 172–96.

Alryyes, Ala (ed.), *A Muslim American Slave: The Life of Omar Ibn Said* (Madison: University of Wisconsin Press, 2011).

Aydin, Cemil, 'After the "Muslim World": Beyond Strategic Essentialism', *The Immanent Frame*, 17 October 2017, available at: https://tif.ssrc.org/2017/10/17/after-the-muslim-world-beyond-strategic-essentialism.

Aydin, Cemil, *The Idea of the Muslim World: A Global Intellectual History* (Cambridge, MA: Harvard University Press, 2017).

Ballaster, Rosalind, *Fabulous Orients: Fictions of the East in England, 1662–1785* (Oxford: Oxford University Press, 2005).

Bilgrāmī, ʿAbdullāh Ḥusain, *Dastan-e Amir Hamza: An Oriental Novel*, ed. Sajjad Husain (Patna: Khuda Bakhsh Oriental Public Library, 1992).

Bin Tyeer, Sarah R., *The Qurʾan and the Aesthetics of Premodern Arabic Prose* (London: Palgrave Macmillan, 2016).

Boase, Roger, *The Origin and Meaning of Courtly Love: A Critical Study of European Scholarship* (Manchester: Manchester University Press, 1977).

Burke, Edmund, *Reflections on the Revolution in France*, ed. Frank M. Turner (New Haven, CT: Yale University Press, 2003).

Chandler, Alice, *A Dream of Order: The Medieval Ideal in Nineteenth-Century English Literature* (Lincoln: University of Nebraska Press, 1970).

Clouston, W. A. (ed.), *The Bakhtyar Nama: A Persian Romance*, trans. Sir William Ouseley (Larkhall: William Burns, 1883).

Clouston, W. A., *A Group of Eastern Romances and Stories from the Persian, Tamil, and Urdu* (Glasgow: Privately printed, 1889).

Damrosch, David, *What is World Literature?* (Princeton, NJ: Princeton University Press, 2003).

Davis, Kathleen, 'Time Behind the Veil: The Media, the Middle Ages, and Orientalism Now', in Jeffrey Jerome Cohen (ed.), *The Postcolonial Middle Ages* (New York: Palgrave Macmillan, 2000), pp. 105–22.

Diouf, Sylviane A., *Servants of Allah: African Muslims Enslaved in the Americas* (New York: New York University Press, 2013).

Dudney, Arthur, 'Keeping the Magic Alive: How Devakīnandan Khatrī's Chandrakāntā, the First Hindi Best-Seller, Navigates Western Modernity and the Fantastical', unpublished manuscript, 2012, available at: http://www.columbia.edu/itc/mealac/pritchett/00urduhindilinks/txt_dudney_chandrakanta.pdf.

Fak̤hr al-Zamānī, ʿAbd al-Nabī, 'The Preface and Introduction to the Ṭirāz Al-Ak̤hbār', in *The Broken Spell: Indian Storytelling and the Romance Genre in Persian and Urdu*, trans. Pasha M. Khan (Detroit, MI: Wayne State University Press, 2019), pp. 219–64.

Fak̤hr al-Zamānī Qazwīnī, ʿAbd al-Nabī, *Ṭirāz al-ak̤hbār* (Patna, 1633. 358; Tehran: Mūzah-i Markaz-i asnād-i Majlis-i shūrā-i Islāmī).

Faruqi, Shamsur Rahman, *Sāḥirī, shāhī, sāḥib-qirānī: Dāstān-i Amīr Ḥamzah kā mutālaʿah*, 4 vols (New Delhi: Qaumī Council barāʾe furoġh-i Urdū zabān, 1999), vol. 1.

Faruqi, Shamsur Rahman, *Sāḥirī, shāhī, sāḥib-qirānī: Dāstān-i Amīr Ḥamzah kā mutālaʿah*, 4 vols (New Delhi: Qaumī Council barāʾe furoġh-i Urdū zabān, 2006), vol. 3.

Fathpūrī, Dildār ʿAlī Farmān, *Urdū kī manẓūm dāstāneṅ* (Karachi: Anjuman-i taraqqī-i Urdū Pākistān, 1971).

Fay, Elizabeth, 'Romantic Medievalism: The Ideal of History', in *Romantic Medievalism: History and the Romantic Literary Ideal* (London: Palgrave Macmillan, 2002), pp. 1–27.

Fāʾiz Dihlawī, Ṣadr al-Dīn Muḥammad b. Zabardast K̤han, 'K̤huṭbah', in *Fāʾiz Dihlawī aur Dīwān-i Fāʾiz*, ed. Sayyid Masʿūd Ḥasan Riẓwī, 2nd edn (Aligarh: Anjuman Taraqqī-i Urdū Hind, 1964), pp. 150–96.

Forbes, Duncan, *The Adventures of Hatim Taï: A Romance* (London: Oriental Translation Fund, 1830).

Frye, Northrop. *Anatomy of Criticism* (Princeton, NJ: Princeton University Press, 1973).

Gabrieli, F., 'Adab', *Encyclopaedia of Islam*, 2nd edn, Brill online, 2012, available at:. http://referenceworks.brillonline.com/entries/encyclopaedia-of-islam-2/adab-SIM_0293?s.num=0&s.f.s2_parent=s.f.book.encyclopaedia-of-islam-2&s.q=adab.

Gallien, Claire, *L'Orient anglais. Connaissances et fictions au XVIIIe siècle* (Oxford: Voltaire Foundation, 2011).

Gallien, Claire, 'From One Empire to the Next: The Reconfigurations of "Indian" Literatures from Persian to English Translations', *Translation Studies* (2019).

Ġhālib Lakhnawī, Mirzā Amān ʿAlī Ḳhān, *Tarjamah-i dāstān-i Ṣāḥib-qirān* (Calcutta: Maṭbaʿ-i Imdādiyyah, 1855).

Gottschalk, Peter, 'The Interpretative Pivot: Hermeneutics and the Contemporary Decline of Islamic Pluralism', *Marginalia: Los Angeles Review of Books* (blog), 26 August 2016, available at: https://marginalia.lareviewofbooks.org/interpretative-pivot-hermeneutics-contemporary-decline-islamic-pluralism-peter-gottschalk.

Grewal, Sara, 'Ghazal as "World Poetry": Between Worlding and Vernacularization', *Comparative Literature* 74(1) (2022): 25–51.

Harb, Lara, *Arabic Poetics: Aesthetic Experience in Classical Arabic Literature* (Cambridge: Cambridge University Press, 2020).

Hodgson, Marshall G. S., *The Venture of Islam: Conscience and History in a World Civilization, vol. 1: The Classical Age of Islam* (Chicago: University of Chicago Press, 1977).

Hole, Richard, *Remarks on The Arabian Nights' Entertainments* (London: Cadell, 1797).

Huet, Pierre-Daniel, *Lettre de Monsieur Huet à Monsieur de Segrais de l'origine des romans* (S. Mabre-Cramoisy, 1678).

Huet, Pierre-Daniel, *The History of Romances*, trans. Stephen Lewis (London: Flower-de-Luce & Sun, 1715).

Jain, Gyān Chand, *Urdū kī naṡrī dāstāneṅ* (Karachi: Anjuman-i Taraqqī-i Urdū, 1969).

Keshavmurthy, Prashant, 'The Limits of Islamic Civility in India', in Milad Milani and Vassilios Adrahtas (eds), *Islam, Civility and Political Culture* (Cham: Palgrave Macmillan, 2021), pp. 105–30.

Key, Alexander, 'Arabic: Acceptance and Anxiety', *ACLA State of the Discipline Report: The 2014–2015 Report on the State of the Discipline of Comparative Literature* (blog), 4 March 2015, available at: https://stateofthediscipline.acla.org/entry/arabic-acceptance-and-anxiety.

Khan, Pasha M., 'What Storytellers Were Worth in Mughal India', *Comparative Studies of South Asia, Africa and the Middle East* 37(3) (2017): 570–87.

Khan, Pasha M., *The Broken Spell: Indian Storytelling and the Romance Genre in Persian and Urdu* (Detroit, MI: Wayne State University Press, 2019).

Khatun, Samia, *Australianama: The South Asian Odyssey in Australia* (London: Hurst, 2018).

Kia, Mana, *Persianate Selves: Memories of Place and Origin Before Nationalism* (Stanford, CA: Stanford University Press, 2020).

Kipling, Rudyard, 'The White Man's Burden', in *Complete Verse* (New York: Anchor Press, 1940), pp. 321–3.

Lawrence, Bruce B., 'Genius Denied and Reclaimed: A 40-Year Retrospect on Marshall G. S. Hodgson's The Venture of Islam', *Marginalia: Los Angeles Review of Books* (blog), 11 November 2014, available at: https://marginalia.lareviewofbooks.org/retrospect-hodgson-venture-islam.

Macaulay, Thomas Babington, *The Complete Writings of Lord Macaulay*, vol. 12 (Boston, MA: Houghton Mifflin, 1900).

Macaulay, Thomas Babington, *Speeches: With His Minute on Indian Education*, ed. G. M. Young, The World's Classics (New York: AMS Press, 1979).

Mahdi, Muhsin, *The Thousand and One Nights* (Leiden: Brill, 1995).

Makdisi, Saree, *Making England Western: Occidentalism, Race, and Imperial Culture* (Chicago: University of Chicago Press, 2014).

Melvin-Koushki, Matthew, 'Powers of One: The Mathematicalization of the Occult Sciences in the High Persianate Tradition', *Intellectual History of the Islamicate World* 5(1/2) (2017): 127–99.

Menocal, Maria Rosa, *The Arabic Role in Medieval Literary History: A Forgotten Heritage* (Philadelphia: University of Pennsylvania Press, 2004).

Mill, John Stuart, *Dissertations and Discussions, Political, Philosophical, and Historical*, 2nd edn, vol. 1 (London: Longmans, Green, Reader & Dyer, 1867).

Miyān Muḥammad Baḳhsh, *Safar al-ʿishq: Saif al-Mulūk*, ed. Muḥammad Sharīf Ṣābir (Lahore: Sayyid Ajmal Ḥusain Memorial Society, 2002).

Mufti, Aamir, *Forget English! Orientalisms and World Literatures* (Cambridge, MA: Harvard University Press, 2016).

Naim, C. M., 'Prize-Winning Adab: Five Urdu Books Written in Response to the Gazette Notification No. 791A (1868)', in *Urdu Texts and Contexts* (Delhi: Permanent Black, 2004), pp. 120–50.

Oesterheld, Christina, 'Entertainment and Reform: Urdu Narrative Genres in the Nineteenth Century', in Vasudha Dalmia and Stuart H. Blackburn (eds), *India's Literary History* (Delhi: Permanent Black, 2004), pp. 167–212.

Omidsalar, Mahmoud, *Poetics and Politics of Iran's National Epic, the Shahnameh* (New York: Palgrave Macmillan, 2011).

Orsini, Francesca, *Print and Pleasure: Popular Literature and Entertaining Fictions in Colonial North India* (Ranikhet: Permanent Black, 2009).

Pritchett, Frances W., *Nets of Awareness: Urdu Poetry and Its Critics* (Berkeley: University of California Press, 1994).

Propp, Vladimir, *The Russian Folktale*, trans. Sibelan Forrester (Detroit, MI: Wayne State University Press, 2012).

Radcliffe, Ann Ward, *A Sicilian Romance* (London: T. Hookham, 1792).

Rana, Junaid Akram, *Terrifying Muslims: Race and Labor in the South Asian Diaspora* (Durham, NC: Duke University Press, 2011).

Reeve, Clara, *The Progress of Romance*, vols 1 and 2 (New York: Facsimile Text Society, 1930).

Sakkākī, Yūsuf b. Abī Bakr, *Kitāb Miftāḥ al-ʿulūm* (Miṣr: Al-Maṭbaʿah al-Maimanīyah, 1900).

Ṣiddīqī, Abū al-Lais̤ and Nasīm Amrohwī, 'Adab', in *Urdū luġhat: Tārīḵhī uṣūl par*, available at: http://udb.gov.pk/result_details.php?word=9714.

Singh, Dharam, 'Saṅpādakī', in *Hātamnāmā*, by Saundhā (Amritsar: Gurū Nānak Dev University, 1982), pp. 9–30.

Smyth, William, 'Controversy in a Tradition of Commentary: The Academic Legacy of Al-Sakkākī's Miftāḥ Al-ʿUlūm', *Journal of the American Oriental Society* 112(4) (1992): 589–97.

Tavakoli-Targhi, Mohamad, 'The Homeless Texts of Persianate Modernity', *Cultural Dynamics* 13(3) (2001): 263–91.

Thum, Rian, 'What is Islamic History?' *History and Theory* 58(4) (2019): 7–19.

Todorov, Tzvetan, *Genres in Discourse* (Cambridge: Cambridge University Press, 1990).

Van Leeuwen, Richard, 'The Canonization of the Thousand and One Nights in World Literature', in Dominique Jullien (ed.), *Foundational Texts of World Literature* (New York: Peter Lang, 2011), pp. 101–18.

Versteegh, Kees, *Landmarks in Linguistic Thought III: The Arabic Linguistic Tradition* (London: Routledge, 2013).

Waldman, Marilyn and Malika Zeghal, 'Islamic World', in *Encyclopaedia Britannica*, 21 August 2019, available at: https://www.britannica.com/topic/Islamic-world.

Warton, Thomas, *The History Of English Poetry*, vol. 1 (London: Thomas Tegg, 1840).

12

INDONESIA'S *SASTERA PROFETIK* AS DECOLONIAL LITERARY THEORY

Nazry Bahrawi

What is the value of literary theory to world literature? Scholars have argued that the idea of world literature is traceable to Goethe's *weltliteratur* formulated in the late 1820s in his conversations with his disciple Eckermann and later elaborated by Marx and Engels in the *Communist Manifesto.* That the discipline began as an abstract concept before it was a practice makes *theory* integral to it. Today, world literary theory is punctuated by the works of Pascale Casanova, David Damrosch, Franco Moretti and several others. Yet the critical contribution of theory to world literature presents a contradiction. The presence of the non-West in literary theory is minimal. Granted, the valuable postcolonial works of Edward Said, Gayatri C. Spivak and Homi K. Bhabha may appear in a typical literary theory course. For instance, they account for two of twelve lessons in my own introductory module at a Singapore liberal arts engineering university where I used to teach. However, these are not inherently non-West as they are post-West. First, they can be said to be a response to theory's seedier side by highlighting the mechanics of asymmetrical power and privilege between world cultures. Secondly, it can be said that postcolonial literary lenses are still fashioned from the poststructuralist and postmodernist frameworks introduced by European continental philosophers like Ferdinand de Saussure, Jacques Derrida and Michel Foucault. This contradiction lies in the lack of 'worldliness' of world literature as works from the non-West are interpreted primarily from lenses and frameworks developed out of the Anglo-American and European continental philosophical tradition. Put simply, it is an ill-fitting venture.

This contradiction has also been expressed by the catchy phrase 'world lit without world lit crit' introduced by Revathi Krishnaswamy in her 2010 path-breaking essay 'Toward World Literary Knowledges: Theory in the Age of Globalisation'. Pointing to similar issues above, Krishnaswamy calls on comparative literature scholars to do the hard work of expanding the field of literary theory to include 'non-Western poetics, criticisms and commentaries'[1] in a bid to determine which aesthetic concepts are universal and which are limited to certain cultural traditions. Responding to Krishnaswamy, Chen Bar-Itzhak in a 2019 article argues for an epistemic shift with regard to how we read literary texts to guard against what she calls 'intellectual captivity' referring to the normative practice by world literature scholars to privilege the Western philosophical tradition when interpreting texts from all cultures.[2]

Accepting Krishnaswamy and Bar-Itzhak's dares, this chapter digs deep into Indonesia's discourse on literary criticism to explore the intricacies, value and cross-cultural applicability of *sastera profetik* (or, prophetic literature) as a literary lens conceptualised by the author and academic Kuntowijoyo in the 1990s. This lens stems from the unique practice of Islam in Indonesia, at once progressive and traditional in its Sufistic leanings. But, while *sastera profetik* hails from within the fold of Islam, Kuntowijoyo describes its third element, transcendentalism, as referring not just to 'a consciousness of Godliness through religion, but also a consciousness of whatever is able to surpass the limits of humanity'.[3] This suggests the possibility of its wider applicability beyond the Muslim world, a hypothesis that I intend to test on two short stories by the Argentine author Jorge Luis Borges. Why Borges?

[1] Revathi Krishnaswamy, 'Toward World Literary Knowledges', in David Damrosch (ed.), *World Literature in Theory* (Malden, MA: Wiley-Backwell, 2013), p. 150.

[2] Chen Bar-Itzhak, 'Intellectual Captivity: Literary Theory, World Literature, and the Ethics of Interpretation', *Journal of World Literature* 5(1) (2020): 92.

[3] Kuntowijoyo, 'Maklumat Sastra Profetik: Kaidah, Etika dan Stuktur', in Abdul Wachid B.S. and Jabrohim (eds), *Maklumat Sastra Profetik Kaidah, Etika dan Strukture Kuntowijoyo* (Yogyakarta: Multi Presindo, 2013), p. 30 (my translation).

A more elaborate answer will follow later. For now, it suffices to say that this decision rests on the view that Borges non-reductively channels aspects of Islamic culture in his prose even though he writes 'from the edge of the West'[4] as the Argentine literary critic Beatriz Sarlo describes it. As prose that is foreign yet familiar to Islam, the short stories of Borges position them as an apt litmus test for the universal relevance of *sastera profetik*.

Decolonial Islam in Theory

We might then also ask: where is the place of Islam in world literature? A quick study of materials that have been published suggests that this is not a major preoccupation among scholars. As an indication, a search of the keywords 'Islam' and 'world literature' on Google Books shows that there is only one book dealing directly with this theme – namely, Mohamed-Salah Omri's *Nationalism, Islam and World Literature* (2006)[5] on the works of Tunisian writer Mahmud al-Masʿadi. In comparison, a search for the keywords 'translation' and 'world literature' returns several titles, including Rebecca L. Walkowitz's *Born Translated* (2011),[6] Emily Apter's *Against World Literature* (2013),[7] and more recently, Susan Bassnett's edited volume *Translation and World Literature* (2018).[8] A work worth mentioning here is Ronit Ricci's *Islam, Translated* (2011),[9] whose subject of study covers both Islam and translation as these relate to the Arabic cosmopolis in South and Southeast Asia. Further, if one considers the spread of the themes in David Damrosch's *World Literature in Theory* (2014)[10] as a microcosmic representation of the state of theory in world literature today, it will quickly become

[4] Beatriz Sarlo, *Jorge Luis Borges: A Writer on the Edge* (London: Verso, 1993), p. 5.

[5] Mohamed-Salah Omri, *Nationalism, Islam and World Literature: Sites of Confluence in the Writings of Mahmud Al-Mas'adi* (London: Routledge, 2006).

[6] Rebecca L. Walkowitz, *Born Translated: The Contemporary Novel in an Age of World Literature* (New York: Columbia University Press, 2015).

[7] Emily Apter, *Against World Literature: On the Politics of Untranslatability* (London: Verso, 2013).

[8] Susan Bassnett (ed.), *Translation and World Literature* (London: Routledge, 2018).

[9] Ronit Ricci, *Islam Translated: Literature, Conversion, and the Arabic Cosmopolis of South and Southeast Asia* (Chicago: University of Chicago Press, 2011).

[10] David Damrosch (ed.), *World Literature in Theory* (Chichester: Wiley-Blackwell, 2013).

clear that there is only one essay that explores Muslim cultures. This was written by Ricci as a 2010 journal article[11] exploring the subject of Islamic literary networks. These examples were not drawn from any rigorous data sets, and cannot therefore be taken as exhaustive. However, they do indicate that the scholarship on theory in world literature suffers from a lack of engagement with Islam. A more specific term that would suit the need of this chapter is 'decolonial Islam' because it gestures to an epistemic schema that is context-specific, indigenous and drawn from Islamic theology, differentiating it from theory derived from European philosophy.

Before going deeper into the concept of 'decolonial Islam', my recourse to it requires some clarification. This means revisiting what Krishnaswamy meant by the word *knowledges* as opposed to 'theory, poetics, aesthetics or criticism' when she introduced her concept of world literary knowledges.[12] Citing the work of indigenous scholar Linda Tuhiwai-Smith,[13] Krishnaswamy outlines that knowledges (in the plural) here refer to the 'various local or indigenous epistemologies that have been marginalised by the universal claims of Western high theory'.[14] True to the spirit of her inquiry, my invocation of decolonial Islam in this chapter is not a denotation of Islam as a religious faith but the idea of Islam as an expression of what Krishnaswamy calls 'culturally situated knowledges' that could help its adherents conceptualise literature or literariness. In a like-minded move, Bar-Itzhak urges scholars of world literature to adopt 'the anthropological practice of reflexivity' which posits that:

> . . . the results of a study are not objective but are shaped by an interaction by the researcher and the researched, implying that the cultural background of a researcher affects the research topic, the research process, and, eventually its outcome.[15]

[11] Ronit Ricci, 'Islamic Literary Networks in South and Southeast Asia', *Journal of Islamic Studies* 21(1) (2010): 1–28.

[12] Krishnaswamy, 'Toward World Literary Knowledges', p. 136.

[13] Linda Tuhiwai Smith, *Decolonizing Methodologies: Research and Indigenous Peoples* (London: Zed Books, 2013).

[14] Smith, *Decolonizing Methodologies*, p. 143.

[15] Bar-Itzhak, 'Intellectual Captivity', p. 24.

To this end, I acknowledge my positionality in this research as a scholar of world literature trained in Anglo-American and European literary modes of reading. Yet I would also like to qualify that I am also familiar with Malay–Indonesian and Arabic literary criticism, and have a keen interest in exploring their scope of use. Thus, my own use of the term 'decolonial Islam' pushes theology centrestage in its articulation of Islam as a knowledge system more than a belief system, though any insistence of a strict binary between the two is complicated by the fact that they share a symbiotic relationship. In this sense, even Ricci's seminal world literature book *Islam, Translated* does not quite qualify as a study of decolonial Islam. While she takes the Arabic theological text *The Book of One Thousand Questions* to be her subject of study, Ricci traces the changes to its translated versions in Javanese, Malay and Tamil to draw insights about the paratextual phenomenon of Muslim literary networks. Through these, she argues for the viability of an Arabic cosmopolis as a cultural sphere that spans from the Middle East to South and Southeast Asia. To this end, her book provides insightful commentaries into the movement of texts within the Muslim world as well as the role that translation plays in the spread of Islam to Asia. It therefore speaks to certain standard themes within world literature – globalisation, circulation and translation. However, the book does not quite delve into the theological mechanisations contained within the *One Thousand Questions* if we take theology to mean the systematic study of divine doctrines and how these shape a person's understanding of other life-spheres as nature, politics and law, to name some.

Decolonial Islam can be seen as a branch of decolonial theology. Given that Islam is part of the Abrahamic faiths, it is apt to situate decolonial Islam within the nascent study of decolonial Christianity and Judaism. With Christianity, the work of Nelson Maldonado-Torres suggests that indigenous and black peoples in Latin America and the Caribbean 'are keener on alternative genealogies emerging in the Southern hemisphere', writes Barreto and Sirvent in their introduction to the edited volume *Decolonial Christianities*.[16] They argue that the foundations of decolonial Christianities can be traced back to liberation theology, a Latin American doctrine concerned with addressing poverty and

[16] Raimundo Barreto and Roberto Sirvent (eds), 'Introduction', in *Decolonial Christianities: Latinx and Latin American Perspectives* (Cham: Palgrave Macmillan, 2019), p. 8.

oppression that was championed in the 1950s and 1960s by organisations such as the Latin American Episcopal Conference (CELAM). According to one of its early propagators Enrique Dussel, liberation theology runs counter to the doctrines of Latino-Germanic Christendom that have peddled the idea that there is one true, universal theology emanating from parts of the Northern hemisphere. Instead, liberation theology harkens back to the openness that characterised the early years of messianic Christianity during the Hellenic-Roman empire when a new religion was introduced to the masses by 'a proselytising Jewish sect open to the *goim* (Hebrew: the non-Jewish)', says Dussel.[17] As a grassroots movement in Latin America, liberation theology therefore represents an attempt to conceptualise a Christian doctrine that does not uphold Eurocentrism, or the idea that Europe is the universal standard marker of civilisation, or any of its associated ideologies of modernity, capitalism and colonialism. But there is a caveat here. While it has been rather adept at addressing the plights of the poor, liberation theology has not quite tackled the issue of how Christians can relate hospitably to the non-Christian Other. And so, Barreto and Sirvent point to a chapter titled 'The Bible and 500 Years of Conquest' by Elsa Tamez,[18] a Mexican biblical scholar, who calls on Christians to move beyond liberation theology and rethink 'its centuries-long complicity in colonialism, conquest and domination at a time when Latin American Christianity was wrestling with the 500th anniversary of its first and tragic encounter with the peoples of Abya Yala'.[19] In effect, where liberation theology draws inspiration from the praxis of early Christianity, the version of decolonial Christianity envisioned by Tamez necessitates the airing of dirty linen within the faith that points to how it might have justified, even encouraged, the persecution of less powerful peoples as it was spread by missionaries to the non-West hand in hand with European imperialism.

There are far fewer works on decolonial Judaism, though the social theorist Santiago Slabodsky easily counts as the leading scholar on the subject. In

[17] Barreto and Sirvent, 'Introduction', *Decolonial Christianities*, p. 9.

[18] Elsa Tamez, 'The Bible and 500 Hundred Years of Conquest', in R. S. Sugirtharajah (ed.), *Voices from the Margin: Interpreting the Bible in the Third World* (Maryknoll, NY: Orbis, 2006), pp. 13–26.

[19] Barreto and Sirvent, 'Introduction', *Decolonial Christianities*, p. 2.

his book *Decolonial Judaism* (2014),[20] Slabodsky observes that, while Jews were once perceived as barbarians plotting the downfall of Europe, they were normalised as 'integral members of Western civilisation'[21] following the Holocaust to signal that a second Holocaust would not happen. This normalisation is most evident with the Jewish community resident in the Global North – America, Europe and Israel/Palestine – that makes up for 80 per cent of global Jewry. Yet this integration of Jews into 'a civilised white society' only serves to 'reinforce racial binarisms in the post-war era'.[22] That is to say, it does very little to dismantle the civilised–barbarian dualism, which is an integral discourse buttressing Western imperialism. The integration of Jews into Western civilisation, says Slabodsky, unveils a paradox: 'Jews became re-inscribed in the same dualistic paradigm that was responsible for the annihilation of one third of their population in World War II.'[23] In his book, he invokes decolonial Judaism as instances of Jewish thought that attempts to draw from non-Western epistemologies. He cited the works of the early Frankfurt School, Emmanuel Levinas and Albert Memmi as cases in point. With Memmi in particular, Slabodsky points out that he was inspired by the Negritude ideas of Aimé Césaire to reclaim the barbarism of blackness in his 'return to Africa' call. Memmi had done likewise to couch barbaric Jewry as a positive valence to oppose the colonial idea. He had defended the creation of the state of Israel as a decolonial struggle, a stance that Slabodsky could not quite condone as he ruminates over the writings of Edward Said and Ella Shohat on Israel/Palestine. For Slabodsky, it appears that 'the positive counter-narratives failed because they were unable to make an internal critique of the new Jewish status'.[24] For the purpose of this chapter though, it appears that Slabodsky's discourse on decolonial Judaism has not quite drawn from theology in the same way that decolonial Christianities have done with liberation theology. Rather, it can be read as an exploration on socio-political theory more than Judaism as a knowledge system.

[20] Santiago Slabodsky, *Decolonial Judaism: Triumphal Failures of Barbaric Thinking* (Cham: Palgrave Macmillan, 2014).

[21] Slabodsky, *Decolonial Judaism*, p. 5.

[22] Slabodsky, *Decolonial Judaism*, p. 5.

[23] Slabodsky, *Decolonial Judaism*, p. 7.

[24] Slabodsky, *Decolonial Judaism*, p. 205.

Moving on to the scholarship on decolonial Islam proper, it can be said that its conception was also fuelled by liberation theology, drawing it closer to decolonial Christianities than decolonial Judaism. Here, the scholarship of Farid Esack is instructional. Esack wrote the seminal work *Qur'an, Liberation and Pluralism* (1997),[25] which details his deep reflection about how South African Muslims can come to terms with values from the Qur'ān to make sense of apartheid. Esack is a regular participant at the annual Granada Summer School on Critical Muslims Studies organised by the Centre of Study and Investigation for Decolonial Dialogues alongside other regulars such as decolonial scholars Slabodsky and Maldonado-Torres, both mentioned earlier. While Esack professes an affinity to the philosophy of Christian liberation theology, he draws on Islamic sources and his own lived experience as a Muslim activist fighting against the apartheid system in South Africa to formulate his own version of Islamic liberation theology. For instance, he reads the Qur'ānic concept of *qist* (equity) from the Qur'ān as the basis for 'the natural order'.[26] According to this view of the cosmos, injustice creates disorder (*fitnah*) and it therefore becomes obligatory that Muslims strive to eradicate it. Apartheid as a legacy of colonialism counts as disorder and so South African Muslims have a religious duty to return to the natural state of *qist*. However, it is important to note that Esack was not the first to have professed liberation theology in Islam. As pointed out by Marco Demichelis, earlier proponents of this movement came in the figures of the Indian scholar Asghar Ali Engineer and British-Pakistani philosopher Sabbir Akhtar.[27] While Esack may be read as conceptualising a decolonial strain of Islamic thought that emerged out of his experience of South Africa's apartheid, the same cannot be said of the Islamic liberation theology conceptualised by Engineer and Akhtar. The latter, for instance, makes the argument that Islamic liberation theology is not a new reactionary movement, but one

[25] Farid Esack, *Qur'ān, Liberation and Pluralism: An Islamic Perspective of Interreligious Solidarity Against Oppression* (London: Oneworld, 1997).

[26] Farid Esack, 'In Search of Elusive Notions of Islamic Justice in Elusive Contexts', *Religions: A Scholarly Journal* 2 (2012): 11.

[27] Marco Demichelis, 'Islamic Liberation Theology: An Inter-Religious Reflection between Gustavo Gutierrez, Farīd Esack and Ḥamīd Dabāšī'', *Oriente Moderno* 94(1) (2014): 128.

that lies at the heart of a faith that possesses 'a scripture whose only theology is liberation theology'.[28] His reasoning lies on the argument that Islam, unlike Christianity, is a religion that affirms legal and political instruments in its very conception in the forms of *shar'ia* and caliphate. The term 'caliphate' carries a certain conceptual weight in the post-9/11 world, primarily in security studies to describe geopolitical jihadi groups like al Qaeda and Islamic State outlined in a number of works, including Abdel Bari Atwan's recently published *Islamic State: The Digital Caliphate* (2019).[29] However, Esack's use of the term gestures to the idea of the caliphate as a premodern political institution from the appointment of Abu Bakr as the first caliph in the wake of Muḥammad's death to the reign of the Ottoman sultans.

Between Esack and Akhtar are then two definitions of liberation theology and, in fact, of Islam. Esack recognises multiple articulations of Islam, while Akhtar seems to suggest a monolithic interpretation of Islam, which appears to be Sunni-centric.

Like Akhtar, Engineer too propounds a similar monolithic interpretation of Islam. Yet the Shi'a Muslim theologian from India has also designed an Islamic liberation theology that is most effective at challenging the elitism of the religious elites. How has Engineer been monolithic? According to Shadaab Rahemtulla in his book *Qur'an of the Oppressed*, Engineer 'essentialises Islam as being a message of peace and only peace, dismissing militant interpretations as being outside the fold of the faith'.[30] This stands in stark contrast to Esack who displays a deep understanding of how the discourse of peace can be made to defend an oppressive status quo. Esack's understanding was shaped by his experience of apartheid South Africa, where apartheid activists were posited as disturbers of peace. Thus, Engineer's peace discourse could in fact prove to be counter-productive to his liberation theology. Still, although Engineer has mounted an apologetic defence of Islam, he has

[28] Shabbir Akhtar, *Islam as Political Religion: The Future of an Imperial Faith* (London: Routledge, 2010), p. 127.

[29] Abdel Bari Atwan, *Islamic State: The Digital Caliphate* (Oakland, CA: University of California Press, 2019).

[30] Shadaab Rahemtulla, *Qur'an of the Oppressed: Liberation Theology and Gender Justice in Islam* (Oxford: Oxford University Press, 2017), p. 89.

also conceptualised a formidable version of Islamic liberation theology that embraces a 'praxis-based approach' as Rahemtulla calls it.[31] For Engineer, the Qur'ān should not be reduced to an abstract philosophical tract or a legalistic document. Rather, taking it to be the most authoritative source of Islamic teaching, Engineer makes the argument that it should be seen as a source of ethical principles whose emphasis is the conduct of life in the contemporary material world as opposed to the heaven and hell realms of the divine hereafter. To demonstrate this, Rahemtulla points to an example of how Engineer interprets *sura* 104 of the Qur'ān which reads:

> Woe to every fault-finding backbiter, who amasses riches, counting them over, thinking they will make him live for ever. No indeed! He will be thrust into the Crusher. What will explain to you what the Crusher is? It is God's fire, made to blaze, which rises over people's hearts. It closes in on them in towering columns.[32]

Engineer interprets the Crusher here to be 'an impending social upheaval, fuelled by popular discontent with the glaring inequalities of Meccan society, which will ultimately destroy the city's elite'.[33] In terms of dealing with colonial structures, Engineer's liberation theology is not so much directed against European colonisation directly as it is an internal critique of the religious elites in Islam. Liberation for Engineer is therefore about giving lay Muslims the agency to interpret the faith for themselves as opposed to handing the clerical class the authority to dictate how others should lead their lives.

Rahemtulla's book is also instructional at highlighting the intersections between female empowerment and Islam through the figures of Amina Wadud and Asma Barlas, both of whom are female exegetes of the Qur'ān known for writing works that challenge misogynistic practices within Islam. It is especially interesting to consider the case of Barlas, whose liberation theology has been described by Rahemtulla as serving a 'double critique'[34]

[31] Rahemtulla, *Qur'an of the Oppressed*, p. 69.

[32] 'The Backbiter/al-Humazah', trans. M. A. S. Abdel Haleem, *The Qur'an* (Oxford: Oxford University Press, 2004), p. 436.

[33] Rahemtulla, *Qur'an of the Oppressed*, p. 71.

[34] Rahemtulla, *Qur'an of the Oppressed*, p. 224.

against oppressive structures within Muslim communities and non-Muslim Western societies, particularly in United States where she is based. With the latter, she rejects the Western conception of feminism because of its blindness to racial politics. In particular, she disagrees with the Western feminist view that the Muslim headscarf signals oppression and that the naked body equates to liberation. With the liberation theology of Barlas, we see a form of decolonial Islam that is intersectional in the way it incorporates 'questions of race and sexuality, class and empire'.[35] While not exhaustive, this short survey of scholarship in decolonial Islam suggests that they have mainly hailed from outside the 'centre' of the Muslim world, that is, the Arab societies of the Gulf and North Africa. There is, however, no mention of developments in the Malay Archipelago, a peripheral region of the Muslim world that has its fair share of liberation theology. In an attempt to address this lacuna, the next section will consider a literary lens fashioned in Indonesia.

Theorising *sastera profetik*

To extend decolonial Islam's challenge to the Arabocentrism of Islamic theology is to factor in discourses from Muslim Southeast Asia, a region also known as the Malay world that has oftentimes been marginal to the discussion. A pertinent term to begin with is 'Islam Nusantara', with Nusantara being an Old Javanese word that roughly translates to 'islands between' referring to the islands beyond Java in the Indian and Pacific oceans. Today, the term Nusantara is widely acknowledged as referring to the Malay world encompassing Indonesia, Malaysia, Singapore, Brunei and the southern parts of Thailand and Philippines.

It stands to reason, then, that Islam Nusantara refers to the practices of Islam in these parts. Azyumardi Azra, a renowned Islamic studies scholar in Indonesia, argues that the concept is not simply geographic in nature in the way one thinks of Turkish Islam or South Asian Islam. Expressing its doctrinal facet, Azyumardi outlines what is perhaps one the most specific definitions of Islam Nusantara. In a 2015 op-ed commentary for the Indonesian daily *Kompas*, he writes that Islam Nusantara is based on the tripartite combination of Ashʿarite theology, Shāfiʿi *fiqh* (or jurisprudence) and al-Ghazālī's *tasawwuf* (or Sufi practice). This mix has resulted in its modest (*wasaṭiyyah*) quality.

[35] Rahemtulla, *Qur'an of the Oppressed*, pp. 214–15.

He writes: 'Ash'arite theology emphasises the attitude of moderation between revelation and reason, Shafi'i *fiqh* coupled with Sufism's *amali-akhlaqi* makes Islamic expression so inclusive and tolerant'.[36] Yet this is perhaps the most specific doctrinal expression of Islam Nusantara. It is important here to acknowledge that the concept of *wasaṭiyyah* has also been professed by Egypt's Al-Azhar University in 2011 when it released *Wathīqat al-Azhar Ḥawla Mustaqbal Miṣr* (*Al-Azhar's Document About the Future of Egypt*). According to the Malaysia-based Islamic law scholar Mohammad Hashim Kamali, the document:

> . . . advocated moderation in Islamic thought (*al-fikr al-Islami al-wasati*) that drew inspiration from famous Azharite reformers, including Hasan al-'Attar, Rifa'a al-Tahtawi, Muhammad 'Abduh, Mahmud Shaltut, Yusuf al-Qaradawi and others.[37]

Ironically, the concept of *wasaṭiyyah* as the modest or moderate practice of Islam can in fact lead to the polarising discourse nuancedly articulated as the 'good Muslim, bad Muslim' thesis by Mahmood Mamdani.[38] Mamdani argues that the way out of this quagmire is to 'shift the focus from doctrinal to historical Islam',[39] something that Kuntowijoyo appears to do with *sastera profetik* which he situates within Indonesia's socio-political climate.

This shift away from doctrine can also be seen in the reception of the idea of Islam Nusantara by Indonesian scholars of Islam such as Mujamil Qomar, K. M. Luthfi,[40] as well as Edy Susanto and Karimullah who had engaged with Azyumardi's definition as method more than doctrine. Edy and Karimullah,

[36] Azyumardi Azra, 'Sustainable Indonesian Islam: A Blessing for the Universe', *Kompas*, 3 August 2015, available at: www.indonesia-nederland.org/archive/azyumardi-azra-sustainable-indonesian-islam-a-blessing-for-the-universe.

[37] Mohammad Hashim Kamali, 'Al-Azhar Stands for Moderation of Thought', *New Straits Times*, 2 March 2018, available at: https://www.nst.com.my/opinion/columnists/2018/03/340471/al-azhar-stands-moderation-thought.

[38] Mahmood Mamdani, 'Good Muslim, Bad Muslim: A Political Perspective on Culture and Terrorism', *American Anthropologist* 104(3) (2002): 766–75.

[39] Mamdani, 'Good Muslim', p. 768.

[40] Khabibi Muhammad Luthfi, 'Islam Nusantara: Relasi Islam dan Budaya Lokal', *Shahih: Journal of Islamicate Multidisciplinary* 1(1) (2016): 1–12.

for instance, argue that Islam Nusantara is a theological mode of interpretation that is 'tolerant, peaceful and accommodating to the cultures of Nusantara'.[41] Mujamil, meanwhile, highlights a laundry list of unique traits of Indonesia that informed the idea of Islam Nusantara, such as its rich biodiversity, its distance from Middle Eastern conflicts and the multiple cultures that make up the nation.[42] Their treatises position Islam Nusantara as a canopy that encompasses a number of more specific theological positions. One of those positions is the idea of *sastera profetik*, or prophetic literature, theorised by Kuntowijoyo.

By way of a short introduction, Kuntowijoyo (1943–2005) was a prolific Indonesian writer, academic and public intellectual who had published prose, poetry, plays and non-fictional works. Trained as a historian in Indonesia and America where he attained postgraduate degrees from Connecticut University and Columbia University, Kuntowijoyo returned to his alma mater, Gadjah Mada University in Yogyakarta, to serve in the departments of literary and cultural studies, among others. Within Kuntowijoyo's oeuvre of work, *sastera profetik* began life under a different guise – *sastera transcendental*, or transcendental literature, a term he introduced in a 1982 essay.[43] There, Kuntowijoyo laid the groundwork for theorising a mode of literary thinking that embraces spirituality as a means of circumscribing the trappings of materialism and technology for the modern Indonesian citizen. According to Mohd Faizal Musa, this concept was driven by the desire to channel *kejawen* (Javanese mysticism), a localised form of Sufism, as the alternative to unbridled modernity.[44] Roughly translated, *kejawen* means the quality of being Javanese. In the context of our discussion, *kejawen* as Javanese mysticism denotes 'syncretic' Islamic practices in Java. For instance, Suwardi Endraswara points to the cultural example of

[41] Edy Susanto and Karimullah, 'Islam Nusantara: Islam Khas dan Akomodatif terhadap Budaya Local', *Al-Ulum* 16(1) (2016): 77 (my translation).

[42] Mujamil Qomar, 'Islam Nusantara: Sebuah Alternatif Model Pemikiran, Pemahaman, dan Pengamalan Islam', *El Harakah Jurnal Budaya Islam* 17(2) (2015): 212–13.

[43] Kuntowijoyo, 'Saya Kira Kita Memerlukan Juga Sebuah Sastra Transendental', *Berita Buana*, 21 December 1982.

[44] Mohd Faizal Musa, 'Islamic Literature Discourse in the Postcolonial Era: The Transcendental Literature of Indonesia and Genuine Literature of Malaysia', *Malay Literature* 25(1) (2012): 60.

shadow puppetry as an instance of *kejawen*.[45] Shadow puppetry, or *wayang kulit*, has been used as a tool for spreading Islam by Sunan Kalijogo, one of the nine saints (*wali songo*) thought to have been responsible for spreading Islam in Java. Previously, shadow puppetry was started by Hindus who came to Java as a narrative form to stage their classic tales such as the *Mahabharata* and the *Ramayana*, according to L. F. Brakel.[46] A feature of *kejawen* thus is the syncretism between Islam and other religious traditions such as Hinduism that was already entrenched in Java. With *kejawen* as its defining feature, we see that *sastera transcendental* shares the same principle as Islam Nusantara in drawing from Islamic teachings that have taken local forms.

According to Suminto A. Sayuti, Kuntowijoyo first used the term *sastera profetik* at a cultural event at Taman Ismail Marzuki in 2016, four years after writing the aforementioned essay.[47] However, his most extensive articulation of the term can be gleaned from a 2005 essay titled *Maklumat Sastra Profetik: Kaidah, Etika dan Struktur* (*An Edict on Prophetic Literature: Principles, Ethics and Structure*). In it, he interprets the adjective 'prophetic' to mean the pursuit of emulating Prophet Muḥammad's conduct. This takes the form of three themes extracted from the Qurʾānic verse 110 of the 'Al ʿImran' (The Family of ʿImran) chapter, Q. 3:110, which Abdeel Haleem translates as: '[Believers], you are the best community singled out for people: you order what is right, forbid what is wrong, and believe in God.'[48] These themes are *ʿamar maʾruf* (the injunction to do right), *nahi mungkar* (the forbidding of wrong deeds) and *tuʾmunina billah* (belief in God).[49] Kuntowijoyo recasts these Islamic themes as Western theoretical frames of humanism, liberation and transcendentalism, respectively. He also qualifies that, while Western societies linked these frames to specific ideologies (humanism to liberalism, liberation to Marxism, and

[45] Suwardi Endraswara, *Mistik Kejawen: Sinkretisme, Simbolisme dan Sufisme dalam Budaya Spiritual Jawa* (Jogjakarta: Penerbit Narasi, 2003).

[46] L. F. Brakel, 'Islam and Local Traditions: Syncretic Ideas and Practices', *Indonesia and the Malay World* 32(92) (2004): 13.

[47] Suminto A. Sayuti, 'Selamat Jalan Kuntowijoyo', in Abdul Wachid B. S. and Jabrohim (eds), *Maklumat Sastra Profetik: Kaidah, Etika dan Struktur* Yogyakarta: Multi Presindo, 2013), p. 5.

[48] 'The Family of ʿImran/al ʿImran', trans. M. A. S. Abdel Haleem, *The Qur'an*, p. 42.

[49] Kuntowijoyo, 'Maklumat Sastra Profetik', pp. 16–17.

transcendence to religiosity), *sastera profetik* encompasses all three at once. To get at what he meant, it is apt at this juncture to delve deeper into each in turn.

With humanism, Kuntowijoyo saw this as a means of challenging the dehumanisation of society brought about by the automation of human activities and the commodification of mass culture. His reading was influenced by two works of Western critical theory. The first is Jacques Ellul's *The Technological Society* (1964), which speculates the notion of *technique* as 'the totality of methods rationally arrived at and having absolute efficiency (for a given stage of development) in every field of human activity'.[50] The widespread adoption of technique leads to the creation of machine man (*l'homme machine*) whose acts in society are reactionary and mechanical. Localising it to Indonesia, he observes that Muslims are prone to expressing remorse, even weeping, at *dzikr* gatherings while reflecting on their sin of forgetting God. This, he believes, signals that Indonesians are disgruntled by the automation that has come to define their lives. Though Kuntowijoyo did not make this explicit, it can also be said that the capability to weep negates the state of automation. The second work to have inspired him is Theodor Adorno and Max Horkheimer's classic essay 'The Culture Industry',[51] which posits that mass culture cultivates a politically apathetic society. Here, Kuntowijoyo expresses concern over young Indonesians. As the primary consumers of mass culture, they are susceptible to the values of exploitation and sensationalism promoted by mass culture, thereby creating in Indonesia a culture of narcissism.

His views on liberation were less theoretical and more grounded in the material realities at the time of his writing. Here, Kuntowijoyo argues that this theme refers to the fight to end oppression by both external and internal forces. The former refers to capitalism, colonialism (he names Palestine as a case in point) and big state aggression towards smaller states. The latter, meanwhile, includes Indonesia's struggles with art censorship, state oppression, as well as income and gender inequality. To this end, it can be said that

[50] Jacques Ellul, John Wilkinson and Robert King Merton, *The Technological Society* (New York: Vintage, 1964), p. xxv.

[51] Theodor Adorno and Max Horkheimer, 'The Culture Industry: Enlightenment as Mass Deception (1944)', in *Dialectic of Enlightenment: Philosophical Fragments*, ed. Gunzelin Schmid Noer (Stanford: Stanford University Press, 2002), pp. 94–136.

this facet of *sastera profetik* comes closest to the objectives of liberation theology common to decolonial Islam, Christianities and Judaism.

The final theme of transcendence is arguably the most nuanced part of Kuntowijoyo's conception, and thus requires some attention. Here, Kuntowijoyo took great pains to qualify that transcendence does not refer solely to a sense of Godliness that can be found in religions. Rather, transcendence denotes the acknowledgement of 'whatever is able to surpass the limits of humanity'[52] as I have described earlier. While *sastera profetik* was born from Kuntowijoyo's observation of Islam in the Indonesian context, it also does *not* appear to be anti-secular. In line with this observation, Kuntowijoyo speculates both theistic and non-theistic forms of transcendence. With the former, Kuntowijoyo channels the concept of 'dedifferentiation' that he had gleaned from Scott Lash's *Sociology of Postmodernism* (1991).[53] According to Lash, European cultures had come to differentiate between faith and the secular from the Renaissance period, a phenomenon that Kuntowijoyo believes had come to define Indonesian modernity too. The theistic transcendental impulse of *sastera profetik* reverses that phenomenon by collapsing what had been held as a clear divide between religious and world institutions. A more generative discussion can be had on the basis of Kuntowijoyo's views on non-theistic transcendence, which he had attempted to express through his novel *Khotbah di atas Bukit* (*Sermon on a Hill*).[54] The novel recounts the tale of a retired diplomat named Barman who is obsessed with the pursuit of peace and happiness. Barman eventually ended up establishing a quasi-religious sect. While Islam may not be the religion embraced by the sect, the book can be described as a spiritual *bildungsroman* of sorts because it details its protagonist's journey from secularism to religiosity. This sense of non-theistic transcendentalism is congruent to Indonesia. Kuntowijoyo observes that even 'secular' Indonesians possess an appreciation of something greater than humanity, whether this is in the form of spiritualism or cosmic consciousness.[55]

[52] Kuntowijoyo, 'Maklumat Sastra Profetik', p. 30 (my translation).

[53] Scott Lash, *Sociology of Postmodernism* (London: Routledge, 2014).

[54] Kuntowijoyo, *Khotbah di atas Bukit* (Jogjakarta: Yayasan Bentang Budaya, 2000).

[55] Kuntowijoyo, 'Maklumat Sastra Profetik', p. 15.

To this end, Kuntowijoyo outlines that all his literary works can be considered transcendental because they capture his sense of wonderment over life's mysteries. To him, *sastera profetik* encompasses literary works that do not reproduce the realist style common to journalistic reports, academic essays and philosophical books. Rather, its prose is better described as non-analytical and descriptive-narrative.[56] He believes that it is important that *sastera profetik* engages with reality from a distance. This does not mean that *sastera profetik* has nothing to contribute to real life. Rather, the critical distance accords *sastera profetik* with the dialectical ability to evaluate and critique the socio-cultural sphere in an ethical manner. He writes: 'The realism of literature is symbolic and not actual or historical. It is through symbolism that literature guides and performs a critique of reality'.[57]

Sastera profetik has been robustly discussed within Indonesia not just by scholars of Islamic studies, some of whom I have referred to above, but also by some of its more popular literary practitioners. Chief among them is Abdul Hadi W. M., a poet and academic, who is known for penning Sufistic literature. There are many points of convergence between Abdul Hadi and Kuntowijoyo on *sastera profetik*, but one area that is pertinent to this chapter concerns the universal applicability of the concept. While Abdul Hadi seems to lean more strongly on the influence of Sufism on *sastera profetik*, he appears to support the idea of non-theistic transcendence when he proposed that non-Muslim authors too can produce works of *sastera profetik*. He identified T. S. Eliot, Rabindranath Tagore, Akiya Yutaka, Choo Byun Hwa, Goethe, Walt Whitman and Khalil Gibran as authors whose works embody what he calls the prophetic spirit. While he did not engage in a close reading of their works, Abdul Hadi theorised certain features that qualify a piece of writing as *sastera profetik*. I will be referring to some of the more salient features that were listed in a 2011 essay by Mohd Faizal who had neatly delineated them based on his interpretation Abdul Hadi's writings.[58]

With form, the feature that defines *sastera profetik* is the deliberate use of symbols and images drawn from real life, nature, historical stories and legends

[56] Kuntowijoyo, 'Maklumat Sastra Profetik', p. 35.

[57] Kuntowijoyo, 'Maklumat Sastra Profetik', p. 10 (my translation).

[58] Mohd, Faizal Musa, 'Javanese Sufism and Prophetic Literature', *Cultura* 8(2) (2011): 189–208.

that are articulated as spiritual experiences by the author.[59] These, he adds, convey hidden truths, beauty and charm that are to be interpreted and enjoyed by the readers. In terms of characterisation, *sastera profetik* should feature characters with a connection to the divine which can be expressed as possessing 'patience and forbearance in dealing with tests and trials in life and at the same time believe in destiny'.[60] In the essay, Abdul Hadi said that the characters in many of Dostoyevsky's novels display such sheer tenacity in the wake of life's obstacles 'just like the prophets in Islam such as Joseph, Jacob, Moses and Jonah'.[61] Thematically, the works should express the oneness of God.[62] One can venture that this is premised on the Islamic precept of *tawḥīd* and is often expressed as the interconnectedness of all things to the Divine. Lastly, *sastera profetik* fulfils several objectives. Two of the most relevant are: (1) to encourage a person to become more humane in their personal life so that they can affect a similar change in their environment; and (2) to urge a community to embrace spirituality as a counter to oppression and colonisation.[63]

If we consider these features, it may appear that *sastera profetik* has a limited application to the interpretation of literary texts. It works best when a text fits some of the characteristics described above, even if they were not the product of writers from Islamic cultures. Borges' short stories are instructive here, as I will show in the next section. This restriction, though, should not necessarily be seen as a weakness to the lens. In line with Krishnaswamy's argument that 'world lit crit' from the Western hemisphere is not universal, the acknowledgement of *sastera profetik*'s limitation serves as an important reminder that any claims of generalisability when it comes to a specific literary lens has to be problematised. Still, it might be generative here to interpret texts that do not overtly display features of *sastera profetik*. As a means of testing its limits, I will also be experimenting on its use on Franz Kafka's short story, *The Metamorphosis* (1915), a modern classical short story penned in German in the early twentieth century with little to no trace of influence by Islamic cultures.

[59] Mohd, 'Javanese Sufism', p. 203.

[60] Mohd, 'Javanese Sufism', p. 201.

[61] Mohd, 'Javanese Sufism', p. 201.

[62] Mohd, 'Javanese Sufism', p. 201.

[63] Mohd, 'Javanese Sufism', p. 202.

Finally, it is worth mentioning that Kuntowijoyo's *sastera profetik* shares some similar traits to the twentieth-century discourse of Islamic metaphysics developed out of Malaysia by Syed Naquib al-Attas in his book *Prolegomena to the Metaphysics of Islam* (1995).[64] In essence, both have mined the Islamic intellectual tradition to propose an alternative approach to epistemology. In doing so, they have turned to Sufism as a source for their discourses. However, two major contrasts exist between them, which makes them distinctly different. First, both emerged out of the socio-political contexts of their nations, which vary in terms of their practices and institutionalisation of Islam. For instance, Islam and Malayness are enshrined in Malaysia's constitution as definitive of each other. This has resulted in the institutionalisation of Islam that is conservative in nature, and that downplays the pre-Islamic Hindu and Buddhist influences on Malay life. This is not the case in Indonesia, where Islam is not the sole religion practised by peoples of Malay descent such as the Javanese, Balinese, Bataks and others. The influence of Hinduism and Buddhism can still be seen in contemporary society. Secondly, al-Attas' discourse upholds a binary between secular and Islamic knowledge, while Kuntowijoyo's *sastera profetik* appears to be syncretic in terms of acknowledging its 'Western' influences as I have described.

Reading Borges through *sastera profetik*

Abdul Hadi has identified a number of international authors whose work qualifies as *sastera profetik*. However, I will be testing its universal applicability on the works of a writer whom he did not name. This is to ensure a more accurate picture of its generalisability, since choosing the work of someone whom Abdul Hadi had identified runs the risk of a foregone conclusion. Yet it is also important to qualify that *sastera profetik* is not relevant to *all* types of writing – only those that seem to embody some form of transcendentalism as they react to the adverse effects of capitalism and automation that began sometime in the early to mid-twentieth century with the emergence of the print industry and mass consumerism within newly formed nation-states in line with what has been described as the 'machine age'. It is therefore also pertinent that my

[64] Syed Muhammad Naquib al-Attas, *Prolegomena to the Metaphysics of Islam: An Exposition of the Fundamental Elements of the World View* (Kuala Lumpur: ISTAC, 1995).

choice settles comfortably within the confines of this theme and time period. To this end, I have opted to consider selected works of the Argentine writer Jorge Luis Borges (1899–1986). Borges figures as a staple author in the discipline of world literature. In the 2019 rendition of the Institute of World Literature summer school, he was the subject of an entire module titled 'Jorge Luis Borges and/as world literature' by Dominique Jullien.[65] Little work has been done though to read him from an Islamic literary lens, a gap which I hope to address in this chapter. His writings fit both the said time period and theme. As an indication of the latter, Alfonso J. García-Osuna describes Borges' writings as disrupting the over-reliance on 'positivist approaches to reality', which García-Osuna defines as 'methods that rely on empirical evidence for any authentication of what is "real"'.[66] Two more additional factors influenced my choice. The first has to do with the fact that Argentina does not qualify as strictly 'Western' in as much as 'the West' can be taken to denote economically developed nations in Europe and the United States with some history of colonisation or hegemony over less economically developed nations. To revisit Sarlo's quote in the opening section of this chapter, Borges is described as writing from 'the edge of the West'. Secondly, my choice is also influenced by Borges' profound engagement with Islam and Muslims. Writing about the depth of his engagement, Ian Almond explicates that Borges has not reproduced the stereotypical view of Islam as a monolithic culture in the way that Richard Burton, D. H. Lawrence and Albert Camus were prone to do in their writings. Rather, Borges portrays 'a myriad of images' about Islam that showcases 'Islam's radical plurality'.[67] Having qualified my reasoning, I will explore two of his short stories, namely, *The Zahir* (1949) and *The Aleph* (1945). While these were not explicitly written in relation to each other, both stories feature fantastical objects that can be found in everyday items, objects

[65] 'Institute of World Literature 2019 Summer School Programme, Institute of World Literature, available at: https://iwl.fas.harvard.edu/july-15-25, last accessed 17 February 2021.

[66] Alfonso J. García-Osuna, 'Introduction: Borges, or the Geography of Sentience', in Alfonso J. García-Osuna (ed.), *Borges, Language and Reality: The Transcendence of the Word* (Cham: Palgrave Macmillan, 2018), p. 1.

[67] Ian Almond, 'Borges the post-Orientalist: Images of Islam from the Edge of the West', *Modern Fiction Studies* 50(2) (2004): 454.

that had a grave impact on changing their respective narrator's perspective about the cosmos.

I will begin by looking at form. Both stories are built on incredulous premises that challenge our empirical experience of reality. In particular, they do not explain away the fantastical objects in this story, leaving the reader to interpret for themselves their meaning as symbols. As highlighted, the use of everyday items as symbols is a defining feature of *sastera profetik*. In *The Aleph*, the narrator encounters the titular celestial phenomenon in the cellar of his poet-friend's house. The latter describes the Aleph as 'the place where, without admixture or confusion, all the places of the world, seen from every angle, coexist'.[68] *The Zahir*, meanwhile, details the narrator's inner monologue as he becomes increasingly besotted with a piece of coin. That coin is, in fact, the Zahir or 'a being or things that have the terrible power to be unforgettable, and whose image eventually drives people mad'.[69] This descent into madness was experienced by the narrator. In these two stories, ordinary objects in the form of a cellar and a coin are rendered extraordinary, and are presented as repository of 'hidden truths' that can reveal the secrets of the universe. It is interesting that the unassuming cellar and coin symbolically correspond to the dyadic concepts of the *zahir* and the *batin* in Sufism. The former denotes the 'external' or 'manifest' reality of an object,[70] while the latter refers to its 'internal' or 'secret' meaning.[71] But what hidden truths do they symbolise?

To attempt to answer this question means considering the themes of the stories. Here, both stories seem to encapsulate the idea of the oneness of God that Abdul Hadi envisioned in *sastera profetik*. The Aleph enables a person to experience the entirety of the universe all at once, while the Zahir causes an individual to be so consumed by it that they cannot think of anything else. As a symbol, the Aleph can be interpreted as the unity of the universe

[68] Jorge Luis Borges, 'The Aleph', in *Collected Fictions Jorge Luis Borges*, trans. Andrew Hurley (New York: Penguin, 1998), p. 281.

[69] Jorge Luis Borges, 'The Zahir', in *Collected Fictions Jorge Luis Borges*, trans. Andrew Hurley (New York: Penguin, 1998), p. 246.

[70] 'Zahir', Oxford Islamic Studies Online, available at: http://www.oxfordislamicstudies.com/article/opr/t125/e2551, last accessed 17 February 2021.

[71] 'Batin', Oxford Islamic Studies Online, available at: http://www.oxfordislamicstudies.com/article/opr/t125/e314, last accessed 17 February 2021.

that connects 'all the ants on earth' to 'every letter of every page', and 'the coils and springs of love and the alterations of death'.[72] This revelation occurs simultaneously to the narrator. It seems to echo what Abdul Hadi observes as the interconnectedness of all things to the Divine, though the Divine is not expressed explicitly in this story as God but as a macrocosmic view of the universe in motion. Meanwhile, the Zahir as a symbol seems to suggest the opposite in terms of scale. The magic of the Zahir lies in its microcosmic appeal – the coin, and nothing else. Soon the coin is all that the narrator can think about, and he likens this to Sufis losing themselves in God as they chant their own names or the ninety-nine names of God. Yet this sense of godliness is not uniquely Islamic because the Zahir can also be found in other forms such as a tiger in eighteenth-century Gujarat and a blind man in a Surakarta mosque. Despite its singular focus, the Zahir may be just as infinite as the Aleph. Both items do not show explicit signs of Islam, a feature that Abdul Hadi argues is also a desirable trait of *sastera profetik*, as indicated by Mohd Faizal.[73]

In terms of characterisation, it is important to note that both stories feature protagonists who are fictionalised versions of Borges. To the discerning reader, this should immediately call attention to the very idea of reality and by extension, our dependency on facts and logic when determining the validity of a literary text. This challenge is magnified by the presence of mundane everyday objects with extraordinary qualities. Abdul Hadi theorises *sastera profetik* as featuring characters struggling with deep existential crises to the point of eventually resigning themselves to destiny. Expanding on Hadi's point, I argue that this sense of existential dread can be expressed symbolically and not just blatantly. The fictionalised Borges in both stories can be said to have gone through this process in differing ways. *The Aleph*'s Borges is a rationalist who is dubious about his poet-friend's claim of encountering the Aleph. In a bid to disprove his friend's theory, he agrees to sit in the latter's cellar where the Aleph was allegedly located. There, he encounters it and becomes a believer. In fact, he is so convinced of this new revelation that he continues researching about the Aleph to the point of speculating the locations of other possible Alephs,

[72] Borges, 'The Aleph', p. 283.

[73] Mohd, 'Javanese Sufism', p. 203.

suggesting a complete transformation from rationalism to transcendentalism. Meanwhile, *The Zahir*'s Borges struggles to maintain his sanity as he tries to rid his mind of this obsession with the Zahir coin, though this is to no avail. Eventually, he gives in to that obsession in the hope that this can stop his relentless obsession. In both their final stances, we see the narrators surrender to a force bigger than themselves. One might even call that force destiny.

Finally, we come to the two objectives that might qualify these stories as *sastera profetik*. There is little doubt that both stories harbour a deep respect for otherworldliness. That is to say, the stories make the case that material conditions are neither the ultimate harbinger of truth nor the primary determinant of how life will turn out. Rather, there appears to be something bigger at work. In both stories, the settled worldviews of their narrators are derailed by a chance encounter with a fantastical object. In *The Aleph*, this is through the death of a former lover whose distant cousin turns out to be the poet. In *The Zahir*, this comes in the form of the coin begotten by the narrator as part of his change after purchasing a brandy and orange juice. Yet this major unsolicited alteration has awakened the narrators of both stories to the true workings of the cosmos. In a sense, they are made privy to a secret knowledge made available only to a select few, signalling that their journeys possess a gnostic dimension. Abdul Hadi speculates that *sastera profetik* counters oppression and colonisation. While the stories do not directly speak of colonisation, the metamorphosis of the narrators seem to empower them. Put simply, the two narrators appear to be in a more informed position than they were before. It is, however, tenuous to conclude that the narrator in *The Aleph* has become more humane, an objective of *sastera profetik* according to Abdul Hadi. While the narrator himself is awed by what he has witnessed, he is driven by envy over his poet-friend to lie about his encounter so as to spite the latter. Meanwhile, the narrator of *The Zahir* has decided to offload the Zahir coin by purchasing a brandy in a random tavern. If we accept that the narrator sees his obsession as an affliction, then his act of offloading the coin is not motivated by kindness and can in fact be considered selfish and potentially harmful to others. The two stories do not seem to fit neatly with the objectives of *sastera profetik*, though there are some congruences.

As a foil for comparison, and to test the limits of *sastera profetik*'s generalisability, it is generative to attempt interpreting a piece of literary work that has little to no connection to Islamic cultures. After considering a few works, I have settled on Franz Kafka's *The Metamorphosis* (1915) here on several grounds. Other than the fact that it is not known to have been inspired by Islamic cultures, the short story conforms to the genre of the short story though it is also sometimes described as a novella. Secondly, it conforms to the time period of Borges' short stories that were penned during the 'Machine Age'. Lastly, it is generally accepted as a modern classic, which makes it one of the most well read, critically appraised pieces of literary work.

Read from the lens of *sastera profetik*, the remarkable story of Gregor Samsa appears to bring together two existing strands of interpretations: materialist, of which there is plenty, and transcendental, which are fewer in number. The former conforms to *sastera profetik*'s feature of humanism. Gregor's dehumanisation in his insect form is symbolic of his role as an oppressed employee of a cloth company. Bill Dodd writes that it is indisputable to read the character's alienation as 'discernibly material and social, and intimately connected with the nature and conditions of employment'.[74] He also cites Walter Sokel's reading of the story as corresponding to the Marxist concept of the '"externalisation" of work under capitalism'.[75] Such reading suggests that Gregor is an automaton that fits the description of the machine man, Ellul's concept that had a strong influence on *sastera profetik*.

While the story seems bleak because it ends with Gregor's death, there is a brief moment of respite to his miserable existence as an insect in the instance when he is drawn to the music played by his sister, Grete, on his last night as a living thing. Ritchie Robertson describes this as a 'spiritual nourishment' for Gregor who did not enjoy music in his human form.[76] This moment of respite is fleeting, but it points to the acknowledgement of something that transcends the human, the third feature of s*astera profetik*. This reading is symbolically represented by the fact that this spiritual nourishment can be enjoyed only when Gregor is no longer in his human form. While the transcendental force is certainly not Godly, it is also not cosmic as suggested in

[74] Bill Dodd, 'The Case for a Political Reading', in Julian Preece (ed.), *The Cambridge Companion to Kafka* (Cambridge: Cambridge University Press, 2003), p. 135.

[75] Dodd, 'A Political Reading', p. 135.

[76] Richie Robertson, *Kafka: A Short Introduction* (Oxford: Oxford University Press, 2004), p. 57.

Borges' short stories. In fact, the force is banal and man-made. This transcendental force in *The Metamorphosis* is neither an instance of theistic nor non-theistic forms. Rather, it is manufactured, thus steering clear of the third tenet of *sastera profetik*.

The story also does not speak neatly to *sastera profetik*'s second feature of liberation. The protagonist starves to death while his sister takes a turn for the worse in her behaviour. Though she has treated him decently in the early days of Gregor's insect life, she grows increasingly indifferent to his plight as she enters into the workforce to become a salesgirl. In the end, she is the one to suggest that family be rid of Gregor, calling him by the pronoun 'it', therefore dehumanising him. Nina Pelikan Straus has argued that the metamorphosis in the story refers to the change in Grete as much as Gregor.[77] If so, this is not so much a spiritual *bildungsroman* in the vein of *sastera profetik* but a descent into the abyss.

A Decolonial Postscript

What can be learnt from our analysis of these selected short stories of Borges? Judging from a purely structuralist angle, a strong case can be made that the two stories conform to a number of features of *sastera profetik*. Yet there are also some shaky parallels. For instance, the stories appear to value epiphany more than humaneness as part of its character's growth. To be clearer, the pursuit of self-reflexivity of a single individual seems like a more desirable objective than the push for societal change against oppression and colonisation as is the point of *sastera profetik*, a quality that it shares with decolonial Islam. Another difference lies in its appeal to the divine. The stories make scant mention of God. When they do, like in *The Zahir*, it is to exemplify rather than pontificate. In both, divinity is steered clear from the monotheistic profession of the One God. Instead, they articulate a sense of divinity that comes across as a mysterious and overpowering cosmic force. When applied to Kafka's *The Metamorphosis*, the lens of *sastera profetik* appears to reveal even starker incongruences as I have outlined above. This brief reading only serves to strengthen the point that theory, from the non-West or otherwise,

[77] Nina Pelikan Strauss, 'Transforming Franz Kafka's "Metamorphosis"', *Signs* 14(3) (1989): 651–67.

cannot be applied universally. It would serve a critic well to be mindful of this limitation.

Still, this experiment suggests that *sastera profetik* can help us interpret works that were not produced in Indonesia. This suggests a measure of 'worldliness' at play. The caveat to note here is that while I have used the term 'universal applicability' to describe *sastera profetik*'s generalisability, I do not mean that it can be applied spick and span to all literary works in the same way a text can be read from, say, the Marxist perspective or the postcolonial angle. Rather, I have made the careful choice of selecting works that I suspect bear enough similar traits to warrant an analysis in the first place. The thrust of this exercise is therefore not to systematise and subsume but to compare and contrast. This insures it from reproducing the contradiction of an ill-fitting venture that I raised at the beginning of this chapter wherein a text is forcibly interpreted from lenses and frameworks that are not befitting of their contexts. Its inclination towards measuredness grants *sastera profetik* its decolonial quality. That it can be considered as one of many 'options' and not a top-down theoretical imposition is another reason why it qualifies as decolonial. To paraphrase the literary theorist Walter Mignolo, one notable difference between the objective of decolonial theory and postcolonial theory is that the former aims to expand an epistemological field while the latter 'claims globality, if not universality'.[78] By way of resisting the impulse to dogmatise, *sastera profetik* can be positioned as a global literary lens from the non-West that is at once counter-hegemonic and accommodating. Its potential contribution to the field of world literary theory looks promising.

Bibliography

Adorno, Theodor and Max Horkheimer, 'The Culture Industry: Enlightenment as Mass Deception (1944)', in *Dialectic of Enlightenment: Philosophical Fragments*, ed. Gunzelin Schmid Noer (Stanford: Stanford University Press, 2002), pp. 94–136.

Akhtar, Shabbir, *Islam as Political Religion: The Future of an Imperial Faith* (London: Routledge, 2010).

[78] Walter Mignolo, *The Darker Side of Modernity: Global Futures, Decolonial Options* (Durham, NC: Duke University Press, 2011), p. 57.

Al-Attas, Syed Muhammad Naquib, *Prolegomena to the Metaphysics of Islam: An Exposition of the Fundamental Elements of the World View* (Kuala Lumpur: ISTAC, 1995).

Alim.org, 'Surah 3. Al-I'Imran', available at: http://www.alim.org/library/quran/surah/english/3/YAT, last accessed 17 February 2021.

Almond, Ian, 'Borges the post-Orientalist: Images of Islam from the Edge of the West', *Modern Fiction Studies* 50(2) (2004): 435–59.

Apter, Emily, *Against World Literature: On the Politics of Untranslatability* (London: Verso, 2013).

Atwan, Abdel Bari, *Islamic State: The Digital Caliphate* (Oakland, CA: University of California Press, 2019).

Azyumardi Azra, 'Sustainable Indonesian Islam: A Blessing for the Universe', *Kompas*, 3 August 2015, available at: www.indonesia-nederland.org/archive/azyumardi-azra-sustainable-indonesian-islam-a-blessing-for-the-universe.

Bar-Itzhak, Chen, 'Intellectual Captivity: Literary Theory, World Literature, and the Ethics of Interpretation', *Journal of World Literature* 5(1) (2020): 79–110.

Barreto, Raimundo and Roberto Sirvent (eds), 'Introduction', in *Decolonial Christianities: Latinx and Latin American Perspectives* (Cham: Palgrave Macmillan, 2019), pp. 1–21.

Bassnett, Susan (ed.), *Translation and World Literature* (London: Routledge, 2018).

Borges, Jorge Luis, 'The Aleph', in *Collected Fictions Jorge Luis Borges*, trans. Andrew Hurley (New York: Penguin, 1998).

Brakel, L. F., 'Islam and Local Traditions: Syncretic Ideas and Practices', *Indonesia and the Malay World* 32(92) (2004): 5–20.

Damrosch, David (ed.), *World Literature in Theory* (Chichester: Wiley-Blackwell, 2014).

Demichelis, Marco, 'Islamic Liberation Theology: An Inter-Religious Reflection between Gustavo Gutierrez, Farīd Esack and Ḥamīd Dabāšī'', *Oriente Moderno* 94(1) (2014): 125–47.

Dodd, Bill, 'The Case for A Political Reading', in Julian Preece (ed.), *The Cambridge Companion to Kafka* (Cambridge: Cambridge University Press, 2003), pp. 131–49.

Edy Susanto and Karimullah, 'Islam Nusantara: Islam Khas dan Akomodatif terhadap Budaya Local', *Al-Ulum* 16(1) (2016): 56–80.

Ellul, Jacques, John Wilkinson and Robert King Merton, *The Technological Society* (New York: Vintage, 1964).

Esack, Farid, *Qur'án, Liberation and Pluralism: An Islamic Perspective of Interreligious Solidarity Against Oppression* (London: Oneworld: 1997).

Esack, Farid, 'In Search of Elusive Notions of Islamic Justice in Elusive Contexts', *Religions: A Scholarly Journal* 2 (2012): 9–16.

García-Osuna, Alfonso J., 'Introduction: Borges, or the Geography of Sentience', in Alfonso J. García-Osuna (ed.), *Borges, Language and Reality: The Transcendence of the Word* (Cham: Palgrave Macmillan, 2018), pp. 1–15.

Institute of World Literature, 'Institute of World Literature 2019 Summer School Programme', available at: https://iwl.fas.harvard.edu/july-15-25, last accessed 17 February 2021.

Khabibi Muhammad Luthfi, 'Islam Nusantara: Relasi Islam dan Budaya Local', *Shahih: Journal of Islamicate Multidisciplinary* 1(1) (2016): 1–12.

Krishnaswamy, Revathi, 'Toward World Literary Knowledges', in David Damrosch (ed.), *World Literature in Theory* (Chichester: Wiley-Backwell, 2013), pp. 134–58.

Kuntowijoyo, 'Saya Kira Kita Memerlukan Juga Sebuah Sastra Transendental', *Berita Buana*, 21 December 1982.

Kuntowijoyo, *Khotbah di atas Bukit* (Jogjakarta: Yayasan Bentang Budaya, 2000).

Kuntowijoyo, 'Maklumat Sastra Profetik: Kaidah, Etika dan Stuktur', in Abdul Wachid B.S. and Jabrohim (eds), *Maklumat Sastra Profetik Kaidah, Etika dan Strukture Kuntowijoyo* (Yogyakarta: Multi Presindo, 2013), pp. 9–40.

Lash, Scott, *Sociology of Postmodernism* (London: Routledge, 2014).

Mamdani, Mahmood, 'Good Muslim, Bad Muslim: A Political Perspective on Culture and Terrorism', *American Anthropologist* 104(3) (2002): 766–75.

Mignolo, Walter, *The Darker Side of Modernity: Global Futures, Decolonial Options* (Durham, NC: Duke University Press, 2011).

Mohammad Hashim Kamali, 'Al-Azhar Stands for Moderation of Thought', *New Straits Times*, 2 March 2018, available at: https://www.nst.com.my/opinion/columnists/2018/03/340471/al-azhar-stands-moderation-thought.

Mohd, Faizal Musa, 'Javanese Sufism and Prophetic Literature', *Cultura* 8(2) (2011): 189–208.

Mohd, Faizal Musa, 'Islamic Literature Discourse in the Postcolonial Era: The Transcendental Literature of Indonesia and Genuine Literature of Malaysia', *Malay Literature* 25(1) (2012): 56–74.

Mujamil Qomar, 'Islam Nusantara: Sebuah Alternatif Model Pemikiran, Pemahaman, dan Pengamalan Islam', *El Harakah Jurnal Budaya Islam* 17(2) (2015): 198–217.

Omri, Mohamed-Salah, *Nationalism, Islam and World Literature: Sites of Confluence in the Writings of Mahmud Al-Mas'adi* (London: Routledge, 2006).

Oxford Islamic Studies Online, 'Batin', available at: http://www.oxfordislamicstudies.com/article/opr/t125/e314, last accessed 17 February 2021.

Oxford Islamic Studies Online, 'Zahir', available at: http://www.oxfordislamicstudies.com/article/opr/t125/e2551, last accessed 17 February 2021.

Quran.com, 'Al-Humazah', available at: https://quran.com/104, last accessed 17 February 2021.

Rahemtulla, Shadaab, *Qur'an of the Oppressed: Liberation Theology and Gender Justice in Islam* (Oxford: Oxford University Press, 2017).

Ricci, Ronit, 'Islamic Literary Networks in South and Southeast Asia', *Journal of Islamic Studies* 21(1) (2010): 1–28.

Ricci, Ronit, *Islam Translated: Literature, Conversion, and the Arabic Cosmopolis of South and Southeast Asia* (Chicago: University of Chicago Press, 2011).

Robertson, Richie, *Kafka: A Short Introduction* (Oxford: Oxford University Press, 2004).

Sarlo, Beatriz, *Jorge Luis Borges: A Writer on the Edge* (London: Verso, 1993).

Slabodsky, Santiago, *Decolonial Judaism: Triumphal Failures of Barbaric Thinking* (Cham: Palgrave Macmillan, 2014).

Smith, Linda Tuhiwai, *Decolonizing Methodologies: Research and Indigenous Peoples* (London: Zed Books, 2013).

Strauss, Nina Pelikan, 'Transforming Franz Kafka's "Metamorphosis"', *Signs* 14(3) (1989): 651–67.

Suminto, A. Sayuti, 'Selamat Jalan Kuntowijoyo', in Abdul Wachid B.S. and Jabrohim (eds), *Maklumat Sasta Profetik: Kaidah, Etika dan Struktur* (Yogyakarta: Multi Presindo, 2013), 1–8.

Suwardi, Endraswara, *Mistik Kejawen: Sinkretisme, Simbolisme dan Sufisme dalam Budaya Spiritual Jawa* (Jogjakarta: Penerbit Narasi, 2003).

Tamez, Elsa, 'The Bible and 500 Hundred Years of Conquest', in R. S. Sugirtharajah (ed.), *Voices from the Margin: Interpreting the Bible in the Third World* (Maryknoll, NY: Orbis Books, 2006), pp. 13–26.

The Qur'ān, trans. M. A. S. Abdel Haleem (Oxford: Oxford University Press, 2004).

Walkowitz, Rebecca L., *Born Translated: The Contemporary Novel in an Age of World Literature* (New York: Columbia University Press, 2015).

INDEX

adab, 2, 14–16, 23, 42, 90, 254–5, 266, 316–19
Aeschylus, 265
Ahmed, Shahab, 1, 33–9, 105, 320–2
ākhira(h), 22, 265; *see also* Hereafter
al-Andalus, 5, 14, 57, 59, 61, 72–3, 77, 79–80, 308
al-Burda, 43, 113–17, 119–27, 130–1, 134, 284–5
al-Būṣīrī, 43, 113, 115, 116, 117, 120, 121, 122, 123, 124, 126, 134, 284
al-Maʿarrī, 20, 23, 34, 35
  Risālat al-Ghufrān, 23
al-Malaika, Nazik, 256
Alfonso X, 3, 57, 81
  Estoria de Espanna, 43, 58, 63, 64
  Siete partidas, 71
Almohads, 61, 63
Arabian Nights, 5, 45, 195, 196, 217–20, 225–30, 236, 237–9, 241–3, 246, 256, 302
Aryan, 221, 225, 227
Asia, 17, 225, 277, 304, 332
  East, 281
  Central, 42, 48, 165, 166, 172, 179, 180, 185, 255, 278, 280, 285, 288
  South, 28, 120, 165, 179, 185, 218, 255, 317, 332
  Southeast, 3, 120, 125, 134, 222, 321, 330, 332, 338
Atomisation, poetics of, 234

badīʿiyyāt, 122
Baizizan 百字赞, 271–2, 274, 281, 284–8, 289, 292
Boochani, Behrooz, 45, 266
Borges, Jorge Luis, 329–30, 345, 346–52
Braidotti, Rosi, 266
Braudel, Fernand, 263
Büwi, 166, 177–9, 182–4

Casanova, Pascale, 10–12, 328
Césaire, Aimé, 256, 257, 258, 260, 334

China, 3, 29, 166, 174, 175, 176, 177, 181, 271, 273, 275, 279, 281, 285, 288, 289, 290, 321
Islam in, 164–86, 273, 281, 288
colonialism, 43, 81, 103, 166, 295, 299, 301, 303, 306, 318, 333, 335, 342
Confucian, 272, 273, 279, 280, 283, 288, 289, 290, 291
neo-, 287

Damrosch, David, 16, 18–20, 26–7, 32, 117, 125, 131, 133, 259, 295, 315, 328, 330
Dao (Way, Tariqa) 道, 283, 289, 290, 291
Darwish, Mahmoud, 256–7, 258, 261, 265
dastan, 47, 164–86, 295–6, 300, 302
Decolonial, 17, 18, 47, 263, 322
Islam, 330–46, 352–3
theory, 47
devotional poetry, 113, 128–9, 133
dīn, 36, 211, 265–6
dunya, 153, 265

Egypt, 13, 31, 44, 120, 123, 218, 228, 235, 240, 339
ancient, 309, 311
Description of Egypt, 222
Manners and Customs of the Modern Egyptians, 240
engaged literature, 139–61
ethnic(-ity), 62, 81, 131, 176, 272
exotic, 6, 67, 70, 72, 195, 219

Ferdowsi, 256, 258, 261
figures, 96, 104
Flesler, Daniela, 69, 76
Fluidity, 44, 167, 172, 178, 185
Fulani, 139, 140, 141, 142, 155, 156
Empire, 140
mystical poetry, 44

Galland, Antoine, 5, 45, 195, 217–18, 220, 222, 223, 236–9, 241–5
genre, 3, 8, 15, 20, 40, 42, 43, 44, 88, 89, 92, 103, 113, 115, 116, 117, 122, 124, 128, 129, 134, 144, 151, 166, 167, 171, 172, 173, 175, 177, 183, 185, 186, 233, 273, 275, 291, 295, 296, 297, 298, 299, 300, 301, 302, 305, 307, 308, 310, 311–17, 351
genre-making, 15, 117, 173, 186
literary genre, 43, 47, 115, 122, 133, 196, 295, 300
subgenre, 121, 122, 124, 134, 298
Ghalib, 258
ghazal, 114, 129, 198–9, 262, 296, 338
global, xiv, 5, 17, 18, 19, 21, 24, 25, 28, 32, 43, 45, 99, 118, 119, 124, 125, 130, 132, 133, 175, 205, 258, 266, 334, 353
Global North, xiv, xv, xvi, xix, 10–11, 21, 26, 28, 41, 42, 46, 47, 48, 134, 257, 334
Global South, 18, 47
globalisation, 15, 21, 24, 38, 43, 263, 300, 329, 332
globalising, 315

Gobineau, Joseph Arthur comte de, 222–5, 236
Goethe, Johann Wolfgang von, xv, xvi, xvii, 7, 8, 16, 44, 104, 114, 117, 131, 132, 194–6, 198, 199, 205, 213, 266, 227, 259, 262, 295, 300, 328, 344
Gothean, xv, xvii, 2, 300, 315, 316, 319
Goytisolo, Juan, 78–9
guiyi (Return to The One) 归一, 282, 286, 289, 290

Hafez / Ḥāfiẓ, xv, xvii, 2, 3, 25, 34, 38, 104, 131, 198, 199, 213, 253, 258, 261, 262
Hammer-Purgstall, Josef von, 197–9, 204, 207, 212, 213, 225–6, 228, 235
hamziyya, 116, 123, 124, 141
Han kitab (Chinese Islamic book), 272, 275
Ḥayy ibn Yaqẓān, 30–8
Hekmat, Nazem, 256, 257, 258, 261
Henley, William Ernest, 229, 230
hikaya, 47, 165, 296
hikmet, 165, 166, 167, 171–2, 173, 175, 177–9, 182, 185, 186
Hodgson, Marshall, 1, 30, 31, 33–5, 59, 264, 196, 320–1
Holocaust, 91, 92, 93, 98, 103, 334
humanism, 104, 131, 255, 341, 342, 351
  literary humanism, 254, 255, 261, 266
Hughes, Langston, 256, 257, 258
Ibn al-Muqaffaʿ, 8, 265
  Kalila and Dimna, 8, 9, 36, 37, 265
Ibn Ṭufayl, 30–3, 34
imagination, 26, 40, 44, 91, 92, 98, 99, 102, 104, 105, 106, 132, 139, 141, 143, 151, 155, 160, 220, 230, 232, 233, 238, 239, 242, 254, 257, 259, 263, 306, 307, 314
imitation, 12, 114, 117, 121, 134, 197, 198–201, 204, 211, 212, 224, 237
Indian Ocean, 48, 272, 279, 319
indigenous Languages, xv, xviii
  Cherokee, xvi
  Dakota, xvi
  Inuttitut, xvii
  Kalaallisut, xvi, xvii, xviii, xix
Indonesian, 332, 338, 339, 340, 342, 343
Intangible Cultural Heritage (ICH), 175, 180, 184
Iqbal, Muhammad, 258, 262
Islam
  and liberation theology, 332–8, 343
  as a floating signifier, 45, 91, 255, 264
Islamic literature, 2, 3, 30, 40, 43, 128, 275
  pre-Islamic, 2, 113, 127, 133, 134, 149
Islamicate, xiv, xv, xvi, xvii, xix, 1, 2, 3, 5, 6, 11, 12, 13, 14, 20, 21, 29, 30–3, 42, 43, 45, 47, 48, 49, 57, 59, 60, 64, 74, 79, 297, 320, 321
  world, xiv, 8, 48, 133, 201
  literature, xiv, xvii, 1, 2, 4, 13, 15–16, 21, 22, 23, 30–3, 42, 46, 47, 118, 121, 196

Islamophobi(a)(c), 43, 60, 68–70, 73–4, 81, 184, 320

Kinoshita, Sharon, 70, 74, 79
Kublai Khan, 276
Kuntowijoyo, 329, 339–44, 346

Lane, Edward William, 228, 231, 236, 239–40, 242–3, 246
Library of Arabic Literature, 40
lineage, xv, 174, 280
literary theory, 11, 47, 132, 262, 328

madīḥ, 43–4, 113–34
Makdisi, George, 253–5, 267
Mamluk, 14, 117, 122, 134
Martí, José, 263
mawlid, 113, 119, 123, 130, 284–5
Mayakovski, Vladimir, 256–8, 260
mazar (festival/pilgrimage), 164, 167, 170–2, 176, 178, 181, 183, 186
meaning of a word, 91, 99
mechanics (of confirmation), 25, 328
meddah, 44, 165–6, 177–84
Medieval, 59, 67–74, 76–7, 219, 236, 240, 244, 301, 303–5, 310, 314
  Medievalis(ation)(ed)(ing), 301, 302, 307, 315
Metcalf, Barbara Daly, 255
Ming (dynasty), 271–91
minority, 57, 70, 71, 275
Mongol, 7, 170, 174–5, 200, 272, 276, 278, 291
Moors (Moros), 58, 64, 67–8, 72–3, 76, 78–81
  Moorish, 68, 73, 80–1, 308
Mudejars, 70–1
Mufti, Aamir, xiv, 25–6, 87, 295, 301, 316
Muḥammad, the Prophet, 2, 16, 44, 46, 64–9, 71, 114–15, 118, 122, 124, 129, 130, 133, 148–50, 154–5, 158–60, 170, 183, 202–3, 271–2, 274, 280–4, 287, 290–1, 293
multilingual, 28, 42, 45, 118
munshid, 123
music(al)(ality), 44, 119, 120, 129, 143–4, 164–5, 168, 169, 172, 174, 176–9, 184–6, 213, 351
muʿāraḍāt, 114, 122
mystical poetry, 44, 116, 126, 141, 144–5, 151, 154, 157, 160–1
mysticism, 340

Neruda, Pablo, 255–8, 260, 261, 265
Nima, Yushij, 258
Nirenberg, David, 59
non-Western, 7, 47, 114, 315, 329, 334
numbers, 81, 87, 91–2, 95–6, 100, 256

oral, 42–4, 89, 123, 142, 164–6, 168–9, 171, 173–4, 176, 182, 185, 279–81, 290, 296, 298, 316
orality, 185
orientalising (self-), 12, 166, 194–5, 197, 296
Orientalism, 1, 15, 37, 42–3, 47, 66, 69, 70, 74, 90, 97, 131, 195, 203, 232, 235, 295, 302–3, 310, 322
  chrono-Orientalism, 296, 301, 307, 313
  pseudo-oriental(ism), 195–6, 201, 221, 224, 238

Orsini, Francesca, 28, 174, 299–300
orthodoxy, 34, 64, 66, 140, 280, 286, 291

pastiche, 70, 80, 114, 122; *see also mu'āraḍāt*
Persianate, 28, 90, 255, 264–5
philology, 45, 193–4, 197–8, 200, 203–4, 223, 235
polycentrism, 13
praise of the Prophet, 43–4, 113, 115, 123, 133, 274; *see also madīḥ*
pseudo-oriental(ism), see orientalism

qaṣīda, 43, 113–14, 116, 121, 126, 149
Qing, 169, 171, 271, 275, 281
qissah / qisse, 165–6, 295–322
qissekhan, 166, 177–8, 180, 182–4
Qur'ān(ic), xvi, xvii, 2, 3, 16, 27, 30, 32–3, 35, 37–8, 45, 113, 127, 130, 141, 143, 152, 155, 178, 179, 193, 197, 200, 201, 203–14, 222, 254, 285, 280, 285–7, 320, 335–7, 341

race, 82, 97, 150, 225, 227–8, 233, 305, 338
  racism, 82, 236
religion, 6–7, 25, 27, 30, 32, 34, 40, 43, 46, 59, 71–2, 88–90, 91, 97, 105, 145, 174–5, 184, 196–7, 202–3, 219, 237, 265, 273–4, 276, 279, 281–2, 285, 287, 289–91, 309, 321, 329, 333, 336, 343, 346, 363
Renan, Ernest, 222–4, 235–6
representation, 3, 28, 39, 45, 48, 72, 87–8, 91, 148, 203, 222, 245, 303, 330
Republic of Letters, 10–14
reworlding Literature 259
rhetoric, 65, 91–2, 122, 198, 225, 236
  rhetorical, 5, 58, 67, 74, 91, 95, 97–8, 122, 129
Rieff, Philip, 253–4
Rodrigo Jiménez de Rada, 61–3, 65
  De rebus Hispanie, 61–2, 64, 66
  Historia Arabum 64–5
romance, 166, 175–6, 183, 185, 295–327
romanticism, 194, 198, 224
romanticist, 203
romantic, 193, 219, 220, 223, 225, 231, 232, 237–9, 243, 310
Rückert, Friedrich, 45, 193–213
Rudaki, 116, 258, 261
Rumi, 2, 3, 36–8, 198, 199, 201, 258, 261, 262, 334

Sa'di, 258, 261
Said, Edward W., 21, 31, 43, 69, 235, 328, 334
  affiliative thinking, 31–3
  contrapuntal, 17
  secular criticism, 32, 90
  The World, the Text, and the Critic, 21, 32
Sánchez-Albornoz, Claudio
sastera profetik, 47, 328, 338–53
secular, 4, 22, 23, 27, 34, 42, 46–7, 90, 103–4, 180, 186, 265, 343, 346
semite, 97, 221, 353

Shamlou, Ahmad, 256–8, 261
Shawqī, Aḥmad, 123
shèng rén (Prophet/sage) 圣人, 281
Sikh, 320–2
Silk Road, 29
Spain, 8, 31, 43, 57–82, 261, 305, 308, 310, 313
Spivak, Gayatri Chakravorty, 87, 263, 328
storytell(er)(ing), 44, 29, 164–86, 222, 226, 237, 245–6, 318
Sufi, xv, 106, 121, 123, 124, 129, 180, 285, 338
  literature, 44, 144, 170
Sufism, 2, 130, 133, 165, 173, 180, 182, 223, 340, 344–6, 348–9

Tamerlane, 271, 276
text as document, 45, 217, 235, 240, 337
thematisation, 24–5
Thousand and One Nights, xvi, 1–3, 5, 8, 16, 29, 36, 104, 218, 222–4, 227, 228, 223, 236–8, 240–1, 245, 302
time
  coevalness, 22–3, 301
  deep time, 21–3
  Hereafter, 22–3, 151, 289, 337; *see also ākhira*(*h*)
  secular time, 22
Torrens, Henry, 218, 225, 227

universalism, 48, 203
  Euro-universalism, 255, 260
Uyghur, 44, 164–86

Wallerstein, Immanuel, 20, 263
Wang Daiyu 王岱輿, 275, 280
Weimar, xv, xix
Weltliteratur, xvi, xviii–xix, 14–16, 131, 195, 328
Wieland, Christoph Martin, xvii
  Oberon, xvii–xix
world
  poetry, 196–7, 213, 296, 308
  romance, 46, 295, 296, 305, 315

Yuan dynasty, 276, 278, 291

Zheng He 郑和, 272, 279
Zhu Yuanzhang (Emperor) 朱元璋, 44, 46, 271, 273–5, 278, 280, 291–2